Management for Professionals

The Springer series *Management for Professionals* comprises high-level business and management books for executives. The authors are experienced business professionals and renowned professors who combine scientific background, best practice, and entrepreneurial vision to provide powerful insights into how to achieve business excellence.

More information about this series at http://www.springer.com/series/10101

Lukas Rieder • Raef Lawson

Management Control with Integrated Planning

Models and Implementation for Sustainable Coordination

Springer

Lukas Rieder
Controller Zentrum St. Gallen
St. Gallen, Switzerland

Raef Lawson
Institute of Management Accountants
Montvale, NJ, USA

ISSN 2192-8096 ISSN 2192-810X (electronic)
Management for Professionals
ISBN 978-3-030-48301-2 ISBN 978-3-030-48302-9 (eBook)
https://doi.org/10.1007/978-3-030-48302-9

The simulation model can be downloaded from https://en.management-control.eu using the password: MCSSim326197. For better orientation we strongly recommend to read Chap. 1 to Sect. 4.7 in Chap. 4 in the book before delving into the simulation model.

Original German edition published by Schðffer-Poeschel, Stuttgart, Germany, 2020

This Springer imprint is published by the registered company Springer Nature Switzerland AG.
The registered company address is: Gewerbestrasse 11, 6330 Cham, Switzerland

Preface

This book provides you with the knowledge needed to develop **holistic, integrated planning and control systems** within your organization. The principles it contains are based on scientific knowledge along with practical experience in developing management support systems in diverse organizations.

Long-term organizational success, perhaps even survival, requires effectively addressing numerous internal and external challenges. This includes, for example, the need for organizations to develop and sell new products and services at appropriate prices on an ongoing basis in order to compete in the marketplace. Management must also control the incurring of costs in a way that results in short- and long-term cost advantage. In order to do so, companies need to design their processes and structures in such a way that overall costs grow at a lower rate than those of their competitors, as price competition is ever present in most markets.

Discussions with our consulting clients regularly confirm that the key to building sustainable competitive advantage is **continuous coordination** within their organizations. Coordination requires an integrated and forward-looking approach, including the development of an integrated planning and control (IPAC) system for the entire organization. Development of such a system requires the creation of instruments that support decision-making by all managers, from the company manager with overall responsibility down to the individual group leader/team leader. Successful implementation of this holistic approach requires:

- Mapping all dimensions of a company and its parts as well as all environmental dimensions to the consequences for internal processes and structures
- Interlinking strategy and operation so that integration can be shown with textual and numerical data
- Determining the data-requirements for managerial decision-making (as opposed to external reporting)
- Disclosing decisions to be made by managers for their respective areas of responsibility and areas where sufficient data are available such that decision-making can be automated.

To ensure full traceability and simultaneously to present the complete system in a replicable way, this publication consists of two parts:

(a) This text, which describes the basics, the models, and their dependencies
(b) A comprehensive, programmed simulation model that supports the examples and discussions in this book. While the model is integrated into the text discussions, the book can also be read without using the simulation model.

The model makes it possible to investigate in detail all the dependencies and structures as well as the calculation methods used while making the necessary numerical calculations much less time-consuming. In this manner, the text becomes illustrative of the actual processes used in modern organizations today. The model also offers the ability to change initial values and to track how these changes affect all associated reports.

The simulation model is built in Excel in the form of databases. Excel was chosen because it is widely available and will be familiar to most readers. Consequently, no additional new knowledge prerequisites will be needed to get from the overall view to the individual data record.

The example company in the database is called Ringbook Ltd. In keeping with its name, it produces and sells ring binders (which are still widely used despite electronic data storage). The ring binder items, as well as related merchandise, are distributed in various sales regions and countries via several sales channels, resulting in a realistically complex overall model. The model in the database comprises more than five hundred thousand data cells. It demonstrates that an integrated planning and control system can be effectively implemented.

St. Gallen, Switzerland — Lukas Rieder
Montvale, NJ, USA — Raef Lawson
2020

Target Audience

This book is meant for those who want to implement integrated planning and control, who want to complete their own systems for it, and for those who teach courses in this area. Specifically, this includes:

- **Managers** from any function and hierarchical level in for-profit companies, both publicly and privately held
- **Executives** from public administration and non-governmental organizations (NGOs), as many elements of integrated planning and control also apply in such organizations
- **Controllers** with the task of designing and operating integrated planning and control systems
- **Consultants,** looking for a blueprint for implementing a management control system that meets the needs of their customers
- **IT specialists** who want to program such systems and build and maintain the interfaces to existing operational systems (especially ERP systems)
- **Teachers** who are involved in business education and training as well as in management training. The combination of management-relevant fundamentals and practical examples is intended to support them in aligning the content of their teaching with today's need for integral planning and control and in presenting the interrelationships to the students in a way they can experience and understand. Many curricula prescribe outdated and non-management-relevant learning content that "eats away" training time necessary for achieving a holistic understanding of this subject.

Notes

For better orientation, we strongly recommend to read Chap. 1 to Sect. 4.7 in Chap. 4 before working with the simulation model.

All figures and tables emanate from the authors. Exceptions are Figs. 2.1–2.5 (Chap. 2). Their origin is cited in the respective texts.

The copyright of the complete simulation model belongs to CZSG Holding AG, St. Gallen, and Lukas Rieder.

As far as possible we cite original publications. The purpose of doing so is to show that many good proposals for supporting integrated and holistic management were presented years ago but have not yet been sufficiently adopted in practice.

The simulation model is based on the years 2011–2015. The reason for using these years in the simulation model instead of years 1–5 lies in the capabilities of Excel. Some Excel functions do not allow calculation with years that lie in the future.

Gender-specific expressions apply equally to women and men.

Management Summary

Many managers want a well-structured system for the holistic and coordinated planning and control of their companies and their parts. In designing such systems, it is necessary to start with an organization's purpose and core values so that individuals as leaders of their organizational units are able to understand the results to be achieved. Additionally, managers need to be able to directly control the input factors they are responsible for and need to be accountable for the results achieved by those factors. This requires the formulation of the results to be achieved in a measurable, or at least a verifiable, form. Aggregation of these results to the overall organizational result should be possible, requiring the performance measures to be quantified in a similar manner.

The proposal presented here for the establishment of a comprehensive management control system is largely centered on discussion of performance and financial data. However, dysfunctional decision-making behavior that impedes the optimal implementation of the system also needs to be considered and addressed as far as possible.

It will be shown how planning from the corporate purpose down to the individual aspects of a project (or a manufactured product, a customer, an employee, a supplier) becomes feasible and how the achieved results can be measured so that they become relevant for organizational control. Every manager, from the foreman up to top management, should recognize which data and parameters they need for planning and controlling their individual area of responsibility.

The designers of the necessary information system (above all controllers and IT specialists) should recognize which planning and piloting figures are to be presented in the planning and control system so that system users can act independently.

The conceptualization of the system presented here is multidimensional in order to achieve general validity and integrated applicability. It includes the following attributes:

- Hierarchical: From the CEO to the group leader
- Planning: From corporate policy and strategy to the individual process
- Content: From the corporate purpose to the production order
- Functional: From sales to production and R&D to support areas

- Comprehensive: From the single project to the exchange of services in corporate groups
- Behavioral: From reluctance to plan to actions to maintain its own hierarchical position
- Time reference: From early warning and piloting information to yearly planning, actuals, and forecast

We use the term AMPLE to represent the five top performance controls of sustainable success and graphically portray these controls as shown in the figure below. AMPLE provides orientation (see Sect. 1.1.1). To be and to remain successful in these areas requires many preliminary achievements that are hard to measure such as appropriate leadership behavior, creative ideas, process productivity, and luck. These aspects are only partially addressed here; our focus is on measuring results achieved from utilization of the inputs.

To obtain decision-relevant parameters, top-down and bottom-up viewpoints are alternately utilized. This changing of perspective provides appropriate scope to the decision-making of the manager involved and ensures that the various aspects of corporate management are mapped in parallel. This process is known as the countercurrent principle (see Glossary).

An objective is a result or state to be achieved. Objectives need to be formulated so that they are measurable and verifiable. Results should be able to be aggregated up to the whole organization, which automatically results in a focus on technical, performance-related, and ultimately financial parameters.

A holistic understanding of the company, the application of fundamental management principles and the consistent application of structural and procedural concepts are prerequisites for integrated corporate management. Particularly relevant terms for system design are developed in Chaps. 1 and 2. In Chaps. 2 and 3, based on AMPLE and findings from the explanation of integrated management models, the requirements for a comprehensive planning and control system are designed top-down. Chapters 4–6 deal with operational annual planning, the recording of achieved results, and tactical management during the year.

The example in the accompanying Excel simulation model will be used as a step-by-step guide to demonstrate:

- The individual segment plans
- Their mutual dependencies
- The system-design requirements resulting from the management processes and the decisions to be taken
- The necessary links that must be established to arrive at the plan result
- The required databases for the recording of real results
- The presentation and interpretation of the individual as well as overall results in plan, target to actual comparison with the purpose of deriving target-oriented corrective measures

Corporate policy, strategic and medium-term planning, and control require instruments with a multi-year horizon and a link to annual performance. Suitable instruments—further based on the accompanying model—are dealt with in Chaps. 7–10.

Additional components of this book include the documentation of the accompanying simulation model as well as an extensive glossary. The simulation model is extensively integrated into the book and is a great resource which shows in detail how this methodology can be implemented in any organization.

Acknowledgments

Many people have made important contributions to the development of this system and publication, including:

- Managers from small to very large internationally operating companies in a wide variety of industries, who have repeatedly held up the mirror to us as counterparts in our consulting projects, providing important ideas for improvement and further development
- Countless students who have intensively questioned our suggestions, examined their applicability, and contributed further ideas
- With their publications, numerous researchers, especially from the fields of system-oriented management and cybernetics, who have provided insights into holistic management that have been incorporated into the development of the system
- Application-oriented consulting colleagues, above all those from CZSG Controller Zentrum St. Gallen, Control Management Information St. Gallen, and IGC International Group of Controlling, who were our sparring partners when it came to questions of the representability of key figures and input variables
- Markus Berger-Vogel who, based on his many years of experience in consulting and training, contributed many improvements to the contents, validated the simulation model and tested its applicability
- Dipl. Ing. ETH/MBA Markus Orengo, who brought in his knowledge concerning the design and implementation of viable systems and checked the consistency of the text
- Ms. B. Rieder, who significantly improved the style, text, and presentation of this material through her editing

All these persons deserve our sincere thanks. Their contributions have made it possible for us to publish this fully integrated management control system.

About This Book

This overview describes how this book will enable you to design planning and control systems so that your organization becomes and remains sustainably successful. Our intention is to provide guidance on the design and practical development of holistic, integrated planning and control systems for company management. The term "**management control systems**" is often used for these types of systems. In order to design such systems, the following basic questions must be answered:

- What requirements for a comprehensive management control system can be derived from internationally recognized management models for holistic corporate management?
- How can the mutual dependencies of the various subprocesses (e.g., strategy development, sales planning, and cost planning) be mapped and considered in planning calculations?
- Which performance figures and which data are necessary to manage a company (system) successfully and sustainably?
- How can planned and actual data be linked in order to become relevant for decision-making?
- How can uncertain or only suspected future developments be integrated into planning and control?
- How should a custom-tailored system be implemented?

The combination of scientific findings with the authors experience in management and consulting forms the basis for the identification of the critical success factors in system design and implementation. Studying the sample company model will help clarify how one's own information systems can be adapted or supplemented to suit management needs, making them relevant for decision-making at all (hierarchical) levels of management.

Objective and Scope

This book describes the systems, data, information, and indicators an integrated and holistic planning and control system should encompass to provide decision-relevant information for all managers and all segments of a company. A complete set of measures appropriate for all types of enterprises can never be compiled. Many developments, values, and external influences cannot be put in simple formulas while others are only partially measurable. Additionally, many key figures are not compatibly denominated (e.g., job satisfaction compared to turnover), which makes their mathematical linking impossible or at least difficult. (This is clear from the Industrial Dynamics movement; see, for example, Forrester, 1961, pp. 55–59.) However, this is good news for the managerial profession, because if an entire company could be described in formulas, it would no longer need managers to control the company, only computers.

A performance planning and control system should be as holistic as possible, i.e., cover all aspects of corporate management. Such a system should be universally valid, meaning that it can be used—in an adapted form—both in privately managed companies across industries and in public administration and other organizations. Furthermore, the system should be suitable for both *planning* and *control* and be suitable for both shorter periods (e.g., 1 month) and longer ones (e.g., a strategy horizon). The system should also be applicable in affiliated companies, e.g., groups of companies.

The focus here is on control-relevant data, as every manager is a customer of their organizations' data systems. So many key performance indicators have been presented in the past that focus on those of primary importance can be lost very quickly. The key figures are those relevant to managerial decision-making. Managers require a set of key performance indicators suitable for their area of responsibility in accordance with their tasks, competencies, and responsibilities.

We pursue a *pure management orientation*: The goal is to present performance indicators and figures that are relevant for managerial decision-making consistent with managers' responsibility. Accounting standards (IFRS, US GAAP, Swiss GAAP FER and similar external reporting standards), and statutory provisions (HGB, OR, code civil, tax law provisions) are only taken into account to the extent they have a direct influence on decision-relevant reporting or if they place requirements on the underlying accounting and process recording systems.

To compare execution with the operational plans a *monthly reporting system* will usually suffice. Daily reports are an option for even shorter-term tactical control (e.g., personnel deployment control, activity recording, or triggering production orders). However, the focus is on the long-term and sustainable success of a company. With regard to the quarterly reporting required of publicly traded companies, we consider this to be largely counterproductive to the long-term successful management of an organization.

Behavioral considerations, such as personal struggles to gain more power or the attainment of personal financial advantages, are not discussed here. While these are important, we focus here on developing a system for defining annual and medium-term objectives for all areas of responsibility with the goal of ensuring an organization's long-term success and alignment of goals within the organization.

Important Basic Terms for Planning and Control

In order to discuss "integrated planning and control," it is essential to first define some terms, including:

Managers: Individuals of all hierarchical levels that lead organizational units are called managers. They are responsible for working with their employees to achieve planned results. Members of the Executive Board, referred to as "executives" in English-speaking countries, are managers at the highest hierarchical levels.

Results: These are measurable states. The measuring unit can be a value, a quantity, a service, a date, or the determination of a condition (occurred or not).

Controllers: Provide management support for managers of all levels. They develop and implement the necessary instruments and systems that managers need for performance and value-based integrated planning and control (see *Controller's Dictionary*).

Controlling: Means having your business "under control." Controlling is therefore a management task. With their instruments and advice, controllers enable managers at all levels to carry out controlling.

Holistic: Integral, integrated, to look at something in its entirety. To be "integrated" in a company requires inclusion of all dimensions of a company's activities, including developments in the current and future environments of the company.

Sustainable: Sustainable means that the company/system will continue to exist successfully while considering changes in all surrounding environments.

Plan: To intend, be determined, be willing, have in mind. "Planning" is a creative act that leads to the determination of the results to be achieved together with the allocation of necessary resources as well as the identification of procedures needed. A plan also serves as a basis for comparing what has been achieved with what has been intended (i.e., creating a feedback loop).

Control (and Regulate): Especially in discussions with technically educated persons, a distinction between control and regulation is often made, although in the English language the word control can be used for both control and regulation. Regulation describes closed-loop control, i.e., with feedback, while control describes open-loop control (see Fig. 1).

From a technical point of view, the main difference between control and regulation is that control is intended to influence the behavior of a result variable without measuring the result variable. Regulation, on the other hand, is intended to influence the result variable in such a way that it corresponds to the control specification. It requires the result variable to be measured regularly.

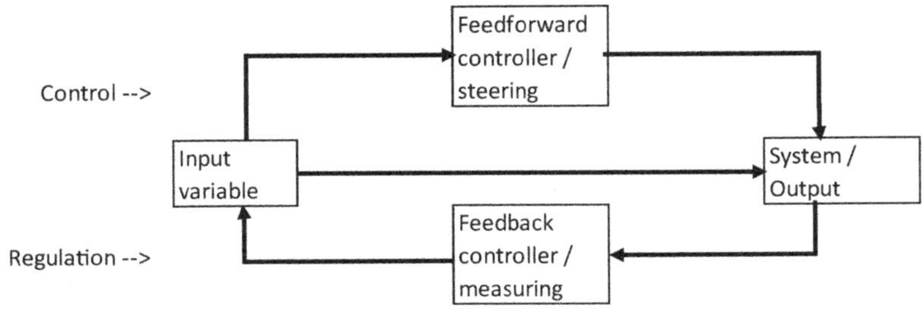

Fig. 1 Difference between control and regulation

With regard to organizational management, control and regulation are almost always regarded as belonging together. Control is directional (where to go?) and is implemented through objectives, plans, and rules. However, since a wide variety of "disturbance variables" can influence the achievement of a goal, management also requires regulation. If a variable to be controlled changes differently than planned, management must recognize this and intervene with corrective measures (new control inputs) to ensure that the planned output is achieved despite disruptions.

Following these definitions, in this book the concept of control is always understood to take place in combination with regulation. After all, it is regularly a matter of evaluating controlling (prescriptive) inputs from management to determine whether they produce the required effect (feedback), considering the changes in the corporate environment that have occurred.

Management control: A part of any management system, aimed at achieving defined objectives within an established timetable, with the following components: ensuring measurable objectives, measuring actual performance, and taking corrective action and forecast.

Management control system: The instruments necessary for the exercise of management control at all levels. These include the *management accounting system*, necessary for operational planning and control. Additional data collection and evaluation is required for medium- to long-term corporate management and addressing strategic issues:

- *Piloting* (see Sects. 9.1–9.3) comes "before control" and thus also before planning. Piloting information is intended to alert managers to medium-term internal developments.
- *Early warning* (see Sect. 9.4) also comes before planning. Early warning information should bring suspected changes in the corporate environment into focus for the company so that opportunities and risks can be identified and assessed and from these strategies developed.

$$\text{Management Control System} = \text{Management Accounting} + \text{Piloting} + \text{Early Warning}$$

The needs of managers determine the contents, methods, and evaluations of a management control system, not legal or reporting-oriented requirements.

How to Ensure the Relevance of a Management Control System

A management control system is only of real help if it meets the needs of its potential users—the managers at all hierarchical levels. Fully integrated management models like the St. Gallen Management Model (SGMM) from Hans Ulrich and the Viable System Model (VSM) from Stafford Beer provide guidance on the necessary dimensions and scope of the management control system that needs to be developed and shaped. These two management models describe the dimensions, structures, cultures, and managerial processes required in an integrated planning and control system. This also includes the interactions between the company's functions and the respective parts of the corporate environment (Fig. 2).

In Chaps. 1–3, the two models are analyzed in order to deduce the contents, procedures, time periods, comparisons, and metrics management control systems need to cover. The resulting insights define the requirements for the management control system. Chapters 3–6 present how the management accounting part of the MCS is to be built to meet these requirements. Chapters 7–11 present how strategic and midrange planning and control can be supported with piloting and early warning data as well as a multi-period analysis showing the development of efficiency. The simulation model accompanying this book provides "proof of concept."

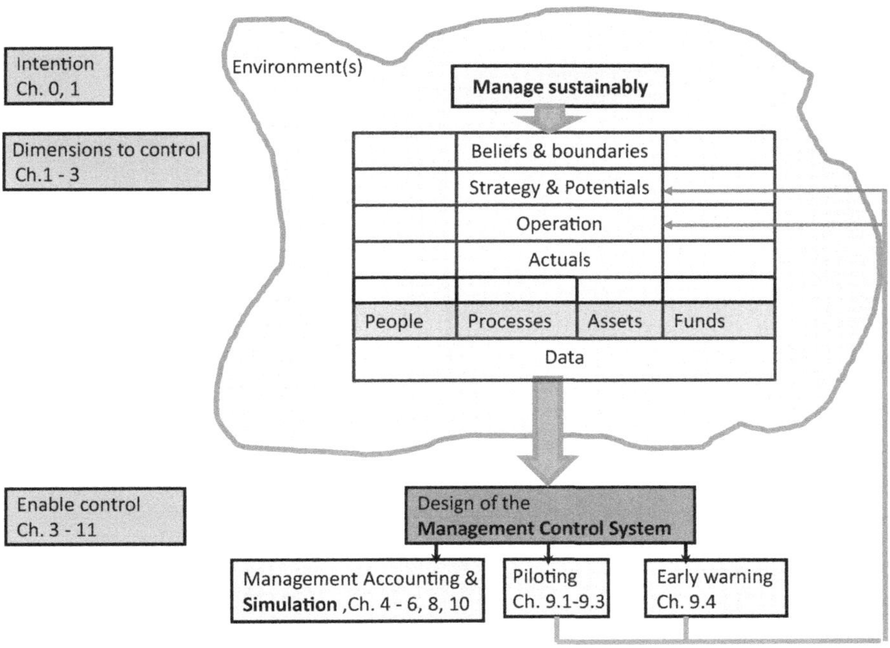

Fig. 2 Management control system = management accounting, piloting, and early warning

Contents

Abbreviations

Ø	Average
AMPLE	Five top target areas of corporate management
BILMOG	German Act of Accounting Modernization
BOM	Bill of materials
BSC	Balanced scorecard
CC	Cost center
CCperf	Performing cost center
CCrec	Receiving cost center
CEO	Chief executive officer
cf.	compare
CFBIT	Cash flow before interest and taxes
CFMC	Conceptual Framework for Managerial Costing
Ch.	Chapter
CM	Contribution margin
CM I	Contribution margin I
CM II, CM2	Contribution margin level 2
COSM	Cost of sales method
CRM	Customer relationship management
CWB	Controller's Dictionary
DSO	Days sales outstanding, debtor target
E&I	Escalation and Intervention (VSM)
e.g.,	for instance
EBIT	Earnings before interest and taxes, operating result
EBT	Earnings before taxes
EDP	Electronic data processing
EOQ	Economic order quantity (optimum order quantity)
ERP	Enterprise resource planning system
EUR	Euro
ex.	Example
FAUF	Production order
FDC	Factory data collection
G	Net benefit

HGB	German Commercial Code
HR	Human resources
i	Interest rate
I	Investment amount
IFRS	International Financial Reporting Standards
IGC	International Group of Controlling
IMA	Institute of Management Accountants, Montvale, NJ, USA
IMS	Integrated management system
ISP	Internal services provided
IT	Information technology
Itemnr.	item number
L	Liquidation proceeds
Ltd.	Public limited company
MBO	Management by Objectives
MCS	Management control system
MIS	Management information system
MRP	Material requirements planning
n	Useful life (of a fixed asset)
NC	Numeric control
NGO	Non-governmental organization
NPO	Not-for-profit organization/non-Profit organization
OR	Swiss Code of Obligations
OU	Organizational unit
P&L	Profit and loss statement
P.	Page
PC	Personal computer
Phours	Personnel hours
PM	Product manager
pmin	Personnel minute
PPSS	Production planning and control system
prop.	proportional
R&D	Research and development
RB&A	Resource bargain and accountability (VSM)
RepV	Replacement value
RFU	Reference factor unit of a cost center
ROCE	Return on capital employed
ROE	Return on equity, return on equity
ROI	Return on investment
ROS	Return on sales
SBU	Strategic business unit
SG	Semi-finished good
SGMM	St. Gallen Management Model
SLA	Service-level agreement
SQL	Structured Query Language
Swiss GAAP FER	Swiss Generally Accepted Accounting Principles

TCM	Total cost method
US GAAP	United States Generally Accepted Accounting Principles
VL	Sales director
VSM	Viable system model
YTD	Year-to-date

About the Authors

Lukas Rieder is founder of CZSG Controller Zentrum St. Gallen/Switzerland, a consultancy for management, controllership, management accounting systems, and MIS. Customers of CZSG are mid-size and large corporations as well as public administrations. He is Co-founder of IGC International Group of Controlling and honorary member of ICV International controller Association. Previously, he was assistant professor at the University of St. Gallen. His main research topics are controllership, management accounting, management information systems, and management control systems. He has published many books on management and controllership.

Raef Lawson, PhD, CFA, CMA, CSCA, CPA, CAE is Vice President—Research & Policy and Professor-in-Residence for the Institute of Management Accountants (IMA) where he leads IMA's global thought leadership efforts and oversees IMA's student and academic relations programs. Prior to joining IMA, he was a professor and Chair of the Department of Accounting and Law at the State University of New York—Albany. He has published several books and over one hundred articles in leading practice and academic journals in the areas of sustainability, business ethics, managerial costing, and cost and performance management systems.

Organizational Purpose and Integrated Control

1

When developing an integrated planning and control system, the linkage between corporate policy and implementation must first be established. Sustainably successful organizations regularly create outstanding results by establishing this linkage, based on five critical performance controls. The development of these key areas needs to be managed holistically, in order to consider all business environments.

Under an integrated planning and control system every manager must know and strive to attain his and the organization's objectives. These should be set using the management cycle (see Sect. 1.2.1), with the following steps: agreeing on objectives, planning, execution, comparison with actuals, and implementing corrective actions.

Plans and objectives are necessarily linked to each other. This can be accomplished using management by objectives (MBO), a management concept primarily geared toward agreeing on results to be achieved in a financial year. MBO spreads from an organization's core values and strategies to the objectives of the individuals in the organization and thus also includes the delegation principle (see Sect. 1.3).

Organizational Purpose

The development of an integrated planning and control system starts with an understanding of an organization's *purpose*. This is the reason for the establishment and further development of a company or any other organization. The purpose communicates what the company "does" for its stakeholders (customers, employees, suppliers, society), what value its services should bring to the customers, what is important for the development of the company (i.e., the core values of the founders and owners), how the company and its services differ fundamentally from its competitors and, finally, where it should develop in the long term.

Corporate Policy

An organization's corporate policy (or mission statement) is often summarized in the form of *guiding principles*. The documentation of corporate policy serves—which is often forgotten—above all to inform managers and employees what the long-term

L. Rieder, R. Lawson, *Management Control with Integrated Planning*, Management for Professionals, https://doi.org/10.1007/978-3-030-48302-9_1

intentions of the company are, which values are considered important. It is intended to promote the organization's purpose both in decision-making and in execution. A corporate policy is valid "from now on" for all employees and remains valid until a revised and approved new version is issued. As corporate policy is meant to be valid for a company's longest time horizon (from now to the distant future); it forms the orientation for all other plans. The contents of a corporate policy are dealt with in Sect. 1.4.

Vision is often mixed up with corporate policy or mission. The first describes (with a short, concise formulation) in what position the company wants to find itself in the future. It is important that managers and controllers differentiate between mission and vision.

1.1 Holistic Corporate Management

Every company, every organization operates in several environments (i.e., technological, social, economic, and natural—see Sect. 1.1.2) and has to consider these various dimensions simultaneously. Changes in the environment in which an organization operates are commonplace and generate new challenges. While some of these changes are expected, some are not, such as:

- The changing wishes of employees or their representatives
- New lifestyles that influence public opinion
- New topics that are discussed in the media
- Enhanced protection of the natural environment
- Stricter legal requirements that impact the organization
- Shifts in the preferences of investors and owners

The importance of each of these impacts at any given moment cannot be completely predicted. Yet observing the development of companies over time shows that no company can neglect addressing changes in its environment if it is to develop successfully in the long term.

Sustainably successful organizations regularly create outstanding results by linking corporate policy with strategies and operational reality. They effectively pursue holistic organizational management, employing performance controls in five key areas. We use the abbreviation AMPLE to represent these five areas because, taken together, they make up the elements essential for sustainable and ample management (similar to Malik 2008, 146 ff.).

1.1.1 AMPLE Top Performance Controls

The five key performance areas include attractiveness for employees, market position, profitability, liquidity, and evolution. These are portrayed in Fig. 1.1 with a

Fig. 1.1 AMPLE for sustainable entrepreneurial success

five-pointed star, indicating their mutual dependency: the development of any one area is dependent on the development of the other four areas. These target areas are the most important performance factors for public and private companies and—with suitable adaptations—for NGOs (Nongovernmental Organizations), NPOs (Not for Profit Organizations), and administrative and political organizations.

Because the five performance areas are mutually dependent, their explanation can be started anywhere. Here we move from the market to the company.

Market Position

Market position is consumers' perception of a brand, product, or company in relation to that of its competitors. A company must strive for a strong market position in order to find enough customers to buy and pay for its products and/or services. A strong market position may also give an organization the chance to enforce technical standards that competitors must adhere to (e.g., operating systems such as Windows or Android). With a strong market position, higher selling prices are often obtainable (e.g., the selling prices of Apple smartphones compared to those of other mobile phone vendors).

Evolution

Experience shows that products and services often lose favor with customers over time. They are then either further developed, replaced by other products or services (possibly those of competitors) or the interest in them disappears (substitution). Companies must therefore continuously adapt their products/services to suit their customers' evolving needs or invent new ones (innovation) so that they can either maintain their market position or enter a new market.

Evolution is also of the highest relevance for internal development by a company. Internally, the focus is on improving, simplifying, and accelerating processes. If a company is not able to sufficiently deliver its products or services on time and according to customer demands it will sooner or later lose its market position. Since it can only adjust its production capacities to a limited extent, it will then produce at a higher cost than its competitors, resulting in it having less ability to meet the price competition common in maturing markets, leading to lower profitability.

Attractive Employer

Innovations, process improvements, and market position are developed by an organization's employees. A company is therefore constantly faced with the question of how to retain those employees whose skills and abilities will be needed in the future or how to recruit them from the labor market. The level of wages paid compared to that offered by other potential employers is only one of the determining factors. Aspects such as management culture, career advancement, educational opportunities, and working-time models play at least as important a role. Conveying the significance of an employee's work and the objectives to be achieved when working also substantially contributes to the attractiveness of a job.

Profitability

When assessing the profitability of an organization we also need to consider improving productivity. Input/output ratios must be in line with standards if an organization is to survive in the long term. While organizations such as NGOs usually do not have to make a profit, they must control expenditures in such a way that they do not exceed revenues (from whatever sources). In the long run, even a public administration cannot consume more than it earns from taxes and fees. Violations of this rule cause the amount of debt to rise, resulting in the need for politicians to concentrate a considerable part of their efforts on reducing these debts. In such organizations, the "profit" must at least be zero in the medium term.

For a privately managed company, the resources invested must achieve a return on equity in line with market conditions. Profitability must not only be enough to cover all resources consumed (including that for evolution), but also to compensate lenders and owners with a return on their investment commensurate with the risk they assume.

The establishment of new market positions and the development or introduction of new products or technologies often require an extended period greater than, say, a year. The profitability consequences of such investments must be assessed, particularly in the case of decisions that are strategic in nature. Investments themselves must be managed in such a way that the company can utilize them to achieve a strong cost position for surviving price reductions from competitors. The knowledge and skills that grow from experience can also be used by other companies to improve their cost position and thus their profitability (see Experience Curve, Sect. 7.5.1). If the opportunities to improve a company's cost position are not implemented by a company itself, its competition will likely do so.

Liquidity

Liquidity can be defined as solvency at any time. An organization must have enough liquid funds, on a timely basis, to pay employees, suppliers, and lenders when debts come due for repayment. If the assets of an organization are tied up in inventory, receivables from customers, and other nonliquid assets, it can become insolvent and lose its independence. For this reason, liquidity is an independent and vital performance area.

Synergies, Obstructions, Contradictions

The five key performance areas are not controllable individually, and none can be omitted from decision-making. The following examples show that these target areas are linked both in the positive sense (working together to improve the success of the company) and in the negative sense (working in contradictory ways that are mutually damaging). Management must evaluate the impact of its decisions on each of the five areas:

- If a company tries to strengthen its market position by granting discounts, it may win market share. The discounts reduce contribution margins, which in turn reduces profitability. It is often argued that higher sales volumes will increase capacity utilization and thus improve the company's profits despite the higher discounts. This is almost always a fallacy, since discounts granted have a direct impact on the cash return, while higher capacity utilization does not lead to a reduction of absolute fixed costs.
- Declining profitability means that less resources are available for the evolution of the organization. As a result, both the market position and the attractiveness for R&D employees are negatively impacted.
- If it is possible to increase market share at constant prices, this will have a positive effect on profitability, attractiveness, and innovation. At the same time, however, trade receivables, inventories, and possibly fixed assets will also grow, which can lead to liquidity bottlenecks. The latter can result in even a highly profitable company getting into difficulties paying wages on time, which in turn reduces its attractiveness for (potential) employees.
- If a company concentrates on maximizing (short-term) profitability, too few resources are available for sales promotion and advertising, which sooner or later leads to a weakened market position. Similarly, if too little is invested in innovation and capacity expansion, this will have a negative impact on all other target areas in the medium term.
- If management becomes too "lean" by approving too few management positions, profitability will increase in the short term but, as a result, faulty processes will accumulate, leading to delayed deliveries and insufficient quality (market position), as well as delayed projects (evolution).
- A popular way to improve liquidity is to reduce inventories of finished goods, semi-finished goods, and raw materials. In this regard it is important to ask questions such as: How much does this reduce the degree of delivery readiness (market position)? By how much does production become more expensive because smaller lot sizes are specified for production orders (thereby reducing profitability)?

Here it is assumed that a company always intends to develop successfully in the long term, taking AMPLE into account. What "successful" means, however, is sometimes open to interpretation!

1.1.2 Corporate Environments and AMPLE

Hans Ulrich (1974, p. 27) divided the corporate environment into four environmental spheres. Other structures are possible, but Ulrich's formulation is described here because all conceivable environments can be depicted in it. It consists of the *natural environment,* which includes all others; the *technological environment* which includes everything that has to do with products, technologies, raw materials, services, and markets; the *economic* environment which includes money, values, and productivity; and the *social environment* which represents the aspects of society and politics, the coexistence of all people in it, laws, rules, and mentalities as well as competition.

As a two-dimensional model, AMPLE is not able to comprehensively map the internal relations and the control-relevant aspects between the five essential control areas. Changes in one of the five key areas will have partially unpredictable effects on the other four. Thus, the development of the five key areas should always be managed holistically. This requirement is omnipresent in the derivation of an integrated planning and control system (see Chaps. 7–9).

For AMPLE to be an effective assessment scheme for measuring sustainable success for an organization or the success of the contributions made by its employees and managers, it should clarify how internal successes can be compared with the environmental developments. This would be simple if it were possible to measure what effects "the doings of the people in a company" had on acceptance in the environments. However, such comparability or measurability is rarely possible.

It is relatively easy to measure and assess whether there is enough **liquidity**, i.e., enough money to cover short-term needs as well as to finance multiyear developments, since "only" money is spoken of. The same applies to **profitability**. The profit figure (e.g., earnings before interest and taxes, EBIT) is usually compared to other quantities expressed in monetary terms, such as the amount of an organization's investments (balance sheet total) or sales (Fig. 1.2).

The assessment of **market position** is more difficult. In the short term, the sales achieved can be related to those of the competitors or the total market volume (technological environment). However, it should be noted that competitors' sales are often only known when the company's own fiscal year has already ended. Measuring actual market shares therefore usually means performing a backward-looking analysis, which has only limited relevance for future-oriented management. Whether the company is doing the right thing to move future sales in the desired direction can only be judged with auxiliary variables, as the sales have not yet been realized.

For these assessment needs, "piloting data"such as the number of sales quotes requested (potential customers interested in a company's service or products) or customer benefit evaluations (benefits provided by a company's product or service to a potential customer relative to those provided by its competition) may be employed. The number of requests for quotations can still be measured (ex post). Whether potential customers assess and evaluate the additional value of the offer for their own benefit only becomes apparent when an inquiry arrives and leads to further

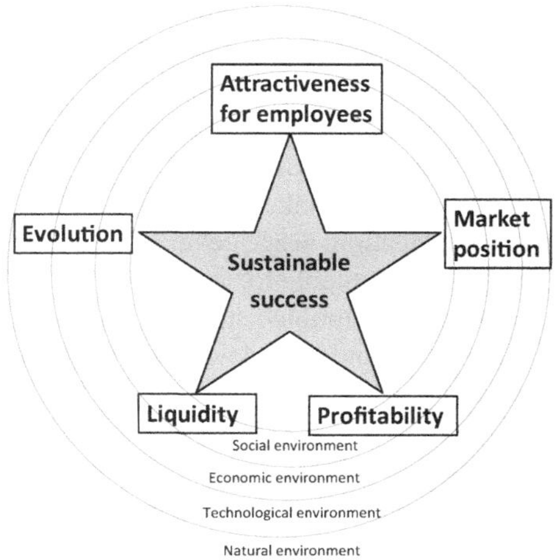

Fig. 1.2 All environments affect the AMPLE elements

negotiations. To measure and subsequently assess this, it is necessary to count the number of requests for quotations and the offers made, their amount, and the period between the request for quotation and the generation of sales. All these variables are not yet facts (actual sales), but only "hopes" (of future sales).

"Soft" estimates are of great importance for the future of the company and for the investments to be made for it, even though they are not based on "hard" data. For integrated planning and control, such variables are just as important as the hard facts about the sales achieved. Estimates must therefore be included in the design of appropriate information systems.

The assessment of **evolutionary developments** becomes even more difficult. If an investment in a process improvement is to lead to lower unit costs, this can be largely assessed with an investment calculation. However, if this improvement is to lead to more customers ordering from the company, assumptions must be made as to the number of customers that can be influenced positively and whether, and to what extent, they will be willing to pay for such improved services. A survey of the market environment is thus necessary.

If innovations in products or services are being considered, their success will only be measurable if they lead to additional sales and profit contributions. However, this information comes too late for corporate management because it must be decided well in advance whether the investment of additional resources in a research and development project is promising and whether the project should be continued. For this management must get information regarding whether the product idea is favored or perhaps approved by potential customers, technical papers, and so on.

Finally, the question arises as to whether focusing on certain skills and knowledge can prepare those employees who need to be able to invent and realize the products and services of the future, create the necessary customer contacts, and ensure the realization of internal process improvements. In this assessment, too, the determination of the measurement parameters depends on the ideas of top management about the future composition of the staff.

Current developments, termination rates, and employee satisfaction often do not help. To assess the attractiveness of an employer, rankings are available today from various providers. But even this information only describes in the medium term whether measures taken in the company (e.g., regarding management methodology, further education, wage level or fringe benefits) have increased its attractiveness. They are not suitable for assessing current efforts.

These descriptions suggest that for the successful application of AMPLE, parameters should be developed that make it possible to describe, measure, and evaluate:

- Predictive control and readjusting regulation (feedforward and feedback)
- Short- and long-term aspects of management (time frame)
- Questions of content control (planning steps)
- The process flow of the management processes (management cycle)
- Objectives, means, and procedures (management phases)
- Function-related questions (which area regulates what?)
- Hierarchical and responsibility issues

It would be easiest if the parameters to be developed and used could all be measured in monetary terms. However, this is not possible because many important variables cannot be expressed or measured in that way (e.g., customer satisfaction, employee satisfaction, quality of in-house training). Piloting variables especially are often measured in nonmonetary terms of such as quantities, outputs, times, and so on.

1.2 Management Means Goal-Oriented Proceeding

Every manager, from group leader to senior manager on the supervisory or administrative board, must know what he and the company *want to realize*. This means it is important to consider:

- What results (objectives) are to be achieved by a defined point in time
- What actions need to be taken
- What means need to be employed
- What process knowledge (know-how) is to be used

to achieve the organization's objectives.

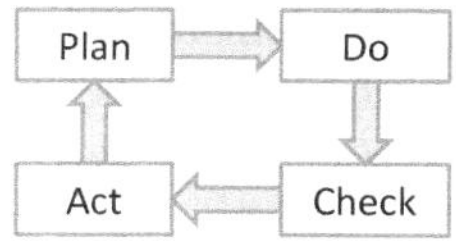

Fig. 1.3 The Deming Cycle: Plan–Do–Check–Act

1.2.1 Management Cycle

The "Deming Cycle," shown in Fig. 1.3, is a well-known management technique for the control and continuous improvement of processes and products. It shows the steps an organization needs to follow in order to achieve process improvements.

In the St. Gallen Management Model (SGMM), Hans Ulrich (1974, p. 30) presented a generally valid description of the management cycle with comparable content (see Fig. 1.4). A comparison of the two figures shows that the management process, whether presented in a process-related or general manner, has a basic pattern one should follow:

- The first subprocess of management is *planning* (PLAN). This requires consideration of the objectives to be achieved as well as the necessary means and procedural knowledge. Based on these specifications a decision is made as to which combinations of objectives, measures, resources, and know-how are to be implemented (referred to as the *management phase* in the SGMM, p. 30).
- Planning for the next period is completed when the (annual) objectives and the target values to be achieved in partial periods have been agreed and decided by overall management. Their validation and approval for implementation usually takes place at the budget meeting of the decision-making body (Board of Directors, Executive Board).

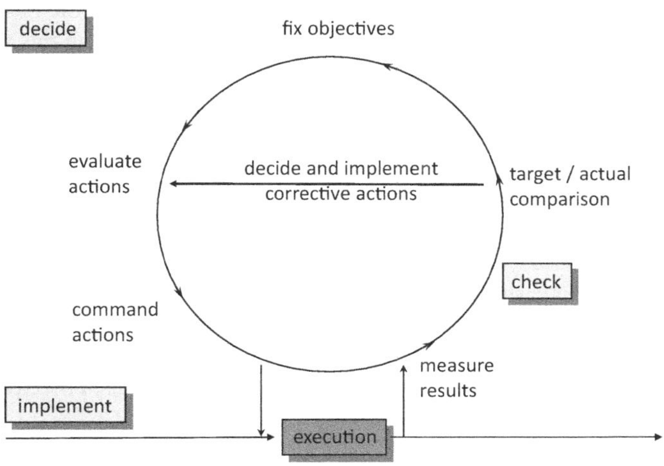

Fig. 1.4 The management cycle in SGMM

- Implementation then begins (DO). Self-execution, delegation, commands, and the like set the execution in motion.
- Since the future rarely unfolds as planned by the manager, target values and goals must be compared with what has been achieved. This makes it possible to determine how successful one's own department or the organization has been in achieving its goals. For this purpose, *actual values* and activities are measured. These are compared with the plan, i.e., the goal described in a measurable form, from which the plan to actual comparison or the flexible budget to actual comparison (see Sect. 6.2.1) results (CHECK). Differences between plan/target and actual should lead to corrective measures that enable a return to the target path (ACT).

Both the responsible manager and his supervisor want to know whether the corrective measures determined in the control process will be enough to achieve the originally defined goal. The *forecast* serves this purpose. It is used to quantify the effects of the corrective measures decided on, so that a result expected for the end of the year or of the project (expected actual) can be determined.

Conceptually, it is important when designing integrated planning and control systems to distinguish between projection, trend, estimate, and forecast:

- In the *forecast*, managers quantify the expected results for the rest of the planning horizon, considering the corrective measures they have decided on and the actual values achieved to date.
- A *trend calculation or projection* statistically determines probable final values based on the actual values to date and the values of past periods. It only considers past experience and not the impact of the corrective actions decided upon. Employing statistical methodologies, it cannot predict a trend break.
- A period-end *estimate* is a quantity that can be calculated in many ways. Most of the time it is calculated as the year-to-date actual results plus the balance of the remaining plan. However, calculating the period-end estimate in this way fails to consider the impact of corrective management actions, which leads to less useful estimates.
- A related term is prognosis. In most cases, this is a forecast of the expected actual value at the end of the year based on actual values from previous periods.

In our experience, projection, trend, estimate, and extrapolation figures are almost always computer-based calculations without considering the expected effects of planned corrective measures (Fig. 1.5).

For management purposes, the forecast is the most suitable for presenting expected values at the end of a year or project. Forecasts can only be made by managers who are aware of their own planned corrective actions. Forecasts based on agreed corrections support forward-looking management.

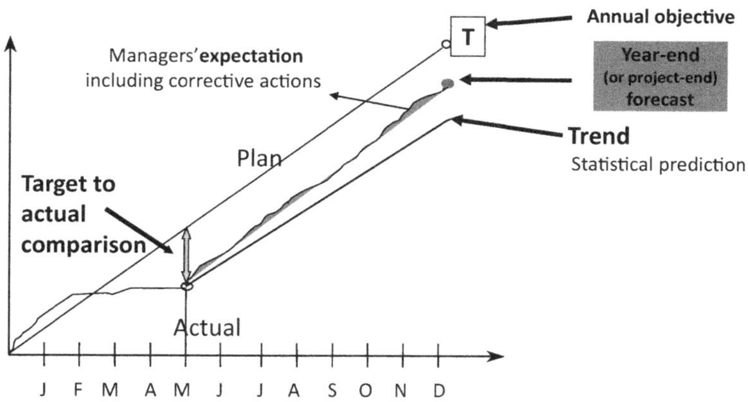

Fig. 1.5 Plan, objective, actual, variance, forecast

1.2.2 Conclusions for Integrated Management

An integrated planning and control system must be able to depict planned, target, actual, and forecast values in a manner appropriate to the given period and to the respective management position. In MIS language, these four characteristics are called "value types."

Adapt Contents and Levels of Objectives?
Objectives, i.e., results or states to be achieved, are recorded in (annual) plans. An objective often proves to be unrealizable during the year (e.g., due to exchange rate shifts, loss of core customers, shortages of raw materials, and accidents). It is often thought that in such cases the objectives need to be adjusted. Such an approach can have counterproductive effects since:

- The annual targets have previously been agreed upon and approved by top management.
- Adjustment of an objective leads to the loss of the benchmark and, in the worst case, targets in the company must be renegotiated.
- As many companies have shown in practice, the possibility of adjusting an objective during the year tempts many people to neglect the quality of the target figures in the planning process ("It is possible to readjust if things do not go as expected").

It is advisable to adjust the forecast, not the original objective.

In the field of strategic planning the situation is different. There it must be possible to adjust strategic goals within the framework of a (long-term) strategy revision. It is possible that the assumptions on which the strategy was originally based are no longer valid or that environmental factors make it impossible to achieve a strategic goal.

Plans and objectives are necessarily linked to each other. Theoretically, the question arises as to whether the goal comes before the plan or vice versa. It is logical to generate the plan from the goal to be achieved, but a manager can only definitively set himself a goal when he realizes that he will also have the resources and procedural knowledge (see Sect. 1.2.1, Management Cycle) at his disposal. In an integrated planning and control system all agreed objectives should be accessible for all managers so that every manager can see on what his colleagues are working on (This is the process installed at Google Corp. (OKR)).

1.2.3 Management by Objectives

Objectives are omnipresent in corporate management and agreement on them is essential for effectively managing an organization. A widely used process for goal fixing is management by objectives (MBO), a management concept that is often used in defining the targets to be achieved in a fiscal period. Whether these objectives are normative, strategic, or operational is only indirectly relevant, because every objective must be achieved operationally "with the feet on the ground." MBO pursues the idea of aligning work efforts and the behavior of each employee with the realization of overall corporate, strategic, and operational targets. This should result in concentration on the essentials, pooling of forces, and mutual coordination of efforts.

The starting point is the clear definition of the term "objective":

> **An objective is a result or a state to be achieved!**
> When fixing an objective think of it as an anticipated result.

An objective is the yardstick for measuring success. An athlete, for example, undertakes a competition with the objective of either breaking his previous record or beating all other competitors. From his point of view, he is successful if he achieves at least one of these two results.

In a similar way, success for an organization occurs when a goal has been achieved. If an organization does not know **what and how much** it wants to achieve, it cannot focus its resources and measures on the "what"—the objective. As a result, employees will not know the extent to which they have been successful.

1.2.3.1 Thinking in Contributions

If a company wants to pursue a market share or profitability target, its employees must deliver coordinated contributions in the form of results. For example:

- Saleable products or services must be developed and tested.

- Products or services must be available on time in the required quality and quantity.
- Products must be familiar to potential customers so that they can buy them.
- There must be a smooth and efficient administrative process, from customer service to accounting to ensure immediate response to inquiries, the timely recruitment of new personnel, the factual, professional, and timely correct preparation of financial statements, and more.

From the point of view of the individual, the key question is:

What results can I contribute that help my manager and my company achieve their objectives?

Are my contributions important to the overall success of my company? How can I judge for myself whether my contributions are satisfactory in the sense of quality, quantity, and timeliness? What is my yardstick of comparison? To succeed in answering these questions it is necessary that the contributions be described measurably in the form of results to be achieved.

Most people find it difficult to describe the results of their efforts. We are used to just working and often ignore the question why something is being done. This failure to understand why is easy to test: explain the difference between an objective and an activity to your employees and then ask them to write down their goals. Most people will still create an activity list.

Even if the objective to be achieved is clearly understood initially, employees often forget it while working. This often happens in stressful situations and when people have a high workload, resulting in their only keeping the correct execution of the activities in mind. Odiorne (1987, p. 56) calls this the **Activity Trap** and shows that the occurrence of the Activity Trap not only means the loss of corporate profits but above all causes people to shrink in their personality and in their activities. Most people are creatures seeking success (ibid., p. 101); their being is purposeful. They define objectives for themselves and on their own initiative (ibid., p. 60) because they intuitively know that those who succeed are those who can compare their results to the yardstick they defined themselves beforehand or that were set by others.

Thinking in contributions is the first basic principle of MBO. It is bottom-up thinking, but it requires that supervisors disclose their own goals top-down so that their employees can derive their appropriate contributions. The derivation of objectives from the overall objective to the objectives of the individual employee cannot be purely mechanistic as the objectives to be adopted vary greatly depending on the function or management level.

From this it can be concluded that the process of finding, defining, and formulating objectives needs to be learned. Objectives must fulfill various criteria so that people want to achieve them and are able to be guided by them.

1.2.3.2 Formulating Qualitatively Good Objectives

The central prerequisite for successful MBO are objectives for which achievement can be clearly determined, which individuals can accept, and which they can achieve given their hierarchical competence. Practical implementation of MBO shows that the ten criteria described in the below paragraphs are essential for the quality of a well-selected and formulated objective (translated from Rieder 2010, p. 158).

Result Orientation

Each objective must describe the result to be achieved or an anticipated situation (the what?). Descriptions of action (the how?) have no place in the objective.

Measurable or Verifiable

Every objective must be checkable, i.e., it must be possible to clearly determine whether the desired situation has occurred. This also applies to behavioral goals!

Time Bound

Each objective must contain the date of realization (or the realization period, if the start time is unclear).

Objectives Are Personal

Results are always the responsibility of individuals. An organization achieves its objectives only if the contributions made by the individuals are great enough. This also applies when a *team* is working together; the target carrier in this case is the team leader (who in turn can agree on specific objectives with individual team members).

Controllability

The person accepting the objective must be able to directly influence the factors that determine the achievement of the objective.

Challenging and Achievable

Every objective should be a challenge, starting from the initial situation. It must be achievable with effort. A goal that beforehand is not achievable will not be accepted and thus not realized.

Derivable

Each objective should contribute to a higher-level objective (or plan) of the organization or be derivable from the job description or functional diagram.

Measured Value and Measuring Method

If there is no written record of the measure and of the method to be used to measure the results achieved, there is a big risk that those who agree on an objective will talk at cross purposes.

Written Form
Objectives are not definitively agreed until both parties have signed the agreement.

Avoid Subsequent Discussions, Beware of Adjectives!
Room for interpretation makes it impossible to clearly determine whether the objectives have been achieved. Therefore, characteristic words such as "appropriate, fast, simple, sufficient, good, flexible, customer-friendly, practical" should not appear in target agreements.

1.2.3.3 The Process of Agreeing on Objectives

Agreement on Objectives
MBO is often translated as "Management by target-setting or target-dictation." Odiorne, the great promoter of MBO, recognized through practical application that management by *setting* or imposing goals is not promising. In the second edition of his book (Odiorne 1987, p. 89), he emphasized that the *goal negotiation process is* the centerpiece of MBO.

This insight is understandable, as a person who is supposed to achieve an objective must be convinced of the:

- Accuracy
- Appropriateness
- Relevance
- Accessibility

of the target.
If a goal is imposed on an employee without his participation, acceptance of the targeted performance level will be lacking. The employee will not personally identify with the result to be achieved and could possibly even try to torpedo realization of the objective (as he has always "known" that its achievement was not possible).

For nonacceptance of goals to be avoided and for management by delegation to be realized, a **process of agreeing on objectives** must be utilized from the beginning, enabling employees assuming objectives to help shape them. This relates especially to:

- The content (factual)
- The amount (how much?)
- The measurement method used (how is the achievement measured?)

of the objective. As part of the process, employees should be asked to contribute their own ideas. In addition, the way a goal is to be achieved should be left as open as possible so that the person taking on an objective can design and choose the most suitable path for achieving that goal.

MBO is closely linked to the *delegation principle*. Under this principle the fulfilment of tasks and the achievement of objectives is delegated to the lowest hierarchical position or person who has the overview and the ability to act autonomously. The decision-making authority required to achieve the objectives must also be delegated to that employee. Joint agreement regarding objectives creates clarity regarding what an employee needs to accomplish. The discussion regarding the results to be achieved and the tasks to be fulfilled also make it clear what authority needs to be delegated to the person in charge in order to achieve the objective.

It is often lamented that agreeing on objectives leads to a "self-service shop." Employees may be tempted to choose the target contributions they like best (with regard to the target itself or its value). If the delegation principle is correctly implemented (i.e., if objectives at all levels are formulated so that they make a direct contribution to the achievement of the objectives of one's manager or the company as a whole), the focus is automatically on the objectives that are most important for the company. During the agreement process, a supervisor has the opportunity to help his employees understand the importance of individual objectives. Space in the definition of personal goals of individual employees and managers should be deliberately kept open in order to address an employee's personal development.

Employees may build in *reserves* when determining target amounts, for example, by indicating costs higher than needed to generate the planned performance or by estimating the achievable performance lower than expected. Many managers say that in such cases goals should be set or imposed instead of agreed on. We do not agree with this approach. If a manager feels that his employee wants to include reserves in his objective, he must explain that reserves should only be planned at the top level of the organization. This is logical because the areas in which reserves are needed to achieve the agreed overall objectives will only become known as time goes by.

In the agreement process, the manager should take care that the levels of objectives are fixed so that they are attainable but challenging, achievable but with effort. To recognize what is possible with effort cannot be calculated in a mechanical way with goals set from top to bottom. Rather it requires knowledge of what employees are capable of as well as negotiation. Employees should not be overwhelmed by the formulation of objectives.

Imposing and setting goals incapacitates employees;
agreeing on objectives involves employees assuming responsibility.

The Process of Defining Objectives 1: Top-Down Development

The yearly objectives top management has drafted are the starting point in the process of defining objectives. Based on these and on existing strategic and medium-term objectives, each executive draws up draft objectives for his area of responsibility. Answering the following questions can help in defining objectives:

"How can I (in my position and with my employees) directly contribute in the coming year to:

(a) Corporate long-term objectives
(b) Strategic and medium-term objectives
(c) Annual company-objectives?"

Additionally, job descriptions and/or functional diagrams may provide ideas regarding goals to be achieved, as these may already contain descriptions of objectives. Finally, each person must also ask themselves what personal development goals they would like to achieve within the company.

The result of this work is a **preliminary catalog of annual objectives**, which should include 37 important goals. A larger number of goals is difficult to keep in mind and it becomes difficult to concentrate on achieving the essential ones. Wherever possible, care should be taken during this phase to ensure that the objectives are formulated as anticipated results and that the target level and the method of measuring target achievement are described at the same time (see Sect. 1.2.3.2). This preliminary list of objectives is presented by the members of senior management to their directly subordinate managers/employees, along with explanations of the background and connections.

At the next stage, goal-defining process begins anew, i.e., the persons concerned begin to design their own provisional list of objectives on the basis of the input received. Since they also ask themselves whether they can make a direct contribution to corporate policy, strategic or medium-term goals, the holistic nature of fixing objectives is promoted. However, the goals of the superior automatically receive a higher weight, since the employee primarily drafts contributions to the objectives of his supervisor.

This process continues step by step until each employee finally has a draft of his own list of objectives.

The Process of Defining Objectives 2: Lateral Coordination

Today, many forms of work and processes cannot be organized by describing processes solely within a function. Often the achievement of a result in one's own area is dependent on input from other areas. Cross-functional coordination is thus increasingly becoming the most important part of MBO. Parallel to the process of formulating their provisional list of objectives, employees must therefore also consider which services and/or behaviors in other areas or from other persons they will require in order to achieve their objectives.

Example

If a controller intends to prepare a customer profitability statement using the management information system, he must first clarify with order entry, invoicing, and IT whether the required data will be available. In addition, the IT department must enable him to access this data directly and ensure that the appropriate evaluation tools are available. If these preliminary services are not provided, the controller will not be able to achieve his objective.

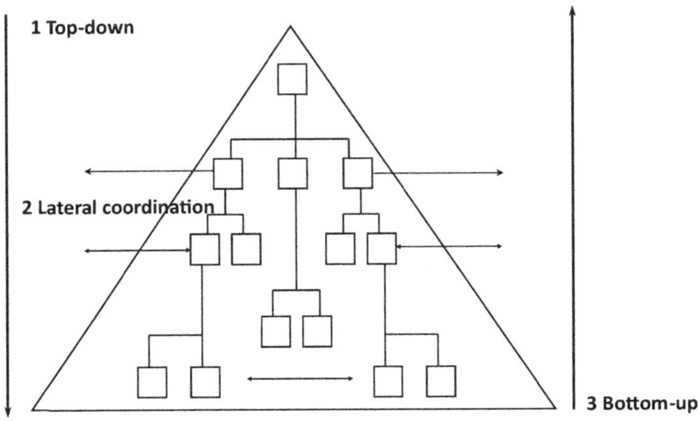

Fig. 1.6 The three main phases of achieving coordinated objectives

Cross-coordination improves the quality of goal fixing and leads to consistent objectives that are not mutually exclusive with other people's goals. Only when one's own draft of objectives is known does it becomes clear with which persons **coordination talks** need to be conducted and whether an objective can be achieved. Lateral coordination helps ensure that all employees "pull on the same rope in the same direction" (Fig. 1.6).

The Process of Defining Objectives 3: Merging from Bottom-Up
Since each employee formulates his own target contributions, it is to be expected that the individual contributions will not add up to the totals that the manager has drafted, or that interesting goals worthy of implementation will be drawn up, but these will not be sufficient to support the achievement of the next level manager's objectives. Due to situations such as these it is necessary to consolidate planned results from bottom to top.

This happens when an employee discusses his own objectives list with his manager. In discussing objectives to be achieved it is up to the employee to disclose his considerations and target contributions to his direct supervisor so that together they can determine the contents, the result, the due-date and the method of result measurement for each agreed objective. This meeting places high demands on the supervisor. He must ensure that:

- His employees do not build up reserves and formulate objectives that are too low.
- His employees do not overestimate themselves or formulate targets that exceed their possibilities or their sphere of influence.
- The agreed contributions are suitable for achieving the totality of his own objectives and correspond to his priorities.

- All objectives are correctly formulated in terms of quality, and that due attention is paid to the measurability of their achievement.
- Employees can personally identify with what has been agreed.

By repeating this process from bottom to top at each level it is possible to see whether the company's annual targets are achievable or not. It may happen that, once bottom-up consolidation has been achieved, a further revision of individual target contributions is required because the planned results are not sufficient. Ultimately, if revision of the individual target contributions is still not enough to achieve the desired corporate goals, adjusting the corporate objectives downwards selectively may be required.

It often happens in this process that nobody wants to further resize cost or investment budgets and that no possibilities for additional sales can be found. In such situations top management often dictates a "haircut" (where all areas must reduce their planned costs by a given amount, say, 10%). However, requiring an across-the-board cost reduction such as this must be avoided. Such a command chokes off the culture of coordinated goal finding and agreement in one fell swoop. The following year most managers will start to build up reserves because they fear that part of their budget will be cut or that their goals will be set higher. In addition, "December fever," otherwise known as "use it or lose it" (in which managers feel they must use their budget completely, or it will not be granted the next year), is promoted.

A "haircut" is poison for Management by Objectives!

The Process of Defining Objectives 4: Definitive Agreement

Once the three phases of defining objectives have been completed, the final agreement is to be set. The agreed objectives become binding through a two-stage procedure:

1. By the signature of the employee and his manager on their agreed list of objectives.
2. By the approval of the annual objectives and the budget of the company by the highest management body (board of directors, supervisory board, possibly owner).

Sales and cost budgets should encourage managers to think carefully about what they intend to achieve with their organizational unit in the next period. The inclusion of new objectives during the financial year or a change in the order of priority should be the exception. If the three phases described above are seriously gone through, the really important results are also recognized and mutually coordinated. The balance resulting from the discussion of objectives should lead to a concentration of forces on achieving the overall objectives. To constantly add new goals disturbs this concentration on the essential objectives.

MBO is a powerful tool for searching for and deriving subgoals to achieve the developments and results envisaged in AMPLE. Above all, the target areas defined in AMPLE can be broken down to the level of the individual. Focus on the financial year allows an organization to present measurable and verifiable interim results. These in turn must be monitored in the management cycle and result in corrective measures if variances occur.

In an integrated information system, the agreed objectives and their metrics should be visible as information for the manager, his superiors, and his employees. Very successful companies, such as Intel, Google, LinkedIn, Zinga, and Bayer, disclose the objectives of their managers to the entire workforce. Smaller German companies such as MyMuesli and Viventura are also users of the OKR (Objectives and Key Results) principle (see Dörner, 4 March 2016). John Doerr, the founder of the OKR principle, published his ideas and insights in his book *Objectives & Key Results* (Doerr and Duggan 2017); the procedures he proposes are fully in line with those outlined in the introduction to this book and Sects. 1.1 and 1.2.

1.3 Tasks, Competencies, and Responsibilities

Those who (co-)decide the content and the levels of objectives assume responsibility for the results according to well-known rules of organizational management (Ulrich and Fluri 1995, p. 146 f.), but they also determine the measures, the use of resources and—if necessary—the corrective measures. Every manager assumes responsibility for the achievement of his objectives. This responsibility can comprehensively be described with four elements (Fig. 1.7):

All actions and behaviors of a manager and his employees should aim at achieving the agreed objectives while adhering to these four elements (QQDR—quality, quantity, deadline, and result).

Responsibility for Action, Managerial Responsibility, and Delegation

Those who pass on part of their management task to others retain managerial responsibility but pass on the *responsibility for action*. The same thing happens at the next lower level. This is the delegation *principle*. *Managerial responsibility* resides with the delegating manager, and responsibility for action arises with the assuming party, i.e., responsibility for action can be delegated, but not managerial responsibility. Consequently, the top manager bears nondelegable responsibility for the whole company. Responsibility for action is transferred to the subsequent hierarchical levels. The latter becomes managerially responsible when tasks are delegated further. This cascade runs through the entire organization. This principle also applies to the achievement of financial targets.

Quantity	Deliver the ordered quantity.
Quality	Achieve the required quality.
Date	Deliver the service on time.
Result	Maintain the flexible budget or the planned result.

Fig. 1.7 The four main elements of responsibility (QQDR)

Delegation Enables Self-Organization

Delegation is an organizational principle designed to help cope with complexity. Delegation passes decision-making freedom to the next level, so that the delegating level no longer has to worry about the details of goal attainment and can use its time to make more comprehensive decisions. The transfer of decision-making freedom to the next level is countered by the assumption of responsibility for action.

> Any manager is committed to achieving the objectives he has assumed. He is taking responsibility for them. In return, he is given the freedom to determine the means by which to achieve the objectives and the use of resources within the defined framework conditions.

To cope with complexity the delegation principle should be implemented as fully as possible. This means that responsibility is always passed on to the lowest possible level. There, the bearers of action and managerial responsibility organize themselves in their areas of work and take responsibility for achieving the goals.

Delegation Requires Indicators to Measure Achievements

In a goal-oriented organization, delegating managers as well those assuming responsibility for action have the need to find parameters that show them quickly and clearly whether the desired objectives of their management area have been or will be achieved.

Following the management cycle (Fig. 1.4), an integrated planning and control system must be able to provide information for planning, decision-making, measurement, target to actual comparisons, and assessment of the impact of intended corrective measures. It is necessary to identify the most important parameters and key figures for the success of a given organizational area. The principle here is that measurement should be carried out with as few parameters as possible to ensure *concentration on the essentials* (the achievement of the objectives).

How the QQDR parameters are determined according to different managerial levels (i.e. for orders, cost centers, projects, inventories) is an important topic in the design of an integrated planning and control system. A parameter is considered **appropriate to the managerial level**, if the responsible person:

- Has the authority to directly influence the levers that can change the value of the performance measure.
- Can define the target value (and the scale) of the key figure together with the superior.
- Does not receive any charges for variances that have their origin in other management areas (i.e., outside the own direct sphere of influence).

Individuals, not organizational units, assume responsibility for the achievement of goals. This is the reason why objectives are assigned to individuals. In practice, if two (or more) people are responsible for the same objective, often neither will be.

1.4 Planning and Management Levels

Achieving the positions aspired to in AMPLE requires not only the application of the management cycle, the delegation principle, and management by objectives, but also the appropriate derivation of the contents of objectives and a suitable planning process.

Section 1.1 described the purpose of the enterprise and its documentation in corporate policy. The interaction of the various management and planning stages of an integrated planning and control system is dealt with there. These are taken from the St. Gallen Management Model (SGMM, p. 29 and Sect. 2.1) but can also be found in a similar form in other discussions of corporate management.

Figure 1.8 shows the four management levels. They are individually identified because they answer different questions. In addition, the relevant time horizon for each is also different.

As mentioned in Chap. 1, *corporate policy* applies "from now on" and remains valid indefinitely. In contrast, a *strategy* to be implemented should have a realization period so that the management can assess whether the targeted positions in the market can also be achieved within a useful period of time.

The field of *operational planning and control* begins with the questions: "How to achieve the goals?" and "How do we react to disruptions?" Operational planning has:

- A medium-term horizon (what resources and potentials are to be made available in the coming years so that the strategies can be implemented?)

Fig. 1.8 The four planning levels

- An annual horizon (what results are to be generated in the planned year so that the ideas from medium-term and strategic planning and corporate policy become reality?)
- A horizon of a year or less (how to act if disturbances from the environment or from the company affect the achievement of annual or longer-term goals?)

1.4.1 Who Do We Want to Be(Come)?

The type of company to be created or further developed and the core values to which it is committed are derived from the purpose of the company. This is the subject of **corporate policy.**

We will use establishing and operating a public transport company as an example of defining business purpose and corporate policy. This example company decides to seek success in long-distance rail transport. It thus delineates its business as excluding air, road, and waterborne transport as well as local public transportation from its business.

A company that defines itself must consider the requirements of the various environments in which it operates and, if necessary, react to changes in these requirements. These adjustments should be reflected in the core values of the owners and senior management to determine whether the whole business can become what it wants to be.

To enable this reflection, top management should formulate its (long-term) main objectives in such a way that they are measurable and thus as assessable as possible. At the same time, it should determine which boundaries are to be adhered to (e.g., remaining a privately owned company, countries that should not be served). These specifications should be known by all employees, but especially by all managers. In line with the environments, the basic corporate policy statements are documented in three corporate concepts (Ulrich 1987, 107 ff.): the performance-based concept, the financial concept, and the social concept (Fig. 1.9).

Corporate concepts		
Performance-based	**Financial**	**Social**
Products / assortments	Profitabilty	Methods of management
Markets / market-position	Liquidity	Promotion of managers & employees
Quality (customer view)	Stability	Behavior towards competition
Price levels	Use of cash flow & profit	Behavior towards government & associations
Our core competencies		
Technologies		Political engagement
Geographic regions served		Behavior towards natural environment

Fig. 1.9 The three corporate concepts for the documentation of corporate policy

The **performance-based business concept** should be in line with the technological and market environments. It is necessary to determine in which product areas, product groups, or application areas the company intends to sell and which basic (raw material and manufacturing) technologies form the basis for producing these products (or, for a service organization, providing these services). Then it must be determined in which markets (sectors, industries, regions, sales channels) the sales should take place. These statements set the course for the search for strategies and for market development. Long-term market share positions to be achieved in the individual market segments are also taken into consideration. These are not yet objectives for absolute market shares to be won but aim at positioning the company in comparison to competition. For this positioning, statements on the price level to be achieved (e.g., low prices for mass products, higher price level for luxury segments) are also of great importance, as these subsequently determine the required investment (advertising, sales promotion, production quality).

The targeted product quality is also decisive for the market positions to be achieved (e.g., leading international supplier with market-satisfactory quality or niche player that can meet the highest quality requirements at any time). It should be noted that quality is not an issue of the company's own manufacturing processes but is defined from the customer's point of view (does the quality offered, combined with price and conditions, provide me as a customer the required benefit?).

The more precisely corporate policy statements are formulated and adopted (e.g., the largest absolute market share as a supplier of steel tube-based products to the European automotive industry), the clearer the starting position for finding and defining strategies will become. These specifications concentrate on the AMPLE elements of market position and evolution.

The **financial business concept** focuses on the liquidity and profitability elements of AMPLE. Anyone engaged in strategic and operational planning must know the order of magnitude of the level of profitability to be achieved (e.g., return on capital employed to be achieved). This is because when assessing a strategic plan, a project, or an investment request the projected financial return must be in line with market requirements. Furthermore, available money, i.e., liquidity, can become a bottleneck factor when many strategies and development projects place high demands on the use of funds. Another factor that severely limits options is stability. The independence of a company from financial backers is a key concern and, for many medium-sized and family-owned companies, maintaining financial independence is the most important corporate policy issue. (Exemplary rule: all fixed assets should always be covered by equity.)

Finally, a highly profitable, stable, and liquid company can jeopardize its future if its owners pay out too much from their earnings in the form of dividends or other disbursements. For this reason, the financial concept must also determine how the level of distributable profit is determined (e.g., after imputed depreciation of the replacement value) and which part of it is to be distributed (enough building of reserves before distribution so that future evolution can be financed).

The attractiveness of the company for existing and newly recruited employees depends to a large extent on how the company is managed and what guidelines are in place in relation to employees and other stakeholders. Topics related to the **social**

business concept include the management methodology to be "lived by" (e.g., consistent management by objectives, continuous further education of managers and employees, professional and hierarchical career opportunities) as well as behavioral aspects of interactions with competitors, the government, and other claimants (e.g., how to react if customers bring arguments of the competitors into discussion).

There is no business concept related to the natural environment as a company can only react to environmental aspects at the technological, financial or social level. Values and measures for the protection of the natural environment are therefore included in the three concepts presented. In a service company, for example, a great distance may be driven by company cars, resulting in significant carbon emissions. A tree planting is to be carried out so that an equivalent amount of CO_2 as emitted by the cars is converted back into oxygen. The company's actions relate to the social level (employees' desire to reduce carbon emissions), the financial level (payment for trees and transportation), and the technological level (physical management of the project). But oxygen cannot be produced by the company directly.

1.4.2 Where Do We Want to Go?

Based on the cornerstones of corporate policy, it is necessary to determine in which markets, with which services or products, with which technology, and in which areas of application the company should apply its technology in order to be successful. These **strategic questions** aim at achieving or maintaining a strong market position (Fig. 1.10).

The example company wants to become at least the second largest provider of long-distance travel in specified countries. This determination will later form the basis for the establishment of Strategic Business Units (SBUs) in the course of the planning process.

The term "strategy" is often used today for everything that somehow has to do with the future. The outcome of a strategic planning process must be more precise because it determines what is to be planned and what results are to be pursued. For this reason, we use the term **strategy** exclusively to answer two questions:

- With *which products or services* does the company want to achieve *what market position* (quantities, turnover, contribution margins) and *by when* (product–market combination)?
- Which existing internal *potentials for success* must be enhanced and which new ones must be built up in order to reach the wanted market positions?

In the functional areas (e.g., research and development, production, marketing, procurement, IT) foundations must be laid so that strategies can become a reality. But these foundations are often also a prerequisite for other successful product–market combinations (e.g., building an internet application that covers all processes from product comparison to actual purchase and payment, or an R&D project that leads to lower raw material consumption for all manufactured products).

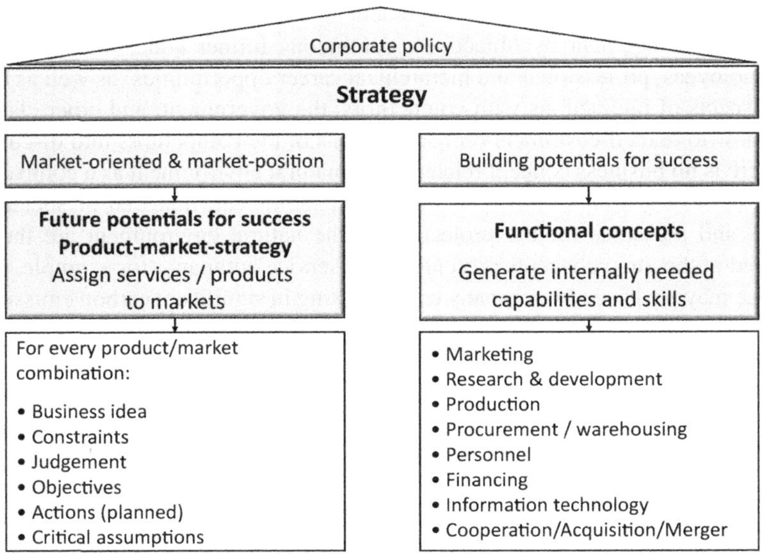

Fig. 1.10 Product/market strategies and functional concepts

We call these types of plans and projects **functional concepts**. In contrast to strategic plans, they are mostly function-related and have the character of medium-term operational plans (IT concept, financing concept, procurement concept, etc.). What they have in common is that they create the conditions to achieve desired strategic market positions but can as well generate benefits in various strategic business units.

The distinction between product/market strategy and functional concept has a practical background. A strategy is focused on:

- What the products and applications to be offered should be able to do.
- Who can buy them and the size of their potential sales markets.
- What benefits they will bring to the customer.
- What sales prices (possibly sales channel or country-specific) can be realized with them.

In addition, it is important to consider and record in the context of devising a strategic plan what developments can be used to maintain a lead over the competition. Achieving all this requires quantity, performance, pricing and cost plans as well as marketing, promotion and product development projects. Whether or not a strategy will pay off must be assessed with a dynamic investment appraisal.

In contrast, **functional concepts** describe how the functions should be developed in the medium term to reach the desired market positions and what evolutionary progress can be achieved in the functions themselves. These concepts are often implemented through projects. Thus they require the same consideration as to whether the investments will be worthwhile. However, since their development affects all business areas, the impact of their implementation on the whole company is relevant for decision-making, not just the impact on a single product–market combination.

1.4.3 How to Reach Objectives?

To attain the desired market positions, as well as to achieve the objectives in all other relevant target areas, an organization's potential must be built up and made to work. The course is set in **operational medium-term planning**, which covers the multi-year planning horizon. This is usually 2–5 years, but there are also companies with a medium-term planning horizon of up to 25 years (e.g., aircraft construction, gravel pits, power plants, and hospitals).

The implementation of **functional concepts** is likewise a topic of **medium-term planning**, as it describes the developments that are necessary for the realization of strategic product/market objectives.

In the example company this includes determination of which routes it wants to use, which of these it must build itself, how it will cover its energy needs, what personnel it will need, etc.

Medium-term planning provides the link between strategic and operational annual planning (Figs. 1.8 and 1.11). The most important task of medium-term planning is the preparation of a comprehensive preview of the foreseeable overall development of the company (market position, evolutionary developments, investments, results, consequences for the working methods of the company, and its employees). This overall view enables corporate management to assess whether everything that is planned to be done (strategically and operationally) appears feasible in terms of available personnel, management capacities, financial affordability, and profitability (more on this in Chap. 10). The whole way from corporate policy to the midrange plan is depicted in Fig. 1.11.

An organization's resources must generate profits which in turn must finance the innovations for the future and be enough to satisfy the demands of employees, suppliers, the government, and investors. The objectives to be achieved, the resources to be deployed and the procedural knowledge required to achieve the results should be coordinated in the **annual plan**. The results of this planning step are the agreed objectives of employees and managers at all levels and the associated plans for investment, cost, performance, revenues, and results.

The example company defines its timetable and all related sectoral plans and achieves agreement regarding the objectives to be achieved with the responsible persons.

Beginning with the start of the financial year, salespeople generate orders, production produces the products/services ordered, and research and development generates new products. All other functional areas ensure that resources and know-how are available as needed, that processes run smoothly and that the objectives can be achieved. To this end, the managers delegate the execution of the planned tasks and processes and set them in motion (the management cycle). This is the actual **execution** or implementation of the plan.

The example company uses its personnel and resources to ensure that trains run and customers are satisfied.

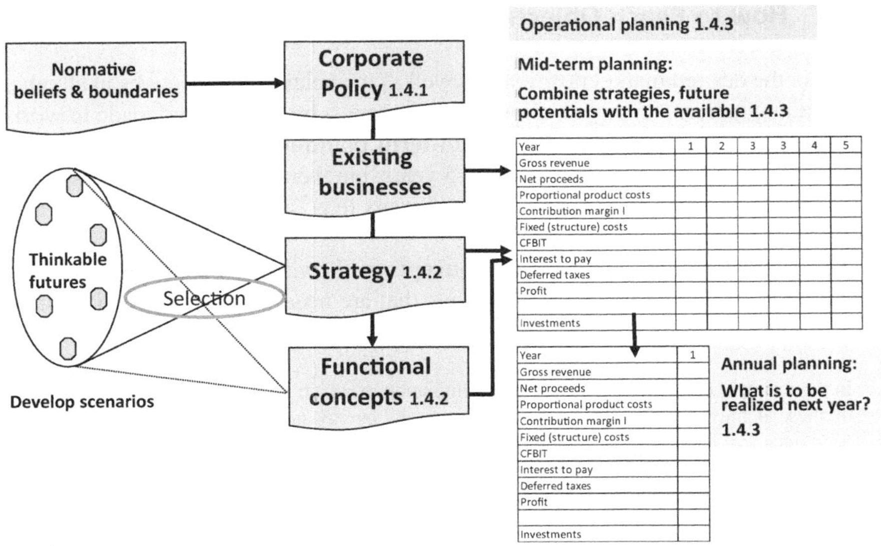

Fig. 1.11 From beliefs and boundaries to the annual plan

1.4.4 Reaction?

Forecasts of business performance will differ from actual outcomes: receipt of incoming orders can be irregular, production must react to that irregularity, and purchasing must adjust raw materials from suppliers accordingly. Employees may be absent due to illness, dismissal, or other reasons, with the need to redistribute work. As a result, a further management level, **tactical planning,** is required for short-term control during the year.

In the example company, train compositions must be changed because more or fewer passengers book and because damage occurs to the rolling stock. Due to delays, detours must be organized, or replacement trains used.

1.4.5 Overview of all Planning and Management Levels

The overall view of the planning levels (Fig. 1.12) serves to recapitulate the connections and at the same time describes the most important tasks to be processed in the individual stages:

- The primary target of corporate policy is managers at all levels; their leadership is essential to ensuring that the principles are implemented. For this reason,

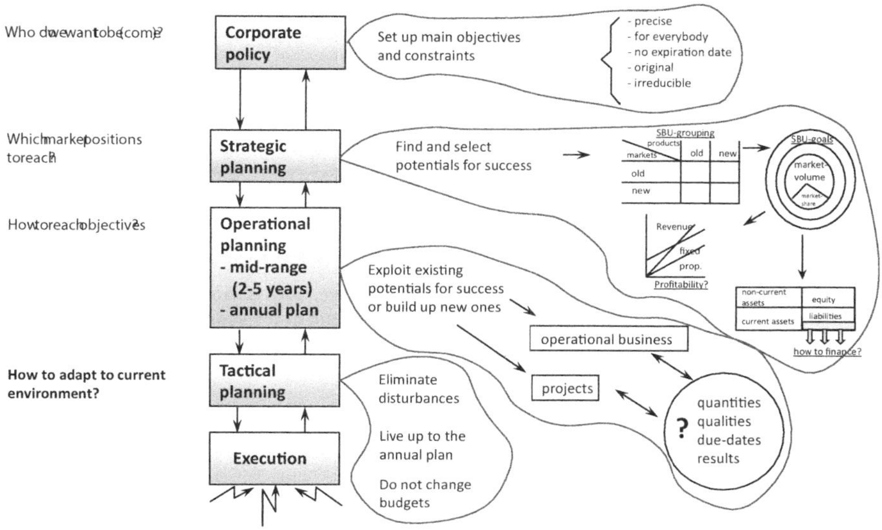

Fig. 1.12 Management steps in SGMM

corporate policy statements must show the characteristics listed in the bubble and the main objectives and constraints must be formulated in a comprehensible manner.

- In a company there are often more ideas for the development of future potentials for success than personnel, capacities, and resources available to implement those ideas. Therefore, strategic planning is essentially a selection process (e.g., which of the presented ideas do we want to develop into new or strengthened market positions?). These decisions must always be taken in relation to expected market developments. Therefore, the bubble shows the expected development of product/market combinations (concentric circles), the formation of strategic business units (SBU) in which the targeted market position is to be achieved and finally the question of the profitability of the strategy as well as its financial affordability.
- In operational planning precautions must be taken to fully exploit the existing potentials for success in the sense of AMPLE. Good utilization generates the profits and the liquidity needed to finance the new capacities for success that are required for strategy implementation. Exploiting existing potentials usually takes place in the existing organizational structures and processes of the business. In contrast, the development of new capacities for success is mainly built up in the form of projects. That requires cross-functional work, interdisciplinary working methods, partly not yet definitively clarified project goals, time pressure, often high financial commitment, and technical "new ground" for the employees in the projects. In projects as well as in existing business the responsible managers assume accountability for QQDR (see Sect. 1.3).
- The job of tactical planning and control is to react to the uncertainty of everyday life and either to eliminate the resulting "disturbances" or, if this does not appear

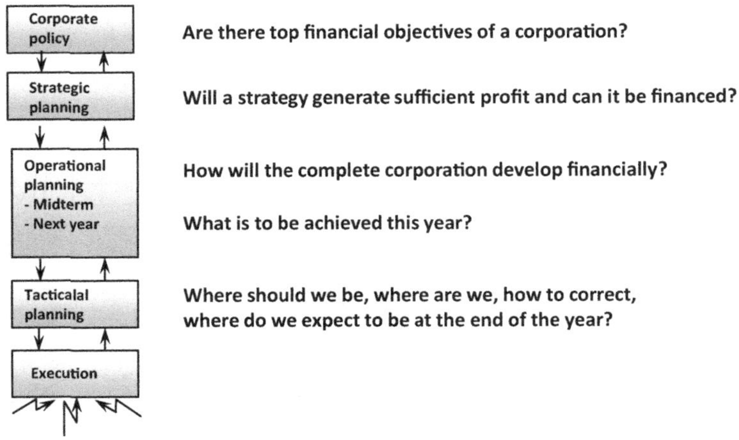

Fig. 1.13 The main questions for financial control

to be practicable, to try to circumvent them by means of corrective measures. The focus is on the management cycle and the annual objectives. A comparison with these objectives is important to assess their achievement for self-control. For this reason, Sect. 1.2.2 called for the adjustment of the forecast rather than objectives in the event of variances.

The application of these management levels to the financial aspects of the management of a company raises key questions as in Fig. 1.13.

1.5 Functions

Functions and functional areas (e.g., accounting, warehouse management, and information technology) are ubiquitous in companies and organizations. They are often (but rarely correctly) the main criterion for the design of the structural organization and result from the fact that their associated tasks must be carried out in a company so that "it can function at all." School-based training and study programs are often similarly structured according to functions and job descriptions. Employees are hired to perform a specific function (e.g., warehouse clerk, salesperson, payroll clerk, researcher and development engineer, controller).

Functional area managers are entrusted with the performance of tasks and the achievement of their area's objectives. For a clear demarcation between functional areas and thus the responsibility for QQDR (results), an overview of the functional areas is necessary. The organizational structure of these areas (also from the SGMM, p.23) starts with procurement as all companies require supplying functions (e.g., staff performing tasks ranging from personnel search to training and further education, management development, personnel support, and wage administration). Subsequently, in executing functions, products and services are invented and further

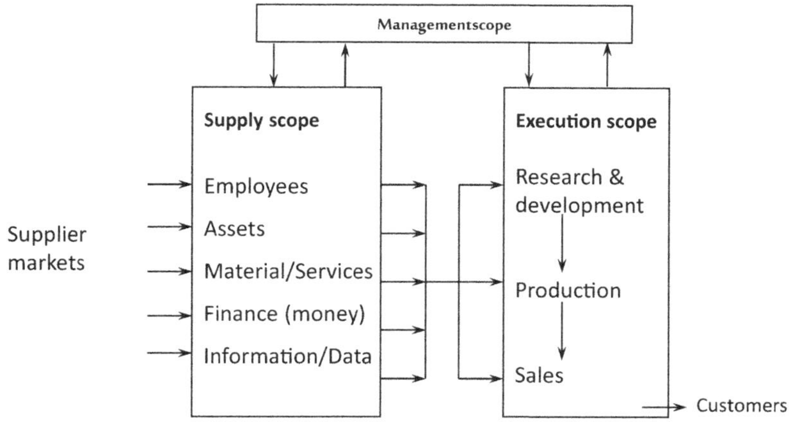

Fig. 1.14 Functional areas (generally, according to SGMM)

developed, manufactured, and sold. Management is also seen as a function securing coordination among the operational functions and leading the organization.

Executing and supporting functional areas are subdivided into departments and other subareas, each depending on the size of the company, with its own responsible manager. These depend on being able to plan and track their performance, costs, and results.

The functional areas (usually also the places where costs are incurred) are managed as *cost centers*. *Projects* or internal orders are set up to control services and costs as well as investments incurred. Whether producing products or services, cost centers and, above all, *production orders* are objects of planning and control. Product orders are manufactured in accordance with the planned or preliminary calculation and are stored as semifinished and finished products; services are delivered as ordered. Production-order data is also required for inventory management in the "material" function (Fig. 1.14).

In the sales area, the customer dimension is added to the product dimension. For the plan-to-actual comparison, the data contained in the individual billing line becomes the central information source for the evaluation of the results achieved according to the management cycle. Linkage with the "finance" area and with accounts receivable accounting is created via the billing totals and terms of payment.

All data necessary for understanding what has happened (the actual) is generated in the functional areas. Thus, when designing the information system it is necessary to ensure that data is always recorded at the most detailed level. Otherwise detailed analysis according to all planning and control dimensions will often be impossible. The most detailed levels are required for:

- Materials (item number)
- Production orders (manufactured product or service)
- Sales orders (units sold)

- Cost centers (activities, cost)
- Projects (services, cost, investments)

Up to now, the structural and process-related characteristics of holistic management have mainly been derived and presented top-down. But looking from bottom-up, when designing a performance management system, it needs to be ascertained whether the control-relevant data can be stored in the proposed system with the necessary granularity and then aggregated and analyzed according to the required dimensions. With the pressure of installing a new ERP-system on time this user requirement is often forgotten. System design must always keep in mind that plans are developed top-down whereas analysis starts from the most detailed level (the countercurrent principle, see Glossary).

1.6 Stocks and Movements

All organizations, whether they trade products or are engaged in the production and sale of products or services, including public administration entities and NGOs, are characterized by a constant alternation between movements and stocks (i.e., inventories). For integrated planning and control, this interplay must be continuously mapped in terms of quantity and value. The timely availability of raw materials, semifinished and finished goods and maintaining liquidity is always a prerequisite for being able to do business.

The sequence of processes, the resulting inventory changes, and their monetary consequences are shown in Fig. 1.15 for a manufacturing company with two production stages. If the two production stages are omitted, the representation is also suitable for a trading company or a pure sales subsidiary of a corporate group. In these cases, stock ingress corresponds roughly to purchases and store exits to sales (except for free samples and non-product-related consumption in cost centers).

For service companies and governmental organizations it is often the case that specific purchases are made directly for orders or that operating materials are procured from the warehouse on an order-related basis. For example, a hospital

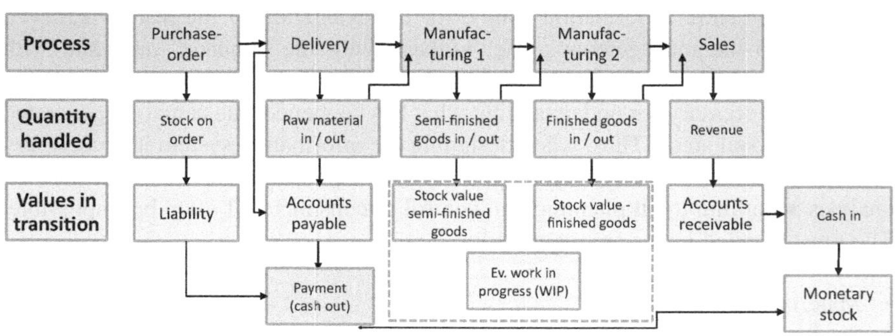

Fig. 1.15 Processes and different stocks in their sequence

may purchase medicines and medical aids, put them in stock, then use them on a case-related basis. Similarly, a building authority may have expert opinions prepared by third parties, which are then charged to applicants for building permits. In these cases the stock "orders in progress" is created, similar to "work in progress" in a manufacturing company.

Knowledge of the quantity and value of stocks is of great importance for integrated planning and control:

- The order stock plus the existing stock provides information on how much can still be sold or produced before reordering.
- Commitments (liabilities) indicate the cash outflows to be expected soon because of orders.
- Semi-finished and finished goods inventories are used to determine range indicators (how long and how much can still be sold before production has to be resumed?).
- By comparing finished inventories with planned sales, it is possible to assess how good the service level is for individual products.
- Sales made on credit generate accounts receivable. These represent the portion of the company's assets that have not yet been collected and therefore need to be financed.

Management-Oriented Inventory Valuation

An information system for integrated planning and control also has the task of informing the appropriate person when corrective actions need to be considered or taken. This is done by target-to-actual comparisons (see Sect. 1.2.1, Feedback-loop), which show how well the plan or target has been achieved to date and whether the resulting variances require corrective action. Every manager needs to be able to compare his own performance with his objectives without the comparison being influenced by performance in other areas of the organization.

Examples include:

- If the actual purchase price of (raw) material differs from the planned values the buyer must react and, in particular, inform the sales department immediately. However, a person responsible for production orders should be able to procure the material from inventory throughout the year at the planned price (standard price). If this rule is not observed, it is not possible to tell the amount of the variance that resulted from purchase price changes and the amount which is the result of input quantity differences.
- Inventory management at planned purchase prices is also important for accrual accounting. This is because the purchase price variance arises at the time of purchasing (when the delivery or invoice comes), not at the time of consumption. Consequently, this variance must be recorded in the month of purchase. If stocks of the same raw material (item number) from deliveries with different purchase prices are in inventory, the price variance can only be distributed randomly

among the production orders, since it would have to be decided which order receives the cheaper material and which the more expensive one.

- In many companies, fluctuating purchase prices are recorded in inventory valuation by means of weighted average purchase prices. For managers, this method has the disadvantage that the input material is charged with a different valuation each time a production order is placed, which in turn makes it impossible to keep the value and quantity effects apart.
- It is therefore advisable to consistently manage inventories at planned purchase prices even if purchases are made in other currencies or if the final purchase price has not yet been determined at the time the materials are sold. The planned purchase prices for 1 year thus become **standard prices** for product costing and inventory movements.
- If manufacturing in several stages (for example, semi-finished products are produced and stored in inventory, and then "purchased" from stock to manufacture the finished products), it is recommended that the intermediate products also be carried at standard value in the semi-finished products warehouse. This standard value is calculated using the standard costing process (with bill of materials items valued at standard cost and standard activities of the production cost centers valued at the proportional planned cost rate).
- If production orders are only partially completed at the end of the period (month or year), only the finished units are delivered to stock at standard value. At the end of the period, production still includes the raw materials and semi-finished products already purchased, as well as the production services already performed for the order. This results in the value of the work in process (WIP).
- When an item is sold, it should also be transferred from stock at the planned value. This is because the sales department wants to be able to recognize which variables within its direct sphere of influence (gross/net price, discounts and sales deductions, etc.) have positively or negatively changed the contribution margin achieved.

Deviations from the plan or standard must always be reported in the period in which they occur to give management quick indications of how to control their own area of responsibility. In accounting, this corresponds to reporting on an accrual basis.

In summary, it is recommended that the following valuation approaches be used for control purposes in accounting for management:

- Planned-purchase prices used for raw materials and other recurring purchases which are significant in terms of amount.
- Raw material inventory (and possibly also auxiliary and consumer goods) valued at standard purchase price.
- Semi-finished goods in the warehouse valued at budgeted proportional standard production cost (see Sect. 4.8).
- WIP valued at standard purchase price for raw materials already related to the order, proportional standard production cost for semi-finished products,

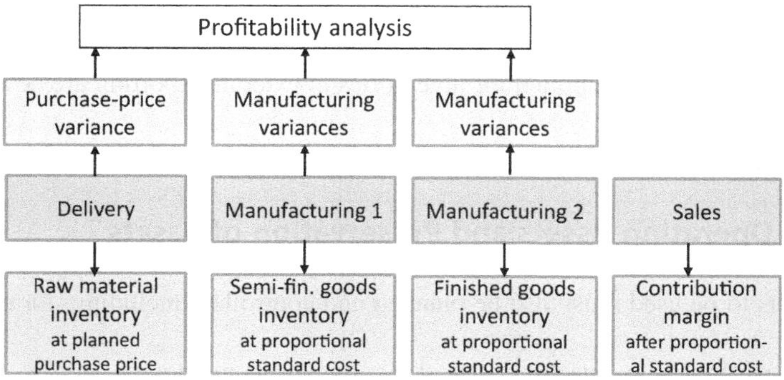

Fig. 1.16 Valuation of inventory rotation always made at proportional (standard) cost of goods

production activities at standard manufacturing cost, less any (partial) finished products already delivered to stock, valued at their proportional cost rates.
- Finished goods (in the warehouse) valued at proportional standard cost.

All inward and outward inventory movements are to be valued at these standard rates. This ensures that variances are always shown where they arose and that recipients always receive their input goods without variances from previous steps, which in turn facilitates the search for improvement measures within their own area.

Variances are to be shown where the cause lies (e.g., cost center or order) as the starting point for corrections is also there. An allocation of variances to other products or cost centers should not take place as the receiving unit is not responsible for them. All variances end up directly in the profitability analysis. This makes sense in an integrated planning and control system because there is no direct cause-and-effect-relationship between the service provider and the subsequent recipients (see Chap. 6) (Fig. 1.16).

At the end of the fiscal year it is necessary to revalue the various inventories without affecting net income. This is because the warehouse receipts and issues for year X are always valued at the standard (planned) values for year X, so the responsible manager has a unique reference point for comparing the actual with the plan and with the target. The year-end closing inventories of raw materials, semi-finished products, WIP (orders in progress), and finished products are thus all valued at the standard proportional cost of year X.

If in year X + 1 the cost of a service or product changes, e.g., because of a streamlined manufacturing process, or if the raw materials to be procured in the following year become more expensive. The proportional standard manufacturing costs of the items concerned can also change. The manager's new comparison standard becomes the planned or standard cost estimate for year X + 1.

In such cases, the inventory at the end of year X should be revalued in the opening balance of year X + 1 with the planned cost of year X + 1. This revaluation must be carried out internally without affecting net income, as the management success of year X is assessed based on the valuations of year X, and that of year X + 1 is assessed by comparison with the plans of year X + 1. The corresponding procedure is shown in Chap. 8.

The valuations to be applied for inventories in external reporting are described in Sect. 6.6.

1.7 Operating Assets and Preservation of Assets

The assets to be used must also be planned and controlled, including, for example:

- Physical: buildings, machinery, fleet, equipment, computers
- Intangible: purchased or self-created IT programs, patents, customer addresses

Determining the current value of the (fixed) operating assets involves making numerous assumptions and estimates. Nevertheless, it is necessary to know the replacement value of these assets as managers need to know how much they must earn to replace assets at the end of their useful life with new ones. Management must assume that the company will continue to exist successfully (i.e., is a going concern).

To plan and control investment in fixed assets and imputed depreciation all technical specifications are relevant plus the following data:

- What is the current (residual) value of an asset and in the aggregate for all investment properties?
- How much would have to be paid at current prices if the complete systems to be used had to be repurchased at the planning time?
- How much of the replacement value of these assets is consumed in a planned year and therefore must be earned in this period to preserve the assets?

These questions cannot be answered with conventional accounting data about fixed assets as these assets and their depreciation expense are calculated from historical acquisition values and depreciated according to tax or external financial reporting rules.

Management's point of view must focus on the preservation of the substance (those assets can be acquired again that are to be used further) and on the knowledge of the assets necessary for operation (how much would have to be paid today for the existing investment objects at current values?). Thus, the starting point for valuation in the integrated and future-oriented system is the replacement value (RepV).

Example: A production hall that was built 50 years ago for 100,000 Euro (without land) has probably been written off in the accounts for many years. If this building were to be replaced (ready for use) today, perhaps 2.1 million would have to be invested (due to inflation and the additional legal and safety regulations that have been added in the meantime). If the planned useful life of the building is assumed to be 30 years, this results in an imputed depreciation of 70,000 for the planned year. From a management perspective, this amount corresponds to the annual asset preservation cost that must be earned before a profit will be generated. The 2.1 million Euro correspond—also from a management point of view—to the assets required for a completely new plant. Management estimates that the existing plant can be used for another 10 years. The residual value of the fixed asset to be shown in the operating balance sheet amounts therefore at 700,000 (i.e., the replacement value (RepV) of 2.1 million less 20 years imputed depreciation of 70,000 per year).

Promoting sustainable and holistic corporate management therefore requires the inclusion of imputed depreciation in the internal income statement and the presentation of the residual values of the assets in the operating balance sheet (RepV minus imputed depreciation for all prior years). The instrument for this is a fixed asset accounting tool in which external accounting values as well as operationally relevant values can be kept (see Sect. 4.7.7 for implementation).

Management-Oriented Balance Sheet

The assessment of profitability (AMPLE) requires that the internal balance sheet also be prepared based on operationally relevant valuations. As shown above, inventory is valued at plan values (for the actual year) and the fixed assets at replacement values. Cash and receivables as well as borrowed capital are usually valued equally in internal and external terms. To ensure that the sum of the assets required for operations corresponds to the sum of all debts, adjustment items must be included in equity (see Sects. 4.10.2 and 6.4.2).

Example: An aging hospital operating without significant new investments can show a higher EBIT for external reporting purposes because it must write off less depreciation than a newer, state-of-the-art hospital.

1.8 Market Dimensions

The marketing of products and services is occurring in increasingly more complex ways. Companies sell physical products or product sets, services, rights (e.g., licenses), and the like to customers. They can reach existing and new customers as well as other interested parties over very different channels:

- Direct sales (via the company's own sales force or mail order)
- Sale via retailers or wholesalers
- Sales via own sales companies or sales partners (distributors)
- Online sales (directly or via online sales providers)

Additional complexity arises because:

- They can sell to different regions and countries.
- They can sell to end customers via processors.
- They can sell through various marketing agents (e.g., architects, trade journals, consultants of all kinds, word-of-mouth communication).
- They can sell to a variety of industries.
- They can sell to different companies of the same group.

The list is not complete. To determine the structures of the planning and analysis dimensions requires a detailed understanding of the company under consideration. In each case, the different dimensions must be provided according to the actual structures of market development:

- Product (item) → Product group →Assortment or product area → Application area
- Customer → Customer group → Country, region, →Industry → Processor
- Customer → Sales channel → Customer corporate group
- Customer → Sales representative → Sales area
- Sales agent → Customer (group)

When designing the planning and control system, the countercurrent principle (see glossary for a definition) must also be applied. The evaluation dimensions required for strategic and operative planning are imposed top-down. Bottom-up, it must be the case that all key performance measures required for multidimensional analysis can be derived from the individual billing line (see Sect. 5.4).

Learning from Integrated Management Models 2

In the previous chapter various dimensions of management were analyzed. Starting from the corporate purpose some basic requirements for an integral management control system were derived. In this chapter, the completeness of the system is examined and, where necessary, supplemented by comparing it to other comprehensive management models.

In our opinion, the *St. Gallen Management Model* (SGMM) and the *Viable System Model* (VSM) currently form the best basis for this comparison. Both design models were developed to present contents, processes, and structures of corporate management in all dimensions and to categorize the relationships between the various elements.

2.1 The St. Gallen Management Model and the Integrated Management System (IMS)

The St. Gallen Management Model has already influenced generations of managers because, as H. Ulrich, the main promotor of the SGMM, wrote, it pursues the purpose of "... consistently extending system-oriented business administration to the management problems of companies and similar social systems. From a practical point of view, we were guided by the insight that the management knowledge available today from practice and science has become so extensive and confusing that it can no longer be learned without considerable efforts to systematize it and without separating the essential from the merely fashionable" (Ulrich and Krieg 1974, p. 5).

Many essential elements of the SGMM have already been addressed in Chap. 1 with regard to their importance for integrated management. These include:

- Structuring the relevant corporate environments
- The management cycle with the management phases

L. Rieder, R. Lawson, *Management Control with Integrated Planning*, Management for Professionals, https://doi.org/10.1007/978-3-030-48302-9_2

- The need for an objective-oriented approach
- The planning/management levels versus the structural hierarchy
- Functional areas

2.1.1 The Integrated Management System

Based on the SGMM, F. Malik (1981, in particular p. 25 f.) developed the Integrated Management System (IMS). It presents the different elements and subsystems, along with their mutual dependencies, that are *necessary* and *sufficient* for correct and effective management. The description of the IMS presented here has been partially adapted by the authors with regard to the terms and the links presented without, however, changing the original content. The adjustments were made to facilitate access to the design of the integrated information system.

Four Quadrants for Classification of Management Topics
As indicated in Fig. 2.1, the structure of the IMS model is divided into *company-related* (left half, quadrants 1 and 2) and *employee-related* elements of management (right half, quadrants 3 and 4). The time horizon of the use of the instruments is displayed horizontally. The upper half groups the topics with time horizons of *more than a year*, the lower half those which result directly from the tactical management *during the year*. **The annual objectives for individual managers appear at the intersection between company- and employee-related specifications and are intended to describe the results to be achieved** (by the respective managers) **in the planned year.** From Fig. 2.1 it can be seen that:

- The planning/management levels (see Sect. 1.4) are contained in quadrant 1 (top left). These range from corporate policy to tactical management.
- Projects are listed on the demarcation line between company-related and employee-related. This is because real projects usually develop from strategic and medium-term planning. For their realization, the partial results to be achieved in a planned year must be reflected in the personal annual objectives of the relevant project managers and employees. For reasons of space, the "Projects" box was placed in the "above one year" area. Projects that can be finished within one plan year should also be included in the personal annual objectives.
- Organizational structures, and very often also processes, should be derived from strategies and from the functional concepts. Too often they are organized according to the availability of people and their abilities or wishes. But since organizational structures influence operational planning, for the assignment of tasks and responsibilities it is wiser to group these and the results to be achieved first and then to assign them to managers. For the documentation of these allocations the **functional diagram** (see glossary) is an easy-to-use instrument and should also be part of the information system.

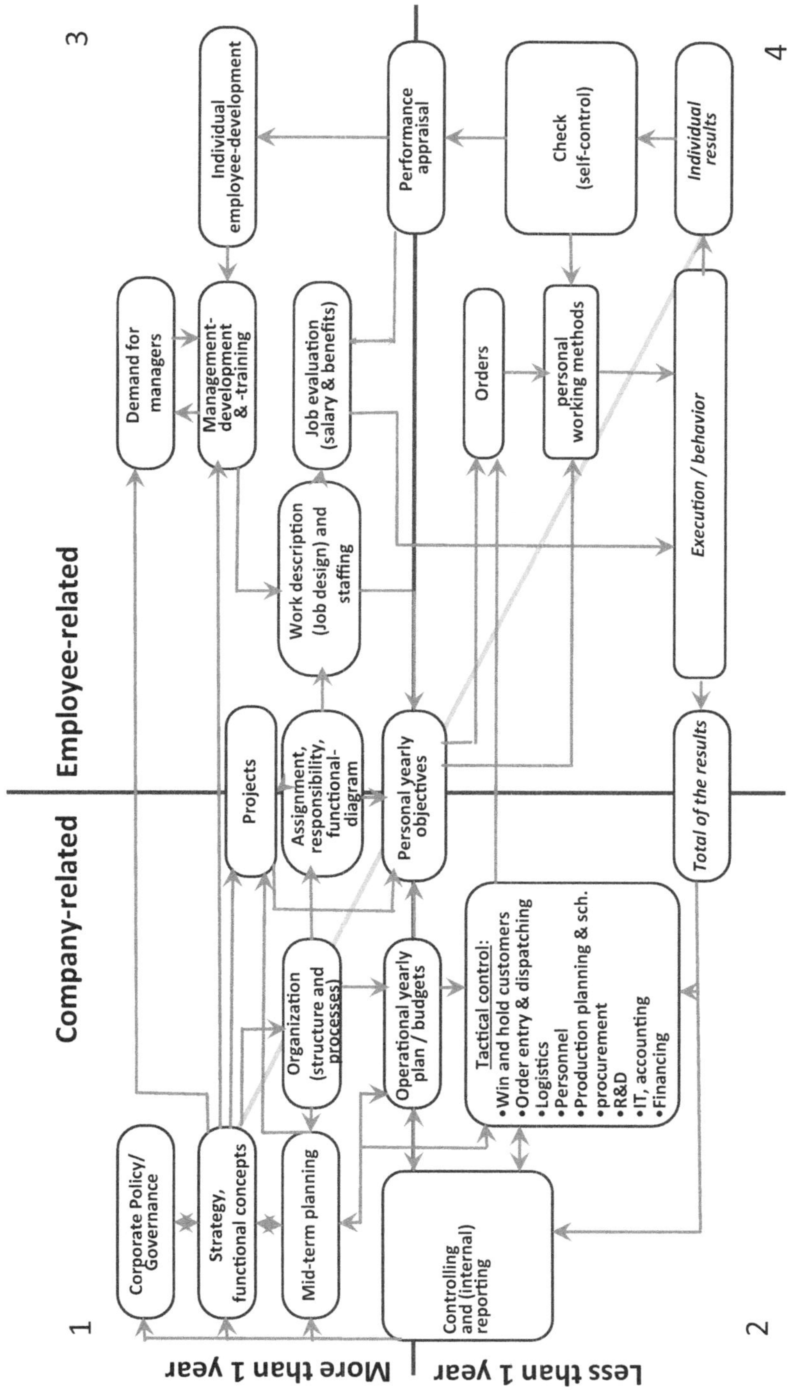

Fig. 2.1 The Integrated Management System, IMS (presentation slightly adapted by the authors)

- The implementation of strategies and functional concepts requires management capacity. Therefore, both the need for managers and the development of junior managers must be quantified and the managers' abilities developed (quadrant 3).
- Quadrant 4, bottom right, shows the way in which the annual objectives of individuals are translated into working results. Personal objectives are derived from higher-level goals or projects through the goal-fixing process and—if necessary—detailed more specifically into orders. The principles of delegation and self-organization are also included in the implementation process. From this arises the responsibility for achieving the objectives and the enabling of self-control (see Sects. 1.2.3 and 1.3). Management control depends on the documentation of all objectives in the information system so that the progress in achieving results (QQDR) can be tracked.
- Performance assessment is the means by which a supervisor gives feedback to a staff member concerning the achievement of results in order to specify the future development of the assessed person (training, education) as well as to judge changes in the eligibility of this person for managerial or technical promotion. All this happens in quadrant 3, top right.
- Questions concerning the need for specialist and management skills are also an important topic of this quadrant as they have to be taken into account in mid-term planning. The (management) potential to be built up is in turn a prerequisite for achieving the strategic and operational goals defined in quadrant 1.
- In quadrant 2, bottom left, the tactical control of the achievement of objectives takes place during the year. Measurement of the results achieved is necessary in order to assess the degree to which objectives have been achieved. The management cycle (Sect. 1.2.1) is thus located in quadrants 1 (target formation) and 2 (measurement of results and feedback). The comparison of actuals to plans requires the use of all planning systems. These prepare the data for planning and control during the year. This ranges from recording an initial contact with a potential customer to the entire provision of services and receipt of payment through to after-sales support for the customer. The main part of this data is collected in the ERP, the Enterprise Resource Planning system. This system must be set up in such a way that the indicators appropriate to each level can be obtained from its output and from the corresponding reports.
- The "tactical control" box mainly involves the determination of the necessary design and dimensioning of the integrated information system. This is because on one hand, all planning must be mapped in terms of quantity and value and, on the other hand, all transactions executed with all their processes and results must be documented in such a way that they can be evaluated in all management-relevant dimensions and compared with the plans.
- The personal annual objectives at the heart of the IMS require a regular plan-to-actual comparison. The necessary actual data must also be prepared in a suitable form in the information system.
- Finally, controlling "... is the entire process of defining objectives, of planning and controlling (in the sense of steering and regulating) and includes all relevant financial and commercial aspects" (CWB 2010, p. 52). With the help of

feedforward (corporate policy and strategy) and feedback (comparison of what was achieved with what was planned), managers try to prepare plans for the future, decide how to implement them, and then assess the extent to which they have already succeeded in implementing them. This also makes it obvious that controlling is not a department, but an essential task of managers at all hierarchical levels. Findings from the controlling process can affect all planning levels. For this reason, the controlling process is arranged overlapping in quadrants 1 and 2.

In our opinion the IMS can very well serve as a blueprint for the meta planning of an integrated management control system. With the development of the necessary (and adequate) instruments of holistic management, it also covers the areas relevant for the design of the information system and is expandable if new requirements arise from changes in corporate environments.

2.1.2 Coordination and Opposition to Planning and Budgeting

The purpose of planning is to align available know-how and resources with what one wants to achieve (objective) and to provide measures and actions that will lead to the achievement of these objectives (see management cycle, Sect. 1.2.1).

In an increasingly division-of-work world a steadily increasing number of people with their own needs and values are involved in the coordination process. This makes it difficult to determine the measures to be taken and the resources to be deployed. Timely availability of (part-time) personnel combined with fixed delivery dates as well as presence times of the staff further complicate this coordination process. In addition, timely input from other areas is often a prerequisite for the successful implementation of a measure. When viewed across organizations, forward-looking **coordination** becomes just as important a component of planning as the allocation of resources.

The organization which effectively masters the coordination of results to be achieved with the tasks to be performed, as well as the organizing of necessary means and process knowledge, will create a significant competitive advantage. Other companies will find it difficult to compete with such an organization.

Example: A construction material supplier which is noted for always delivering exactly at the agreed time at the construction site will be awarded the contract during negotiations even if he is slightly more expensive than his competition. This is because ordering contractors will take into account the cost of their employees waiting for deliveries when deciding where to place their orders.

Well-integrated planning, from corporate policy to tactical management, is labor-intensive, but enables coordination and thus the acquisition of competitive advantages. Coordination involves all management levels joining forces in such a way that each individual and the entire company achieve the agreed results.

The time and effort required for the planning job speaks against coordination. "Budgeting takes too long, goes too much into detail, costs too much time and gets done too late." These and similar statements can be heard in many companies, mostly connected with the desire to abolish or at least simplify planning and budgeting. Jack Welch (1995, p. 73), then CEO of General Electric, gave an additional impetus to this idea with his statement: "The budget is the bane of corporate America".

Also starting from the feeling that conventional budgeting is no longer relevant, the Beyond Budgeting movement recommends the annual budgeting process be abolition. N. Pfläging, former president of the Beyond Budgeting Round Table, postulated at a presentation in Zurich on February 13, 2007 that processes be geared much more toward short-term to immediate-term market success, that resources should be made available "ad hoc" according to need, and that planning should be understood as a purely action-oriented process.

Increasing volatility of the economies leads many managers to ask: "Why should we plan at all? - tomorrow everything will be different anyway." But looking at the planning levels in the SGMM (see Sect. 1.4) and the IMS shows that planning and budgeting are indispensable because different questions are answered in different planning levels. In addition, these levels determine which resources are to be procured and installed and to whom they will be made available.

Budgeting is generally understood as the determination of planned amounts (e.g., revenues, expenses, investments) for the next plan year. This understanding falls short in several respects. Planning must also take place for the medium term and for the long term, i.e., for strategy formulation. In this process services are to be planned in quantities and activities so that coordination becomes possible. A plan purely based on money is only enough for the preparation of planned profit and loss statements and budgeted balance sheets.

Budget = Fight for Funds for Future Development

For a budgeting process to be effective it must lead to tough discussions within the company! Only the struggle for the limited means within an organization leads to a balance between strategic and operational goals. The Board of Directors or the Executive Board/Supervisory Board act as arbiters in this fight. These must stand above divisional egos and take the AMPLE areas (market position, innovation, attractiveness for employees, profitability, and liquidity) into account as the future viability of the company is decided.

Why?

- The release of a budget for the development of specific resources means that no investments can be made elsewhere unless operating costs are reduced elsewhere.
- If the construction of a new factory building or even an entire plant is approved, or if a budget is released calling for the acquisition of a new market segment, this usually has multiyear consequences for liquidity and profitability. Once the work

has begun, it becomes very costly to leave the factory half-finished or to use it for a different purpose. This means that budgeting must always be done over multiyear horizons.
- Investment in training and marketing can be halted in the short term (as is the case in any crisis). But training and marketing are central to the long-term viability of a business, whether in terms of market position, innovation, or profitability. The corresponding expenditure should therefore also be included in the multiyear plans.
- Project budgets should specify for each milestone what investments and costs may be consumed by the time the milestone is reached. During each milestone meeting, it is to be asked whether the project should be continued or discontinued (i.e., a go/no go decision). Increasing complexity of projects means that the project duration is likely greater than 1 year.
- Annual planning provides orientation on the results to be achieved in the planning year and the resources to be used for this purpose. It also forms the benchmark for the achievement of objectives. The 1-year horizon has proved particularly useful for recurring targets.
- An annual horizon is also an important orientation period with regard to maintaining solvency (liquidity). This is because the CFO must be able to control the liquidity of the company as a whole, taking into account both short-term liquidity bottlenecks during the year and the reporting of adequate liquidity ratios at the end of the financial year.

In a nutshell:

An approved budget is a license to spend.

If a position is released for filling and an employee is hired, costs and expenses are the consequence of this budget decision. It is more effective to "ruffle feathers" in the planning process before a budgeted position is approved than to correct it afterward.

In other words:

The battle for money must be fought (with the necessary rigor) **in the planning phase; later it is too late.**

This insight is the main reason why the emphasis in the design of a management control system is on planning questions and why key figures are also defined and selected according to these questions.

2.1.3 Conclusions from the IMS for System Design

The IMS lists the necessary and sufficient elements and subsystems for holistic management. With a view to setting up an integrated planning and control system, various requirements for the necessary contents of the data system can be deduced:

- Objectives are at the heart of the IMS. For this reason, the agreed objectives with their metrics and the results achieved should be documented and tracked in the integrated planning and control system. The extent to which a manager has access to the objectives of other units should be a result of the need for cross-coordination.
- Self-organization and self-responsible management are core elements of integrated management. To enable conversion, the holders of the objectives must have access to all data relating to quantities, services, dates, cost, and revenues for their range of responsibility.
- From the management cycle it follows that the integrated system must always present planned, actual and variance data. Also, forecast values should be included to consolidate the complete forecast for the end of the year or of a project. This defines the contents of the data structure (plan, actual, variance, forecast).
- Being better than in the previous year is only of limited use as a target template. The annual targets are derived from corporate policy, strategies, and medium-term planning. Eugen Schmalenbach, an icon of business administration, postulated in his book, *Kostenrechnung und Preispolitik* (1963, p. 447) that one should not compare "jog trot with jog trot." What he meant by this was the fallacy of comparing the inefficiencies of the current year with those of the previous year.
- Projects are also components of the integrated planning and control system. Their data is therefore also to be displayed in the management control system with objectives and plans as well as with interim results (results, performance, investments, cost, deadlines, and milestones).
- If investment projects are included in strategic or medium-term plans, their profitability must be clarified in the decision-making stage. Once a project has been decided, implementation and thus also the expenses to provide the resources begins. Therefore, it must be clarified before taking the decision to commence a project whether it will be sufficiently profitable and whether it can be financed. The appropriate instrument for this is the dynamic investment appraisal.
- If you cannot deliver, you do not make a deal! This means that the level of planned and current inventories from raw material to finished products must always be available in the information system.
- Agreeing on objectives and operational annual planning are mutually dependent. Thus, to include a reduction in processing time in the objectives only makes sense if the necessary investment is approved. Consequently, objectives should only be entered into the information system when the required resources have been released. Definitive fixing of objectives and budgets can only accurately take place if decided at the same time.

- The same applies to the project business. Before fixing a project goal it is necessary to clarify that the necessary capacity, knowledge, and skills of the project members are available.
- The level of detail in the various management or planning levels varies. Corporate policy and strategic decisions usually contain a lot of descriptive text, but only a few key parameters to which direct reference is to be made in the subsequent levels (e.g., market shares or net sales to be achieved, profitability to be achieved, or targeted equity ratios). This information can be documented in text form in the data system. However, if values to be achieved are determined in operative planning, these target quantities and values should be stored in the information system at least by product group, possibly even per item, so that plan-to-actual comparisons are possible.

2.2 The Viable System Model (VSM)

Designing a comprehensive system of indicators requires more than just thinking in hierarchies and overall goals. Consideration must be given to how a company can be made viable and maintained as a productive socio-technical system. "Cybernetics is the science of effective organization" (Beer 2008, p. IX). Based on this definition Stafford Beer describes an organization as viable if it can survive in its specific environment (business environment, group of companies, people). Even if it is independent and has a great deal of autonomy, it cannot survive in a vacuum (ibid., p. 1).

From a management point of view, it is interesting to recognize how such independent systems can be defined in a company and how they can be successfully controlled internally and externally. Nature itself has developed the best-known control system, the human nervous system. It ensures that the functioning of the various subsystems in the body are coordinated and that the overall system thus maintains itself. Comparisons with this system provides useful and essential insights for the development of integrated control management systems.

Beer developed the VSM to present such interrelationships in a way that is recognizable and transferable to companies. He also provided a presentation notation, a good introduction to which is provided in his book *Diagnosing the System for Organizations* (2008).

The purpose of this section is not to explain the VSM in detail as there is already very good literature (including an intensive blog, (see https://www.linkedin.com/groups/3680613/)) on this subject. However, the basic elements and some important contents of this control system are examined here in order to derive design recommendations for integrated planning and control systems from them.

2.2.1 Five Partial Control Systems

The basic unit of a viable unit is the operating unit, OU (Beer 2008, 21). It consists of the totality of the environments of the unit (free form/amoeba), the actual operation (circle), and the management of the unit (square) (Fig. 2.2).

Operating Units Are Customer-Oriented (Systems 1)
An OU does what customers pay for or fulfills the purpose of the organization; it is called System 1. It needs autonomy in its behavior toward the environments that are important to it and for its own management and resources (employees, facilities, material, money). However, because the OU is also integrated into an overall system that must compare competing interests, it must also adhere to rules "from above". People in the operating unit bring in ideas and different behaviors which, from management's point of view, must be supported, promoted, or restricted (with rules or indicators) for the cooperation to work. The greater the number of distinguishable behavioral states an operation can adopt through cooperation of people and resources, the more difficult it becomes to control and maintain viability.

Variety
The unit for measuring the number of distinguishable states was introduced by W.R. Ashby (1956, p. 20). Here are three simple examples:

- A stop signal has three lamps, each of which can theoretically be on or off. Thus $2^3 = 8$ states are possible. In road traffic, usually only three of these options are used to control traffic: red, yellow, or green individually. The control system, in this case legislation and/or regulations concerning the operation of vehicles, has defined that of all eight possible states only three are permissible. It thereby reduced the variety of the operation.
- A car factory has three car bodies, can use five different engines and paints the cars in ten different colors. This theoretically results in 150 models (states). In the case of the Ford Model T around a hundred years ago, the rule was that cars were only supplied in black because at the time all other available paints dried too slowly. This requirement also reduced the variety of the operation.

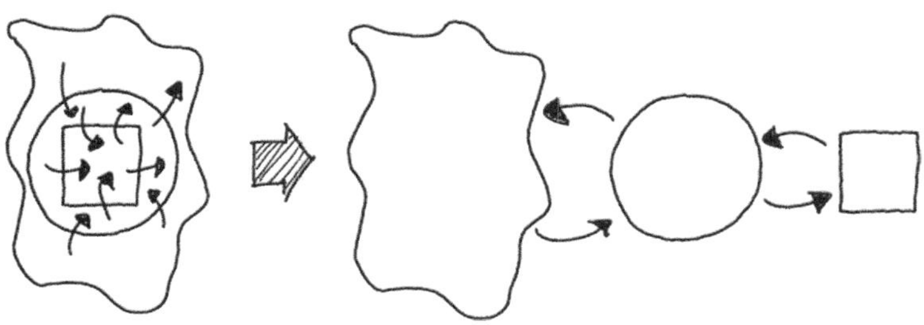

Fig. 2.2 Notation of an operating unit in the VSM (taken from Beer 2008, p. 21)

- A pharmaceutical company sells only one product. It is to be sold in ten countries, which requires ten country-specific packagings and leaflets. For implementation, the control system, in this case the ERP, must be able to map the ten-fold variety (e.g., how many different package inserts must be printed per country?).

From this it can be deduced that a control system must be able to deal comprehensively with the permissible variety of the system to be controlled. Too simplistic key performance metrics can have a negative impact on viability.

If, for example a CFO fixes the rule that the total value of stocks may never exceed one-twelfth of the annual consumption of materials, he wants to ensure that stock values remain low. However, this rule does not consider the fact that a large part of the stock value is invested in "shopkeepers." This can have the consequence that the fast turning parts are only stocked in insufficient quantities, which leads to delays in production and the consequence that delivery dates to customers cannot be met.

OUs Operate in Overlapping Environments

A company usually has several OUs operating in different, partly overlapping environments. A food supplier can supply both a retailer with a comprehensive range of foodstuffs for the customer's weekly purchases and the neighborhood shop, where short-term "ad hoc purchases" are made. In such cases, the assortments to be delivered are different in terms of item size and packing size, and possibly also in terms of prices, although they are physically the same products. For both sales channels, management organizations are needed which, based on the planning and control systems, can control the actions of their operations in such a way that each OU develops correctly in the sense of viable.

More Freedom for the OU Increases the Need for Coordination

The variety of the overall system is not only increased by the fact that several OUs exist side by side, but also by the fact that they have to intensively coordinate themselves (Fig. 2.3). For example:

- Should it be permissible for two OUs to compete in the same sales market?
- Does an OU obtain services or products from other OUs and, if so, at what price and at what delivery conditions?
- Is an OU dependent on the fact that developments in another OU are completed on time (product releases)?

System 2 Coordinates the Operating Units

Ensuring coordination between systems 1 (the OUs) is the task of system 2. It comprises all supporting functions, processes, instruments, and rules which regulate the interaction of the OUs, enable the resolution of emerging conflicts and—as far as possible—facilitate self-coordination of the OUs in the sense of self-organization. This includes various things that are often not recognized as a coherent system:

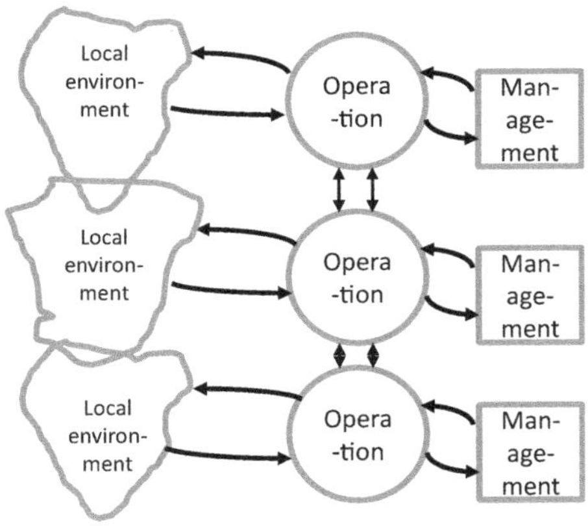

Fig. 2.3 Several operating units working side by side

- "Soft factors" such as common language and terminology, traditions, implicit "rules of the game"
- Mission statement and corporate policies
- Meetings, work groups, secretariats
- Planning and control systems including their IT-based tools (e.g., ERP)
- Rules for valuating positions and movements
- Charts of accounts
- Other written rules and standards

This coordination work is mainly performed in the functional areas of support, e.g., personnel, procurement, maintenance, IT, finance, and above all the controller area, but also through the production planning and steering system (PPSS). These areas therefore require the content and hierarchical competence to define the design, functioning, and associated application rules of the planning and control systems. However, the rules are issued from system 3.

System 3 Corresponds to the Operational Management of a Group of Companies

System 3 (S3) has the mandate to manage all OUs and System 2 considering the overall environment of the organization. It is usually referred to as operational management. It ensures that cooperation between Systems 1 is optimized (e.g., the production departments are served with the orders that they can handle most favorably and best). It looks for opportunities to find synergies between the various OUs and to implement them in the overall company as cost advantages or as comprehensive market accesses (e.g., cross-selling or joint purchasing of raw materials). In addition, through coordination of the agreed-upon objectives, it ensures that existing success potentials (e.g., well-running products or strong customer loyalty) generate positive financial results (ROI) in the OUs.

This management task and the associated task of keeping an eye on the overall environments of the company with their developments means that S3 must also

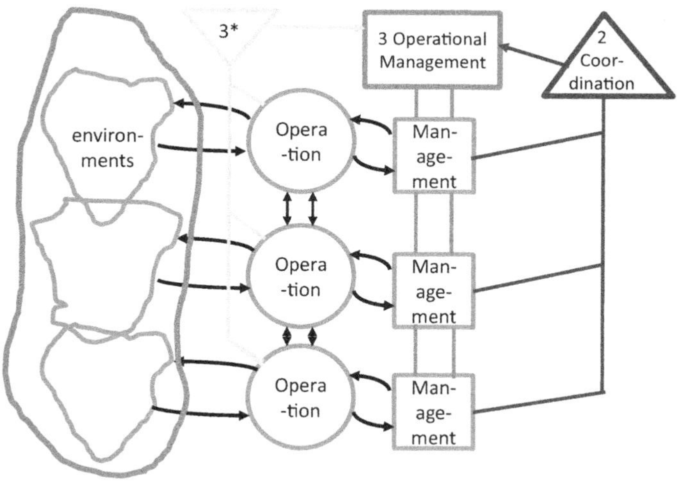

Fig. 2.4 Overview of Systems 1 to 3

allocate resources (investments, headcounts) to the individual OU in the sense of managing the whole.

For these decisions to succeed, operational management needs to be able to intervene directly in all Systems 1, while maintaining as far as possible the autonomy of Systems 1. This influence is represented in Fig. 2.4 by the two vertical lines from S3 to the management areas of Systems 1. One line stands for Resource Bargaining and Accountability (RB&A) processes, the other for Escalation and Intervention (E&I) processes.

As the name suggests, in the communication channel RB&A the OUs' demands for resources of all kinds are weighed against each other and allocated to Systems 1 in accordance with the ideas of S3. In return, S3 wants to be able to recognize the extent to which an S1 has achieved the planned successes with the resources allocated (accountability meant as reporting on results, not as pure accounting). Budget negotiations are a good example of the R&B process, periodic reporting is an example of the accountability (the A in RB&A) process. As a side note, it can be inferred from this that the head of a unit reports, not the controller. The latter's role is to prepare reports and interpret them from a business point of view.

Finally, with regard to operational management, S3 is also responsible for validating System 2 rules and regulations and ensuring that they are followed. System 2 should determine the rules according to which resources are assigned to the OU in the event of a conflict. If these rules are not enough in individual cases, the operational management (S3) must enter via the E&I channel and—again in the sense of the larger whole—regulate the right of way. The E&I channel is used for individual cases, while the RB&A channel is also used in individual cases, but mainly in the planning process when objectives, means, and procedures are coordinated (the management phases in SGMM).

System 3 Requires an Independent Information Channel (System 3*)
For S3 to be able to perform both the designing and the monitoring tasks correctly, another independent system, System 3*, is required. System 3* is mainly an information channel with the task of procuring unfiltered information on actual events, i.e., ensuring that information is neither "manipulated" by employees of Systems 1 and 2 nor by representatives of System 3 itself. This information can be generated both by direct observation through S3 managers (such as front tour, mystery shopping, unannounced visits, collaboration in projects) or through commissioned units such as internal audits. Internal audits should ascertain whether compliance rules, contracts, account assignment and depreciation rules, and inventories are being applied in accordance with the rules, and also whether risks and potential threats to the company are being observed. In the simple case, the information to be obtained by System 3* is actual data. Direct contacts of the S3 managers with individuals in System 1 can also provide insights that will influence the next planning rounds. To prepare the reports and to compare them with the plans is the task of Systems 1 and 2.

However, it is better to avoid bypassing the official channel through direct intervention. If instructions are given directly "from above," omitting the locally responsible person, that person's authority and personal responsibility will be undermined. System 3* is thus a "read only" channel.

System 3 Is Contemporary and Internally Oriented
Operational management guides the existing OUs operating in the currently relevant environments. But environments change as new developments and technologies become available, new ways of life emerge, and new needs arise as a result. This can lead companies to include new or additional environmental developments in their planning considerations and begin to look for suitable new applications to maintain the company's viability.

Strategic Leadership (System 4) Is Future and Externally Oriented
The fusion of automotive technology with electronics has already extensively taken place, ranging from electronic engine control and navigation systems to distance meters. Will a viable automotive company of the future also have to get involved in road construction so that data transmission will be linked in real-time to the cars driving on the roads? Will future means of transportation be more "work-spaces" or more "pastime facilities," and in which of the affected areas does the company want to build up new potentials for success?

These are the type of strategic leadership questions addressed in System 4. Strategic management has the task of seeking opportunities and determining for which products and services strong market positions shall be achieved in which future markets. To this end, System 4 develops ideas and plans for strategies that in turn are to be implemented by existing or new OUs. The realization of these plans requires various kinds of resources and the necessary budgets. To realize the strategies part of the available investment budget must be diverted for the development of new success potentials. This creates a potential contradiction in the minds of operational managers and their employees. They are the ones who earn the money today. So, they request that the generated cash flows be invested in the further development of their business. If operational management has too many objections against the strategic plans, none of the strategic plans will ever be implemented.

This risk is particularly high in organizations employing the Beyond Budgeting approach, because there resources are to be made available "ad hoc" according to immediate need as the short-term improvement of market success is a priority (see Sect. 2.1.2).

A strategy can only be implemented through operational actions.

- If a project results from a strategic plan, it must be implemented operationally on schedule and within budget with a measurable and verifiable goal (see Sect. 2.1).
- If the market position in a given region (say, South America) is to be strengthened, real increases in sales in these countries are necessary.

A management control system that is appropriate for the various management levels must primarily concentrate on supporting the entire operational management. Whether a strategy develops as planned can only be measured by operating results.

System 5 Is Referee and Identity Donor

System 3 assesses the company's prospects from **inside and now**, while System 4 assesses the company's prospects from **outside and toward the future** (Beer 2008, p. 136). This can lead to friction and requires a referee.

This **arbiter function is** assumed by System 5. Top management and representatives of the owners must bring strategic opportunities and risks into balance with the operational requirements and results. System 5 has the authority to issue commands to both System 3 and System 4 (direct vertical line). As a prerequisite, it must recognize and assess the different views from the systems (monitoring).

Unplanned developments can disturb the equilibrium in a life-threatening way. An (operational) liquidity squeeze due to an economic downturn can result in top management having to impose severe restrictions on expenditure, which affect all systems. In such situations decisions about who must renounce investments or planned engagements for new employees can only be taken quickly enough in System 5.

System 5 should always provide **orientation**. It should disclose to all employees the fundamental core values which the company represents and intends to uphold, as well as the results that are to be achieved within the scope of fulfilling the purpose (AMPLE). This is the normative (legislative) leadership of the entire organization. It

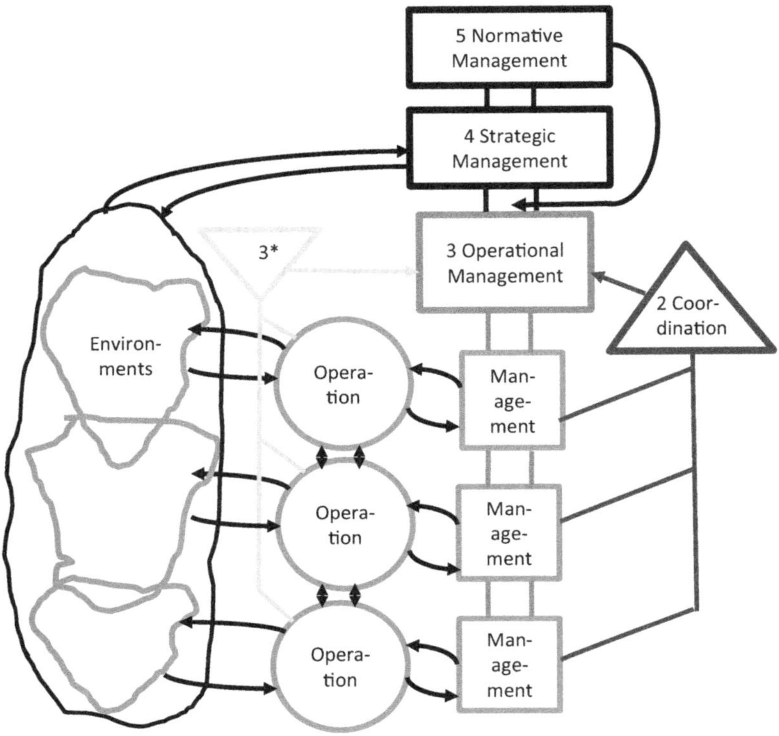

Fig The VSM with its five subsystems

takes place through the definition of corporate policy and, as part of it, the mission statement. Since corporate policy guidelines often cannot be formulated comprehensibly for every situation, they also require explanation, training, and interpretation. This is best achieved when managers live the postulated core values themselves.

It should be noted that the VSM describes vital processes and content, but not people and positions. Many employees wear a variety of "hats" and work in several systems. A senior manager who mainly deals with normative management issues in System 5 can also make significant contributions to System 1, e.g., when accompanying customer visits. When the same person goes to the warehouse and talks to the warehouse staff, he gets unfiltered information and works in System 3*. A specialist in group consolidation is responsible for maintaining the chart of accounts for group consolidation (System 2). In addition, internal auditing in subsidiaries can be part of his duties, which corresponds to a System 3* function. For the understanding of VSM it is essential to understand that the same person can and should move in several systems so that all survival-relevant processes can function.

It is a good idea to think in terms of **hats**, not **heads.**

2.2.2 Recursiveness and Autonomy

A central construction principle of viable systems is that they repeat themselves within themselves, i.e., are nested. Orengo (2011, p. 6) explains the concept using the example of the corporation in such a way that the overall economy is at the top of the list, followed by the industry, the company itself, and finally the division or subsidiary. Each of these parts must itself be modeled as a viable system, if the various (recursion) levels are to function in the long term.

This means that the individual systems **must in turn contain Systems 1–5.** Normative and strategic decisions must also be taken in the subsidiary to make the local operation work successfully in the sense of viability. Furthermore, every viable system should be able to act as autonomously as possible and control itself.

Autonomy should only be restricted by higher recursion levels "if this is indispensable for the cohesion of the whole" (ibid., p. 11). For example, a corporation defines a minimum chart of accounts structure to be followed by all internal reporting units. This makes consolidation easier and the values contained in the accounts more comparable.

The rule of the greatest possible autonomy corresponds to the principle of subsidiarity in political leadership (a central authority should only perform those tasks which cannot be performed at a more local level). For the design of management control systems this means, on one hand, finding indicators that are as universally valid as possible and, on the other hand, noticing if a quantity to be measured is not adequate for an OU or a subarea within it. Equally relevant for the design is the question whether a part of a company, in particular a functional area, can still be regarded as an independent viable system in the sense of recursiveness:

- An IT department is an enabler and facilitator. It enables and facilitates the operation and management of a viable system but is not a viable system itself. The department was established as a service provider for the company. Only when it becomes an independent company that can operate freely on the market will it also need Systems 1–5. The same applies to a human resources department, accounting, building management, and other support functions.
- A plant that is only allowed to supply its own sales companies is not an independently viable system. Without a sales organization, no production orders would be placed.
- The sales and distribution function of an OU is an enabler and facilitator as well, and thus not an independent viable system. The same applies to pure sales subsidiaries abroad. In contrast to a distributor or a pure trading company, they are only there to sell a company's own products or services.

These remarks are by no means intended to cast doubt on the importance of hierarchical ranks. What is of interest here is how decision- and responsibility-oriented performance indicators are to be set up based on the findings from the VSM. Beer (2008, p. 8) states that a viable system must be a **true profit center:** It must be able to continue to exist if it is "cut out" of the current system and sold.

Direct market access, i.e., sales to external customers, thus becomes the constituent characteristic for the definition of a profit center (see Deyhle and Hauser 2011, pp. 82 f).

This clear and logical derivation stands in stark contrast to the practice in many companies, especially in corporate groups:

- In an effort to deploy as many managers as possible who act on their own responsibility and are responsible to achieve a profit, organizational units such as plants, logistics, and IT departments are created as shared service centers and defined as "profit centers."
- These profit centers invoice their services to internal recipients at a transfer price that enables them to achieve their (internal) profit target.
- Therefore, the prices charged must be justified by complicated cost allocations to the recipients.
- Transfer prices are influenced by national tax authorities, which have an interest in ensuring that as much profit as possible is taxed in their country. They want to see exactly which services were performed in which subcompany of the group. Thus they support this back and forth allocation of fixed costs additionally.

If this practice also finds its way into the key figure system of a viable system, incorrect decisions are inevitable:

> The Portuguese sales manager wonders how he can generate a positive local result when he compares the sales price realizable in Portugal with the transfer price demanded by the parent company in Germany. He will tell the operational management at headquarters that he is throwing in the towel and giving up sales because he sees no chance of selling enough at the required prices and achieving a satisfactory result locally. What then happens in the manufacturing plant in Germany?

In our opinion, the dilemma lies in the attempt to use the same parameter (the transfer price) for both tax optimization and the holistic management of a viable group of companies.

The link between recursiveness and the question of under what circumstances can one still speak of a viable system is intended to make clear that the design of management control systems focuses on decision-making and responsible corporate management, not on accounting and external reporting.

2.2.3 Conclusions for the Design of Management Control Systems

The VSM design model supports the following rules for the development of planning and control systems and the associated management-oriented reporting:

- Restrict the autonomy of the executive systems only if this appears indispensable for the cohesion of the overall system. Even the best Systems 3 and 5 cannot generate as much variety as the operational units and not as much as the relevant environments. Self-responsive steering at all levels should be the dominant basic principle.

- The plan is the result of decision-making. It is therefore also the yardstick for assessing the achievement of objectives. This requires level-specific segment plans. A cost center in an OU plans differently than a product manager in sales promotion, so planning instruments are needed that are set up appropriately.
- **In planning and control, units and time always take precedence over values:** Work and material quantities must be planned and measured before they can be evaluated with a financial approach. Every management control system should therefore first be based on the planning and measurement of quantities, services, and time consumption.
- In multiyear (mid-term) operational planning it is necessary to plan based on a quantity and services basis. Today medium-term planning is often limited to the updating of profit and loss accounts and budgeted balance sheets. But decisions such as the staffing of cost centers or investments in machinery, vehicles, and buildings are based on the underlying volume developments, especially sales and production volumes.
- Resource bargaining and use of resources must be mapped in the planning and control system with quantities to be consumed and their costs. This is necessary both for reporting (accountability) and as a basis for tactical management intervention. Since managers are responsible for implementing the plan or corrective actions, areas of responsibility must be clearly defined. The system must therefore be structured in such a way that variances occurring in one area are not passed on to subsequent areas. Otherwise it is not possible to determine who has to decide corrective actions or to escalate, if the differences become too large (see the plan, target, and actual comparisons in Chap. 6).
- **Investment decision:** Investment planning takes place where investments will subsequently be implemented, mainly in Systems 1 and 3. However, the final allocation of the investment budget should always take place in System 5. This is the only system that has a complete overview over strategic and operational developments. If this insight is not followed, the company risks never being able to implement a strategy. Systems 1–3 will always have enough ideas for investments in their areas and want to implement them.
- Budgeting also means the reduction of variety for the OU (one budget position is accepted which means that another cannot be realized).
- Coordination System 2 must ensure comparability. Therefore, it is predestined to design the planning and control systems. It should be noted that at different recursion levels (System 1 and 3) and in the organizational units, different parameters can also be relevant to management. For the overall view, crosswise comparable measurement units must be found. These should not be limited to profit and loss and balance sheet accounts. The comparison between two plants (OU) producing the same product must be based on the same data collection and evaluation rules if useful findings are to be obtained from it.
- For this purpose, rules that apply to everyone should also come from System 2 (account assignment rules, depreciation rules, inventory valuation rules,

planning calendar, planning specifications, calculation method for headcount, requirements for operational reporting). This enables better comparability between the OUs as well as "learning from others."

- **Request only indispensable information**: System 2 representatives (and their principals in System 3) should always keep in mind that any information request they make to System 1 leads to additional work there. The time used for this is no longer available for local support.
- Where internal controls and risk assessments are localized as a task of System 3* in a separate department, this department should also be set up in such a way that it can collect its data as far as possible without causing additional work for Systems 1. Evaluations and statistics, which the Systems 1 do not need for their own control should be compiled in System 3* itself (also applies to the external audit).
- The transfer pricing problem also belongs to the domain of System 2 tasks. A distinction must be made between the purpose of tax optimization (setting transfer prices in such a way that the whole corporation can reduce tax expenditure) and the purpose of internal control (only charging each other for those services the recipient can directly influence himself).
- Key figures on market development are just as important as financial indicators. This is the basis for the decisions of all five systems.
- Making plans a reality is always the task of Systems 1 (fulfillment of purpose). Systems 1 and the leading system 3 are therefore the ones that must first formulate the requirements for level-specific key figures. As mentioned above, strategies (prepared in System 4) are always implemented through operational actions of Systems 1.
- **Adapt key figures to decision-making needs:** Within and between the systems different key figures can be of relevance. If System 3 can report the capacity utilization of its plants, this does not help the individual plant. In the plant it must be known which cost centers have exhausted their available capacity because these cost centers form the bottleneck for further development. Key figures must therefore be defined and applied at the appropriate level.
- The introduction of profit centers only makes sense if they can act on their own responsibility directly on the market. To "construct" profit centers for internal plants and support areas with the help of cost-allocations only leads to an internal shift in results. The company earns nothing from this.
- With regard to planning the following applies to all systems: Operational and strategic management are responsible for the "contents" (contents of objectives and their target level) and the actors in System 2 (above all controllers) are responsible for "procedures and systems" (procedures, integration, and information systems required for this).

From the IMS as well as from the VSM it can be seen that management-relevant information systems must provide both internal data for the target to actual comparison (feedback loop) and data on changes in the environment (of each OU or of the corporation as a whole). The latter can be classified as **early warning information.**

It provides indications that external changes could give rise to internal need for action. Further action may be required because of information regarding the medium- to long-term internal changes. Examples include:

- If certain reasons for employees' dismissal increase over time, this can be an indication of management problems.
- Continuously decreasing production lot sizes lead to a decrease in competitiveness as unit costs rise.
- An increase in supplier concentration may indicate future cluster risks.
- Rising average age in top management can trigger a demand for management development.

External early warning information and **piloting information** obtained from internal data are indispensable for corporate management in Systems 1, 3, and 5.

The purpose of Chaps. 1 and 2 was to gain a comprehensive overview that not only considers the multidimensionality of corporate management but also reveals concrete requirements for the design of management-relevant information systems. In the following chapters, the insights gained above for the design of the contents and parameters of the integrated management control systems are explored.

3 Further Requirements for Integrated Planning Systems

Every viable organization has to think from the customer, buyer, or market into the company and proceed accordingly when planning. This is because customers decide whether they want to evaluate an offer at all and whether they want to purchase the product or service offered and pay the requested price for it.

This also applies to existing products and services as well as new ones about which potential buyers do not yet know. In the latter case interest in the new product or service must first be generated. Public administrations or NGOs similarly need to consider how to offer services in such a way that they are purchased (and paid for) by customers.

Summarized, the application of the SGMM and the VSM results in the following sequence of the planning process:

Feedback and feedforward are always necessary in the planning process between the different planning levels. For example, when it becomes apparent in operational planning that strategic intentions cannot be implemented, or at least not within the planned timeframe, because of production bottlenecks, changes in the plan may be required.

The sequence of the main planning elements in Fig. 3.1 shows that the objectives to be achieved and the services to be provided in all areas are also the decisive factors for cost and results and ultimately for changes in available cash. Therefore, management relevant integrated planning must always start from the planning of services and costs, revenues, and investments. The focus is on performance planning with its mutual dependencies and forms the guideline for the design of the integrated planning and control system.

L. Rieder, R. Lawson, *Management Control with Integrated Planning*, Management for Professionals, https://doi.org/10.1007/978-3-030-48302-9_3

Ideas (Strategic Planning and Corporate Policy)	What does the company want to offer at what price and when? How does it want to position itself to optimally meet customer needs? To be answered: • What kind of company do we want to become (corporate policy)? • What positions do we want to achieve with our offerings in the various market segments (strategic planning)? • How do we differentiate ourselves from competition? • Can we finance these future developments, and will they yield enough profitability? • What personnel requirements, in particular what management capacities, result from the plans?
Products/Services (Operational Planning)	Which products or services should be sold in what quantities, at what prices and with what qualities? To be answered: • From which items/services should what quantities be sold? • How much remains of the price offered as net cash inflow into the company (net revenues, contribution margins, cash flow)? • Which products/services are to be provided (reconciliation with the inventory to be held)? • How much demand for work results from this for the individual functional areas in production? • Which internal tasks are to be fulfilled by all functions not directly involved in the production process to ensure that sales are made, and the company can develop further (specially working time requirements for internal tasks)?
Capacities (Operational Planning)	What is the size and the quality of capacities to be provided so that quantities, qualities and deadlines can be met? To be answered: • What personnel and machine capacities are required to be available in the various functions in a timely manner? • What capacity reserves are needed to cushion fluctuations in demand?
Cost (Operational Planning)	Costs are the result of units to be sold and manufactured and the capacity required to do so. To be answered: • What costs are directly caused by the units to be manufactured and sold (proportional costs)? • What costs are caused by management decisions and not directly attributable to the individual unit manufactured or sold (fixed costs)? • How are projects and assets under construction valued? • How can the organization reach a cost-position that maintains or develops a cost advantage over competition?
Results (Operational Planning and Disposition)	To be answered: • Which product or customer groups contribute sufficiently to the payment of the costs not directly caused through the products? • Is the result enough to finance the reproduction of the available capacities (i.e., to ensure the maintenance of the substance at replacement values)? • Does the complete company achieve a result in line with the market (i.e., is it worthwhile for the owners to remain invested in this company or even to invest more)?
Money Flows (Operational and Strategic Planning)	Will the liquid funds required to implement the above key points be available and in good time? To be answered: • What are the expected money-inflows from sales each year and when? • What are the cash outflows in the coming years for investments, purchases, payments to personnel and debt repayments? • Are there always enough cash reserves (liquid assets or open credit lines) available (continuous maintenance of solvency)?
Stocks (Inventories) (Operational and Tactical Planning)	Which fixed assets and inventories should a company invest in to maintain delivery readiness? To be answered: • What is the optimal amount of inventory of raw materials, semi-finished and finished products necessary to maintain readiness for delivery while tying up as little capital as possible? • What are the correct lot sizes for production considering setup cost, capacity restrictions and investment volume? • What is the replacement value of the assets required for operation and the amount required to maintain its substance, to be recorded as imputed depreciation? • The valuation rules should also apply to projects and assets under construction.

Fig. 3.1 Sequence of the most important planning contents

3.1 Principles and Methods to Apply in Management Accounting

Having an uncompromising management orientation in the design of the planning and control system requires the application of the following principles and methods in management accounting (see definitions of revenue terms in Sect. 4.3.2 and cost terms in Sect. 4.7.1):

1. **Work with standards:**
   Management means goal-oriented proceeding (see Sect. 1.2). This requires that all objectives be transformed into a measurable format. As far as management accounting is concerned this requirement can be met with a **standard costing system.** It can be applied to prices, services, cost, and revenues. Standards and the standard cost system are not new. They are often described in literature and installed in practice (see Horngren, et al. 1999, p. 575 ff.). New is the importance these methods gain in a management-oriented design of the planning and control system.

   A planned purchase price for a raw material determines for the plan year the expected average purchase price to be paid for raw material or supplies. For the responsible purchaser, this value is the yardstick against which he can measure the achievement of his price objectives. By displaying purchase price variances, procurement can see how well it succeeded in realizing the target prices.

   For the users of an item (e.g., production), the internal standard purchase price remains unchanged during the whole year. This equally applies for merchandise in the sales organization.
2. **Plan and record direct costs:**
   A manager will rightly insist that his area of responsibility only be charged for services, consumption, and revenues that he or his employees can **influence directly** and thus for which he should be held responsible. That includes withdrawals from inventory (raw material, semi-finished and finished goods), external purchases directly for one's own cost center (area of responsibility), services from other cost centers (if the consumption can be determined directly by the receiver, i.e., real internal activity charging), as well as costs that can be clearly assigned to an item/product.
3. **Clear distinction between proportional and fixed costs:**
   Proportional costs are caused directly by the production of units. Fixed or structural costs are the result of decisions concerning capacities or the structure of the organization. These decisions are always made by managers. Proportional costs can be clearly compared with the units produced and the sales achieved. **Proportional costs are driven by quantity and product structure. Fixed costs are the result of management decisions** and are the responsibility of the deciding manager.
4. **Plan and record sales deductions according to source:**
   Bonuses and reimbursements are usually granted retrospectively based on sales achieved in a given period. Whether cash discount conditions were used can

only be determined after receipt of payment. All sales deduction items should be subtracted monthly from the monthly billings. This has the advantage of not overstating a company's profits during the year. As the actual amounts of many sales deductions are not yet known at the reporting date, **standard rates** should be applied and deducted from sales. These standard rates should thus be presented in the monthly reports.

5. **Always value inflows to and outflows from inventory at standard:** Similar to the valuation of raw material issued to production at the planned purchase price, standard rates should also be applied to the valuation of receipts to and issues from the semi-finished or finished goods warehouse as well as to the valuation of goods in production, WIP. This means that all production activities performed on production orders are always valued at proportional standard cost (proportional planned cost rate of the respective performing cost center). Additions to the semi-finished goods warehouse are valued at the planned proportional product cost, as are withdrawals of finished products for sale.

   This principle results from the management orientation. If in a cost center the actual costs deviate from plan, the cost center manager is charged with taking corrective action so that the variances disappear in future reporting periods. He must ensure that these deviations are rectified by means of corrective measures. Recipients of his services, be they a person responsible for production orders or a cost center manager who receives internal services, cannot directly influence these variances. From a management point of view, it is appropriate that **variances are always reported at the point of origin** and not passed on to the purchasing or consuming units. They are only to be presented in the overall result of the operating unit. In any case, the allocation of variances to subsequent cost centers or to products is inappropriate as there is no direct causal link between the cause of the deviation and the actions of the recipients.
6. **Present contribution margins after deducting proportional standard product costs:** The planned and the realized revenues (gross and net) should always be compared to the proportional standard cost of goods sold. Production managers and their cost center managers are responsible for variances on the manufacturing side; sales stand for the realized net revenues.
7. **Revalue year-end inventories:** The application of the standard system for the calculation of proportional standard costs requires that, in the transition from the old to the new year, all inventories must be valued with the planned proportional unit cost for the new year. If, for example, an item becomes more expensive in the new year due to price increases in purchasing or due to higher proportional cost rates (e.g., higher wages), the inventories available at the end of the year are to be revalued with the new standard rates. This prevents "comparing apples to oranges" in the planned year.

   This **revaluation** at year-end is to be implemented **without affecting net income**. The assessment of net income for the current year is based on the standard rates for the current year, while the assessment for the following year is based on the new rate. How this change can be transferred to external reporting is described in Sect. 6.6.

8. **Value fixed assets at replacement value and use imputed depreciation**:
It is advisable to value fixed assets at **replacement value.** This gives the responsible managers a more realistic feeling about the investment needed to produce and sell their products. Replacement value is estimated with the question: "How much would have to be paid today if the asset in question were bought and installed **newly** and what is the planned useful life of this new asset? From these specifications, one can calculate **imputed depreciation** for each asset and therefore also for each cost center. Imputed depreciation is a fair guess of the cost of the use of the presently invested assets and should, therefore, be deducted when presenting the internal EBIT to management. The total of all replacement values minus the cumulated imputed depreciation roughly shows management the necessary net investment in fixed assets to run the business.
9. **Do not allocate fixed cost:**
Fixed costs should neither be passed on from one cost center to another nor allocated to manufactured or sold items. The amount of fixed costs is determined by the decisions of the respective cost center manager and his superiors. They are therefore responsible for these amounts.
Since there is no direct "cause–effect relationship" between fixed cost and units produced and sold, any allocation of fixed cost to other cost centers and from there to product units is not appropriate.
The so-called "as realistic as possible causal relationship" does not actually exist. It can only be constructed with an arbitrary allocation basis. Because of this, neither full manufacturing costs nor cost-prices per unit should be calculated in accounting for management. Fixed costs are passed on as cost blocks in the step-by-step contribution margin accounting.
10. **Include in reports only revenue and cost figures that can be directly influenced by a manager:**
A manager should only be held responsible for what he can directly influence himself. All plans and reports about revenues and costs should be presented in a performance-related way so that the addressee recognizes the connection immediately. Items that cannot be influenced (e.g., allocations) are not to be shown. Input services from other areas should always be valued at proportional standard rates, as the influence is exerted through the service provider. Additionally, the receiver of the report should be able to derive the time-period in which he can change individual items from the report.

Insofar as external reporting requirements, local tax law, or the determination of transfer prices require the disclosure of full manufacturing costs, these calculations should be performed outside of the management accounting system. External financial statements should only be shown to those managers who bear (co-)responsibility for these external statements so that the different valuation approaches do not create confusion within the company.

Overall, the decision- and responsibility-oriented design of the management accounting system should always be structured in a way that each manager can immediately recognize for his area which items he is directly responsible for and thus has to react to if actual results do not proceed according to plan and require corrective measures.

These 10 principles contradict in many ways those used in common accounting practice. But most ERP-systems can be rearranged to reflect this management orientation without requiring a change of software. The way to get there will be presented in detail in Chaps. 4 to 6.

3.2 System Design: Inside-Out or Outside-In?

Setting up an integrated planning and control system immediately raises the question of where to start.

Starting with an entire company, the focus is on sustainable, long-term success. This speaks in favor of an **outside-in approach** to system design: "How should the company and thus also the appropriate data system be set up today so that we can successfully survive in changing environments?"

Since the future of the company is also based on the status quo it can also be argued that the data system is to be developed based on the existing organization with its processes and capacities as well as the existing customers and products. In this **inside-out approach,** existing customers, products, structures, and processes dominate.

The use of the outside-in approach is supported by the fact that newly founded or realigned companies must think consistently from the market (environment, VSM) into the new company. The planning and control systems and, as a result, the data systems will be a consequence of this realignment.

However, existing companies have customers, products, organization, and capacity. They prefer the inside-out approach because the structures from which they can develop successfully are already there. This suggests that the planning and control system should be set up inside-out and thus bottom-up.

Here a combination of both approaches is pursued. This matches with the **countercurrent principle** (defined in the Glossary) which is so important in planning and in the agreement of objectives. It is the logical consequence of the procedures described in Sect. 1.2 (Management by Objectives), according to which a superior explains to his employees which goals he wants to achieve, and the employees then consider what contributions they can make in their areas.

Plans should be designed top-down, plausibility-checked, and agreed with corresponding objectives bottom-up.

The structure of the data system is built bottom-up, starting from the individual customer and item, because it must be ensured that analyses of the development of individual customers or items can also be obtained. The bottom-up approach is coordinated with the needs of strategic and medium-term planning in the development of more aggregated evaluations.

Function	Trade	Production	Service Provider	Public & NGO
Sales	yes	yes	yes	partly
Procurement/warehouse	yes	yes	partly	partly
Production	no	yes	partly	partly
Research & development	possible	yes	possible	possible
Human Resources	yes	yes	yes	yes
Fixed assets	yes	yes	yes	yes
Finance	yes	yes	yes	yes
Information Technology	yes	yes	yes	yes

Fig. 3.2 Functional areas in different types of corporations

3.3 Different Types of Enterprises

The type of company to be represented by an integrated planning system also has an influence on the system design. A comparison of different types of enterprises shows that the supply and service functions (Fig. 3.2) are necessary in more or less all types of enterprises and therefore have also been mapped.

Service providers, public institutions, and NGOs often also have a limited production function. Service providers working on customer-specific orders know the situation where several cost centers work on the same order and make specific purchases for it. As in production, these items must then be entered for the order and, if several months are spent working on this order, must be valued at the end of each month as work in process (WIP), which corresponds to inventory in a production process. The often-heard definition that a service company distinguishes itself by not requiring inventory is therefore not universally valid. Only the pure **trading company** does not have a production function as it does not physically change the products.

The following overview shows that working on customer- or product-specific orders can occur in all types of companies (including banks and insurance companies) except for pure trading companies.

Due to this and because production planning and control in conjunction with inventory management places extensive demands on the functionality of the ERP-software, the discussion of the contents and the procedures in integrated planning and control will always start from those used by a manufacturing company.

Elements and Contents of Integrated Annual Planning

4

Most figures in the following chapters and sections refer to the worksheets in the simulation model. We often refer to the name of the worksheet (i.e., *sheet "Regionalsales")*.

4.1 The Example Company: Ringbook Ltd.

Ringbook Ltd. produces and sells, in accordance with its name, various formats and designs of folders with flap mechanisms. Headquarters, production, and group management are in St. Gallen, Switzerland.

According to the market environment, and for production control, different dimensions of consideration are required for the structure and coordination between sales and production (Fig. 4.1).

Product Ranges

Producing finished goods is the main business of Ringbook Ltd. These are divided into six product groups (PG). Ring binders permanently available in stock are divided into four product groups. Distinguishing features are the width of the back (7.5 cm or 4 cm) and the built-in closing mechanism (4 or 2 rings). Two further product groups are available for customer-specific special designs, which are only manufactured to order. The ring binders are available in various colors. This dimension is not shown here to simplify the model.

The range of goods offered for sale is supplemented by merchandise purchased from other companies. These are office supplies that are usually used by customers in combination with ring binders. Examples include index-registers, foil pouches, transparent envelopes, follow-up files, and archive boxes. An eighth product group consists of semi-finished goods (Fig. 4.2).

L. Rieder, R. Lawson, *Management Control with Integrated Planning*, Management for Professionals, https://doi.org/10.1007/978-3-030-48302-9_4

Fig. 4.1 The Ringbook Ltd. product ranges

PR#	Year	Product range abbreviation	Product range desc	Sales promotion cost center
1	2011	SG	Semi-finished goods	
2	2011	FG	Finished goods	101
3	2011	Raw	Raw material	
4	2011	WIP	Work in progress	
6	2011	Mer	Merchandise	102

Fig. 4.2 Product group structure of Ringbook Ltd.

PG	Product group description
1	2Ring normal (stock)
2	4Ring normal (stock)
3	2Ring special designs
4	4Ring special designs
5	2Ring special formats (stock)
6	4Ring special formats (stock)
7	Merchandise
8	SG

In detail, Ringbook Ltd. sells the items in Fig. 4.3, to which reference will repeatedly be made in the example application.

Sales Channels

Sales are made through three sales channels. Dealers (resellers) and direct customers currently account for the bulk of sales. In 2011, the "onlineshop" project is to be developed, enabling the company to make its first sales directly to end consumers via the Internet in January 2012 (Fig. 4.4).

Sales Regions, Sales Promotion, and Countries

The sales organization consists of three sales representatives (ADM), the office staff, and the sales manager. The latter also handles all exports from Switzerland to the subsidiary and sales partners. Sales representative Sahli looks after all corporate customers in Switzerland; the other sales representatives take care of the dealers. Sales promotion is also part of the sales organization. It has a section for finished products (its own products) and one for merchandise (Fig. 4.5).

Distribution agreements with local distributors or separate subsidiaries exist in the countries shown in Fig. 4.6.

Customer Groups

The customers served are divided into the following eight groups for the purposes of customer service and sales planning. Depending on the customer group to which they belong, different discounts are granted on the list prices of the sales items (Fig. 4.7).

Itemnr	Item description	L = stock K = customer	Range description	Product group description
101010	4ring 7.5 back glued	L	Finished goods	4Ring normal (stock)
101020	4ring 4 cm back glued	L	Finished goods	4Ring normal (stock)
101030	4 ring 7.5 back welded	L	Finished goods	4Ring normal (stock)
101040	4ring 4 cm back welded	L	Finished goods	4Ring normal (stock)
101050	4ring 7.5 plasticized	L	Finished goods	4Ring normal (stock)
101060	4ring 4 cm plasticized	L	Finished goods	4Ring normal (stock)
101070	4 ring 7.5 plasticized	L	Finished goods	4Ring normal (stock)
101080	4ring 4 cm plasticized	L	Finished goods	4Ring normal (stock)
101090	4ring 7.5 special design	K	Finished goods	4Ring special designs
101100	4ring 4 cm special design	K	Finished goods	4Ring special designs
101110	4ring 7.5 special design	K	Finished goods	4Ring special designs
101120	4ring 4 cm special design	K	Finished goods	4Ring special designs
103000	2ring special format A5 7.5	L	Finished goods	2Ring special formats (stock)
104000	4ring special format A3 7.5	L	Finished goods	4Ring special formats (stock)
105010	2ring 7.5 back glued	L	Finished goods	2Ring normal (stock)
105020	2ring 4 cm back glued	L	Finished goods	2Ring normal (stock)
105030	2ring 7.5 back welded	L	Finished goods	2Ring normal (stock)
105040	2ring 4 cm back welded	L	Finished goods	2Ring normal (stock)
105050	2ring 7.5 plasticized	L	Finished goods	2Ring normal (stock)
105060	2ring 4 cm plasticized	L	Finished goods	2Ring normal (stock)
105070	2ring 7.5 plasticized	L	Finished goods	2Ring normal (stock)
105080	2ring 4 cm plasticized	L	Finished goods	2Ring normal (stock)
105090	2ring 7.5 special design	K	Finished goods	2Ring special designs
105100	2ring 4 cm special design	K	Finished goods	2Ring special designs
105110	2ring 7.5 special design	K	Finished goods	2Ring special designs
105120	2ring 4 cm special design	K	Finished goods	2Ring special designs

Itemnr	Item description	L = stock K = customer	Range description	Product group description
120010	Index A-Z	L	Merchandise	Merchandise
120020	Index A-Z	L	Merchandise	Merchandise
120030	Index 1-31	L	Merchandise	Merchandise
120040	Index 1-31	L	Merchandise	Merchandise
120050	Transparent envelopes	L	Merchandise	Merchandise
120060	Transparent envelopes	L	Merchandise	Merchandise
120070	Transparent envelopes	L	Merchandise	Merchandise
120080	Follow-up file 1-31	L	Merchandise	Merchandise
120090	Follow-up file A-Z	L	Merchandise	Merchandise
120100	Follow-up file 1-31	L	Merchandise	Merchandise
120110	Follow-up file A-Z	L	Merchandise	Merchandise
120200	Archive boxes	L	Merchandise	Merchandise

Fig. 4.3 Sales items of Ringbook Ltd.

The planning and control system must be able to map this multidimensionality of market cultivation in a way that can be planned and evaluated. These evaluations are carried out with multidimensional contribution margin calculations.

Fig. 4.4 Sales channels

sc#	Sales channel description
0	unassigned
1	Dealers
2	Direct customers
3	Onlineshop

Fig. 4.5 Sales regions

Persnr	Last name	First name	Cost center	Customer region
201	Bauer	Marcel	151	Eastern Switzerland
202	App	Peter	152	Western Switzerland
203	Sahli	Helmut	153	Business clients (direct)
204	King (SM)	Pius	100	Sales mgmt. & office

Parent and daughter companies, distributors

Nr.	Name	Country	Country name	Function	Type of partner
1	Ring binder Ltd.	CH	Switzerland	Production, R&D, sales	Parent company
2	Ring binder distribution Ltd.	D	Germany	Sales	Distributor
3	Classeurs Sarl.	F	France	Sales	Distributor
4	Ringbuch Ges.m.H.	A	Austria	Sales	Daughter company
5	Ring binder Ltd.	THAI	Thailand	Production, sales	Under construction
6	Ring binder Ltd.	CN	China	Sales	Distributor
7	Ring binder Ltd.	SG	Singapore	Sales	Distributor

Fig. 4.6 Sales partners and subsidiaries of Ringbook Ltd.

CG	Customer group description	invoice discount	Sales channel	
1	Office products dealers	0	1	Dealers
2	Wholesalers office products	5%	1	Dealers
3	Mass retailers & department stores	5%	1	Dealers
4	Companies (direct sales)	5%	2	Direct customers
5	Public administrations (direct sales)	15%	2	Direct customers
6	Export	28%	2	Direct customers
7	Schools (direct sales)	10%	2	Direct customers
8	Onlineshop (direct customers)	0%	3	Onlineshop

Fig. 4.7 Customer groups of Ringbook Ltd.

Production Levels

The production of the ring binders takes place in three production stages:

- Production level 1 = Production of wire brackets and base plates for the locking mechanism.
- Production level 2 = Assembly of the mechanisms and production of the ring binder envelopes.

Fig. 4.8 List of manufactured semi-finished products

Semi-finished goods SG

Item nr	Quantity unit (QU)	production level (PL)	Item description
11	unit	1	Base plate 4Ring
12	unit	1	Base plate 2Ring
13	unit	1	7.5 cm-brackets
14	unit	1	4.0 cm-brackets
21	unit	2	4-Ring-mechanism 7.5
22	unit	2	2-Ring-mechanism 7.5
23	unit	2	4-Ring-mechanism 4cm
24	unit	2	2-Ring-mechanism 4 cm
31	unit	2	7.5 cm-envelope
32	unit	2	4.0 cm-envelope

- Production level 3 = Completion of assembly and refinement of the ring binders, making them ready for sale.

Since each semi-finished product can be contained in different end products, the semi-finished products are produced in larger batches and stored in the semi-finished goods (SG) warehouse. Their further processing always takes place in production level 3. Currently, it is not planned to sell these parts to other producers as well (Fig. 4.8).

Production and Supply Areas (Cost Centers)
Production is carried out in the following cost centers:

220 Stamping shop
231 Wire rolling
232 Wire bending and forming
240 Cardboarding
250 Assembly
260 Foil welding shop

Since the production employees are trained in such a way that they can work in different cost centers, a **personnel pool is** created. Cost center 245 comprises all employees who can be deployed in cost centers 240, 250, and 260. All employees in the wire rolling and bending shop are assigned to cost center 232 but are also assigned to cost center 231. The stamping shop has its own staff. Cost centers 220–240 produce semi-finished goods.

The work of purchasing and the entire warehouse management (incoming and outgoing raw materials and auxiliary materials, incoming and outgoing goods in the semi-finished and finished goods warehouse and delivery to the end customers) is carried out in cost center 210.

Cost center 200 contains all functions required for production planning and control as well as the management of the entire production operation.

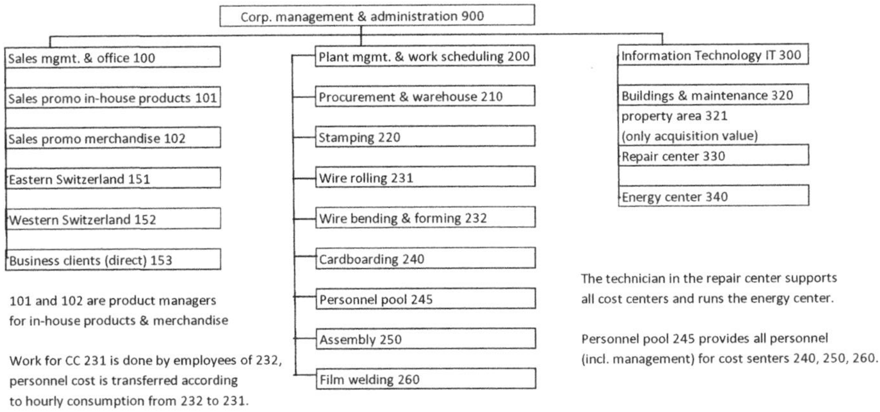

Fig. 4.9 Organizational chart and cost center plan of Ringbook Ltd.

All administrative work (personnel, controller and financial department, general administration), as well as the corporate management, are combined in cost center 900. The Directorate also includes the IT department (300), buildings and maintenance (320), the repair center (330), and the energy center (340).

The sales area (100) includes the above-mentioned sales areas of Eastern Switzerland (151), Western Switzerland (152), and direct sales to companies (153) as cost centers. Sales promotion is structured according to product ranges (own products = 101, merchandise = 102).

The complexity resulting from the basic structures described shows that even in smaller companies integrated planning places high demands on the system and thus on the suitable ERP programs. The task of this example and the simulation model is to map these requirements in structures and processes in such a way that the management-relevant parameters can be planned and measured.

Overall, the organizational chart of Ringbook Ltd. is as shown in Fig. 4.9.

In the simulation model accompanying this book, all planned and actual data are prepared with four-digit figures (from 2010 to 2015). This enables medium-term changes to be mapped and tracked, and also enables annual evaluations and comparisons to be made. In addition, evaluations can be created more easily using four-digit annual figures, since the dates can be used for calculations.

4.2 Planning Dependencies

The representation of the interrelations in an operational unit (OU) in the Viable System Model shows that the environments (amoeba) and particularly the expected demand from the respective sales markets are the starting point for plan integration.

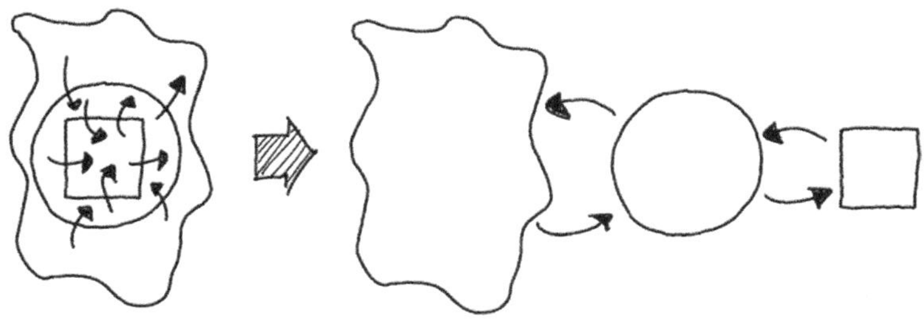

Consequently, the resources to be provided for the operation (circle), the consumption incurred during production, and the work in the management of the OU (square) must be dimensioned in terms of time, quantity, and finances according to the demand. Simultaneously the OU should achieve a profitability in line with market requirements. Figure 4.10 shows part of the individual plans to be created and their inputs for the next stage (The necessary feedback is not yet discussed). The focus is on the services to be provided and the resources required.

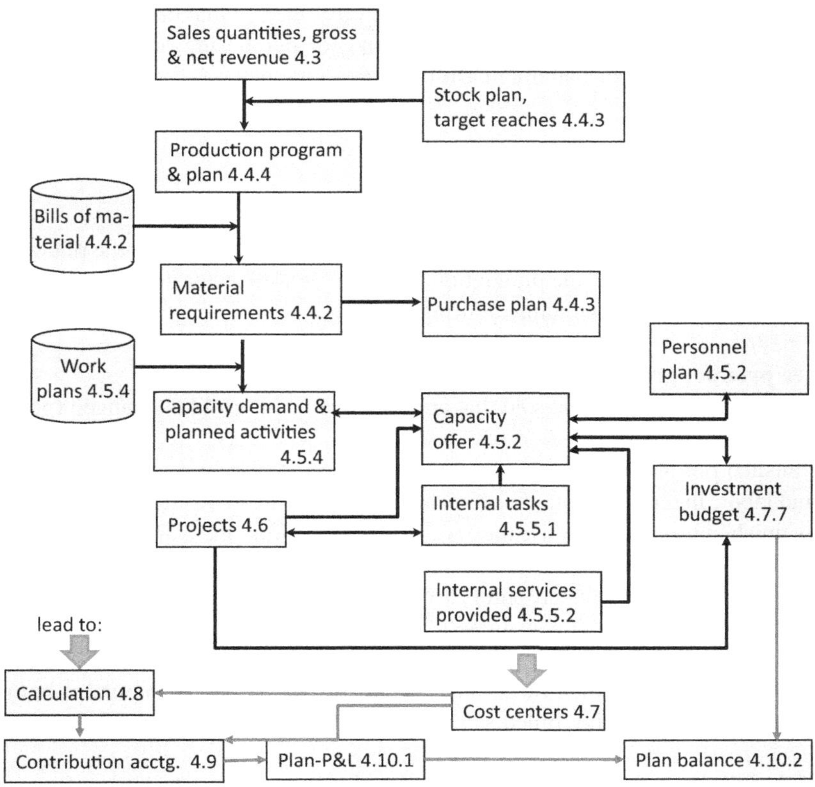

Fig. 4.10 Partial overview of the planning process (with reference to the corresponding subchapters)

Sales and revenue planning provides an indispensable basis for planning integration. This is particularly important in "buyer's markets" for the subsequent internal coordination of resources. In a buyer's market, customers determine whether, when, and how much they want to buy and at what price.

The sequence of topics for the presentation of planning dependencies in the following chapters is derived from these interrelationships. From the arrows connecting the planning topics, it can be concluded that quantity and performance planning is an indispensable prerequisite for financial planning up to the budgeted balance sheet. This applies not only to annual planning, but also to multi-year operational planning.

In the following Sects. 4.3–4.6, the "technical" basics are created. The connection of performance with monetary quantities is made in Sects. 4.7–4.10.

4.3 Sales, Revenue, and Net Revenue Planning

In most cases, a company—including Ringbook Ltd.—sells various products and services (items) at varied prices to multiple customers. Quantities to be sold are relevant for planning production activities and for purchasing; net revenues to be realized are relevant for planning cash flows from the market.

4.3.1 Sales Volume Planning

The annual sales volume planning forms the market-related input for the planning of the units to be produced (the production program) as well as for determination of the inventory levels to be maintained during the year.

Three product group types are to be planned:

1. Merchandise (items to be sold that are purchased and resold unchanged (possibly repacked)).
2. Finished products (products manufactured by the company itself using materials and labor. In terms of data, semifinished products that are resold are also regarded as finished products because they are sold directly from the warehouse. (This also applies to tools to be delivered to customers.)
3. Services (products created purely by work, without material, for sale to further processing units or end consumers).

The distinction between these three product group types is important both for planning and for reporting billed sales:

1. If the planned sales quantities of merchandise are known, the quantities can be used directly for material requirements planning and, as a result, for purchasing plans.

2. The planned sales quantities of finished products manufactured in-house, corrected for any planned inventory changes, are the initial values for the annual rough production planning. The quantities to be produced are broken down into the various production levels until the planned requirements are calculated for each semi-finished product/single item required for the finished products. The planned requirements are then input values for the material to be purchased on the one hand and for the determination of the capacities required in the production cost centers on the other (using work plans).
3. Although services usually do not require material purchases from the warehouse, they also occupy the capacities available at the production sites. The knowledge of the service quantities to sell enables the calculation of the working times required and thus of the requested capacities.

For the direct derivation of material consumption and requested cost center capacities, there should be a 1:1 relationship between the item sold and the item produced. With larger assortments, however, it is no longer possible for those responsible for sales to plan sales quantities on an item-by-item basis. The quantities are then often planned for each product or product subgroup. Statistical distributions are then used for the resolution to individual items.

Sales Quantity Planning in the Example Company

For Ringbook Ltd., the planned sales volumes for the 38 finished products to be sold (see Fig. 4.11) are to be determined. However, this planning would have to be carried out per customer, since the expected ordering behavior of individual customers can change. Only a few companies create such a level of detail (items per customer) in operational planning. Even in the small Ringbook Ltd., for example, the sales managers would resist such a request for planning as they would have to estimate the planned sales quantities of the 38 items for 54 customers, resulting in 2052 estimates (=54*38) needed for the planned year 2011.

The responsible representatives are therefore expected to plan the **sales quantities per product group** in their territories. As an orientation, they receive the information on the quantities for the previous year (2010). They enter their estimates in the column "Planned quantity 2011" and provide them with their comments.

Fig. 4.12 is the result:

This level of detail is not yet enough for production and warehouse planning, since item-related purchasing or production must be carried out. By using the previous year's (2010) sales distributions, the shares of the individual items in their product group are determined for each sales region (column "item share of PG 2010" in Fig. 4.12). The resulting percentage shares are then multiplied by the planned sales quantities per product group and sales area determined by the sellers in Fig. 4.11. This produces—purely mathematically—the planned sales volume per item and sales area (column "planned quantity 2011" in Fig. 4.12). For sales area 201, the planned sales quantities are shown for each item from the finished goods

Planned quantities

Sales representative	Last name	PG#	Product group	Year	**Planned quantity 2011**	Quantity previous year
201	Bauer	1	2Ring normal (stock)	2011	317,000	308,000
201	Bauer	2	4Ring normal (stock)	2011	136,000	131,800
201	Bauer	3	2Ring special designs	2011	12,000	12,000
201	Bauer	4	4Ring special designs	2011	12,000	11,400
201	Bauer	5	2Ring special formats (stock)	2011	28,000	26,800
201	Bauer	6	4Ring special formats (stock)	2011	42,000	40,500
201	Bauer	7	Merchandise	2011	13,500	13,380
202	App	1	2Ring normal (stock)	2011	76,000	73,300
202	App	2	4Ring normal (stock)	2011	119,000	116,000
202	App	3	2Ring special designs	2011	146,000	142,000
202	App	4	4Ring special designs	2011	74,000	72,000
202	App	5	2Ring special formats (stock)	2011	55,000	53,500
202	App	6	4Ring special formats (stock)	2011	60,000	58,200
202	App	7	Merchandise	2011	6,000	5,780
203	Sahli	1	2Ring normal (stock)	2011	13,500	13,000
203	Sahli	2	4Ring normal (stock)	2011	25,000	24,000
203	Sahli	3	2Ring special designs	2011	51,500	50,000
203	Sahli	4	4Ring special designs	2011	31,000	30,000
203	Sahli	5	2Ring special formats (stock)	2011	4,000	-
203	Sahli	6	4Ring special formats (stock)	2011	4,000	-
203	Sahli	7	Merchandise	2011	2,000	440
204	King (SM)	1	2Ring normal (stock)	2011	55,000	52,700
204	King (SM)	2	4Ring normal (stock)	2011	190,000	184,000
204	King (SM)	3	2Ring special designs	2011	88,000	85,400
204	King (SM)	4	4Ring special designs	2011	102,000	98,000
204	King (SM)	5	2Ring special formats (stock)	2011	26,000	25,000
204	King (SM)	6	4Ring special formats (stock)	2011	-	-
204	King (SM)	7	Merchandise	2011	1,000	600
					1,689,500	1,627,800

Fig. 4.11 Planned sales quantities per product group and sales territory (sheet "Regionalsales"). (Note: References to "sheet" are to sheets in the Excel simulation model accompanying this book)

range. In the column "PG totals" it can be seen that the item shares for 2010 per product group and sales area add up to 100% again. The overall table for all sales areas can be found in the simulation model. Summarized across all sales territories, the planned sales quantities for 2011 are calculated per item number (Fig. 4.13).

These calculated planned sales quantities must be revised again by the sales staff. It is possible that individual products will sell better or worse in the planned year from the viewpoint of the sales staff, that new products will be added to the range for which no previous year's figures are available, or that changes will occur in the customer base (new customers arrive or old customers leave) or that the area allocation changes. All these influences cannot be derived mathematically. They require the intervention of the responsible sales representative by adjusting his

Fig. 4.12 Extract from the calculation of planned sales quantities per item (sheet "Plansales")

(without merchandise)				Plan year: 2011		
Sales rep	Itemnr.	PG#	PG-sales planned	item share of PG **2010**	Planned quantity **2011**	PG-totals
201	105010	1	317,000	31.43%	99,629	
201	105020	1	317,000	19.74%	62,577	
201	105030	1	317,000	17.01%	53,931	
201	105040	1	317,000	1.20%	3,808	
201	105050	1	317,000	14.29%	45,286	
201	105060	1	317,000	2.92%	9,263	
201	105070	1	317,000	4.97%	15,747	
201	105080	1	317,000	8.44%	26,760	100.00%
201	101010	2	136,000	4.55%	6,191	
201	101020	2	136,000	11.08%	15,065	
201	101030	2	136,000	18.21%	24,765	
201	101040	2	136,000	44.16%	60,055	
201	101050	2	136,000	3.79%	5,159	
201	101060	2	136,000	0.46%	619	
201	101070	2	136,000	15.93%	21,669	
201	101080	2	136,000	1.82%	2,476	100.00%
201	105090	3	12,000	0.00%	-	
201	105100	3	12,000	40.00%	4,800	
201	105110	3	12,000	28.33%	3,400	
201	105120	3	12,000	31.67%	3,800	100.00%
201	101090	4	12,000	70.18%	8,421	
201	101100	4	12,000	0.00%	-	
201	101110	4	12,000	29.82%	3,579	
201	101120	4	12,000	0.00%	-	100.00%
201	103000	5	28,000	100.00%	28,000	100.00%
201	104000	6	42,000	100.00%	42,000	100.00%

Aggregation: Planned sales quantities per item number Plan year: 2011

Itemnr.	Quantity	Itemnr.	Quantity	Itemnr.	Quantity
Finished goods		**Finished goods**		**Merchandise**	
105010	138,023	101060	82,688	120010	5,718
105020	82,276	101070	116,778	120020	830
105030	70,527	101080	2,476	120030	161
105040	3,808	105090	85,833	120040	2,623
105050	99,534	105100	5,417	120050	1,322
105060	15,484	105110	150,950	120060	3,410
105070	19,894	105120	55,300	120070	1,019
105080	31,952	101090	112,242	120080	1,329
101010	47,496	101100	80,333	120090	525
101020	91,276	101110	7,690	120100	326
101030	30,920	101120	18,735	120110	581
101040	60,055	103000	113,000	120200	4,655
101050	38,312	104000	106,000	Total units	1,689,500

Fig. 4.13 Planned sales quantities for 2011

objective. Without this input, which is based on decisions made by those responsible, the planned sales quantities cannot be reliably determined.

> An integrated planning system cannot be programmed as "fully automatic". This is one of the situations in which management decisions must be taken before the program can continue to calculate.

The definitive planned sales quantity per item is only calculated once the sales staff have entered their adjustments manually in the template (see column "Sales rep adjustments in the sheet 'Plansales'"). The consolidated planned sales are shown per item in the sheet "Revenueplan" in column Sales quantity. These quantities are the starting point for determining the units to be produced in the planning year (Sect. 4.4).

4.3.2 Planning from Sales to Net Proceeds

Differences between the gross and the net revenue of a unit sold occur for a variety of reasons, including:

- Increasing division of labor between trade and producer functions.
- Price and condition pressure on the part of buyers.
- Fluctuating exchange rates.
- Discounts of various kinds that affect the invoiced sales volume.
- Sales deductions and "gifts to customers," which also reduce net revenue after discounts.

In an integrated planning and control system, it is important to map all possible sales deduction items both in planning and in the presentation of the actuals, as they have a negative influence on the overall result on the one hand and quantify the effects of many important marketing instruments on the other.

Without claiming completeness (as new "gifts" are always invented), the following types of revenue deductions can be assumed (Fig. 4.14).

The multidimensionality of market cultivation requires evaluations according to items or customers and aggregated to product and customer groups or sales areas, regions, and countries as well as according to sales channels. This multidimensionality must already be considered when setting up **invoicing:**

- Per billed item, the gross price minus any discounts or surcharges that can be assigned uniquely to the item sold.
- If surcharges or discounts are calculated for the entire delivery/billing document rather than by item, they should each be assigned their own item number so that they can be displayed in their own category or product group (examples include

Pos.		Element	Description	Capture per:	Proceeds calculation
		Gross sales price	The sales price to the final consumer.	position	actual
1	-	Item discount	Basic discount for the customer/dealer, often depending on the customer group to which they belong	position	actual
2	-	Order volume or invoice discount	Granted depending on order volume or customer group.	Item or invoice line	actual
3	+	Extra charge for small quantities	"Penalty" for insufficient order quantity per order item, own item number	position	actual
4	+	Logistics or express extra charge	Surcharges for passing on freight and insurance costs to customers, item on its own	invoice	actual
5	+	Extra charges for tool costs	Charges for customer-specific tool costs, item on its own	position	Standard
6	-	Planning discount	Granted to encourage customers to plan sustainably.	invoice	actual
7	-	Advertisement subsidy	Sales promotion element for product groups	position per PG	actual
	=	**Invoiced sales**	The net value on the invoice, equal to what is billed (net) for the delivered goods.	invoice	
8	-	Cash discount	Discount for prompt payment of the invoice, known only after payment.	invoice	Standard
9	-	Refunds / Bonus	Additional remuneration to customers for buying more than the minimum turnover in a given period (e.g., + 3% discount, for all sales over 1 million). Only known in a subsequent period.	end of period	Standard
10	-	Commissions to licensors/patent providers	Payments to be made directly because of the sales	position	Standard
11	-	Commissions to distributors	Payments to be made directly because of the sales (only known in a subsequent period)	position	Standard
12	-	Sales commissions	Based on the contribution margins or turnover achieved, unfortunately usually only shown in wage slips but to be included in CM	position	Standard
	=	**Net proceeds**	Net cash return to the company to cover all costs and target profit	per item in contribution acctg.	

Fig. 4.14 From gross to net sales

invoiced freight, insurance, surcharges for logistics costs of all kinds, surcharges for small quantities or tools). This makes it possible to evaluate which part of the logistics costs can be passed on to the customer independent of the item. In this case, the actual item result is more appropriate.

- In the case of advertising, exhibition, promotion, or planning discounts, it must also be determined whether these are granted on an item- or invoice-related basis, since the latter can no longer be clearly assigned to a specific article.
- In the case of surcharges and discounts for material price changes or currency shifts, a distinction must be made between surcharges that are uniquely assigned to the item and the ones that are not granted on an article basis.
- All plans and evaluations down to the net revenue are always to be presented *without VAT* (value-added tax) or other sales tax since the latter is to be delivered to the government and therefore does not count as sales revenue.

Most items after invoiced sales are not known in their final amount until after the end of the reporting period (for example, after month-end). The amount of cash discount taken by customers can only be determined after receipt of payment, and the reimbursements or bonuses to be paid can only be determined when the relevant cumulative sales can be calculated. In monthly reporting, these sales deductions should nevertheless be deducted from the invoiced sales at the planned (standardized) rate, as otherwise, the managers would "show themselves too good" during the year.

This standardization is also supported by the fact that the bonuses, rebates, and cash discounts definitively granted are often not known until after the annual financial statements have been prepared. The new financial year with new opportunities and risks has long since begun, and managers regard the past as insignificant "history."

The differences between the gross price and the net revenue are also essential elements for the management of the customers' interest in its sales of the delivered products. If the customer himself sells at gross prices, rebates, commissions, and discounts received determine his own contribution margin and thus his profit.

If planning is to be integrated, all deduction types must be considered in the planning process, since they reduce item sales (discounts) or result in subsequent cash outflows (most sales deductions). In a similar way, this also applies to surcharges.

Net Revenue Planning in the Example Company

In order not to complicate the numerical model too much, in our example Ringbook Ltd. only provides for two types of discounts and no further sales deductions:

- *Item discounts* are granted in different percentages per customer group and product range. The discount rates are determined by the management of Ringbook Ltd. Because the margin on merchandise is lower, they also allow lower discount rates. The purpose of the item discounts is to control the interest of customers in carrying Ringbook Ltd. products in their assortments and to give preference to any competing offers.
- No item discounts are provided for deliveries to administrations and schools as well as for exports. To improve the competitiveness of both own products (FG) and merchandise, *invoice discounts* can be granted in addition to the discount for office supplies and online sales. This should encourage the larger customers to procure as much of their office supplies as possible from Ringbook Ltd. In addition, the invoice discount makes it easier to control distribution partners and sales subsidiaries.

The following discount rates are planned for 2011 (Figs. 4.15 and 4.16):

The sales manager determines the gross sales prices (list prices) together with his area managers for the planned year in the annual article master and has them validated by corporate management. The list prices are also the starting point for

Product range	Customer group	Description	Item discount
Finished goods	1	Office products dealers	14%
Finished goods	2	Wholesalers office products	19%
Finished goods	3	Mass retailers & department stores	14%
Finished goods	4	Companies (direct sales)	10%
Finished goods	5	Public administrations (direct sales)	0%
Finished goods	6	Export	0%
Finished goods	7	Schools (direct sales)	0%
Merchandise	1	Office products dealers	10%
Merchandise	2	Wholesalers office products	14%
Merchandise	3	Mass retailers & department stores	10%
Merchandise	4	Companies (direct sales)	5%
Merchandise	5	Public administrations (direct sales)	0%
Merchandise	6	Export	0%
Merchandise	7	Schools (direct sales)	0%

Fig. 4.15 Item discounts for the individual customer groups and assortments (sheet “itemdiscounts“)

Fig. 4.16 Invoice discounts as an additional incentive to buy (sheet “Salesstructure”)

Customer group	Customer group description	invoice discount
1	Office products dealers	0%
2	Wholesalers office products	5%
3	Mass retailers & department stores	5%
4	Companies (direct sales)	5%
5	Public administrations (direct sales)	15%
6	Export	28%
7	Schools (direct sales)	10%
8	Onlineshop (direct customers)	0%

invoicing the distributors. During the year the sales representatives cannot change list prices or discount rates.

The average item and invoice discounts granted can be calculated from the invoicing of the previous year (actual sales sheet). This was 19.75% for the assortment of own products and 15.74% for merchandise (see sheet “Avgdiscounts”). These discount rates will also be used for budgeting 2011. Since different discount rates than in the previous year are granted in the planned year and both the planned sales quantities per customer group and product range change, the planned discounts cannot be calculated for each item level. The planned net sales for 2011 are therefore calculated based on the above-mentioned average figures for the previous year (see Fig. 4.17).

As a result, the net revenues for the planned year are planned by item and can later be transferred to contribution margin accounting. The company’s salespersons receive a commission based on the contribution margin achieved. This commission

Sales Rep	Itemnr	PG#	Planned quantity	List price	Gross sales	Planned discounts	Net sales
201	105010	1	99,629	3.60	358,663	19.7%	287,842
201	105020	1	62,577	3.40	212,761	19.7%	170,749
201	105030	1	53,931	3.80	204,938	19.7%	164,472
201	105040	1	3,808	3.60	13,709	19.7%	11,002
201	105050	1	45,286	4.90	221,900	19.7%	178,084
201	105060	1	9,263	4.60	42,610	19.7%	34,196
201	105070	1	15,747	4.90	77,161	19.7%	61,925
201	105080	1	26,760	4.60	123,095	19.7%	98,789
201	101010	2	6,191	3.20	19,812	19.7%	15,900
201	101020	2	15,065	3.00	45,196	19.7%	36,272
201	101030	2	24,765	3.60	89,153	19.7%	71,549
201	101040	2	60,055	3.50	210,191	19.7%	168,687
201	101050	2	5,159	4.40	22,701	19.7%	18,219
201	101060	2	619	4.20	2,600	19.7%	2,087
201	101070	2	21,669	4.40	95,344	19.7%	76,518
201	101080	2	2,476	4.20	10,401	19.7%	8,347
201	105090	3	-	5.50	-	19.7%	-
201	105100	3	4,800	5.50	26,400	19.7%	21,187
201	105110	3	3,400	5.50	18,700	19.7%	15,008
201	105120	3	3,800	5.50	20,900	19.7%	16,773
201	101090	4	8,421	5.60	47,158	19.7%	37,846
201	101100	4	-	5.60	-	19.7%	-
201	101110	4	3,579	5.60	20,042	19.7%	16,085
201	101120	4	-	5.60	-	19.7%	-
201	103000	5	28,000	6.80	190,400	19.7%	152,804
201	104000	6	42,000	6.80	285,600	19.7%	229,206
201	120010	7	1,877	25.00	46,917	15.7%	39,531
201	120020	7	-	25.00	-	15.7%	-
201	120030	7	161	28.70	4,633	15.7%	3,904
201	120040	7	2,623	29.20	76,601	15.7%	64,543
201	120050	7	1,322	14.40	19,033	15.7%	16,037
201	120060	7	3,410	14.40	49,109	15.7%	41,378
201	120070	7	1,019	14.40	14,674	15.7%	12,364
201	120080	7	706	39.60	27,969	15.7%	23,566
201	120090	7	525	39.60	20,777	15.7%	17,506
201	120100	7	202	39.60	7,991	15.7%	6,733
201	120110	7	-	39.60	-	15.7%	-
201	120200	7	1,655	1.20	1,986	15.7%	1,673
			560,500	433	2,629,125		**2,120,783**

Fig. 4.17 Item discounts for the individual customer groups and assortments (sheet "itemdiscounts")

also has the character of a sales deduction but cannot be determined until the contribution margins have been calculated. For this reason, the commission is only shown in contribution accounting (see Sect. 4.9.1).

4.4 Production Plan, Material Requirements, and Inventory Levels

The successful sale of the planned quantities requires that raw materials, semi-finished, and finished goods, as well as merchandise, be available in a timely manner at the (delivery) warehouse. However, when planning inventory levels, consideration must also be given to the facts that they must be financed, occupy storage space, and run the risk of having to be disposed of if they are not sold.

4.4.1 Production Plan

Depending on the source, the term production plan is used for different plan types, including:

- Definition of the quantities to be produced per item during the planned year (also called annual rough planning).
- Definition of production capacities in the individual cost centers.
- Short-term planning of production orders and thus capacity utilization (usually for 1–3 months).
- Determination of the production program for the next day or week.

Conceptually, only the first item is considered here as a **production plan** or annual rough-cut plan**.** The second item is derived from the production plan, during which the last two items are counted for dispositional (tactical) management during the fiscal year (see Sect. 1.4.5, SGMM planning levels).

The simulation model shows how the production plan for the planned year is developed based on the sales quantity planning and the resulting requirements from this for procurement. The task of annual rough-cut planning is to derive from sales quantity and inventory planning the activities of the entire production area, including the quantities to be produced, material requirements, and planned activities of the manufacturing cost centers.

The starting point is sales quantity planning. Since material consumption and the use of production activities of the cost centers are different for each manufactured item, sales quantity planning must already be detailed to the level of the individual item number (see Fig. 4.13) if a meaningful planning is to develop. Secondly, information is needed as to what the (expected) final stock level will be in the warehouse at the end of the current year. Thirdly, the target stock of the item at the end of the year to be planned must be considered (see Sect. 4.4.3).

The following formula is calculated for each item:

  Planned sales volume
+ Planned final balance (at the end of the planned year)
− Opening balance (at the beginning of the planned year)
= Planned production quantity

It should be noted that in many cases equipment must first be set up to produce a specific item, which results in material and work consumption for setup. Furthermore, it often happens that production generates rejects (pieces of insufficient quality). The material consumption for setup and process-related rejects (scrap) is also taken from the warehouse and increases the cost of the item to be produced.

A production manager is therefore interested in having a machine setup to produce a specific item run for as long as possible so that setup and scrap costs are spread over as many good pieces as possible, i.e., become cheaper per unit. He will argue in favor of placing orders for the largest possible production lots. Since the machine stands still during setup and is not producing good pieces, the demand for large batch quantities is further supported.

The head of finance will not welcome big lots. This increases average inventories and thus the financing required and the interest payable on loans. Salespeople will also have their problem with large lot quantities, since small lots must be possible occasionally, such as when a customer demands a very short delivery date but existing stocks are not sufficient to fill the order.

For the creators of the annual production plan, it is therefore, necessary to find a compromise or, even better, optimum production quantities that consider the planned quantities, the setup and scrap consumption, the number of planned lots, and the average inventory levels in parallel. This is integrated planning in their area. For this purpose, the information is entered and maintained in the sheet "Articlemaster" (Fig. 4.18). To be recorded for each item are the number of planned lots per year, the planned material consumption for setup and process-related scrap per lot, as well as the reach targets for inventory (e.g., to have the units to be sold in an average month on hand; see Sect. 4.4.3).

The derivation of the planned production quantity for a finished good can take place using the calculations in Fig. 4.19. As described, the planned sales quantities, the opening inventory, the reach targets and thus the target inventory at the end of the year, the consumption for setup and scrap, and the planned number of lots for a specific item are considered. As is so often the case, the entire planning process cannot be expressed as a comprehensive planning formula, which is then automatically calculated. Other factors not encompassed by the planning formula could play a role:

- Insufficient planning quality or planning depth in the definition of planned sales quantities.
- Uncertainty in scrap quantities because the production process is still new and subject to strong fluctuations.

Itemnr	Quantity unit	Production level	Item-description	Year	Opening units	Reach in months planned	planned lots p.a.	Setup units per lot	Scrap / lot
101010	unit	3	4ring 7.5 back glued	2011	4,000	2.0	4	10	40
101020	unit	3	4ring 4 cm back glued	2011	4,000	1.0	4	10	40
101030	unit	3	4 ring 7.5 back welded	2011	5,000	1.0	3	10	40
101040	unit	3	4ring 4 cm back welded	2011	4,000	2.0	6	10	40
101050	unit	3	4ring 7.5 plasticized	2011	4,000	1.0	4	10	50
101060	unit	3	4ring 4 cm plasticized	2011	4,000	1.0	11	10	50
101070	unit	3	4 ring 7.5 plasticized	2011	6,000	1.0	11	10	50
101080	unit	3	4ring 4 cm plasticized	2011	2,000	12.0	1	10	50
101090	unit	3	4ring 7.5 special design	2011	-	-	11	10	50
101100	unit	3	4ring 4 cm special design	2011	-	-	11	10	50
101110	unit	3	4ring 7.5 special design	2011	-	-	2	10	50
101120	unit	3	4ring 4 cm special design	2011	-	-	2	10	50
103000	unit	3	2ring special format A5 7.5	2011	8,000	2.0	11	10	20
104000	unit	3	4ring special format A3 7.5	2011	7,000	2.0	11	10	20
105010	unit	3	2ring 7.5 back glued	2011	10,000	1.0	6	10	40
105020	unit	3	2ring 4 cm back glued	2011	11,000	1.0	6	10	40
105030	unit	3	2ring 7.5 back welded	2011	7,500	3.0	4	10	40
105040	unit	3	2ring 4 cm back welded	2011	1,200	6.0	2	10	40
105050	unit	3	2ring 7.5 plasticized	2011	8,000	2.0	6	10	50
105060	unit	3	2ring 4 cm plasticized	2011	5,000	3.0	4	10	50
105070	unit	3	2ring 7.5 plasticized	2011	3,500	3.0	4	10	50
105080	unit	3	2ring 4 cm plasticized	2011	4,000	4.0	3	10	50
105090	unit	3	2ring 7.5 special design	2011	-	-	11	10	50
105100	unit	3	2ring 4 cm special design	2011	-	-	2	10	50
105110	unit	3	2ring 7.5 special design	2011	-	-	11	100	200
105120	unit	3	2ring 4 cm special design	2011	-	-	11	100	200

Fig. 4.18 Planned lots, setup and scrap requirements for finished products (sheet "Articlemaster")

- Machine standstills or tool breakages, which require large batches to be broken off and replaced.
- Problems with the timely procurement of raw materials of conform quality.

Due to such uncertainties, a production manager must be able to adjust the definitive planned production quantity and the planned number of lots to be produced according to his expectations, while taking note of all the above-mentioned aspects. This is because the production manager and his employees are measured against the deviations of the actual production from the plan and the resulting cost variances.

For this reason, Fig. 4.19 (sheet "Productionplan") contains the column "Planned production p.a.net." Since production management can adjust the planned production quantities, there is a **break in the automatic simulation**, like in Sect. 4.3.1. The planned production quantities determined by the production management form the starting point for calculating the product cost (see Sect. 4.8). Since special designs are only manufactured to customer orders, they should not have any inventory.

The sequence of steps for determining the planned production quantities shows that increasing the quality of planning is almost always worthwhile. The more

Determination of the planned production per article, based on planned sales, opening inventories and reach in months planned													Decided production volume		
Year	Itemnr	Production level	Description	QU	Opening inventory	Net planned sales quantity	Reach in months planned	Target inventory year end (units)	Net good units to produce (inventory entry)	Lots p.a.	Setup per lot	Scrap per lot	Setup &scrap all lots p.a.	Gross input in units, prod. level 3	Planned production p.a. (net good units)
2011	101010	3	4ring 7.5 back glued	unit	4,000	47,496	2.0	7,916	51,411	4	10	40	200	51,611	47,600
2011	101020	3	4ring 4 cm back glued	unit	4,000	91,276	1.0	7,606	94,882	4	10	40	200	95,082	94,800
2011	101030	3	4 ring 7.5 back welded	unit	5,000	30,920	1.0	2,577	28,497	3	10	40	150	28,647	28,500
2011	101040	3	4ring 4 cm back welded	unit	4,000	60,055	2.0	10,009	66,064	6	10	40	300	66,364	61,200
2011	101050	3	4ring 7.5 plasticized	unit	4,000	38,312	1.0	3,193	37,504	4	10	50	240	37,744	37,600
2011	101060	3	4ring 4 cm plasticized	unit	4,000	82,688	1.0	6,891	85,579	11	10	50	660	86,239	85,800
2011	101070	3	4 ring 7.5 plasticized	unit	6,000	116,778	1.0	9,731	120,509	11	10	50	660	121,169	121,000
2011	101080	3	4ring 4 cm plasticized	unit	2,000	2,476	12.0	2,476	2,953	1	10	50	60	3,013	800
2011	101090	3	4ring 7.5 special design	unit	-	112,242	-	-	112,242	11	10	50	660	112,902	112,310
2011	101100	3	4ring 4 cm special design	unit	-	80,333	-	-	80,333	11	10	50	660	80,993	80,400
2011	101110	3	4ring 7.5 special design	unit	-	7,690	-	-	7,690	2	10	50	120	7,810	7,700
2011	101120	3	4ring 4 cm special design	unit	-	18,735	-	-	18,735	2	10	50	120	18,855	18,800
2011	103000	3	2ring special format A5 7.5	unit	8,000	113,000	2.0	18,833	123,833	11	10	20	330	124,163	124,300
2011	104000	3	4ring special format A3 7.5	unit	7,000	106,000	2.0	17,667	116,667	11	10	20	330	116,997	116,600
2011	105010	3	2ring 7.5 back glued	unit	10,000	138,023	1.0	11,502	139,525	6	10	40	300	139,825	139,800
2011	105020	3	2ring 4 cm back glued	unit	11,000	82,276	1.0	6,856	78,133	6	10	40	300	78,433	78,000
2011	105030	3	2ring 7.5 back welded	unit	7,500	70,527	3.0	17,632	80,659	4	10	40	200	80,859	68,800
2011	105040	3	2ring 4 cm back welded	unit	1,200	3,808	6.0	1,904	4,512	2	10	40	100	4,612	3,000
2011	105050	3	2ring 7.5 plasticized	unit	8,000	99,534	2.0	16,589	108,124	6	10	50	360	108,484	99,600
2011	105060	3	2ring 4 cm plasticized	unit	5,000	15,484	3.0	3,871	14,355	4	10	50	240	14,595	11,600
2011	105070	3	2ring 7.5 plasticized	unit	3,500	19,894	3.0	4,974	21,368	4	10	50	240	21,608	18,000
2011	105080	3	2ring 4 cm plasticized	unit	4,000	31,952	4.0	10,651	38,603	3	10	50	180	38,783	30,600
2011	105090	3	2ring 7.5 special design	unit	-	85,833	-	-	85,833	11	10	50	660	86,493	85,910
2011	105100	3	2ring 4 cm special design	unit	-	5,417	-	-	5,417	2	10	50	120	5,537	5,500
2011	105110	3	2ring 7.5 special design	unit	-	150,950	-	-	150,950	11	100	200	3,300	154,250	151,030
2011	105120	3	2ring 4 cm special design	unit	-	55,300	-	-	55,300	11	100	200	3,300	58,600	55,330

Fig. 4.19 Planned production quantities per finished item (sheet "Productionplan")

reliably the planned sales quantities are determined, the more needs-based the planned production quantities are determined. This results in lower proportional manufacturing costs and thus a competitive advantage.

4.4.2 Bills of Material

A bill of materials (BOM) must be created for each item to be produced. To produce a finished ring binder the example company needs:

- An envelope with a spine width of 7.5 or 4.0 cm, semi-finished product of level 2, item number 31 or 32.
- A locking mechanism with 4 or 2 rings, which fits the back widths 7.5 or 4.0 cm, again semi-finished products of production level 2, item numbers 21–24.
- Individual materials such as rivets, stick-on labels, adhesive transparent film, adhesive, and edge reinforcements, which are incorporated into all manufactured products and grouped together as consumables sets with item number 5 (raw material at production level 1).
- In the case of film-coated ring binder versions, also the film to be welded on and the consumables for welding (raw material of production level 1, item number 6) (Fig. 4.20).

The BOM describes which raw materials, individual parts, and semi-finished products are to be removed from stock to produce (normally) one of these item units. For each of these input items, it is determined how many units will be consumed if the production process is properly executed from the start. This is the **preset quantity**. It is a goal for execution: those who master the process can cope with the specified quantity. Each item to be sold, each finished or semifinished good,

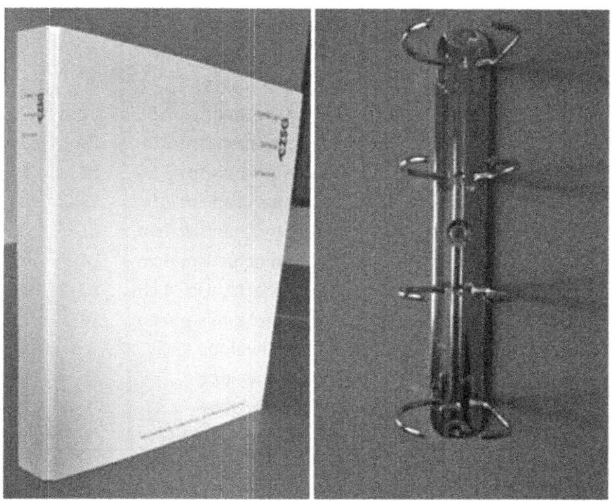

Fig. 4.20 Assemblies of a finished ring binder

as well as each individual part or raw material to be procured requires an item number for unique referencing.

If—as in the example company—there is a multilevel production process, the final stage (finished products) determines the production requirements of the preliminary stages. The 7.5-cm closing mechanisms are used in all finished items with a back width of 7.5 cm, as are the envelopes with a back width of 7.5 cm. This means that the planned production quantity of a semi-finished product is to be derived from the planned production quantities of all finished products that contain this semi-finished product (plus any direct sales of semi-finished products). This enables larger lots to be produced.

The standard quantities contained in the BOMs of the semi-finished goods are multiplied by the planned production quantities for the finished products determined by the head of production. It is also necessary to consider the materials consumed by setup and scrap in the subsequent production levels (Fig. 4.21).

The bill of materials, combined with the calculations in the sheet "Yearlybillofmat," provide the information needed for deriving the production plan (calculated in the sheet "Productionplan") over all levels of production stages down to the raw materials. Also for semi-finished goods, the production manager must have the opportunity to make the final decision on the number of lots to be produced and the total planned production quantity (also to be entered in the sheet "Productionplan").

The example of the 2-ring base plate shows that the net requirement resulting from the production plan for finished products is 881,100 pieces. Since a

Semi-finished goods					**Material positions**			
Itemnr	Year	QU	production level	Description	Itemnr 2	Position	Description 2	preset quantity / unit
11	2011	unit	1	Base plate 4Ring	4	1	Sheet metal	0.024
12	2011	unit	1	Base plate 2Ring	4	1	Sheet metal	0.006
13	2011	unit	1	7.5 cm-brackets	3	1	Wire	20
14	2011	unit	1	4.0 cm-brackets	3	1	Wire	16
21	2011	unit	2	4-Ring-mechanism 7.5	11	1	Base plate 4Ring	1
21	2011	unit	2	4-Ring-mechanism 7.5	13	2	7.5 cm-brackets	4
22	2011	unit	2	2-Ring-mechanism 7.5	12	1	Base plate 2Ring	1
22	2011	unit	2	2-Ring-mechanism 7.5	13	2	7.5 cm-brackets	2
23	2011	unit	2	4-Ring-mechanism 4cm	11	1	Base plate 4Ring	1
23	2011	unit	2	4-Ring-mechanism 4cm	14	2	4.0 cm-brackets	4
24	2011	unit	2	2-Ring-mechanism 4 cm	12	1	Base plate 2Ring	1
24	2011	unit	2	2-Ring-mechanism 4 cm	14	2	4.0 cm-brackets	2
31	2011	unit	2	7.5 cm-envelope	1	1	Cardboard	0.2101
31	2011	unit	2	7.5 cm-envelope	5	2	Consumables (Set)	1
32	2011	unit	2	4.0 cm-envelope	1	1	Cardboard	0.2
32	2011	unit	2	4.0 cm-envelope	5	2	Consumables (Set)	1

Fig. 4.21 Bill of materials cut-out for the semi-finished products (sheet "Billsofmat")

Year	Itemnr	Production level	PR#	Description	QU	Opening inventory (units)	Lots p.a.	Setup per lot	Scrap per lot	All lots p.a. setup& scrap	Gross input in units, prod. level	Gross input in units, prod. level 1	Planned production p.a. (net good units)	Gross input material year
2011	21	2	1	4-Ring-mechanism 7.5	unit	30,000	11	-	-	-	476,880	-	484,000	484,000
2011	22	2	1	2-Ring-mechanism 7.5	unit	30,000	11	-	-	-	715,682	-	691,900	691,900
2011	23	2	1	4-Ring-mechanism 4cm	unit	30,000	11	-	-	-	350,546	-	343,200	343,200
2011	24	2	1	2-Ring-mechanism 4 cm	unit	30,000	11	-	-	-	200,560	-	188,100	188,100
2011	31	2	1	7.5 cm-envelope	unit	100,000	11	20	50	770	952,172	-	924,000	924,770
2011	32	2	1	4.0 cm-envelope	unit	50,000	11	20	50	770	551,875	-	531,300	532,070
2011	11	1	1	Base plate 4Ring	unit	90,000	11	50	200	2,750		830,176	816,200	818,950
2011	12	1	1	Base plate 2Ring	unit	110,000	11	50	200	2,750		918,992	881,100	883,850
2011	13	1	1	7.5 cm-brackets	unit	120,000	11	100	200	3,300		3,342,185	3,275,800	3,279,100
2011	14	1	1	4.0 cm-brackets	unit	75,000	11	100	200	3,300		1,806,602	1,750,100	1,753,400

Fig. 4.22 Planned production quantities for the semi-finished products

consumption of 2750 for setup and scrap of this semi-finished product is expected for all planned lots, the gross input for this item 12 amounts to 883,850 units (Fig. 4.22).

Because the semi-finished products are produced almost continuously, it was decided not to fix any range targets and target inventories. Therefore, these columns are not presented here. The last stage of the BOM explosion is the raw material requirement (in the simulation model this can also be read in the sheet "Productionplan" in column "Gross demand in units"). This result is the most important input for Material Requirements Planning (MRP).

Note: Bills of materials also occur in trading companies when various items usually purchased individually are packed together and offered as a sales set.

4.4.3 Planning Purchases and Inventory Targets

The raw material requirements table (Fig. 4.23) is the starting point for raw material procurement. The planned sales quantities for merchandise can be found in the sheet "Revenueplan." The initial stock levels of all items are recorded in the opening balance sheet for the first planning year (2011). For the following years, these can be found in the "Stockplan" sheet. According to the formula already mentioned in Sect. 4.4.1, there is still no information as to which quantity of each item (raw materials,

Year	Itemnr	Production level	PR#	Description	QU	Opening inventory	Demand raw material for planned production
2011	1	0	3	Cardboard	sqm	40,000	350,718
2011	2	0	3	Film	running	50,000	424,946
2011	3	0	3	Wire	gram	2,000,000	93,636,400
2011	4	0	3	Sheet metal	sqm	10,000	24,958
2011	5	0	3	Consumables (Set)	unit	200,000	2,173,820
2011	6	0	3	Welding consumables (Set)	unit	80,000	688,170

Fig. 4.23 Raw material requirements for planned production

semi-finished products, finished products, and merchandise) should be available at the end of the planned year. The amount of the target closing inventory for the planned year depends on the reach targets for the individual items.

Inventory Targets

When setting inventory targets the dilemma between readiness to deliver, safety stocks, production cost, and necessary investment in warehousing must be resolved:

- The CFO wants a "lean" balance sheet and low capital costs. If the invested assets are kept small, the balance becomes slimmer, which results in a higher ROI-percentage. Lending banks and potential investors pay attention to this. In addition, the head of finance needs to borrow less from banks.
- On the other hand, maintaining the ability to always deliver products on time, the production of large batches, and the procurement of large quantities require higher inventories. From a purely factual basis, the arguments of the sellers, producers, and purchasers are to be given a higher weight, since their efforts are aimed at keeping the cost of the products low (cheaper purchase through larger order quantities and lower unit cost through lower setup cost thanks to large batches).
- Because of the greater investment in inventories mentioned above, most CFOs will focus on setting an upper limit on the percentage of inventory value in relation to sales. If this key figure is applied to all warehouse stocks, it often has a counterproductive effect. This is because the stocks of slow-moving items for the shopkeepers are only declining slowly, with the consequence that there is no longer enough permissible stock value available for the fast-moving items that must always be available.
- In addition, a "percentage-stock from turnover rule" restricts the choice of optimal lot sizes, since low stock specifications automatically require small lot sizes; regardless of the setup cost that can be saved as a result that can be higher than the financing costs saved.
- If purchasing can obtain lower purchase prices through larger order quantities (but fewer orders per year), this can lead to a reduction in product costs, which is greater than the financing costs caused by higher average inventory levels.

For these reasons, Ringbook Ltd. sets its inventory targets as quantitative reach targets. These are determined as a function of the following parameters:

- For finished goods, an average monthly sales quantity (based on planned sales) should always be kept in inventory. Exceptions with 2 months inventory are special formats, because these are produced less often (insufficiently large lot sizes).
- Special designs are only produced to customer orders and are not in stock. The reach target is therefore 0.0 months.
- For merchandise 0.6 months range is enough, since the items concerned are standard products which the suppliers can deliver immediately.

- No stock targets are set for semi-finished products, as they are produced each month and the production quantity is set monthly based on the expected consumption. The year-end balance should therefore not differ significantly from the opening balance.
- In the case of raw materials and individual parts to be purchased, the Purchasing Department shall report which periods of time are to be estimated by the suppliers for replacement. So far, however, no anomalies have been detected, which is why the purchasing department has set a safety stock of an average monthly consumption for all items to be purchased.

With these target stock rules, Ringbook Ltd. tries to reconcile the requirements of always being ready to deliver sales given its multilevel production process along with the need for safety stocks and the financial goal of keeping average stocks as low as possible.

All calculation details can be seen in the simulation model:

- The specifications are entered and maintained in the sheet "Articlemaster" by item and year.
- From there, they are transferred to the sheet "Productionplan" so that the target closing stocks can be calculated depending on the planned sales or planned production quantities.
- The difference between the target closing stock and the opening stock indicates whether more units are to be produced or purchased than are specified in sales/production quantity planning (or vice versa).
- The gross input for the semi-finished and finished products is calculated from the planned production quantities determined by the head of production plus the necessary setup and scrap material.
- The requirements for merchandise items are calculated based on the planned sales quantities, corrected by the planned stock changes resulting from warehouse stock planning.
- Finally, the raw material requirement is derived from the planned consumption recorded in the bills of materials, condensed over all the products to be manufactured, in accordance with the planned production for the year.

All data are collected in the sheet "Productionplan," see Fig. 4.19.

Purchase Planning

The planned requirements for raw materials result from the BOM explosion and from the planned requirements for merchandise items resulting from sales planning (column "Demand planned p.a."). These create the starting point for purchase planning.

The person responsible for procurement considers suitable purchasing quantities based on the reported requirements. In the negotiations with the supplier's delivery times, suitable delivery quantities (1 whole pallet, 1 complete truckload, etc.) and the

Year	Itemnr	PR#	Description	QU	Demand planned p.a.	Planned purchases in QU	Standard purchase price	Planned purchase value
2011	1	3	Cardboard	sqm	350,718	352,000	0.2800	98,560
2011	2	3	Film	runningm	424,946	430,000	0.2000	86,000
2011	3	3	Wire	gram	93,636,400	95,000,000	0.0020	190,000
2011	4	3	Sheet metal	sqm	24,958	25,000	2.0000	50,000
2011	5	3	Consumables (Set)	unit	2,174,020	2,200,000	0.1000	220,000
2011	6	3	Welding consumables (Set)	unit	688,170	690,000	0.0400	27,600
2011	120010	6	Index A-Z nature	10 units	5,718	5,700	13.5000	76,950
2011	120020	6	Index A-Z blue	10 units	830	800	13.7000	10,960
2011	120030	6	Index 1-31 nature	10 units	161	100	14.2000	1,420
2011	120040	6	Index 1-31 blue	10 units	2,623	2,600	14.4000	37,440
2011	120050	6	Transparent envelopes nature	100 units	1,322	1,200	7.6000	9,120
2011	120060	6	Transparent envelopes blue	100 units	3,410	3,400	7.6000	25,840
2011	120070	6	Transparent envelopes red	100 units	1,019	1,000	7.6000	7,600
2011	120080	6	Follow-up file 1-31 blue	unit	1,329	1,300	24.6000	31,980
2011	120090	6	Follow-up file A-Z blue	unit	525	550	24.6000	13,530
2011	120100	6	Follow-up file 1-31 red	unit	326	300	24.6000	7,380
2011	120110	6	Follow-up file A-Z red	unit	581	580	24.6000	14,268
2011	120200	6	Archive boxes	unit	4,655	4,000	0.7000	2,800
								911,448

Fig. 4.24 Definition of the purchase plan

planned prices dependent on these play an important role. The aim is to find the least expensive combination of these aspects. The number of deliveries per year also has an influence, as inventory targets must also be considered. The results of these considerations lead to the planned purchasing quantity, which the purchasing department enters in the yellow column on the "Purchaseplan" sheet. The conscious decision about the planned purchasing quantities again interrupts the automatic planning process. Once the planned purchasing quantities have been determined, the last column can be used to calculate the purchasing budget that is coordinated with the planned sales and planned production, a figure that is important for liquidity and cash flow planning (Fig. 4.24).

The average purchase prices expected by Purchasing for the planned year are entered in the "Articlemaster," since they are also used later for product costing (standard cost). The number of purchase orders per year is only determined during the year when the incoming order is known (tactical management).

4.5 Capacity Planning

Providing services requires personnel capacities, machines and factories. Their ready-for-use procurement and preparation requires different periods of time and generates a need for coordination. Planning is therefore indispensable. If one thinks from market into company, the available capacity or the capacity to be procured must be reconciled with the capacity demand resulting from sales and production planning.

4.5.1 Machine Capacities

The capacity offered should be measured according to the intended use of the facilities. In the case of a single machine, the available working time (machine time or operating hours) will usually be sufficient. If different machines are assembled to form a machining center, the available time of the entire system can also be measured. The possible performance of a machine or plant is usually determined by the possible daily running time (single or multi-shift). If all items running through the plant consume exactly the same amount of power, the number of processed units can also be used as a measure. However, if different products can be manufactured in the same installation, machine time required must be used to measure capacity utilization.

The following formula is used to calculate the machine capacity of a cost center:

Number of similar machines (1) × shift duration (8 h × 60 min = 480 min) × number of operating days (227 in the planned year, see sheet on annual working times) = 108,960 machine minutes capacity available.

Usually, capacities are given in hours or, if processing times per piece are very short, in minutes. This calculation is only necessary for cost centers whose installed machines (groups) are directly responsible for the product creation and could, therefore, can become a bottleneck. The number of shifts and the number of installed machines are recorded in the sheet "Costcenterplan" (Fig. 4.25).

The personnel-related data for the individual production sites (also Fig. 4.25) are described in the next section.

CCnr	RFU	Description	CC-manager	Personnel needed for mgmt. & organization	Opera-tional personnel	Serving person-nel pool	Personnel multiplier (Pmin/ unit)	Num-ber of shifts	Installed machines	Serving only other cost centers	Machine capacity in min. per shift	Normal-capacity all employees
220	Pmin	Stamping	Vogel	0.3	3.7		1	1	4		435,840	408,000
231	Units	Wire rolling	Berger	0	0		0.0375	1	2		-	-
232	Pmin	Wire bending & forming	Berger	0.9	5.5		1	1	1		108,960	652,800
240	Pmin	Cardboarding	Toscano	0		245	1	1	2		217,920	-
245	Pmin	Personnel pool 240-260	Wilhelm	2.5	19		1	1		ISP	-	2,193,000
250	Pmin	Assembly	Wilhelm			245	1	1	6		653,760	-
260	Units	Film welding	Womberger			245	0.25	1	1		-	-
330	Phours	Repair center	Temmel	0.1	0.9		1	1	0	ISP	-	1,700
340	KWh	Energy center	Temmel	0	0		1	1	0	ISP	-	-
300	Phours	IT	Stelker	2.5	0			1			-	4,250

RFU = Reference factor unit to measure the activity of a cost center

Only cost centers dirctly working on the products and ISP-cost centers are shown.

Fig. 4.25 Extract from the cost center list with planned personnel levels and installed machines

4.5.2 Personnel Capacities

The available personnel capacity of a cost center is determined by the net presence time of an employee and the number of persons required. Figure 4.26 shows the determination of the output values. These must be adapted to the conditions in the company and in the cost center to be planned, since the average number of vacation days, the average value for absences due to illness or other absences can change depending on the composition of the workforce of a cost center. The example company assumes a net annual presence of 1700 h per employee. These hours are used as the initial value because they represent the time during which an employee is available to the company.

There will be other planned average absences (holidays, sick leave, military service, and other absences) in the individual cost centers. The cost center manager can enter these yearly in the cost center sheet.

The input for the cost center manager to plan the required personnel capacity is:

- The hours or minutes required by the capacity demand for production (Sect. 4.5.4).
- The planned working hours needed for the internal tasks (Sect. 4.5.5.1).
- Possible reserve capacities for fluctuations in incoming orders.
- The hours needed for planned internal services provided (ISP) to other cost centers (Sect. 4.5.5.2).

On this basis, the cost center manager determines the planned headcount of employees that will be required to fulfill all planned tasks. The following columns are provided in Fig. 4.25 and in sheet "Costcenterplan" for entering these planned full-time equivalents (FTE):

- Personnel management (including the cost center manager) for internal tasks.
- Operational personnel for the work on production orders.
- Personnel multiplier for consideration of multiple machine operation or simultaneous needs of several persons for the operation of a system.

Fig. 4.26 Determining the planned presence time per employee and year (sheet "Workingtime")

Presence time planned 2011	
Target presence time per employee	
Days of the year	365.0
Saturdays / Sundays	105.0
Holidays	11.0
Vacation	24.0
Illness & other absences	7.6
Army service	4.9
Net working days	212.5
Work hours per day	8.0
Target presence time in hours	1700

The indication of the personnel multiplier is necessary because it co-determines the level of personnel requirements in full-time positions (FTEs). The planned number of employees must, therefore, be defined taking this factor into account.

The planned presence time multiplied by the planned number of FTE of the cost center results in its normal capacity. To the extent that the cost center managers are partly also directly involved in the production process, they are also counted as productive FTEs. The normal capacities of the production cost centers planned for the time being according to this procedure can be found in the last column of Fig. 4.25.

Here, again, **automatic planning is interrupted** by a necessary management decision. Each cost center manager must decide what headcount he wants to apply for his cost center plan, since management must determine which budgeted FTEs are approved when the plan is released (entry of the planned headcount in the sheet "Costcenterplan").

The simulation model is structured in such a way that the capacity demand of a cost center is automatically recalculated if changes are made to planned activities or internal tasks. If the demand exceeds the available time, the corresponding cells are displayed in red. The cost center manager decides whether to increase the planned headcount or to cover the shortfall by overtime or other measures.

4.5.3 Reference Factor Units

To match the capacities of a cost center to the ones required a comparable unit needs to be found. In most cases, especially for service companies, this is the employee hour (or minute), because personnel costs are the main cost factor of the cost center. If all product units processed in a cost center consume the same performance from the cost center, the demand and supply of capacity can be quantified in a simplified manner in units, running meters, or similar reference units.

If, on the other hand, the machine—together with the employees—accounts for most of the performance-related cost center costs—the machine hour is the appropriate reference factor unit (RFU). Using the machine hour as an RFU is also recommended if one employee can operate several machines at the same time, or if several employees work simultaneously to operate one machine.

In the example company, the RFU "unit" applies for rolling and punching the wires (cost center 231) and for foil welding (260), because each product running through these cost centers takes the same output quantity. All other cost centers in production have the RFU "Pmin" meaning employee minutes. The internal repair and maintenance cost center (330) and IT (300) plan and control their operations in hours, which is why the "Phour" RFU is used there (see second column in Fig. 4.25).

The definition of the RFU per cost center is an important prerequisite for building the work plans for the individual products to be manufactured and thus also for the comparability of the demand for capacities offered.

4.5.4 Work Plans and Capacity Requirements

The section on Material Requirements Planning (Sect. 4.4.3) showed that the planned production quantities and the corresponding BOMs contain the information required to calculate material requirements. The units to be produced and the cost center services consumed for them form the basis for calculating the required capacity per cost center. These cost center activities are recorded in work plans. The latter serves a variety of purposes:

- Planning of setup times per lot (production order).
- Planning of the activity to be performed in each cost center per unit (*allowed time*, also known as *standard time*).
- Defining the sequence of the processing steps and thus the sequence of the cost centers in the production process (routing).
- Calculating the capacity demand and therefore the planned capacity utilization for each production cost center. Planned activity level is the denominator for calculating the planned cost rate of a cost center.
- Providing the basis for occupying the capacities of the individual cost centers when a production order is triggered (dispatching of the order).
- Providing the basis for calculating the manufacturing cost of an item.

Work plans are also required in service companies and public administrations since capacity requirements planning must also be conducted there and the cost of services must be calculated. Examples include IT service providers or software developers and companies working on a mandate basis (lawyers, consultants, auditors, architects, and engineers). Hospitals also have work plans. These are integrated into the treatment pathways. Pathways may also contain a bill of materials listing medicines, aids, and other case-related consumptions.

In service companies and public administrations product definition is a great challenge for the practical application of quantity and performance planning as well as calculation. Where it is not defined which activities of the different cost centers are causally necessary to create a service unit, no work plan can be created (see Rieder 2004).

Planning Cost Center Activities in the Example Company

The last two lines of Fig. 4.27 show for item 101060 the two work plan positions to be processed to produce the finished product (Film welding and Assembly). For this purpose, the pre-products 4.0 cm cover (item no. 32) and the mechanism (item no. 23, consisting of the base plate (11) and brackets (14)) are obtained from the semi-finished goods warehouse.

In the last two columns of the table, for each process the standard and setup times are entered that will be used for the planned year. The **standard time** applies to each piece produced, the **setup time** is incurred for each new batch of a production order. Both times are in turn very close to execution goals; they indicate how long a cost center should take if its employees master the process.

Work plan positions

Itemnr	Year	QU	Production level	Description	Cost center nr	CC-name	RFU reference factor unit	Standard time/unit	Setup-time (in RFU) per lot
11	2011	unit	1	Base plate 4Ring	220	Stamping	Pmin	0.25	120
14	2011	unit	1	4.0 cm-brackets	231	Wire rolling	Units	1	50
14	2011	unit	1	4.0 cm-brackets	232	Wire bending & forming	Pmin	0.05	120
32	2011	unit	2	4.0 cm-envelope	240	Cardboarding	Pmin	0.2	120
101060	2011	unit	3	4ring 4 cm plasticized	250	Assembly	Pmin	1	120
101060	2011	unit	3	4ring 4 cm plasticized	260	Film welding	Units	1	20

Fig. 4.27 Work plan positions and standard times for the production of item 101060

Figure 4.28 contains all routing items for all semi-finished and finished products to be produced. The good parts to be produced were copied from material requirements planning or BOM explosion (fourth-to-last column). The third last column contains the standard times from the work plan sheet. In the second-to-last column, the planned setup times were taken and multiplied by the planned number of lots per year. From this, the capacity requirements for each individual item in its reference unit are calculated in the last column. By summing all these requirements per cost center, the total capacity demand per production cost center is created. In management accounting, these values correspond to the **planned activity level of** the cost center.

In summary, capacity requirements are derived along the following chain:

Sales quantity planning → Inventory planning → Production quantity planning utilizing bill of materials, including consideration of planned lot sizes → Determination of capacity requirements by cost center using work schedules and planned production quantities.

This planning process is consistently developed from the market into the company. The plan employment represents the market demand or sales planning converted to the cost centers. The question as to whether the available personnel and the automatic available capacity match the capacity demand is processed in cost center planning (Sect. 4.7), together with the planning of personnel costs.

4.5.5 Capacity Requirements Planning for Internal Provision of Services and Internal Tasks

When planning, it is essential to distinguish between internal tasks and internal services provided. An **internal task** is defined as all work performed in cost centers that are neither directly caused by the manufactured and sold products, nor requested by other cost centers with a direct service relationship. These include:

Work plan-positions

Year	Itemnr	QU	Pro-duc-tion level	Description	CCnr	Description	RFU	Plan-ned lots	Planned production good units	Standard time /unit	setup-time (in RFU) per lot	Capacity required / position (in RFU)
2011	11	unit	1	Base plate 4Ring	220	Stamping	Pmin	11	816,200	0.25	120	205,370
2011	12	unit	1	Base plate 2Ring	220	Stamping	Pmin	11	881,100	0.15	120	133,485
2011	13	unit	1	7.5 cm-brackets	231	Wire rolling	Units	11	3,275,800	1.00	50	3,276,350
2011	13	unit	1	7.5 cm-brackets	232	Wire bending & forming	Pmin	11	3,275,800	0.08	120	263,384
2011	14	unit	1	4.0 cm-brackets	231	Wire rolling	Units	11	1,750,100	1.00	50	1,750,650
2011	14	unit	1	4.0 cm-brackets	232	Wire bending & forming	Pmin	11	1,750,100	0.05	120	88,825
2011	31	unit	2	7.5 cm-envelope	240	Cardboarding	Pmin	11	924,000	0.25	120	232,320
2011	32	unit	2	4.0 cm-envelope	240	Cardboarding	Pmin	11	531,300	0.20	120	107,580
2011	101010	unit	3	4ring 7.5 back glued	250	Assembly	Pmin	4	47,600	0.40	120	19,520
2011	101020	unit	3	4ring 4 cm back glued	250	Assembly	Pmin	4	94,800	0.40	120	38,400
2011	101030	unit	3	4 ring 7.5 back welded	250	Assembly	Pmin	3	28,500	0.40	120	11,760
2011	101040	unit	3	4ring 4 cm back welded	250	Assembly	Pmin	6	61,200	0.40	120	25,200
2011	101050	unit	3	4ring 7.5 plasticized	250	Assembly	Pmin	4	37,600	1.00	120	38,080
2011	101050	unit	3	4ring 7.5 plasticized	260	Film welding	Units	4	37,600	1.00	20	37,680
2011	101060	unit	3	4ring 4 cm plasticized	250	Assembly	Pmin	11	85,800	1.00	120	87,120
2011	101060	unit	3	4ring 4 cm plasticized	260	Film welding	Units	11	85,800	1.00	20	86,020
2011	101070	unit	3	4 ring 7.5 plasticized	250	Assembly	Pmin	11	121,000	1.00	120	122,320
2011	101070	unit	3	4 ring 7.5 plasticized	260	Film welding	Units	11	121,000	1.00	20	121,220
2011	101080	unit	3	4ring 4 cm plasticized	250	Assembly	Pmin	1	800	1.00	120	920
2011	101080	unit	3	4ring 4 cm plasticized	260	Film welding	Units	1	800	1.00	20	820
2011	101090	unit	3	4ring 7.5 special design	250	Assembly	Pmin	11	112,310	1.00	120	113,630
2011	101090	unit	3	4ring 7.5 special design	260	Film welding	Units	11	112,310	1.00	20	112,530
2011	101100	unit	3	4ring 4 cm special design	250	Assembly	Pmin	11	80,400	0.70	120	57,600
2011	101100	unit	3	4ring 4 cm special design	260	Film welding	Units	11	80,400	1.00	20	80,620
2011	101110	unit	3	4ring 7.5 special design	250	Assembly	Pmin	2	7,700	0.70	120	5,630
2011	101110	unit	3	4ring 7.5 special design	260	Film welding	Units	2	7,700	1.00	20	7,740
2011	101120	unit	3	4ring 4 cm special design	250	Assembly	Pmin	2	18,800	0.70	120	13,400
2011	101120	unit	3	4ring 4 cm special design	260	Film welding	Units	2	18,800	1.00	20	18,840
2011	103000	unit	3	2ring special format A5 7.5	250	Assembly	Pmin	11	124,300	1.00	120	125,620
2011	104000	unit	3	4ring special format A3 7.5	250	Assembly	Pmin	11	116,600	2.50	120	292,820
2011	105010	unit	3	2ring 7.5 back glued	250	Assembly	Pmin	6	139,800	0.30	120	42,660
2011	105020	unit	3	2ring 4 cm back glued	250	Assembly	Pmin	6	78,000	0.30	120	24,120
2011	105030	unit	3	2ring 7.5 back welded	250	Assembly	Pmin	4	68,800	0.30	120	21,120
2011	105040	unit	3	2ring 4 cm back welded	250	Assembly	Pmin	2	3,000	0.30	120	1,140
2011	105050	unit	3	2ring 7.5 plasticized	250	Assembly	Pmin	6	99,600	0.30	120	30,600
2011	105050	unit	3	2ring 7.5 plasticized	260	Film welding	Units	6	99,600	1.00	20	99,720
2011	105060	unit	3	2ring 4 cm plasticized	250	Assembly	Pmin	4	11,600	0.30	120	3,960
2011	105060	unit	3	2ring 4 cm plasticized	260	Film welding	Units	4	11,600	1.00	20	11,680
2011	105070	unit	3	2ring 7.5 plasticized	250	Assembly	Pmin	4	18,000	0.30	120	5,880
2011	105070	unit	3	2ring 7.5 plasticized	260	Film welding	Units	4	18,000	1.00	20	18,080
2011	105080	unit	3	2ring 4 cm plasticized	250	Assembly	Pmin	3	30,600	0.30	120	9,540
2011	105080	unit	3	2ring 4 cm plasticized	260	Film welding	Units	3	30,600	1.00	20	30,660
2011	105090	unit	3	2ring 7.5 special design	250	Assembly	Pmin	11	85,910	0.70	120	61,457
2011	105090	unit	3	2ring 7.5 special design	260	Film welding	Units	11	85,910	1.00	20	86,130
2011	105100	unit	3	2ring 4 cm special design	250	Assembly	Pmin	2	5,500	0.70	120	4,090
2011	105100	unit	3	2ring 4 cm special design	260	Film welding	Units	2	5,500	1.00	20	5,540
2011	105110	unit	3	2ring 7.5 special design	250	Assembly	Pmin	11	151,030	0.70	120	107,041
2011	105110	unit	3	2ring 7.5 special design	260	Film welding	Units	11	151,030	1.00	20	151,250
2011	105120	unit	3	2ring 4 cm special design	250	Assembly	Pmin	11	55,330	0.70	120	40,051
2011	105120	unit	3	2ring 4 cm special design	260	Film welding	Units	11	55,330	1.00	20	55,550
									Total for comparison			8,285,723

Aggregated planned activities per cost center

220	Stamping	338,855
231	Wire rolling	5,027,000
232	Wire bending & forming	352,209
240	Cardboarding	339,900
250	Assembly	1,303,679
260	Film welding	924,080
	Total for comparison	8,285,723

Fig. 4.28 Work plan items, capacity requirements and planned activity for all manufactured products

- All management tasks from cost center management to the overall management of the company.
- All personnel administration services from recruitment to payroll and personnel administration to care for retired employees.
- Expenses for company-related training and further education.
- All tasks in the areas of purchasing and warehouse management.
- All tasks for the administration of buildings and company premises.
- All tasks for the maintenance and further development of the complete IT operation (without work for projects, see Sect. 4.6.2).
- All tasks of the controller and finance departments.
- All tasks of production planning and control and work preparation.
- Basic research in the fields of research and development.
- All tasks of sales, distribution, and marketing including communication, sales promotion, and advertising.
- All other administrative tasks.

All these internal tasks are also services. However, they are never directly causally related to the products manufactured and services provided (there is no direct cause-and-effect relationship). What they have in common is that they always support the products and the company's uninterrupted readiness to perform. In every company we know, the proportion of working hours required for internal tasks increases faster than the total number of hours worked in the company. Some reasons for this increasing share of total hours include:

- Various legal regulations.
- Safety regulations.
- More comprehensive personnel support.
- Proof of origin and enabling batch tracking in the event of complaints.
- Workload to acquire new customers and orders and maintain existing ones.
- Record keeping of business processes.
- Warranty services, handling of complaints, and return deliveries.

It is therefore becoming increasingly important for the viability of an organization that the time and cost required for this work is planned and monitored and, whenever possible, reduced (improvement of the cost position compared to the competition).

Internal services provided (ISP), on the other hand, occur when and only when the following two criteria are met:

- The service recipient (a cost center) can decide whether and how much service is to be obtained from the internal service provider (e.g., repair services) or there is an automatic relationship between the services of the (internal) provider and the (also internal) service recipient. This is the case, for example, if 100 kWh of electrical energy per hour of operation of a machine (user) is always obtained from the company's own energy center. The activity level of the performing cost center is then directly dependent on the consumption of the receiving cost center.

- The providing cost center must have direct consumption dependent on the activity of the receiving cost center and, therefore, costs. The performance-related costs of the ISP are then directly dependent on the requirements of the recipients.

In the case of a genuine internal exchange of services, the internal service provider replaces an external provider for security, integration, or cost reasons. The service recipient should therefore actually have the freedom to obtain the required service at the planned rate from the internal service provider or more cheaply from an external provider. This, however, is often not permitted by internal group rules (e.g., to better utilize one's own service capacity or to enforce quality regulations).

It is important not to define internal service cost centers as profit centers, since they can show themselves "profitable" via the transfer price of the internal service (see Sect. 2.2.2).

In sum, all activity types occurring in a company belong to one of the following three categories:

- *Services performed directly for the product unit.* These are documented by bills of material and work plans (or surrogates thereof) in a plannable and measurable way and are causally necessary for the genesis of the products or services.
- If the work performance is causally determined by the receiving cost centers (by the cost center manager or by a direct cause-and-effect relationship), there is a *genuine internal service provided.* The cost dependent on the provided activity can be charged to the receivers according to the costs-by-cause principle.
- The remaining *internal tasks* represent the work that is necessary for the organization's capability to perform at any time and ultimately the prerequisite for the company to be able to function at all, to be willing to perform, and to deliver its products to its customers. The cost incurred for these tasks is called in Sect. 4.7.1 fixed cost or structural cost. They cannot be allocated to the individual product units on a causal basis. Both the internal tasks and the resulting costs are defined without exception by management decisions. These decisions define the personnel and capacity structures of an organization so that it is prepared to perform as needed.

4.5.5.1 Planning Internal Tasks

Internal tasks must be carried out so that the organization's capability to perform is permanently maintained and sustainable further development is also made possible. For this purpose, the time required for internal tasks must be planned in the individual cost centers to derive the required personnel capacity. It is advisable to specify a grouping of the essential activities to facilitate the planning task and to enable cross-comparisons between the cost centers.

In practical application, it has proven successful to use the task groups for each cost center shown in Fig. 4.29.

Internal tasks Of all employees of a cost center (including management)		Frequency per year	Avg. time in min.	Demand in hours
Management	Organisation, planning, steering, promotion of employees	48	300	240
Information / communication	Meetings, mails, phone	48	420	336
Further education	Internal and external (for the company), personnel development	4	1,440	96
Travelling time		52	360	312
Administrative tasks	Execute the multicity of everyday tasks in a cost center	222	1,260	4,662
Unforeseen		222	90	333
Capacity demand				5,979

Fig. 4.29 Planning capacity requirements for the main internal tasks of a cost center (example)

These six working groups occur in almost every cost center and can, therefore, be planned for in every organization. The tasks can be divided into subgroups for a clearer representation in each cost center. An example for a sales representative:

- Find potential customers, enter and maintain data, generate leads (invitation to customer visit), and set visit appointments.
- General communication with potential customers.
- Preparation of visits (data, brochures, ordering, and payment behavior of the customer, updating or evaluating technical customer data, and travel planning).
- Customer calls, follow-up, reports.
- Coordination with sales promotion and marketing.

Since the various task areas contain many tasks and each cost center requires a slightly different share of time, the planned hours will not arrive with the same precision as that of the standard times in the work plans. The hours determined are not targeted values either but are the basis for equipping the cost center with full-time equivalents (available capacity) and form the benchmark for comparing the actually performed work during the year. This comparison is particularly useful when the company's cost position needs to be improved in the medium term (see Sect. 7.5. 2.2).

Our experience shows that the personnel costs incurred for internal tasks in manufacturing companies are higher than the personnel costs that are causally necessary for the actual production. This underlines the fact that the planning and monitoring of time and resources spent on internal tasks are becoming increasingly decisive for success.

4.5.5.2 Planning Internal Services Provided

Internal services provided (ISP) are activities for which the receiver either orders from the internal supplier (cost center) or which are procured automatically depending on the activity of the receiving cost center. In addition, the performing cost center must have portions of the planned cost that are directly caused by its actual activity. This is the only basis on which a planned cost rate can be obtained that is the consequence of a direct cause-and-effect relationship (see Sect. 4.7.4). These conditions are only met in a few cases, as can be seen from the following examples for Ringbook Ltd.:

- Services of personnel pools for machine cost centers (CC 245).
- Maintenance and repair services of machinery, buildings, and other equipment (CC 330).
- Internal energy supplies (kWh electrical energy), CC 340.
- Workshop work (mechanics, electrical, painter, garage, and other craftsmen).
- Laboratory work that is not already contained in work plans but is carried out in the laboratory for a cost center on order.
- Fleet costs (per operating hour or km).
- IT development services that are explicitly ordered by the receiving cost center or are written to assets (capitalized projects) (CC 300).

Services within the framework of a Service Level Agreement (SLA, see Glossary) do not, in most cases, meet these requirements. In such cases, the capacity requirements must be planned by the service provider.

Internal Services Provided in the Example Company
The Repair center (330) performs all preventive maintenance work and repairs for the other cost centers that are not outsourced.

The Energy center (340) supplies all internal consumers with electricity. Supervision of the cost center is the responsibility of the repair manager. Activity planning for this cost center is based on the electricity consumption table. This table contains the activity-dependent consumption per operating hour of the production cost centers and the activity-independent consumption of all cost centers (see sheet "ISPplan," activity-independent and activity-dependent columns).

The Personnel pool (245) provides the workforce for the cost centers Cardboarding, Film welding and Assembly. The employees move from one to another cost center according to the demand of the processes.

The IT cost center (300) ensures the ongoing operation of computers, telecommunications, applications, and data storage and develops the entire IT system. Additionally, its employees carry out development work within the framework of projects on order.

The recording of the planned genuine internal services is shown in Fig. 4.30. Purchases independent of activity quantity, e.g., for lighting and heating or for regular maintenance, are entered in column "Non performance-related." If the reference is an automatic consequence of the activity performed in the receiving cost center (here the energy consumption in the production centers), the consumption per RFU of the receiving cost center is recorded in the column

Year	Ser-ving CCnr	Description	RFU	Activ-ity type	Description	Pro-ject	Recei-ving CC	Description	Non perfor-mance-related	Perfor-mance-related /RFU	Perfor-mance-related sum	Work for pro-jects	Total consumption by receiving CC's
2011	330	Repair center	Phours	22	maintenance & repair services		220	Stamping	240	0	-	-	240
2011	330	Repair center	Phours	22	maintenance & repair services		231	Wire rolling	180	0	-	-	180
2011	330	Repair center	Phours	22	maintenance & repair services		232	Wire bending & forming	160	0	-	-	160
2011	330	Repair center	Phours	22	maintenance & repair services		240	Cardboarding	120	0	-	-	120
2011	330	Repair center	Phours	22	maintenance & repair services		250	Assembly	300	0	-	-	300
2011	330	Repair center	Phours	22	maintenance & repair services		260	Film welding	50	0	-	-	50
2011	330	Repair center	Phours	22	maintenance & repair services		330	Repair center	0	0	-	-	-
2011	330	Repair center	Phours	22	maintenance & repair services		340	Energy center	180	0	-	-	180
2011	330	Repair center	Phours	22	maintenance & repair services		200	Plant mgmt. & work scheduling	24	0	-	-	24
2011	330	Repair center	Phours	22	maintenance & repair services		210	Procurement & warehouse	24	0	-	-	24
2011	330	Repair center	Phours	22	maintenance & repair services		320	Buildings & maintenance	144	0	-	-	144
2011	330	Repair center	Phours	22	maintenance & repair services		300	IT	36	0	-	-	36
2011	330	Repair center	Phours	22	maintenance & repair services		900	Corp. management & administration	36	0	-	-	36
2011	330	Repair center	Phours	22	maintenance & repair services		100	Sales mgmt. & office	36	0	-	-	36
2011	340	Energy center	KWh	21	internal energy consumption		220	Stamping	2000	0.002	678	-	2,678
2011	340	Energy center	KWh	21	internal energy consumption		231	Wire rolling	5000	0.006	30,162	-	35,162
2011	340	Energy center	KWh	21	internal energy consumption		232	Wire bending & forming	2000	0.047	16,554	-	18,554
2011	340	Energy center	KWh	21	internal energy consumption		240	Cardboarding	5000	0.082	27,872	-	32,872
2011	340	Energy center	KWh	21	internal energy consumption		250	Assembly	3000	0.032	41,718	-	44,718
2011	340	Energy center	KWh	21	internal energy consumption		260	Film welding	5000	0.02177	20,115	-	25,115
2011	340	Energy center	KWh	21	internal energy consumption		330	Repair center	400	0	-	-	400
2011	340	Energy center	KWh	21	internal energy consumption		340	Energy center	0	0	-	-	-
2011	340	Energy center	KWh	21	internal energy consumption		200	Plant mgmt. & work scheduling	1500	0	-	-	1,500
2011	340	Energy center	KWh	21	internal energy consumption		210	Procurement & warehouse	1500	0	-	-	1,500
2011	340	Energy center	KWh	21	internal energy consumption		320	Buildings & maintenance	12000	0	-	-	12,000
2011	340	Energy center	KWh	21	internal energy consumption		300	IT	12000	0	-	-	12,000
2011	340	Energy center	KWh	21	internal energy consumption		900	Corp. management & administration	6000	0	-	-	6,000
2011	340	Energy center	KWh	21	internal energy consumption		100	Sales mgmt. & office	1000	0	-	-	1,000
2011	330	Repair center	Phours	22	maintenance & repair services	P					-	120	120
2011	300	IT	Phours	24	Ordered IT-Services (internally)	P					-	550	550
2011	245	Personnel pool 240-260	Pmin	23	Personnel pool services		240	Cardboarding	0	1	339,900	-	339,900
2011	245	Personnel pool 240-260	Pmin	23	Personnel pool services		250	Assembly	0	1	1,303,679	-	1,303,679
2011	245	Personnel pool 240-260	Pmin	23	Personnel pool services		260	Film welding	0	0.25	231,020	-	231,020

Planned activity of the internal service providers		
245	Personnel pool 240-260	1,874,599
300	IT	550
330	Repair center	1,650
340	Energy center	193,498

Fig. 4.30 Plan of the internal services provided at Ringbook Ltd.

"Performance-related/RFU." The specifications for the column "Work for projects" are created in the project planning (see Sect. 4.6) and are automatically imported from there. The sum of the plan activities per performing cost center results in the planned activities of the ISP cost centers (at the bottom of Fig. 4.30).

This performance-based planning differs clearly from the usual cost allocation! The receiver as operator of a cost center determines whether and how much of a certain service he wants to consume from the internal supplier. Because of the direct causal connection, the term "genuine internal services provided" is used here. For the internal tasks described above, this direct cause-and-effect chain does not exist, which is why the costs of the internal tasks and the capacities available can never be passed on according to the cause (see Sect. 4.5.5.1).

4.6 Project Planning

From a data structure viewpoint, projects can be planned and tracked in a manner similar to production orders for products. To make planning manageable, the first question to be addressed is under what circumstances a project should be opened and its development monitored.

Increasingly rapid changes in the corporate environment and more diverse interdependencies (higher complexities) lead organizations to constantly demand the establishment of new projects (projectitis acutis). Since a project requires capacities, skills and abilities as well as money, it should therefore first be decided whether a project should be commenced at all.

4.6.1 Open a Project?

In our opinion, the answer to the question of whether to start a project should depend on the fulfilment of the following criteria (see Stöger 2011, p. 3 ff.):

- Clear order with defined objective to be achieved.
- Fixed start and completion dates.
- It is something new, something we have never done before.
- The task is complex and can only be solved through interdisciplinary cooperation of several persons and involving several cost centers.
- It requires extensive use of resources (working time and investments).

These criteria should be considered cumulatively in the planning of projects as a project entails:

- Project organization
- Project planning
- Measurement of achievement targets
- Project control
- Partial separation of employees from their traditional areas of responsibility.

Projects can have time and processing horizons ranging from a few days to several years. Integrated annual planning must therefore ensure that larger project parts to be processed in the planning year are included in procurement and capacity planning as well as in cost, result, and cash flow planning (see IMS, Sect. 2.2.1). The basis for this is the planning of the project schedule with its subprojects, tasks, and processes therein, with regard to milestones, investments, and cost.

4.6.2 Integrating Projects into the Annual Plan

Creating a project budget is comparable to the methodology of material requirements planning. A project must also record what is to be procured externally and, if necessary, what inventory usage (raw materials, auxiliary, and operating materials up to semi-finished and finished products) are to be planned for project implementation. This also includes services to be procured externally.

If a project generates capacity requirements in the cost centers involved in the conversion, this is comparable to capacity requirements planning. The planned time consumption in the individual project steps replaces the work plans with their allowed times.

Instead of the item with its BOM for the products to be manufactured, the project order with its material requirements for the planned year is used (purchase order processing usually via purchasing).

The routing is replaced by the planning of internal services provided ISP. The recipient is the respective project, the service providers are employees of cost centers. They should also enter their planned times for the project in the "ISPplan" table (Fig. 4.30) or, in the case of pure project support, take them into account when planning internal tasks.

Until the completion of a project, the project-related investments, all raw material, semi-finished, and finished product consumptions, as well as the services received from cost centers, are to be charged to the project at the planned cost rates. This also applies, once the necessary changes have been made, to projects whose implementation period will last more than one year. This approach is recommended because the manager in charge of the project can observe and control the development of investments, costs, and services undistorted over the entire course of the project.

As a result, projects are to be included in the operating balance sheet as an independent fixed asset item until they are officially declared completed. Only then the decision is made as to whether the accumulated project value should be capitalized and depreciated from this date or immediately charged to the current annual financial statements. Whether and to what extent a project is to be activated for external reporting (commercial law and accounting standards) is largely independent of the management-oriented operational view.

Projects in the Example Company

Ringbook Ltd. plans to carry out two extensive projects for the planned year 2011:

- Project 1 (P1): Automated material positioning in assembly.
  The exact positioning of the supplied materials (envelopes and pre-assembled mechanics) is to be designed using an automatic handling system with process control so that half the setup time per order and around 35% of the specified time per unit can be saved. This means that the system can also be operated with fewer personnel. The project planning envisages that automated material positioning will be practically applicable to all items to be produced from the beginning of 2012. The head of the Assembly cost center (250) is responsible for the project and its implementation.
- Project 2 (P2): Establishment and development of the *onlineshop* for the direct sale of ring binders (excluding merchandise) to end consumers.
  A standard onlineshop application is to be purchased and linked to the existing ERP, in particular its customer and invoice data, inventory management, and payment processes. The evaluation of the software is already well advanced. It is assumed that preparatory work on the ERP side can begin in February 2011. The onlineshop should be operational from 1/1/2012. To assess success, all online orders are to be recorded in sales channel 3 (direct customer onlineshop). The sales manager is the project and sales channel manager.

The chronological course of the two projects is recorded in the project planning sheet (Fig. 4.31).

The expected material consumption for testing the handling machine was planned on P1. This is necessary because the intended consumption of consumables and semi-finished products must be in stock. These have already been counted in the planning of material requirements, as can be seen from the Inventory draft plan sheet in the "Quantity" column (Fig. 4.32).

The most important positions to purchase are expected to include concept development and implementation for the two projects, the necessary machines and software licenses, and adjustments of the existing ERP software (Fig. 4.33).

At Ringbook Ltd., the cost centers of sales management, IT, and repair/maintenance will be significantly responsible for project implementation. The sales office staff will operate the online shop and will, therefore, be constant companions of IT in the planning and implementation of the project. IT and the repair center also

Year	Pro-jectnr.	Description	Recei-ving CC	Kickoff	Milestone1	Milestone 2	Milestone 3	Planned project end
2011	1	Automatic material positioning	250	2011-05-08	2011-10-31	2011-11-30		2011-12-23
2011	2	Installation onlineshop	100	2011-01-31	2011-04-30	2011-08-31	2011-11-15	2011-12-23

Fig. 4.31 Projects of the planned year 2011 (sheet "Projectplan")

Planned material consumption

Year	Project	Description	Itemnr	Description	Quantity	prop.cost	Amount
2011	1	Automatic material positioning	5	Consumables (Set)	200	0.1000	20.00
2011	1	Automatic material positioning	21	4-Ring-mechanism 7.5	200	0.7335	146.69
2011	1	Automatic material positioning	32	4.0 cm-envelope	200	0.3181	63.62
2011	1	Automatic material positioning	24	2-Ring-mechanism 4 cm	200	0.3345	66.89
2011	1	Automatic material positioning	31	7.5 cm-envelope	200	0.3599	71.99
				Total material consumption for projects			369.19

Fig. 4.32 Planned material consumption of the projects (sheet "Projectplan")

Planned purchases (external)

Year	Pro-jectnr.	Description	Description of the purchases	Amount
2011	1	Automatic material positioning	Auxiliary material	500
2011	1	Automatic material positioning	Concept and implementation	28,000
2011	1	Automatic material positioning	Software development & testing	-
2011	1	Automatic material positioning	Software (licences & implementation)	-
2011	1	Automatic material positioning	Machinery / equipment	22,000
2011	2	Installation onlineshop	Machinery / equipment	12,000
2011	2	Installation onlineshop	Concept and implementation	25,000
2011	2	Installation onlineshop	Software (licences & implementation)	20,000
			Total planned purchases for projects	107,500

Fig. 4.33 Planned purchases for projects (sheet "Projectplan")

Planned Cost center services (ISP)

Year	Pro-jectnr.	Description	Serving CC	Description	Quantity	Prop. cost-rate	Amount
2011	1	Automatic material positioning	330	Repair center	100	38.9488	3,894.88
2011	1	Automatic material positioning	300	IT	50	52.4047	2,620.24
2011	2	Installation onlineshop	330	Repair center	20	38.9488	778.98
2011	2	Installation onlineshop	300	IT	500	52.4047	26,202.35
						Total ISP for projects	33,496.45

Fig. 4.34 Planned services of the cost centers involved in the projects (ISP, sheet "Projectplan")

estimated the hours needed for their contributions and included them in the project budget. These internal services will be charged to the projects at their planned proportional cost rate (Fig. 4.34).

The planned hours are already included in the planned internal exchange of services (see Fig. 4.30). All listed positions will be integrated into the summary of the plans.

Since project completion is not expected until the end of the planned year, the actual accrued expenses and consumption will be included in the balance sheet under "assets under construction/projects." Whether these values are capitalized and depreciated or charged directly to annual costs should only be decided after the actual figures are available. The capitalized part of the project consumption is not included in the fixed asset accounting ("Invest&depr" sheet) until after the project has been completed and is then depreciated. Services, consumption, and investments for projects are thus considered in the integrated planning system.

4.6.3 Will the Projects and the Planned Investments be Profitable?

Before the two projects could be included in the annual planning, it was necessary to assess whether the planned investments would pay off. The **dynamic investment calculation** was used for the assessment.

An investment calculation is used to prepare decisions. It is a **pure cash flow statement**. The cash outflows resulting from the investment are compared with the expected cash inflows or reduced expenses resulting from the investment. This pure cash flow statement is of central importance for decision making, both strategically and operationally:

- The decision is made based on the estimated cash flows as no actual data is available yet.
- All revenues and consumption of resources are estimated as the investment has not yet been made.
- Consumption prior to the decision is not relevant, as the necessary funds have already been used (i.e., they are sunk costs).
- In the same way, residual asset values in the balance sheet are not relevant for decision making, since depreciation would continue to appear in profitability analysis even if the investment were not made (the expenses for this were incurred earlier).
- The decision-making body decides on the appropriateness of future expenditures.

As cash inflows and cash outflows do not occur simultaneously, the fair value of money must be taken into consideration. This is done by discounting the cash flows at the interest rate required by management:

- If, for example, the financial business concept (see Sect. 1.4.1) requires an ROI of 10% (earnings before interest and taxes in relation to invested assets), the total investment amount for each planned investment must generate at least 10% interest. Otherwise, the company would invest in insufficiently profitable businesses and miss its profitability target. (An exception not discussed here: legally required investments.)
- If the cash outflow for an investment takes place more or less immediately after the decision has been made, it roughly corresponds in terms of value to the decrease in the bank account. However, a cash inflow that will not occur until one year after the release of the investment is worth less at the time of the decision because it has not generated the required EBIT for one year.

Date	Money flow	Amount	ROI-target	Discounted value as per 01/01/2011
01/01/2011	Investment (outflow)	1,000.00	10%	1,000.00
01/01/2012	Benefit (inflow)	1,000.00	10%	909.09

The longer it takes for discounted (net present value) cash inflows to cover (mostly) immediate cash outflows, the less profitable an investment becomes.

For the **onlineshop development project,** this analysis was carried out using the investment calculation template (sheet "Investmentappraisal"). The results are shown in Fig. 4.35.

To determine the expected additional money flows:

- The sheet "Plansales" also includes the additional sales quantities in 2012 to be sold via the onlineshop (25,240).
- The planned sales volumes 2013–2016 are estimated by the sales manager (the sum of finished goods).

Fig. 4.35 Calculation basis for the investment calculation of P2 (onlineshop)

Calculation basis (taken from "CMplanitems")		
Finished goods only	Value	Per unit
Sales quantity plan		1,667,000
Net proceeds	6,417,950	3.85
Planned prop. Cost	2,800,560	1.68
CM I (no commissions)	3,617,390	2.17

Personnel costs for sales support of the online shop	
Estimated hours p.a.	360
Planned presence-rate 2011 / hour	48.00
Personnel costs p.a.	17,280

- From sheet "CMplanitems," the average CM I per unit for 2011 is calculated (2.17) and maintained for all years.
- 360 h per year are estimated for the support of the onlineshop. These were valued at the planned presence hour rate of the sales office staff of 48.00. There are no plans to recruit additional staff. However, the 17,280 (360 × 48) personnel costs are included as an opportunity cost in the investment calculation, since the working time is no longer available for other assignments.
- The data for the investment in fixed assets as well as for in-house services from the investment planning in Sect. 4.6.2 (Fig. 4.33) were taken over and transferred to column 0 (decision year 2011).
- Because the additional sales will lead to higher accounts receivable and inventories and, to a lesser extent, to more accounts payable, the invested assets are valued at 10% of the net proceeds and deducted from the cash inflows (only the change from the previous year).
- The annual cash flows are discounted with the required target ROI of 10% (present value factor in the line "Target ROI").

The annual cash return from the expected project is the difference between the additional CM I and liquidity-related fixed costs directly caused by the project (CFBIT or net benefit of the project). If the cash outflows for investments and higher net current assets are also included, the results are the annual cash flows (Fig. 4.36).

The cumulation of the present value annual cash flows shows that the project should generate surpluses above the required 10% from the third year onwards. The return requirement from corporate policy is more than fulfilled. This is also demonstrated by the internal rate of return of 40.27%. If the onlineshop can continue to operate in 2017 and subsequent years without significant new investments, surpluses will continue to grow.

Note that **depreciation should never be included in an investment calculation**, since the acquisition cost is included in the discounted cash flows. Income taxes resulting from the investment are already included in the target ROI rate, i.e., they are not to be added.

For the Automatic Material Positioning project, the investment consideration is somewhat simpler:

- According to cost center planning (sheet cost centers), a planned employment of 1,303,679 personnel minutes is to be assumed for 2011 in assembly. For the project, it is assumed that savings of around 35% of the target times will be achieved, which means around 456,000 personnel minutes. One minute taken from the personnel pool costs 0.756, which should result in savings of around 344,700 personnel costs. The planned halving of setup times was not counted.
- According to Sect. 4.6.1, the total investment amounts to 57,493. Even if start-up difficulties should arise, it can be assumed that the project will pay for itself after 6–9 months through personnel cost savings.

Investment calculation model		2011	2012	2013	2014	2015	2016
Year		0	1	2	3	4	5
Target-ROI / present-value-factor	10.00%	1.000	0.909	0.826	0.751	0.683	0.621
Delta sales quantity, see "Plansales"			25,240	28,000	31,000	34,000	38,000
Average price / unit			3.85	3.85	3.85	3.85	3.85
+ Delta net revenue			97,174	107,800	119,350	130,900	146,300
- Rate for other sales deductions		none	0%	0%	0%	0%	0%
= **Net proceeds**			**97,174**	**107,800**	**119,350**	**130,900**	**146,300**
Prop. production cost (per average unit			1.68	1.68	1.68	1.68	1.68
- Prop. production cost of the units to sell			42,403	47,040	52,080	57,120	63,840
= **Contribution margin I**			**54,771**	**60,760**	**67,270**	**73,780**	**82,460**
Additional fixed costs caused directly by the investment project							
- Production, R&D							
- Procurement, warehousing, services	what will be additional expenditures in the years that are independent of produced and sold units?						
- Sales and marketing			17,280	17,280	17,280	17,280	17,280
- Management, administration, IT							
= **Controllable and liquidiy effecting fixed costs of the project**			**17,280**	**17,280**	**17,280**	**17,280**	**17,280**
= **CFBIT (net cash-in)**			**37,491**	**43,480**	**49,990**	**56,500**	**65,180**
Increase of current assets minus increase of shortrange liabilities minus liquidation proceeds							
+ Change accounts receivable							
+ Change stocks	10%		9,717	1,063	1,155	1,155	1,540
- Change acc,. payable and provisions							
+ Investment/divestment in fixed assets		57,000					
Investment through captalized own work		28,073					
- Liquidation proceeds							0
= **Money flow investment/divestment**		**85,073**	**9,717**	**1,063**	**1,155**	**1,155**	**1,540**
= **Jearly money flows**		**-85,073**	**27,773**	**42,417**	**48,835**	**55,345**	**63,640**
Present value of the money flows		-85,073	25,249	35,056	36,690	37,801	39,515
Cumulated present value of the investment project		**-85,073**	**-59,824**	**-24,769**	**11,922**	**49,723**	**89,239**
Internal rate of return							**40.27%**

Fig. 4.36 Dynamic investment calculation for the setup and operation of the online shop

The investment calculation model used above is a universally applicable Excel model (sheet “Investmentappraisal”). Its use is particularly recommended when investments will be made at different timepoints during the course of the project and when the cash flows will be different in the individual years of use (e.g., growth).

4.7 Cost Center Planning

The activity planning procedure described in Sects. 4.4–4.6 has shown the following for the cost centers:

- The capacity demand for each production cost center can be determined from the work plans and the planned production quantities. In cost center planning, it is called planned activity.
- Planning of the internal services to be provided leads to the determination of the planned activity level of the internal service cost centers. This also includes the performance requirements resulting from the projects or parts of projects planned for the planning year.

- By planning internal tasks, one can determine for each cost center how many working hours are to be reserved for the accomplishment of these tasks. This also includes working hours, which are required for internal tasks in projects.

These three elements result in the capacity demand for each cost center either in reference factor units or in working hours. The determination of the available capacity in the plan year asks for new decisions from the cost center manager:

- How many FTEs (full-time equivalents) are to be made available to the cost center to meet demand (including any personnel reserves to cover fluctuations in demand)?
- Which machines or machine groups will be required to meet demand (considering expected downtimes of the equipment)?

Section 4.5.2 and Fig. 4.25 described how to determine and record personnel requirements. Figure 4.37 summarizes the planned capacity and planned activity data of all cost centers.

It is only now that in cost center planning the planned consumption for the capacities to be held ready is evaluated with money. The purposes of this valuation include:

- The determination of the planned costs for a year.
- The determination of planned cost rates for internal activity calculation and product costing.
- To provide a basis for plan, target, and actual comparison.
- To provide a basis for reconciliation with the expenses in financial accounting.

Planned costs and planned cost rates are of central importance for decision-making in integrated planning and control. The prerequisite for their determination is the consistent application of management-relevant cost and revenue terms. These cost terms are decisive for the design of a cost, performance, revenue, and result accounting that is appropriate for decision-making. They are described in detail below, before actual cost planning is started.

4.7.1 Cost Terms for Decision-Making

For managers, three dimensions are relevant for the planning and control of and responsibility for cost:

- Controllability of costs
- Direct versus indirect costs
- Proportional versus fixed costs

Year	CCnr	RFU	Description	CC-manager	Person-nel for mgmt. & admin.	Opera-tional person-nel	Serving person-nel pool	Person-nel multi-plier	Num-ber of shifts	Installed machines	Serving only other CC (ISP)	Avg. vaca-tion days	Ill-ness p.a.	Army ser-vice days	Other ab-sences p.a.	Total absen-ces	Machine capacity in min. per shift	Normal-capacity all employees	Planned activity p.a.	Planned still-stand p.a.	Min./hours demand for inter-nal tasks	Derived planned activity p.a. (ISP)	Total demand personnel time (min./hours p.a.)
2011	220	Pmin	Stamping	Vogel	0.3	3.7		(Pmin/ 1	1	4		24	7.6	4.9	0	36.5	435840	408,000	338,855	4,400	65,000	-	403,855
2011	231	Units	Wire rolling	Berger	0	0		0.0375	1	2		24	7.6	4.9	0	36.5	0	-	5,027,000	6,600	-	-	188,513
2011	232	Pmin	Wire bending & forming	Berger	0.9	5.5		1	1	1		24	7.6	4.9	0	36.5	108960	652,800	352,209	6,600	91,000	-	443,209
2011	240	Pmin	Cardboarding	Toscano	0		245	1	1	2		24	7.6	4.9	0	36.5	217920	-	339,900	4,400	-	-	339,900
2011	245	Pmin	Personnel pool 240-260	Wilhelm	2.5	19		1	1		ISP	24	7.6	4.9	0	36.5	0	2,193,000	-	-	193,900	1,874,599	2,068,499
2011	250	Pmin	Assembly	Wilhelm			245	1	1	6		24	7.6	4.9	0	36.5	653760	-	1,303,679	-	-	-	1,303,679
2011	260	Units	Film welding	Womberger			245	0.25	1	1		24	7.6	4.9	0	36.5	0	-	924,080	3,300	-	-	231,020
2011	300	Phours	IT	Stelker	2.5	0			1		ISP	24	7.6	4.9	0	36.5	0	4,250	-		3,700	550	4,250
2011	330	Phours	Repair center	Temmel	0.1	0.9		1	1	0	ISP	24	7.6	4.9	0	36.5	0	1,700	-		120	1,650	1,770
2011	340	KWh	Energy center	Temmel	0	0	330	1	1	0	ISP	24	7.6	4.9	0	36.5	0	-	-		-	193,498	193,498
2011	200	empty	Plant mgmt. & work scheduling	Fichter	2	0			1			24	7.6	4.9	0	36.5	0	3,400	-		3,400	-	3,400
2011	210	empty	Procurement & warehouse	Grantl	2	0			1			24	7.6	4.9	0	36.5	0	3,400	-		3,400	-	3,400
2011	320	empty	Buildings & maintenance	Huber	1	0			1			24	7.6	4.9	0	36.5	0	1,700	-		1,700	-	1,700
2011	900	empty	Corp. management & administration	Hofmann	6	0			1			24	7.6	4.9	0	36.5	0	10,200	-		10,400	-	10,400
2011	100	empty	Sales mgmt. & office	Küng (VL)	4	0			1			24	7.6	4.9	0	36.5	0	6,800	-		6,780	-	6,780
2011	101	empty	Sales promo in-house products	Luginbühl	1	0			1			24	7.6	4.9	0	36.5	0	1,700	-		1,567	-	1,567
2011	102	empty	Sales promo merchandise	Vonäsch	0.9	0			1			24	7.6	4.9	0	36.5	0	1,530	-		800	-	800
2011	151	empty	Eastern Switzerland	Bauer	1	0			1			24	7.6	4.9	0	36.5	0	1,700	-		1,600	-	1,600
2011	152	empty	Western Switzerland	App	1	0			1			24	7.6	4.9	0	36.5	0	1,700	-		1,600	-	1,600
2011	153	empty	Business clients (direct)	Sahli	1	0			1			24	7.6	4.9	0	36.5	0	1,700	-		1,600	-	1,600

Fig. 4.37 Planned staff, networking hours and planned activities per cost center

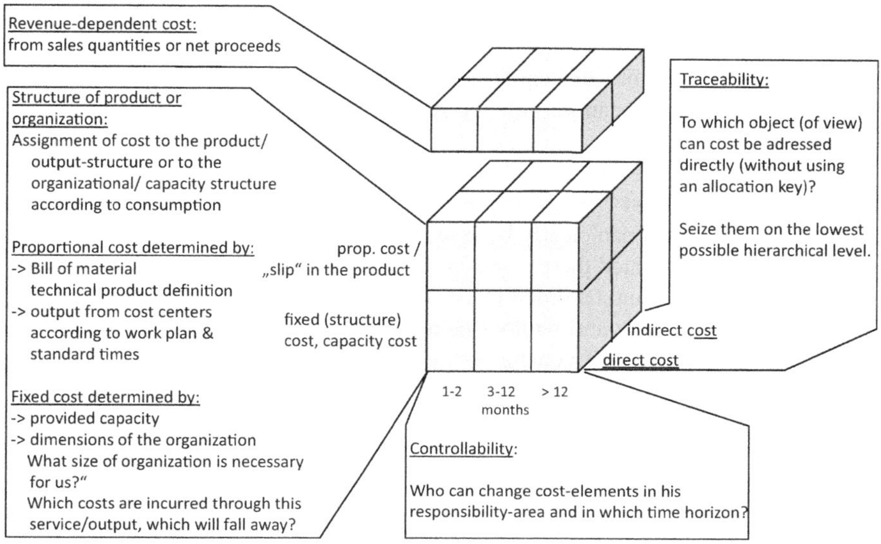

Fig. 4.38 The three most relevant cost dimensions for management (CWB 2010, p. 146)

These three dimensions are interrelated, which is why the connections can be represented as a cube (Fig. 4.38):

Controllability of Cost

Since all managers are responsible for QQDR (quantity, quality, deadlines, and results) in the areas they manage (see Sect. 1.3), they want to know which costs they can directly influence and thus for which they are responsible. In addition, it is important for them to recognize in what period of time they can change these costs. The front side of the cost cube is therefore divided into 3 parts:

- Costs which can be influenced within 1–2 months.
- Costs which can be influenced between 3 and 12 months.
- Costs which can be influenced only in a period of more than one year.

This is a contract and procurement oriented way of thinking. Which ties to employees and suppliers have to be considered, if the cash outflows resulting from the costs are to be changed? If a supplier can be changed at short notice, the costs arising from its deliveries can also be influenced within, say, one month. If a supply contract exists with longer commitment periods, the costs or purchase prices can only be influenced in the medium to long term (e.g., contracts). The same applies if the supplier is the sole supplier of the good or service. Personnel costs can only be influenced with short notice, if the period of notice is a maximum of 1–2 months. It is also possible that the influence can only be exerted in a period of more than one year because social plans must first be implemented. The (imputed) cost element depreciation can only be influenced over a period greater than a year, since it is the result of investments over several years.

To enable responsible managers to control their costs, they must be able to recognize the costs that can be influenced by cost element in both plan and actual evaluations.

Direct or Indirect Cost

All costs of a company can clearly be assigned to one specific object so accountability needs to also be located there. Translated to cost planning and control this means that costs are planned and recorded in all cases at the level to which they can still be assigned unambiguously and without using an allocation basis. Consequently, the assignment of an actual cost voucher to the relevant account must always take place at the lowest possible hierarchical level. A cost center manager will rightly argue that he is not responsible for charges that are not clearly attributable to his area.

Some application examples:

- In a central magazine, 1 kg of M6 screws are purchased and kept ready. If you need any, help yourself. Material slips are not filled in, as their production would cost more than the screws. The lowest possible clear account assignment is thus the central magazine and its boss is responsible for these costs. For him, these are the direct costs of his cost center, for all recipients they are indirect costs.
- Each employee is assigned to one and only one cost center (he only has one employment contract). For the manager of this cost center, the personnel costs of this employee are direct costs. Since the employee works on different production orders during the year and therefore on different products, his personnel costs are indirect costs from the point of view of the products.
- A product manager holds an event to promote his new product line. The resulting external advertising costs and expenses are direct costs of his product management cost center. These are overhead costs for the sales force and sales channels as well as for the individual product in the product range. They are created for the whole product group and can therefore not be uniquely assigned to a sales area or an individual article.
- External consulting and support costs, as well as work in the IT department, are incurred for the improvement of the materials management module in ERP. These are direct costs of the IT department, since it makes the entire ERP available to all users at the same time. From the point of view of the users in the departments, these are overhead costs, since different departments can use the resulting planning and control options in parallel.
- The Personnel department wants to install a computer workstation for each of its employees, each with office applications, mail, Internet connection as well as ERP connection. The necessary hardware and the workplace-related license fees can be clearly assigned to the personnel department as direct costs. The costs for the operation of the various ERP modules, the administration of the licenses, and the costs of general IT operations for ERP, Internet and email, however, remain

direct costs of the IT department and are indirect costs from the point of view of the recipients. Consequently, the head of the HR department can take responsibility for the hardware installed in his area and the licenses necessary for operation, but not for the costs directly incurred in IT, as these are overhead costs for him.
- All material consumptions related to production orders are assigned directly to the order. They are called direct material costs because they can be clearly assigned to the products. Direct material costs therefore never run through the cost center.

These examples are intended to show that consistent planning and recording of all costs as direct costs at the lowest possible level is a central element of independent control. If this idea is implemented consistently it is always the case that only one person is responsible for any cost voucher. This is essential to the concept of holistic management and self-responsiveness.

Proportional or Fixed Cost

Proportional costs are the direct result of the units produced. They arise because an additional unit of a product or service is created. They are determined based on the BOMs and work plans (as explained in material requirements planning and capacity requirements planning) as well as based on the activities planned for internal services to be provided.

Proportional costs are thus directly caused by the quantities produced. There must be a direct cause-and-effect relationship. For this reason, the proportional cost can be clearly assigned to the units produced (material consumption according to bill of materials items, services of the production sites according to the work plans). In other words: Only BOM and work plan items, as well as genuine internal services provided, can lead to proportional cost.

Fixed costs are the complement to proportional costs. What is not proportional is fixed. Fixed costs are the costs of an organization's capability to perform. The capability to perform must be present before production can start. Fixed costs are therefore not driven by production quantities, but by the capacities and requirements of the organization. These capacities are determined by managerial decisions. Because the capacities offered can change as needed, there are also *stepped fixed* costs.

Some application examples:

- The materials required to manufacture a product are defined in the BOM. It specifies how much material of a certain type (item number) is to be consumed per unit to be produced. This standard quantity is multiplied by the planned purchase price of the raw material for each item. In technical terminology, these are the direct material cost, because their consumption can be clearly assigned to a production order and thus to the manufactured item individually via a material procurement slip. The same applies to the setup material for a production order as well as for the process scrap or the material consumed for it.

- If processing steps are assigned externally and the costs for the external service are billed to the company quantity-dependently, these costs also have the character of direct material cost. They are called proportional external service costs (e.g., external coating or painting of parts manufactured in-house).
- Of the costs of a production cost center, only the portion that is directly caused by the product is included in the manufactured product. The consumption that determines this is contained in the work plan of the product to be manufactured as the standard time. Consequently, a production activity can only be valued with the activity-dependent proportional planned cost rate of the performing cost center. The fixed cost of capacity and readiness to perform are not included in these planned cost rates because they are incurred even if no production orders are released for execution. The most important share of proportional manufacturing cost is the personnel costs included in the product according to the work plan, the energy consumed per unit, the performance-related consumption of auxiliary, consumable, and packaging materials as well as the performance-related services from internal cost centers (including preventive maintenance and process-related tool wear).
- The costs of buildings and their maintenance are always fixed costs since these are the consequence of the decisions about the available buildings.
- In most cases, depreciation costs are also fixed, since the depreciation stands for the maintenance of the substance invested in a cost center. Most assets are technically obsolete before they no longer function. Depreciation is therefore mainly time-related and is charged at the same rate each year from a business point of view.
- The amount of work required to organize a cost center, to improve the processes it handles, and the time required to train its employees is also not directly determined by the number of units produced in the cost center, but by management decisions on how this cost center should fulfil its mission and improve its own processes. The cost of these is fixed since they are not included in the work plans.
- On the other hand, setup times are part of the proportional product cost, since without the setup of the production machine and the resulting time and material consumption, the order cannot be completed.
- The cost of downtime is a fixed cost. It arises because the process sequence is not yet completely under control or because a machine fails.

An important distinction between proportional and fixed costs: without exception, fixed costs are the result of **management decisions**. Managers decide whether additional equipment should be purchased and used, whether an additional shift leader is necessary (a stepped fixed cost), whether an IT project should be implemented, whether product management should be expanded, whether an additional sales channel should be implemented and operated, and what scope the consulting and auditing assignment should have for the audit.

Proportional costs are caused directly by the quantities produced and thus also by the **structure of the products manufactured and sold.** Material consumptions are multiplied by their respective cost prices and the work plan items by the proportional planned cost rate of the performing cost center.

In production cost centers, the **splitting of costs** into their proportional and fixed portions is a prerequisite for the management-relevant target to actual comparison in the cost center and for product costing according to the costs-by-cause principle, thus also for Profitability Analysis. In the internal service providing centers cost splitting is a prerequisite for the target/actual comparison, and also for debiting consumed services to the receiving cost centers. This is because the recipient wants to pay for the service purchased, not for the unused capacity of the internal service point or for services not explicitly ordered.

The same three cost dimensions result from the analysis of **revenue-dependent costs**. These no longer depend on the units produced, but on the units sold (for example, commissions, freight, and order-dependent distribution costs). They are presented here as a separate part of the cost cube, since they were already structured as revenue reductions in Sect. 4.3.2.

In our view, the cost cube with its clear structure of the three decision-relevant cost dimensions is a central element for the design of the integrated planning and control system. All our consulting and support assignments have shown that the consistent application of this cube massively improves the quality of management decisions.

4.7.2 Planning Primary Cost Center Costs

Primary costs are defined as all costs that originate from outside the enterprise. They are always entered in the subledgers of the accounting system and can be assigned to cost centers, projects, or production orders by means of additional coding.

- In the simplest case, an external invoice can be assigned directly to a cost center, a project, or an order in accounts payable.
- If the purchased parts are put into stock before consumption, the stocking-in results as an intermediate step (no consumption yet, therefore no costs). The material withdrawal slip documents the consumption for the order, project, or cost center.
- Capital goods acquisitions increase the asset balance, the incoming invoice is therefore assigned to the asset object or to the project (no costs yet). The consequence of its use is a decrease in net asset value. This consumption is charged to the cost centers as primary costs in the form of imputed depreciation. Each asset is assigned to one and only one cost center (see the detailed presentation in Sect. 4.7.7).
- Payroll accounting is the instrument used to determine personnel costs. Gross and net wages, all bonuses, and non-wage deductions are calculated and posted there.

External supplier/service provider	Recorded in:	Account coding to:
Settlement of: - salary, non wage personnel cost, - time bonus	Payroll accounting	Cost centers (aggregated to personnel costs)
Material purchases: - raw material - merchandise - supplies - auxiliary materials	Materials accounting	Production orders/ cost centers/ projects
Investment goods	Asset administration	Cost centers / projects
All other external : - services - energy - insurances, legal costs - fees, licenses	Accounts payable accounting	Cost centers/ projects

Fig. 4.39 Account assignment of primary costs to cost centers, projects, and orders

The details of these statements are of limited interest to a cost center manager, since the amount of social benefits/non-wage labor costs is almost entirely determined by law. To control his cost center, a manager only needs to know the total personnel costs of his employees.

Planning, as well as account coding of primary costs, requires the complete recording of direct costs at the lowest possible level (cost center, project, or order), i.e., to where they can be directly influenced. This is where the responsibility for this cost is located (see the dimension direct cost recording in the cost cube, Fig. 4.38). The consistent application of this rule results in one person being uniquely responsible for each cost and revenue document in the organization (Fig. 4.39).

Explanatory Examples from Ringbook Ltd.

Production cost center punching shop:

Cost center manager Vogel considers which primary costs will be incurred in the Stamping shop in the planned year given he and his staff are to provide the required planned employment of 338,855 personnel minutes (RFU) for the units to be produced and 65,000 minutes for internal tasks (see cost centers sheet):

- He learns from the personnel department that personnel costs of 337,560 will be incurred for the 4 people in the stamping shop. These are the wage totals of all employees assigned to this cost center (which, including himself = 291,000), increased by the planned cost for non-wage personnel costs of 16%, which corresponds to 46,560. The rate of 16% was determined by the Human Resources Department based on the statutory provisions and the previous year's accounts. It applies to the entire company (sheet "Workinghours").

- He plans the costs for office supplies, auxiliary and operating materials, maintenance and repair costs of external suppliers by analyzing the consumption of the previous year, and considering whether procedural changes compared with the previous year could also influence the amount of the plan.
- The cost element Other Overhead Costs is the collective item for consumptions, for which it is not worthwhile to have an extra cost type.
- The controller derives the imputed depreciation from the data in Asset Accounting and makes it available to the cost center manager. The respective process is described in Sect. 4.7.7 and in sheet "Invest&depr." To include imputed depreciation in cost center planning makes sense because after the planned useful life has expired, the asset is to be replaced by a new one at the then current replacement value (from a management point of view, this is about maintaining the substance of the potential, not the acquisition value).
- The total is the primary planned costs of the stamping cost center. Control of these costs is part of the management task of the cost center manager (Fig. 4.40).

Planning of the plant management cost center (Fig. 4.41) is carried out in the same way as in the stamping shop. The differences are striking:

- No planned employment is planned for the Plant Management cost center. This results from the job of the cost center employees being to take care of the organization, management and further development of the entire production process, the production planning and scheduling system (PPSS), and the entire work preparation. The two employees are thus part of the capacity and

Fig. 4.40 Primary costs plan of the stamping shop for 2011

	Cost center	**220 Stamping**	
	Manager:	Vogel	
	Number of shifts	1	
	RFU reference factor unit	Pmin	
	Planned FTE's	Mgmt.	0.3
		Operation	3.7
	Normal capacity employees	408,000	
	Installed machines:		4
	Annual capacity per machine & shift:		108,960
	Personnel multiplier (Pmin/ unit)		1
	Planned activity inl. Setup	338,855	
Nr.	Cost type	Planned	
1	Personnel costs	337,560	
5	Office supplies	440	
6	Auxiliary and operating materials	12,980	
12	External maintenance & repair	17,500	
13	Other expense	4,800	
31	Imputed depreciation	13,063	
	Total primary costs	386,343	

Fig. 4.41 Primary costs plan of the plant management

	Cost center	**200**	**Plant mgmt. & Work scheduling**
	Manager:		Fichter
	Number of shifts		1
	RFU reference factor unit		empty
	Planned FTE's		2
	Normal capacity employees		204,000
	Cost type		Planned amount
1	Personnel costs		197,200
5	Office supplies		1,200
6	Auxiliary and operating materials		360
7	Telephone, communication		720
13	Other expense		3,000
31	Imputed depreciation		5,250
	Total primary costs		209,730

organizational structure. They make the work on the products possible but do not execute it. The primary costs planned here are therefore clearly fixed costs.

- The imputed depreciation for this cost center includes their own computer workstations and the licenses required for them but does not include the software costs for the PPSS and materials management software. These software costs are planned in the cost center IT (300), since they are incurred for the whole company but are controlled by IT.

In all other cost centers, primary costs were planned using the same procedure (Fig. 4.42). As mentioned above, the employees of cost center 245 Personnel Pool can be used as jumpers in production cost centers 240, 250, and 260. Personnel costs are completely planned in cost center 245 and from there charged as internal services provided according to the demand of the served cost centers (see Sect. 4.7.4, Fig. 4.42).

The total of all primary cost center costs plus the direct material costs must correspond to the accrual-based expense totals in financial accounting (before interest and taxes) because there are no-cost allocations and no other valuations.

4.7.3 Cost Splitting for Decision-Making

The splitting of cost center costs into their proportional and fixed portions is an indispensable prerequisite for the design of an integrated planning and control system. The manager who is to make offers or to decide on the acceptance of customer orders must know which costs are directly caused by the manufactured or sold product. These are the proportional costs of goods manufactured, which are made up of the direct material costs, any proportional external activity costs, and the

CCnr	Description	Cost type	Description	Planned amount	prop. planned / RFU
100	Sales mgmt. & office	1	Personnel costs	464,000	
100	Sales mgmt. & office	4	Advertisement	30000	
100	Sales mgmt. & office	5	Office supplies	3,600	
100	Sales mgmt. & office	6	Auxiliary and operating materials	2,480	
100	Sales mgmt. & office	7	Telephone, communication	14400	
100	Sales mgmt. & office	12	External maintenance & repair	3,600	
100	Sales mgmt. & office	13	Other expense, non-activated project cost	11,400	
100	Sales mgmt. & office	31	Imputed depreciation	12,000	
101	Sales promo finished goods	1	Personnel costs	110,200	
101	Sales promo finished goods	4	Advertisement	40000	
101	Sales promo finished goods	5	Office supplies	440	
101	Sales promo finished goods	31	Imputed depreciation	8,000	
102	Sales promo merchandise	1	Personnel costs	104,400	
102	Sales promo merchandise	4	Advertisement	40000	
102	Sales promo merchandise	5	Office supplies	440	
102	Sales promo merchandise	31	Imputed depreciation	8,250	
151	Eastern Switzerland	1	Personnel costs	111,360	
151	Eastern Switzerland	5	Office supplies	440	
151	Eastern Switzerland	31	Imputed depreciation	8,313	
152	Western Switzerland	1	Personnel costs	83,520	
152	Western Switzerland	5	Office supplies	440	
152	Western Switzerland	31	Imputed depreciation	8,000	
153	Business clients (direct)	1	Personnel costs	97,440	
153	Business clients (direct)	5	Office supplies	440	
153	Business clients (direct)	31	Imputed depreciation	8,000	
200	Plant mgmt. & work scheduling	1	Personnel costs	197,200	
200	Plant mgmt. & work scheduling	5	Office supplies	1,200	
200	Plant mgmt. & work scheduling	6	Auxiliary and operating materials	360	
200	Plant mgmt. & work scheduling	7	Telephone, communication	720	
200	Plant mgmt. & work scheduling	12	External maintenance & repair	2,000	
200	Plant mgmt. & work scheduling	13	Other expense, non-activated project cost	3,000	
200	Plant mgmt. & work scheduling	31	Imputed depreciation	5,250	
210	Procurement & warehouse	1	Personnel costs	139,200	
210	Procurement & warehouse	3	Purchasing & shipping costs	20,000	
210	Procurement & warehouse	5	Office supplies	2,400	
210	Procurement & warehouse	6	Auxiliary and operating materials	600	
210	Procurement & warehouse	7	Telephone, communication	940	
210	Procurement & warehouse	12	External maintenance & repair	480	
210	Procurement & warehouse	13	Other expense, non-activated project cost	2,300	
210	Procurement & warehouse	31	Imputed depreciation	15,000	
220	Stamping	1	Personnel costs	337,560	
220	Stamping	5	Office supplies	440	0
220	Stamping	6	Auxiliary and operating materials	12,980	0.03
220	Stamping	12	External maintenance & repair	17,500	0.033
220	Stamping	13	Other expense, non-activated project cost	4,800	0.003
220	Stamping	31	Imputed depreciation	13,063	
231	Wire rolling	5	Office supplies	110	
231	Wire rolling	6	Auxiliary and operating materials	3,120	0.0005
231	Wire rolling	12	External maintenance & repair	33,000	0.005
231	Wire rolling	13	Other expense, non-activated project cost	6,000	0.001
231	Wire rolling	40	Internal clearing (personnel for other CC)	152,918	
232	Wire rolling	40	Internal clearing (personnel for other CC)	-152,918	
231	Wire rolling	31	Imputed depreciation	14,000	
232	Wire rolling	1	Personnel costs	529,540	

CCnr	Description	Cost type	Description	Planned amount	prop. planned / RFU
232	Wire bending & forming	5	Office supplies	110	
232	Wire bending & forming	6	Auxiliary and operating materials	2,930	0.0005
232	Wire bending & forming	12	External maintenance & repair	36,000	0.07
232	Wire bending & forming	13	Other expense, non-activated project cost	6,000	0.0025
232	Wire bending & forming	31	Imputed depreciation	12,000	
240	Cardboarding	5	Office supplies	440	
240	Cardboarding	6	Auxiliary and operating materials	6,200	0.002
240	Cardboarding	12	External maintenance & repair	33,500	0.02
240	Cardboarding	13	Other expense, non-activated project cost	9,000	0.003
240	Cardboarding	31	Imputed depreciation	15,000	
245	Personnel pool 240-260	1	Personnel costs	1,662,280	
250	Assembly	5	Office supplies	880	
250	Assembly	6	Auxiliary and operating materials	8,800	0.005
250	Assembly	12	External maintenance & repair	31,400	0.02
250	Assembly	13	Other expense, non-activated project cost	12,000	0.0004
250	Assembly	31	Imputed depreciation	16,000	
260	Film welding	5	Office supplies	220	
260	Film welding	6	Auxiliary and operating materials	9,800	0.008
260	Film welding	12	External maintenance & repair	40,400	0.042
260	Film welding	13	Other expense, non-activated project cost	12,980	0.008
260	Film welding	31	Imputed depreciation	13,750	
300	IT	1	Personnel costs	222,720	
300	IT	5	Office supplies	440	
300	IT	6	Auxiliary and operating materials	960	
300	IT	7	Telephone, communication	12200	
300	IT	12	External maintenance & repair	6,500	
300	IT	13	Other expense, non-activated project cost	3,400	
300	IT	14	Software (licenses & maintenance)	24000	
300	IT	31	Imputed depreciation	24,625	
320	Buidlings & maintenance	1	Personnel costs	52,200	
320	Buidlings & maintenance	5	Office supplies	980	
320	Buidlings & maintenance	6	Auxiliary and operating materials	480	
320	Buidlings & maintenance	8	Cleaning & conserving supplies	4,080	
320	Buidlings & maintenance	9	El. energy, water, fuel oil	23,400	
320	Buidlings & maintenance	10	Rent	30,000	
320	Buidlings & maintenance	12	External maintenance & repair	2,400	
320	Buidlings & maintenance	13	Other expense, non-activated project cost	3,700	
320	Buidlings & maintenance	31	Imputed depreciation	24,400	
330	Repair center	1	Personnel costs	64,496	
330	Repair center	5	Office supplies	270	
330	Repair center	6	Auxiliary and operating materials	1,080	0.56
330	Repair center	12	External maintenance & repair	480	0.24
330	Repair center	13	Other expense, non-activated project cost	1,680	0.21
330	Repair center	31	Imputed depreciation	7,625	
340	Energy central	9	El. energy, water, fuel oil	44400	0.2
340	Energy central	12	External maintenance & repair	12,000	
340	Energy central	31	Imputed depreciation	2,567	
900	Corp. Management & adm	1	Personnel costs	626,400	
900	Corp. Management & adm	5	Office supplies	440	
900	Corp. Management & adm	6	Auxiliary and operating materials	2,480	
900	Corp. Management & adm	7	Telephone, communication	6600	
900	Corp. Management & adm	12	External maintenance & repair	3,315	
900	Corp. Management & adm	13	Other expense, non-activated project cost	6,600	
900	Corp. Management & adm	31	Imputed depreciation	11,000	
Total primary cost center costs planned				5,691,533	

Fig. 4.42 Primary plan costs of all cost centers

proportional manufacturing costs. Cost splitting is the prerequisite for determining the proportional planned cost rate of a production or internal service center.

The work plan of an item to be produced specifies how much activity of a particular cost center is to be consumed per unit, if the performers have the process under control (i.e., standard time). The necessary planning work was documented in Sect. 4.5.4. In Fig. 4.28, the planned activities of the production cost centers were obtained by adding the planned consumption of all items to be produced. Because setup work and setup times are also causally necessary to be able to produce a production lot, these times were also included in the time specifications and therefore in the planned activities. Work for scrap quantities must also be included, if these are given by the production process. The planned activity thus indicates which directly product-related activities (measured in RFU) a cost center is to perform in the plan year.

To determine the planned proportional costs, it is necessary to define per cost type which part of the cost will depend from the activities. For **each cost type, the planned consumption based on the reference factor unit (RFU) is to be**

measured or estimated (see the last column in Fig. 4.42). In manufacturing plants, activity-dependent consumption is usually found in the following cost types:

- Personnel costs.
- Consumables and supplies, energy.
- Consumables that properly should be listed in the bill of material, but which would require a disproportionate effort to be recorded (screws, wire, possibly paints and varnishes, separating, and packaging materials for storage).
- Tool costs (activity-dependent).
- External maintenance (benefit-dependent).
- Internal services provided (internal maintenance and repairs).

Personnel costs can be influenced more or less quickly, depending on the period of notice (although they are often erroneously regarded as fixed costs). Proportional personnel costs are incurred (independent of the employee's contract with the company), if the time consumed is directly caused by the manufactured product, that is, if a standard time is defined in a work plan.

Costs other than direct material costs are to be included if their consumption is directly dependent on the operating hours, machine hours, or running times of the plants (e.g., electricity kWh per operating hour, maintenance minutes (external or internal) per operating hour, and lubricant consumption).

The sum of all proportionally planned cost center costs is divided by the planned activity. The result is the *proportional planned cost rate*. This rate is used to calculate the proportional manufacturing cost of a product unit or for charging internal services provided to other cost centers.

Fixed or structural costs are then calculated automatically. The planned cost amount of a cost type minus the proportional planned cost results in the planned fixed costs. Fixed costs are not caused by the quantity produced, but by management decisions (usually as part of the planning process). Because there is no direct cause-and-effect link between fixed costs and manufactured quantities, fixed costs should never be allocated to product units, consistent with the cost-by-cause-principle.

Example: Cost Center Stamping

The cost-splitting for the primary costs in cost center 220 Stamping was done as follows:

- The procedure for personnel costs is easy to understand: Employee attendance will be 408,000 minutes in the plan year. For these 337,560 in personnel costs are planned. Thus, presence time costs 0.8274 per minute or 49.64 per hour. This 0.8274 of costs slip into the finished products with every minute spent on an order. As employment of 338,855 min is planned, proportional personnel costs of 280,353 (338,855 × 0.8274) result. The fixed costs are the complement to the total primary personnel costs (57,207). This approach corresponds to the entrepreneur's way of thinking. He is interested to know how much an hour of

	Cost center	**220 Stamping**			
	Manager:	Vogel			
	Number of shifts	1			
	RFU reference factor unit	Pmin			
	Planned FTE's	Mgmt.	0.3		
		Operation	3.7		
	Normal capacity employees	408,000			
	Installed machines:		4		
	Annual capacity per machine & shift:		108,960		
	Personnel multiplier (Pmin/ unit)		1		
	Planned activity inl. Setup	338,855			
Nr.	Cost type	Planned amount	Propor-tional	Fixed	Consump-tion / RFU
1	Personnel costs	337,560	280,353	57,207	0.8274
5	Office supplies	440	-	440	
6	Auxiliary and operating materials	12,980	10,166	2,814	0.0300
12	External maintenance & repair	17,500	11,182	6,318	0.0330
13	Other expense	4,800	1,017	3,783	0.0030
31	Imputed depreciation	13,063		13,063.00	
	Total primary costs	386,343	302,717	83,626	

Fig. 4.43 Cost splitting in the cost center 220 Stamping

real presence time of his employees costs him, considering all personnel-related costs and after deducting all absences such as holidays, vacation, illness, and the like ($60 \times 0.8274 = 49.64$).

- Measurements in the cost center, notes, and estimates are used to determine the proportional share of consumables and supplies as well as other primary costs. Here, too, a cost rate that specifies the planned consumption per RFU (minute) needs to be defined.
- In the case of maintenance services, whether they are provided externally or by the company's own repair workshop (see next section), a distinction must be made between services that are caused by the activity of the cost center stamping and services that are regularly performed after a certain period (i.e. every 3 months). The former are to be planned as proportional costs, the latter as fixed costs (Fig. 4.43).

If the application of the simulation model results in a negative planned fixed cost value, either the planned value consumption/RFU is too high or the total planned amount of the cost type is too low. The cost center manager makes the necessary adjustments in the sheet "Primarycostplan." If the planned fixed cost for personnel turns negative, the planned headcount in the sheet "Costcenterplan" is to be adjusted. Such changes are again based on decisions from the cost center manager and cannot be automated in the simulation model.

Many textbooks and ERP programs recommend the (simpler) **variator method** for cost splitting. Instead of fixing the proportional consumption rate per RFU, they recommend determining the percentage of the planned cost behaving proportionally to the activity. If in such a system, the planned activity changes while the planned cost amount stays the same, the absolute proportional share of the cost changes and thus also the proportional cost rate. This does not correspond to reality. The same number of minutes or the same amount of auxiliary materials are still consumed per activity minute of the cost center. The planned cost rate must thus stay the same. Therefore, and in order not to place managers in the inexplicable situation that the same performance should cost more or less per unit depending on the planning status, the variator method should not be applied.

4.7.4 Costing Internal Services Provided

Secondary costs are the counterpart to primary costs. They arise when primary costs of a serving cost center are charged to receiving cost centers using a cost rate. However, this internal activity charging can only be carried out in a decision- and management-friendly manner, when there is a direct causal relationship between the activity consumption of the receiving cost center and the cost of the performing cost center.

In Sect. 4.5.5.2, it was stated that a genuine exchange of internal services only exists if two criteria are met:

- The service recipient (a cost center) can either decide how much service it wants to receive from the internal provider (e.g., maintenance services) or there is an automatic relationship between the services of the (internal) provider and the activity level of the service recipient. In this case, the activity of the performing cost center is directly dependent on the activity of the receiving cost center.
- In the performing service center, the activity-dependent consumption has respective proportional costs as a consequence. These costs become part of the cost rate of the serving cost center.

Only the proportional cost of the internal services provided can be charged to the service recipient, since the latter is responsible for the consumption of the services, but not for the structure and thus the fixed costs of the providing cost center.

The application of the two criteria reveals that management-relevant charging of internal service costs only occurs in a few cases. Examples include:

- Workshops of all kinds that work to order.
- Internal energy centers whose consumption depends on the power consumption of the receiving cost centers (which can be determined by measurement or consumption tables).
- Personnel pools.

- In-plant transports (if dependent on the production quantity of the cost center), possibly activity-dependent costs of fleet use.
- IT development services that are directly ordered by the receiving cost center.
- Construction and development departments (service on order for another cost center) for service on a project or an order, if ordered by the project or order manager.

If the service center cannot plan proportional cost and the recipient cannot order according to his needs, then charging costs is pure **fixed cost allocation**. This allocation is always executed with the help of an **allocation basis**, i.e., a mathematical distribution basis that simulates a **nonexistent causal relationship**. It is often argued that the allocation basis should be chosen "as far as possible according to the cause." However, this does not help the receiving manager any further, since the fixed cost allocated is to be planned and controlled in the issuing cost center. The responsibility for the fixed cost lies there, not in the receiving cost center.

For this reason, a management-relevant planning and control system must work completely without allocation of fixed cost to other cost centers or to products.

Examples from Ringbook Ltd.

Cost center 330 Maintenance and Repairs:

Cost center 330 has only one employee. It performs maintenance and repair work for all other cost centers. Its manager is also responsible for Energy center 340. Figure 4.30 shows that all cost centers in the plan year want to obtain 1530 hours from cost center 330. In addition, there are 120 h for the collaboration on the two projects. The planned activity level thus amounts to 1650 h.

- The primary planned costs were taken from Fig. 4.42.
- The planned personnel costs for cost center 330 amount to 64,496, which corresponds to a planned presence hour rate of (64,496/1700 presence hours = 37.94).
- If the 1650 h are caused by the planned services for other cost centers, proportional planned personnel costs of (1650 × 37.94 = 62,599) result. The difference of 1897 corresponds to the budgeted fixed personnel costs (organization of the repair and the energy center).
- The last column in Fig. 4.44 shows the consumption of consumables and supplies (0.56), external maintenance and repair costs (0.24), and other expenses (0.21) per hour of activity. If these amounts are multiplied by the planned activity, the proportional shares of these three cost types result (they accrue with each repair hour performed).
- In total, there are 74,209 controllable plan costs for the manager of cost center 330. For these he is responsible, since he can also influence them himself. This also includes the 83 energy consumption, as these are incurred for the operation of his workshop.

Cost center plan	for year:	2011		
Cost center:	**330**	**Repair center**		
Manager:	Temmel			
Number of shifts	1			
Normal capacity employees	1700			
RFU:	Phours			
Derived planned activity	1,650	(from ISP-planning)		

Cost type	Planned amount	Propor-tional	Fixed	Per RFU
1 Personnel costs	64,496	62,599	1,897	37.94
5 Office supplies	270	-	270	
6 Auxiliary and operating materials	1,080	924	156	0.56
7 Telephone, communication				
9 El. Energy, water, heating fuel				
12 External maintenance & repair	480	396	84	0.24
13 Other expense	1,680	347	1,334	0.21
31 Imputed depreciation	7,625	-	7,625	
Total primary costs	75,631	64,266	11,365	
ISP energy	80	-	80	0.20
ISP int. Repair & maintenance				
Total controllable cost	75,711	64,266	11,445	
Prop. planned cost-rate		**38.95**		

Fig. 4.44 Complete plan of cost center 330 Repairs and Maintenance

- The proportional planned cost rate (38.95) of cost center 330 finally results obtained by dividing the proportional planned cost of 64,266 by the planned activity of 1650 h.

Cost Center 340 Energy Center

To ensure a continuous and demand-oriented supply of electrical energy to all cost centers, some investments were made for which imputed depreciation is charged to cost center 340. Energy is purchased from the local power station at the correct voltage and according to the current demand. The planned price in 2011 from the power plant is 0.20 per kWh.

Electricity consumption is driven by the consumption per RFU of the manufacturing cost centers (proportional cost) and by the consumption for heating, lighting, computers, and office machines (a fixed cost). Together with the consumption of water and heating fuel, which cannot be clearly allocated, the total planned costs for energy and water is planned to be 44,400. The proportional planned cost for electricity amounts to ($193{,}498 \times 0.20 = 38{,}700$). The remaining fixed costs for electricity, water, and heating oil will be 5700 (Fig. 4.45).

Cost center plan	for year:	2011		
Cost center:	**340**	**Energy center**		
Manager:	Temmel			
Number of shifts	1			
Normal capacity employees				
RFU:	KWh			
Derived planned activity	193,498	(from ISP planning)		

Cost type	Planned amount	Propor-tional	Fixed	Per RFU
9 El. Energy, water, heating fuel	44,400	38,700	5,700	0.20
12 External maintenance & repair	12,000		12,000	
13 Other expense	-			
31 Imputed depreciation	2,567		2,567	
Total primary costs	58,967	38,700	20,267	
ISP energy		-	-	
ISP int. Repair & maintenance	6,979		6,979	
Total controllable cost	65,946	38,700	27,246	
Prop. planned cost-rate per kWh		**0.20**		

Fig. 4.45 Cost center plan of the Energy center

Cost Center 245 Personnel Pool

The employees assigned to the personnel pool are trained as jumpers. They can work in the Cardboard cost center as well as in the Film Welding shop and in Assembly. They earn comparable wages. Because each employee has only one employment contract, he can only be assigned to one cost center. The head of the personnel pool and the Assembly cost center (Wilhelm) decides on the assignment of employees to the three production cost centers and is therefore also responsible for their personnel costs.

Personnel costs will be 1,662,280 for the 2,193,000 min. the planned FTE's will work. Dividing the two figures generates the presence-time rate of 0.7580 per minute. This is also the proportional plan cost-rate of the personnel pool as there are no other proportional costs to be planned.

The planned activity of the personnel pool is 1,874,599 personnel minutes (see sheet "ISPplan"). This corresponds to 1,420,934 proportional costs charged to the three receiving manufacturing centers. The remaining fixed cost of 241,346 stands for

- Internal tasks (also in the receiving cost centers)
- Capacity reserves and waiting times
- Management of the personnel pool

	Cost center:	**245 Personnel pool 240-260**			
	Manager:	Wilhelm			
	RFU:	Pmin			
	Planned FTE's	Mgmt.	2.5		
		Operation	19		
	Normal capacity employees	2,193,000			
	Planned activity	1,874,599			
Nr.	Cost type	Planned amount	Propor-tional	Fixed	Per RFU
1	Personnel costs	1,662,280	1,420,934	241,346	
	Total controllable costs	1,662,280	1,420,934	241,346	0.7580

Fig. 4.46 Plan costs of the Personnel Pool cost center 245 and proportional cost rate

To plan with the total amount of personnel costs also has the advantage that the confidentiality of the wages of individual employees is maintained (Fig. 4.46).

The use of personnel pools is recommended when:

- The employees assigned to it perform work that requires comparable competencies.
- The wage differences between individual employees are mainly due to age differences (manufacturing contracts are not "penalized" for being carried out by more experienced employees).
- The employees in the personnel pool work at different production sites as required.
- Legal regulations require keeping wages paid confidential and make it impossible to draw conclusions about the performance of an individual (e.g., only cost centers with at least 3 employees may be set up).

4.7.5 Internal Settlements

In practical application and thus also in planning, situations occur in which the service of a cost center is not charged to another cost center, but only individual cost factors are transferred. In such cases, an internal cost clearance by cost element is required. Examples include:

- Employees of one cost center are made available to another cost center for some time. They change the working place but remain assigned to the original cost center.
- Working time of employees is transferred from the issuing cost center according to the requirements of the receiving center.
- Incorrect account codings are corrected in a subsequent period.
- A cost center purchased auxiliary material and passes part of it to another cost center (not via stock).

Year	Cost type	Description	Sender CC	Receiver CC	Consumption / RFU	Planned activity	Consumption in min.	Planned presence rate / min.	Prop. amount	Amount charged
2011	40	Internal clearing (personnel for other CC)	232	231	0.0375	5,027,000	188,513	0.8112	-152,918.06	152,918.06

Fig. 4.47 Example of internal clearance

In such cases, the proportional planned cost rate of the performing cost center cannot be used, since only the personnel activity, and not the entire cost center activity, is transferred to the receiving center. Respective amounts are planned as minus costs in the sending and as plus costs and in the receiving cost center as new (primary) costs. This is not a cost allocation, but a transfer posting.

In the example company, this situation occurs in cost centers 231/232. All personnel are assigned to cost center 232. However, for a small part of their working time (0.0375 min per piece), the employees of 232 also monitor the automatically functioning rolling and punching machines of cost center 231. This corresponds to a planned time of 188,513 min. for the planned year. Multiplied with the planned presence rate of the personnel in cost center 232, this results in a charge of 152,918 personnel costs in cost center 231 and a corresponding cost reduction in center 232 (Fig. 4.47).

4.7.6 Purchasing and Forwarding Costs

a) **Procurement costs.**

External costs for the procurement of raw materials and auxiliary materials are essentially part of the raw material costs. In most countries, they can be capitalized, i.e., added to the pure material costs and included in the valuation of the stock receipt.

The difficulty lies in the fact that several purchased items often come with the same delivery, but the procurement costs charged by the supplier refer to the total delivery. The delivery costs can then not be assigned to an account as direct costs of a material type, or only partially. In many accounting departments, an average markup rate is defined for each material type. This markup is then added to the purchase price of the material during planning and when the material receipt is posted. From the point of view of the material users (production or sale of retail items), this is not completely cause related, since Purchasing negotiates the procurement costs with the vendors and tries to achieve an optimal price/performance ratio.

To charge procurement costs as simple as possible but still taking responsibility into account, the following procedure is used in the sample company:

- Delivery costs that are directly dependent on the quantity and price of a purchased good are already included in the standard purchase price. They are added to the bill for purchased material in the case of incoming raw materials. Some examples: weight-dependent shipping costs, import duties, and item-related fees. This procedure has the advantage that purchase price variances can be isolated immediately when new material is stored in the warehouse.

- Delivery costs that cannot be entered as direct costs of a specific item (for example, from collective deliveries) are planned as fixed costs in the Purchasing and Warehouse cost center and entered as actual costs.

b) **Forwarding charges.**

When the company's own products are delivered, a consignment often contains several items with different dimensions and weights. In addition, there are express deliveries with higher forwarding costs (including air freight). If these shipping costs can be invoiced separately to the customer, it is advisable to create a separate article (with item number, see Sect. 4.3.2) for each of the different forwarding items to be invoiced. This allows a comparison of the invoiced freight forwarding costs with the costs to be paid to the external freight agents. In addition, the separate item number for invoiced forwarding services is also recommended for correctly billing VAT (or sales tax) charged to customers.

In the example company forwarding expenses can only rarely be charged to the customers. They are included when the planned sales prices are determined. Since the Purchasing and Warehouse cost center is also responsible for the freight forwarding costs, the latter are also planned and recorded in this cost center as fixed costs (not item-related).

4.7.7 Depreciation Planning and Fixed Assets

From a pure management point of view, statutory or tax depreciation regulations and accounting principles are largely irrelevant. As described in Sect. 1.7, the aim is to take into account the consumption of fixed assets valued at replacement value (RepV) in cost center and profit planning with imputed depreciation.

The determination of the RepV and thus the imputed depreciation can in many cases only be an estimate. One aspect is that the useful life of the asset can only be definitively determined when the asset is dismantled. Another is that fixing the current replacement value appears to be a costly and time-consuming process. For a cost center manager responsible for an asset or for corporate management, an estimate of the RepV and the resulting imputed depreciation gives a better indication of how much is to be earned for preserving the substance before a profit arises than just the depreciation of the original acquisition value.

In management accounting, therefore, **imputed depreciation** should be calculated from the estimated replacement value and based on the **useful lives** planned by management. Examples include:

- When investing in new ERP software or a new release, management must consider how many years it plans to use the installation without significant changes before switching to a new release or another application. This decides the planned useful life. The replacement value consists of the current prices for the purchase of the entire installation (new software, introductory consulting and support, hardware renewal, and any one-time licenses).
- In the case of a handling robot, the question arises as to whether the technical obsolescence of the robot and its operating software will occur more quickly than its purely mechanical usability is exhausted. If the possible operating time is more important than the technical overhaul, the robot must be depreciated based on performance.
- In our opinion decreasing depreciation should be avoided in management accounting because it is not the sale value of an asset that is relevant for the decision, but the benefit that the existing asset can generate. For example, the handling robot can provide the same benefits in the fifth year of operation as in the first year if it is maintained and ready for operation.

4.7.7.1 Planning Imputed Depreciation

In 2010, the investments and projects for 2011 and, if already discernible in the medium term, for the years 2012 to 2015 are loaded in the planning database to calculate the imputed depreciation for 2011. This is what is needed:

- The estimated replacement value RepV for the completely new acquisition of the existing assets as of 12/31/2010.
- New investments planned for 2011.
- The projects to be carried out in 2011 with their budgets.
- The planned useful life of the assets.

Explanations:

- Estimate of the current replacement value RepV:
  What amount would have to be invested today (at the time of planning) for an equivalent new asset with the capacity of the previous one? Can a clearly quantified offer be obtained from suppliers? For the replacement of a company car, the determination of the RepV is relatively simple. If, however, the asset to be assessed is a combination of many individual facilities and if development and installation work must also be considered for the (re)construction, it will be difficult to determine an expected new price for the entire plant. Examples include replacement of a complete production line, replacement of a complete bacteriological laboratory, and modernization of the entire ERP installation (without additional new applications).
- Correctness of the current replacement value RepV:
  The correctness of the estimated RepV can only be verified after the fact. But that is too late, as the valuation of the necessary assets as well as their depreciation

a	b	c	d	e	f	g	h	i	j
Year	CCnr	Planned useful life in years	RepV new end of previous year	Investments in plan year	Project values plan	RepV for completely new asset	Planned imputed depr. Including invet and projects	Cumulated planned depreciation	Planned RepV after depreciation
2010	100	8	-		-		-	-	96.000
2011	100	8	96.000	-	-	96.000	12.000	12.000	84.000
2012	100	8	96.000	-	83.981	179.981	22.498	34.498	145.484
2013	100	8	185.482	2.500	-	182.481	22.810	57.308	125.173
2014	100	8	191.691	55.000	-	237.481	29.685	86.993	150.488
2015	100	8	250.525	5.000	-	242.481	30.310	117.303	125.178

Fig. 4.48 Planned investments in fixed assets, replacement values, and imputed depreciation (CCnr 100)

must be fixed during the planning process. For decision-making, however, good estimates are enough, as planning is always based on expected values or prices.

- Which new investments are to be planned in the 2011–2015 budgets as consequences of the strategic and medium-term plans?
- Which projects with planned completion in the respective planning year are to be included? (investments, material consumption, and internal services, see sheet "Projectplan").
- Determining the useful life of a planned investment is primarily a management decision. This is due to the fact that most capital goods are technologically obsolete before they come to their "physical end." The decision about the useful life of an asset should, therefore, be taken during the preparation of the investment appraisal. This is the time when the managers decide how long they want to use the new asset (see the examples above).

Figure 4.48 shows how to enter the basic data:

- The RepV as of 1/1/2011 is stored in the sheet "CClist" as it is also relevant for the opening balance sheet. The same applies to the planned useful lives of the different assets.
- The planned investments for the years 2011–2015 are recorded in the "Invest&depr" sheet (column e).
- The project budgets are taken from the Project Planning sheet (column f).

These specifications are used to calculate the planned depreciation base and the planned amounts for imputed depreciation per year and cost center (columns and in the simulation model). These amounts will also appear in the cost center plans.

4.7.7.2 Planning Replacement Values

When the planning for 2012 fiscal year is revised in 2011, the forecast for the end of 2011 will also be used as a basis. The planned values for 2012 in 2010 will, therefore, have to be adjusted in the planning rounds for the coming years. In the simulation model this is possible, but it should be noted that the plan values entered in the previous years can change as a result of the new findings. The annual plan for

2012 will contain different values, if it is prepared based on the expected actual values for 2011 rather than the one prepared in 2010 for 2012.

Such planning updates are also necessary for replacement values. Many existing fixed assets will become more expensive over the years because of inflation and due to new technical and legal requirements, although they will provide the same performance as before. This also applies to new investments and projects. The acquisition value can be used at the beginning of their deployment, but higher prices for replacement are to be expected in subsequent years.

However, the effort involved in determining replacement values as a basis for planning would increase immeasurably, as new offers would have to be obtained every year and the project costs would have to be recalculated. To simplify the estimation of new replacement values the **index method** is often used. The expected price change compared to the previous year is estimated as a percentage so that the initial value can be corrected by this percentage in the plan.

Probably the best-known indices are the consumer price index (only suitable for companies to a limited extent) and the construction cost index. Further application-specific indices are developed by industries (e.g., steel processing companies). The indices are used to measure the price change that has occurred (actual) or is expected (estimate) compared with the previous period.

- The updated RepV, e.g., for 1/1/2012, is obtained by multiplying the RepV by the estimated price increase (columns d, g, and h in Fig. 4.49).
- New investments of the plan year and the projects completed by the end of the previous year do not yet have to be inflated because they are included in the fixed assets of the planned year with their new actual value. These positions can be found in the columns e and f.
- Column i shows the total RepV at the beginning of the plan year including the revaluation of the RepV (new depreciation base). From this, the updated imputed depreciation of the planned year in column j is calculated by dividing it by the planned useful life.
- From a business point of view, in the internal balance sheet one should find the sum of the RepV's including index correction and after deduction of the cumulated imputed depreciation (column l = column i - total previous depreciation in column k).

a	b	c	d	e	f	g	h	i	j	k	l	m	n	o	p	q
Year	CCnr	Planned useful life in years	RepV new end of previous year (column "m")	Planned investments of the year	Finished and acti-vated projects from last year	Index-change for replacement (compared to previous year)	Revaluation of RepV previous year	RepV for completely new installation	Imputed depreciation from RepV for plan year	RepV previous year	RepV in balance plan year	Opening RepV for next year	Cumulated index revaluations	Imputed depreciation from revaluations	Cumulated repurchase reserve (end year)	Backlog (not yet charged imputed depreciation)
2010	100	8	-		0	-	-	-	-	-	-	96,000	-	-	-	-
2011	100	8	96,000	-	0	-	-	96,000	12,000	-	84,000	96,000	-	-	-	-
2012	100	8	96,000	-	86601.6	3.0%	2,880	185,482	23,185	84,000	150,296	185,482	2,880	360	360	2,520
2013	100	8	185,482	2,500	0	2.0%	3,710	191,691	23,961	150,296	132,545	191,691	6,590	464	824	5,766
2014	100	8	191,691	55,000	0	2.0%	3,834	250,525	31,316	132,545	160,063	250,525	10,423	479	1,303	9,121
2015	100	8	250,525	5,000	0	2.0%	5,011	260,536	32,567	160,063	137,506	260,536	15,434	626	1,929	13,505

Fig. 4.49 Inflation consequences for RepV and imputed depreciation (CCnr 100, sheet "Invest&depr")

- The imputed (annual) depreciation thus also includes the annual portion for the change of the RepV. This is shown separately in column o. In the example shown for cost center 100, this share for 2012 is 360 monetary units (2880/8). The remaining 7/8 will be written off in subsequent years. The balance of 2520 is to be included in the calculation of planned depreciation for the following year (2013). In the internal balance sheet (see Sect. 6.4.2) the totals of these not yet written off revaluations will have to be shown in the fixed assets as a net increase of RepV's on the one hand, and as so-called "backlog depreciation" in equity on the other.

The procedure described for planning imputed depreciation and the assets required for operations is by no means "art pour l'art." It should disclose to managers at all levels that all factor consumption must first be valued at replacement conditions before an EBIT is realistically earned. Often the argument is heard that sales prices could be lowered because the machines have already been written off, i.e., they work "free of charge." This works well until new prices have to be paid for the maintenance of the production capacity. The question will then arise as to whether the revaluation reserves have been built up accordingly. In the same way, higher profitability is "lying to oneself" if the profit is related to a balance sheet total based on historical values instead of residual replacement values.

4.7.8 Planned Cost Totals and Cost-Rates

The explanations in Sects. 4.7.1–4.7.7, together with the performance-related planning in Sects. 4.1–4.6, provide the complete basis for the completion of cost center planning.

Using the example of cost center 220 Stamping, the interaction between activity planning and the various possible origins of planned costs becomes clear (Fig. 4.50):

- The total costs that can be influenced and for which the cost center manager is responsible can be found in the "Planned amount" column (dimension 1 of the cost cube). Primary costs plus the cost for internal services provided form the total controllable cost.
- Cost types and the primary cost amounts are presented in such a way that the actual costs can also be coded as direct costs in the same line (dimension 2 of the cost cube).
- All ISP values are based on planned and measurable activities that are valued with the planned proportional cost rate of the performing cost center. This ensures that no fixed cost is allocated from one cost center to another.
- The columns "proportional and fixed" contain the cost splitting up to the resulting proportional planned cost rate of the cost center (dimension 3 of the cost cube).
- The resulting planned proportional cost rate is used for product costing throughout the year for plan and actual because it specifies which costs are to be incurred per RFU (minutes) in the stamping shop if the responsible cost center manager (Vogel) acts in accordance with the plan and thus with his objective (Fig. 4.50).

Nr.	Cost type	Planned amount	Propor-tional	Fixed	Consump-tion / RFU
	Cost center		220 Stamping		
	Manager:	Vogel			
	Number of shifts	1			
	RFU reference factor unit	Pmin			
	Planned FTE's	Mgmt.	0.3		
		Operation	3.7		
	Normal capacity employees	408,000			
	Installed machines:		4		
	Annual capacity per machine & shift:		108,960		
	Personnel multiplier (Pmin/ unit)		1		
	Planned activity inl. Setup	338,855			
1	Personnel costs	337,560	280,353	57,207	0.8274
5	Office supplies	440	-	440	
6	Auxiliary and operating materials	12,980	10,166	2,814	0.0300
12	External maintenance & repair	17,500	11,182	6,318	0.0330
13	Other expense	4,800	1,017	3,783	0.0030
31	Imputed depreciation	13,063		13,063.00	
	Total primary costs	386,343	302,717	83,626	
21	ISP energy	536	136	400	0.0004
22	ISP int. Repair & maintenance	9347		9348	
	Total controllable cost	396,226	302,853	93,374	
	prop. planned cost-rate		0.8938		

Fig. 4.50 Complete cost center plan of the Stamping shop

Cost Centers 231 and 232

(Fig. 4.51) Here the brackets of the ring binder mechanisms are made from the raw material steel wire. Wire rolling in 231 is largely automated. The deployment of personnel is limited to setup, refilling and final inspection. Employees from cost center 232 perform this work (they are assigned to 232). For correct debiting, the internal clearance explained in Sect. 4.7.5 is applied. The system multiplies the planned minutes to be drawn (188,513) by the planned average presence-time rate of cost center 232 (0.8174). The resulting 152,918 is planned as cost type 40 (internal clearing personnel for other cost centers). In cost center 231, the amount is planned proportionally (necessary for the creation of the activity). In cost center 232, the same amount is deducted (cost reduction).

Cost Centers 240–260

The interaction between the Personnel Pool 245 and the cost centers Cardboarding, Film Welding and Assembly can be seen in Figs. 4.52 and 4.53. Since the employees in the Personnel Pool can be used in all three production centers, the planned activity of the personnel pool is derived from the activity exchange table in Fig. 4.27 (derived planned employment 1,874,599 min.).

Nr.	Cost center plan		2011				2011		
	Cost center:		231 Wire rolling				232 Wire bending & forming		
	Manager:	Berger				Berger			
	Number of shifts	1				1			
	RFU:	units				Pmin			
	Planned FTE's	Mgmt.	0			Mgmt.	0.4		
		Operation	0			Operation	6		
	Normal capacity employees	0				652,800			
	Installed machines:		2				1		
	Annual capacity per machine & shift:		108,960				108,960		
	Planned activity incl. setup	5,027,000				352,209			
	Cost type	Planned amount	Propor-tional	Fixed	Per RFU	Planned amount	Propor-tional	Fixed	Per RFU
40	Internal clearing (personnel for other CC)	152,918	152,918	-	0.0304			-	
40	Internal clearing (personnel for other CC)					-152,918	-152,918		
								-	
1	Personnel costs					529,540	285,706	243,834	0.8112
5	Office supplies	110	-	110		110	-	110	
6	Auxiliary and operating materials	3,120	2,514	607	0.0005	2,930	176	2,754	0.0005
12	External maintenance & repair	33,000	25,135	7,865	0.005	36,000	24,655	11,345	0.07
13	Other expense	6,000	5,027	973	0.001	6,000	881	5,119	0.0025
31	Imputed depreciation	14,000		14,000		12,000	-	12,000	
	Total primary costs	209,148	185,594	23,555		433,662	158,499	275,163	
21	ISP energy	7,032	6,032	1,000	0.0012	3,711	3,311	400	0.0094
22	ISP int. repair & maintenance	7,011	-	7,011	0	6,232	-	6,232	0
	Total controllable cost	223,191	191,626	31,565		443,605	161,810	281,795	
	Prop. planned cost-rate		0.0381				0.4594		

Fig. 4.51 Cost center plans Wire Rolling (231) and Wire Bending and Forming (232)

Nr.	Cost center plan												
	Cost center:		240 Cardboarding				250 Assembly				260 Film welding		
	Manager:	Toscano				Wilhelm				Homberger			
	Number of shifts	1				1				1			
	RFU:	Pmin				Pmin				units			
	Planned FTE's	Mgmt.	0			Mgmt.	0			Mgmt.	0		
		Operation	0			Operation	0			Operation	0		
	Normal capacity employees	0				0				0			
	Installed machines:		2				6				1		
	Annual capacity per machine & shift::		108,960				108,960				108,960		
	personnel multiplier (Pmin/ unit)									0.25			
	Planned activity incl. setup	339,900				1,303,679				924,080			
Nr.	Cost type	Planned amount	Propor-tional	Fixed	Per RFU	Planned amount	Propor-tional	Fixed	Per RFU	Planned amount	Propor-tional	Fixed	Per RFU
5	Office supplies	440	-	440		880	-	880		220	-	220	
6	Auxiliary and operating materials	6,200	680	5,520	0.002	8,800	6,518	2,282	0.005	9,800	7,393	2,407	0.008
12	External maintenance & repair	33,500	6,798	26,702	0.02	31,400	26,074	5,326	0.02	40,400	38,811	1,589	0.042
13	Other expense	9,000	1,020	7,980	0.003	12,000	521	11,479	0.0004	12,980	7,393	5,587	0.008
31	Imputed depreciation	15,000	-	15,000		16,000	-	16,000		13,750	-	13,750	
	Total primary costs	64,140	8,498	55,643		69,080	33,113	35,967		77,150	53,597	23,553	
21	ISP energy	6,574	5,574	1,000	0.0164	8,944	8,344	600	0.0064	5,023	4,023	1,000	0.0044
22	ISP int. repair & maintenance	4,674	-	4,674	0	11,685	-	11,685		1,947	-	1,947	
23	Personnelpool services	257,642	257,642	-	0.7580	988,180	988,180	-	0.7580	175,112	175,112	-	0.1895
	Total controllable cost	333,030	271,714	61,316		1,077,889	1,029,637	48,251		259,232	232,731	26,501	
	Prop. planned cost-rate		0.7994				0.7898				0.2519		

Fig. 4.52 Cost center plans Cardboarding, Assembly and Foil Welding

	Cost center:	**245 Personnel pool 240-260**			
	Manager:	Wilhelm			
	RFU:	Pmin			
	Planned FTE's	Mgmt.	2.5		
		Operation	19		
	Normal capacity employees	2,193,000			
	Planned activity	1,874,599			
Nr.	Cost type	Planned amount	Propor-tional	Fixed	Per RFU
1	Personnel costs	1,662,280	1,420,934	241,346	
	Total controllable costs	1,662,280	1,420,934	241,346	0.7580

Fig. 4.53 Personnel Pool (245) cost center plan

The fixed plan costs remaining in the personnel pool (241,346) represent the personnel costs for managing the four cost centers, for all their internal tasks, and for any planned personnel overcapacities.

The proportional planned manufacturing costs and the resulting proportional planned cost rates are therefore known for all production centers that work directly on the products. These will be necessary for product costing.

ISP Cost Centers

(Fig. 4.54) In addition to the personnel pool, three cost centers are defined to charge their proportional cost to cost centers according to the services the latter consume. As mentioned above, only the proportional costs are charged to the receiving cost centers, since the receivers do not directly influence the fixed cost and thus the capacity of the ISP cost centers. The corresponding plan amounts are already planned in all receiving cost centers and are shown in their plans. For the calculation of these exchanges the cost-rates in Fig. 4.54 were multiplied with the planned consumption of the receivers, cited in Fig. 4.30, Sect. 4.5.5.2. Cost center IT (300) only planned chargeable internal services for projects whereas the Repair center (330) works for all other cost centers and for projects.

Fixed Cost Centers

All remaining cost centers of Ringbook Ltd. are purely fixed cost centers, as their services are not directly related to the products or services to be manufactured. A cost split is therefore not necessary in these cost centers. Therefore, only one column for planned amounts is to be presented per cost center. The planning of all cost elements was carried out in the same way as described for the cost centers with planned proportional cost. In addition, there are some cost types that did not occur in the production cost centers.

Cost center plans	2011											
Cost center:	330 Repair center				340 Energy center				300 IT			
Manager:	Temmel				Temmel				Stelker			
Number of shifts	1				1				1			
Normal capacity employees	1700											
RFU:	Phours				KWh				Phours			
Derived planned activity	1,650 (from ISP-planning)				193,498 (from ISP planning)				550 (from ISP-planning)			
Cost type	Planned amount	Propor-tional	Fixed	Per RFU	Planned amount	Propor-tional	Fixed	Per RFU	Planned amount	Propor-tional	Fixed	Per RFU
1 Personnel costs	64,496	62,599	1,897	37.94					222,720	28,823	193,897	52.40
5 Office supplies	270	-	270						440		440	
6 Auxiliary and operating materials	1,080	924	156	0.56					960		960	
7 Telephone, communication									12,200		12,200	
9 El. Energy, water, heating fuel					44,400	38,700	5,700	0.20			-	
12 External maintenance & repair	480	396	84	0.24	12,000		12,000		6,500		6,500	
13 Other expense	1,680	347	1,334	0.21	-				3,400		3,400	
14 Software (licences & maintenance)					-				24,000		24,000	
31 Imputed depreciation	7,625	-	7,625		2,567		2,567		24,625		24,625	
Total primary costs	75,631	64,266	11,365		58,967	38,700	20,267		294,845	28,823	266,022	
ISP energy	80	-	80	0.20		-	-		2,400	-	2,400	
ISP int. Repair & maintenance					6,979		6,979		1,402		1,402	
Total controllable cost	75,711	64,266	11,445		65,946	38,700	27,246		298,647	28,823	269,824	
Prop. planned cost-rate		38.95				0.20				52.40		

Fig. 4.54 Cost center plans of the ISP cost centers 300, 330, and 340

All ISP charges were planned as fixed cost as no activity is to be planned in these receiving cost centers. Still, the responsible cost center manager can influence the consumption of ISPs during the fiscal year by his orders.

There are two groups of fixed cost centers:

1. Cost centers for the entire company: These work for all product areas and for the entire company (Fig. 4.55)
2. Sales-related cost centers: These can be assigned to individual product groups or individual sales channels depending on the analyzed dimension (see stepwise contribution accounting in Sect. 4.9.1).

The cost plans of the sales-oriented cost centers also contain the marketing budgets (for the entire company) and the product-group-related sales promotion budgets (for the company's own products as well as for merchandise) (Fig 4.56).

4.8 Planned Product Cost

With the completion of activity and cost center planning, the data is ready for the plan calculation of product cost. The following basic lists are applied:

- Item list with product descriptions and information on planned production quantities, planned purchase prices for raw materials, merchandise, and product-related external services as well as the planned lot sizes.
- Bills of material with specifications, list of which raw materials and external services are to be included in what planned quantity of the products to be manufactured.

Cost center plan					
	Cost center:	**200**	**210**	**320**	**900**
		Plant mgmt. & work scheduling	**Procurement & warehouse**	**Buildings & maintenance**	**Corp. mgmt. & admin.**
	Manager:	Fichter	Grantl	Huber	Hofmann
	Number of shifts	1	1	1	1
	RFU reference factor unit	empty	empty	empty	empty
	Planned FTE's	2	2	1	6
	Normal capacity employees	204000	204000	102000	612000
	Cost type	Planned amount	Planned amount	Planned amount	Planned amount
1	Personnel costs	197,200	139,200	52,200	626,400
3	Purchasing & shipping costs		20,000		
4	Advertisement	-	-	-	-
5	Office supplies	1,200	2,400	980	440
6	Auxiliary and operating materials	360	600	480	2,480
7	Telephone, communication	720	940	-	6,600
8	Cleaning & conserving supplies	-	-	4,080	-
9	El. Energy, water, heating fuel	-	-	23,400	-
10	Rent	-	-	30,000	-
12	External maintenance & repair	2,000	480	2,400	3,315
13	Other expense	3,000	2,300	3,700	6,600
31	Imputed depreciation	5,250	15,000	24,400	11,000
	Total primary costs	209,730	180,920	141,640	656,835
21	ISP energy	300	300	2,400	1,200
22	ISP int. repair & maintenance	935	935	5,609	1,402
	Total controllable cost	210,965	182,155	149,649	659,437

Fig. 4.55 Cost center plans for the central services

- Work plans with information on how the manufacturing process for the various products is to run, with the specifications for the allowed times per process and individual item plus the setup times per item and lot.
- Proportional planned cost rates of the production cost centers.

4.8.1 Proportional Product Costs in the Sample Company

Figures 4.57 and 4.58 show how the proportional planned manufacturing cost per unit is calculated. The cost of finished product 101060 is derived from the individual parts as follows:

	Cost center plan						
	Cost center:	**100**	**101**	**102**	**151**	**152**	**153**
		Sales mgmt. & office	**Sales promo finished goods**	**Sales promo merchan-dise**	**Eastern Switzerland**	**Wester n Switzerl and**	**Business clients (direct)**
	Manager:	Küng (VL)	Luginbühl	Vonäsch	Bauer	App	Sahli
	Number of shifts	1	1	1	1	1	1
	RFU reference factor unit	empty	empty	empty	empty	empty	empty
	Planned FTE's	4	1	0.5	1	1	1
	Normal capacity employees	408000	102000	51000	102000	102000	102000
	Cost type	Planned amount	Planned amount	Planned amount	Planned amount	Planned amount	Planned amount
1	Personnel costs	464,000	110,200	104,400	111,360	83,520	97,440
4	Advertisement	30,000	40,000	40,000	-	-	-
5	Office supplies	3,600	440	440	440	440	440
6	Auxiliary and operating materials	2,480	-	-	-	-	-
7	Telephone, communication	14,400	-	-	-	-	-
12	External maintenance & repair	3,600	-	-	-	-	-
13	Other expense	11,400	-	-	-	-	-
31	Imputed depreciation	12,000	8,000	8,250	8,313	8,000	8,000
	Total primary costs	541,480	158,640	153,090	120,113	91,960	105,880
21	ISP energy	200	-	-	-	-	-
22	ISP int. repair & maintenance	1,402	-	-	-	-	-
	Total controllable cost	543,082	158,640	153,090	120,113	91,960	105,880

Fig. 4.56 Cost center plans of the functional area sales

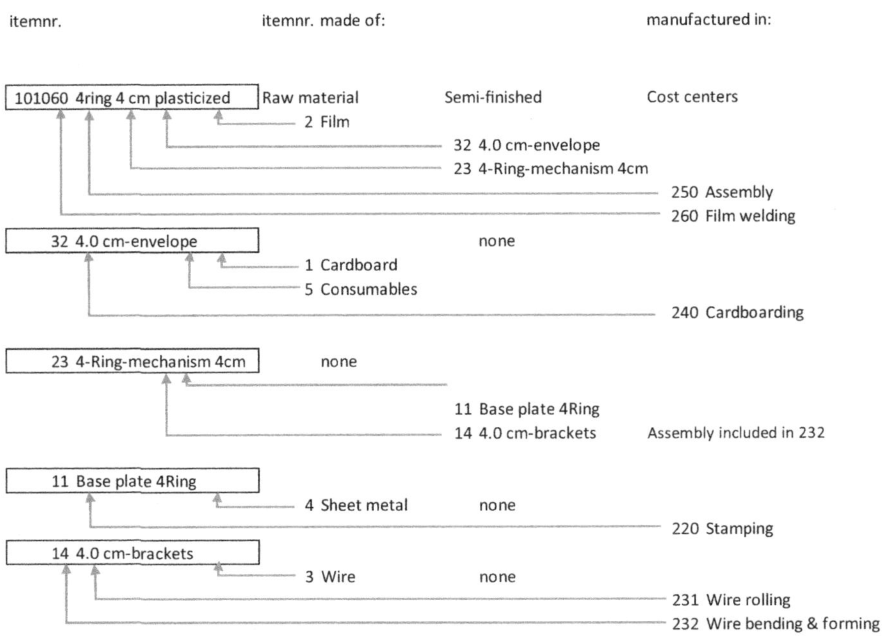

Fig. 4.57 Structured bills of material over three production levels (top-down)

Itemnr	101060
Description	4ring 4 cm plasticized
Planned sales quantity	82,688
Planned production	85,800
Number of lots p.a.	11
Planned lot-size	7,800
Setup/lot	10
Scrap/lot	50
Gross input/lot	7,860

Itemnr	32	23	2	
Bill of material	4.0 cm-envelope	4-Ring-mechanism 4cm	Film	Total item 101060
Preset quantity / unit	1	1	0.44	
Planned cost or price	0.3181	0.6470	0.2000	
Direct material cost	2,500.19	5,085.42	691.68	8,277.30
Workplan/cost center	260	250		
Allowed time	1	1		
Setup	20	120		
Demand Pmin.	7820	7920		
Prop. cost-rate planned	0.2519	0.7898		
Prop. manufacturing/lot	1,969.86	6,255.22		8,225.07
Prop. product cost/lot				16,502.37
Per good unit				2.1157

Itemnr	32
Description	4.0 cm-envelope
Planned production	531,300
Number of lots p.a.	11
Planned lot-size	48,300
Setup/lot	20
Scrap/lot	50
Gross input/lot	48,370

Bill of material/itemnr	1	5	direct mat./unit
Description	Cardboard	Consumables	
Preset quantity / unit	0.2	1	
Planned cost or price	0.2800	0.1000	
Direct material cost	2,708.72	4,837.00	0.1562
Workplan/cost center	240	Cardboarding	
Allowed time	0.2		
Setup	120		
Demand Pmin.	9780		
Prop. cost-rate planned	0.7994		
Prop. manufacturing/lot	7,818.07		
Prop. product cost/lot			15,363.79
Per good unit	*		0.3181

Itemnr	23
Description	4-Ring-mechanism 4cm
Planned production	343,200
Number of lots p.a.	11
Planned lot-size	31,200
Setup/lot	-
Scrap/lot	-
Gross input/lot	31,200

Bill of material/itemnr	11	14	
Preset quantity / unit	1	4	
Planned cost or price	0.2730	0.0935	
Direct material cost	8,519.02	11,667.40	20,186.42
Assembly of mechanisms in 232, no addtional manufacturing cost			
per good unit			0.6470

Itemnr	11
Description	Base plate 4-Ring
Planned production	816,200
Number of lots p.a.	11
Planned lot-size	74,200
Setup/lot	50
Scrap/lot	200
Gross input/lot	74,450

Bill of material/itemnr	4	sheet metal	
Preset quantity / unit	0.024		
Planned cost or price	2		
Direct material cost	3,573.60		0.04816
Workplan/cost center	220		
Allowed time	0.25		
Setup	120		
Demand Pmin.	18670		
Prop. cost-rate planned	0.8938		
Prop. manufacturing/lot	16,686.37		0.22488366
Prop. product cost/lot	20,259.97		
Per good unit	0.2730		

Itemnr	14
Description	4.0 cm-brackets
Planned production	1,750,100
Number of lots p.a.	11
Planned lot-size	159,100
Setup/lot	100
Scrap/lot	200
Gross input/lot	159,400

Bill of material/itemnr	3 wire		
Preset quantity / unit	16		
Planned cost or price	0.002		
direct material cost	5100.8		0.0321
Workplan/cost center	231	232	
Allowed time	1	0.05	
Setup	50	120	
Demand Pmin.	159150	8075	
Prop. cost-rate planned	0.03810	0.4594	
Prop. manufacturing/lot	6,063.62	3,709.66	
Prop. product cost/lot			14,874.07
Per good unit			0.0935

Fig. 4.58 Standard calculation of a finished product with its semi-finished products included

- Production stage 3: One unit of product 101060 consists of 1 unit each of items 32 and 23 as well as 0.44 sqm film (raw material itemnr. 2). For their completion, the Foil Welding shop 260 (plastic coating) and the Assembly 250 (final assembly and final inspection) areas are in use.
- Production stage 2: The ring binder sleeve (itemnr. 32) is made from the raw materials cardboard and consumables. All ring binder sleeves are manufactured in the cost center Cardboarding (240) and placed in the semi-finished product warehouse before further processing.
- A further result of production stage 2 is the assembly of the ring binder mechanisms (itemnr. 23). These are also sent to the semi-finished goods warehouse after inspection.
- Production stage 1: The mechanisms each consist of a base plate (itemnr. 11, produced in cost center 220) and 4 brackets (itemnr. 14), which are processed in cost centers 231 (Wire Rolling) and 232 (Wire Bending & Forming). These items are also delivered to the semi-finished products warehouse, since they can be used for various end-products at production level 3.

Standard calculation starts from the lowest level (raw material) and goes upwards, since independently planned lot sizes were provided for each item based on the annual production plan and since material consumption and scrap as well as allowed setup and manufacturing times were defined. All these consumptions are directly caused through manufacture of the product.

For each item to be produced, the proportional planned cost (value) is calculated based on the planned lot size. This amount is divided by the number of good units to be produced. The result is the planned proportional cost per unit of an item, also called standard cost. This standard cost-value is also used for the valuation of inventory rotation.

The calculations of all semi-finished and finished products are stored in sheet "Propcostitem." This is the consolidation of the sheets "Directmatcalc" and "Capacityplan" (Fig. 4.59).

4.8.2 Conventional Calculation Scheme and Full Cost

The product calculations presented up to here show the planned proportional production costs (also called product cost, see CWB, p. 198) of the individual items to be produced.

In cost accounting education, almost all schools and universities place a great deal of emphasis on the methods of calculating the full product costs and the cost-based price. Often models for the calculation of sales prices are also taught. The following costing sheet is often used (Fig. 4.60):

Full product costs per unit are required in many countries for the preparation of external financial statements under commercial and tax law. It is legally stipulated that semi-finished and finished goods inventories be valued at *full product*

Itemnr	Year	Prop. cost semiF & raw	prop. cost manu-facturing	prop. production cost / good unit	Good units	prop. cost of production
11	2011	0.04816	0.2249	0.2730	816,200	222,860
12	2011	0.01204	0.1354	0.1474	881,100	129,909
13	2011	0.04004	0.0751	0.1151	3,275,800	377,059
14	2011	0.03206	0.0614	0.0935	1,750,100	163,650
21	2011	0.73346	-	0.7335	484,000	354,996
22	2011	0.37765	-	0.3776	691,900	261,295
23	2011	0.64708	-	0.6471	343,200	222,078
24	2011	0.33446	-	0.3345	188,100	62,911
31	2011	0.15895	0.2010	0.3599	924,000	332,589
32	2011	0.15623	0.1619	0.3181	531,300	169,002
101010	2011	1.09800	0.3239	1.4219	47,600	67,682
101020	2011	0.96721	0.3199	1.2871	94,800	122,019
101030	2011	1.13937	0.3259	1.4653	28,500	41,760
101040	2011	1.01010	0.3252	1.3353	61,200	81,721
101050	2011	1.19341	1.0523	2.2457	37,600	84,437
101060	2011	1.06127	1.0544	2.1157	85,800	181,528
101070	2011	1.19231	1.0507	2.2430	121,000	271,407
101080	2011	1.13216	1.1664	2.2986	800	1,839
101090	2011	1.23305	1.0514	2.2845	112,310	256,569
101100	2011	1.10215	0.8184	1.9205	80,400	154,409
101110	2011	1.24495	0.8306	2.0756	7,700	15,982
101120	2011	1.10015	0.8153	1.9155	18,800	36,011
103000	2011	0.61349	0.7982	1.4117	124,300	175,470
104000	2011	1.22023	1.9834	3.2037	116,600	373,547
105010	2011	0.73918	0.2410	0.9802	139,800	137,029
105020	2011	0.65506	0.2442	0.8993	78,000	70,144
105030	2011	0.77985	0.2424	1.0223	68,800	70,334
105040	2011	0.71563	0.3001	1.0158	3,000	3,047
105050	2011	0.83303	0.4948	1.3278	99,600	132,252
105060	2011	0.75587	0.5232	1.2791	11,600	14,837
105070	2011	0.84110	0.5110	1.3521	18,000	24,337
105080	2011	0.74490	0.4986	1.2435	30,600	38,050
105090	2011	0.87671	0.8175	1.6942	85,910	145,549
105100	2011	0.79758	0.8410	1.6386	5,500	9,012
105110	2011	0.88904	0.8120	1.7010	151,030	256,904
105120	2011	0.82710	0.8246	1.6517	55,330	91,386

Fig. 4.59 Proportional planned product cost (standard cost) 2011 for each item (sheet "Propcostitems")

(or manufacturing) cost. The same valuation guideline is also part of various accounting standards such as IFRS, US GAAP, and Swiss GAAP FER (see also Sect. 6.6.2).

Many executives want to know the *cost-price per unit* which should, in their eyes, represent how much a certain item costs after offsetting the total costs of the

+	Proportional product costs	Direct material, proportional external services costs, proportional manufacturing cost	Bills of material/ Work plans
+	Material overhead markup	Fixed cost for the purchasing and storage functions	% markup
+	fixed cost of production	Fixed cost of the production sites and all production-supporting areas	Fixed cost rates of the cost centers
=	Full product cost	Sum	
+	Administrative markup	Fixed cost of all administration cost centers	Total cost of the cost centers
+	Sales expenses markup	Fixed cost of all sales and distribution cost centers	Total cost of the cost centers
=	Cost-price	Sum	

Fig. 4.60 Conventional calculation scheme (see CWB, p. 134)

company, including interest. To arrive at these parameters, all fixed costs must be allocated "appropriately" to the individual products. The entire planning chapter showed that only the performance requirements resulting from the BOM and from the work plan of an item can be assigned to the product units directly according to a cause-and-effect relationship. This direct relationship between activity and the resulting cost can only be mapped for the proportional cost of goods manufactured. For the allocation of all items from material overheads to sales overheads, one must use arbitrarily selected allocation bases because there is **no causal link**.

To allocate the functional costs for warehousing and purchasing, it is often suggested to divide the functional costs for material procurement and handling by the direct material costs and add the resulting material overhead-rate to the direct material cost of the product unit. To generate an hourly full cost-rate of a production cost center (including all allocations) it is recommended to divide them by the planned activity. Such procedures are to be avoided as they proportionalize fixed costs. As shown in Sect. 4.7.1, fixed costs are driven by managerial decisions and never directly through the units produced (recommended, for example, by Seiler 1999, p. 213 f.).

Even an allocation basis selected to the best of one's knowledge and belief cannot establish a causal connection that does not exist.

In addition, the costs of the production-supporting areas (production management, workshops, up to the proportionate costs of personnel administration, buildings and IT) must first be allocated to the production cost centers so that these costs are also included in the fixed cost rates of the production centers and can from there be allocated to the product unit. This makes it clear that full product costs are a **fiction**, as fixed costs are the result of management decisions on structures and capacities and do not automatically build up or decrease as employment increases or decreases.

Since there is no direct causal link between the fixed costs of administrative plus selling overheads and the costs caused by the products, it is recommended that one divides the total of the respective cost group by the full product costs to obtain the markup-rates for administrative and selling overheads.

Conclusion: Both the **full product costs** and the **cost-price** of a product unit are **fictitious parameters**. The proportional product costs can be calculated correctly, but the amount of the fixed cost surcharges depends on the selection of the allocation basis.

In the following example, fixed product costs are apportioned once according to the production hours consumed (fixed cost rate = 10.00/h) and once according to the units produced per product. The results are different full product costs per unit. This clearly demonstrates that the choice of the allocation basis has a decisive effect on the derived full product costs per unit (Fig. 4.61).

The example makes it clear that full product costs and, as a result, full costs of goods sold have no place in a management-oriented planning and control system, which is decision oriented. Managers decide on the level of structural costs (in the cost centers), while proportional product costs are defined by the consumption of material and production services per product.

This insight must always be considered when designing an integrated planning and control system. It applies independently of accounting standards and legal requirements. The first step is to successfully manage the company and only then to report on the successes achieved to outsiders.

Since neither full product costs nor cost-based sales prices should serve as a basis for decision-taking, they are *not* mentioned in the management accounting

Product	Total	A	B	
Quantity produced	1,000	700	300	
Allowed hours in manufacturing		1	2	
Planned activity of the cost center	1,300			
prop. cost center-rate/hour	20	20	20	
prop. manufacturing cost of product	26,000	14,000	12,000	
Direct material cost / unit		5	10	
Direct material cost of product	6,500	3,500	3,000	
prop. product cost	32,500	17,500	15,000	
prop. product cost/unit		25	50	
Fixed cost manuf. cost center	13,000			
Fixed cost-rate of manuf. cost center	10	10	10	(13000/1300)

Different allocation keys for fixed manufacturing cost			
by hours	13,000	7,000	6,000
by units produced	13,000	9,100	3,900
Full product cost /unit			
by hours		35	70
by units produced		38	63
Total full product cost			
by hours	45,500	24,500	21,000
by units produced	45,500	26,600	18,900

Fig. 4.61 The selected allocation basis determines the amount of the full product costs

system explained here. Only when preparing the external income statement and balance sheet under external reporting requirements is full product cost calculated.

4.8.3 Integration and the Consequences of Production-plan Simulations

Changes to the planned production quantity for one or more items have far-reaching consequences for the planned cost and the planned results. The impact can be followed in the simulation model. An increase in the planned production quantity of an item to be produced influences the following related subplans:

- The proportional planned product costs per unit decrease if the number of lots remains the same, since the setup costs are distributed among more units.
- This results in the warehouse stock being valued at a slightly lower standard cost per unit, which is also reflected in the value of the total inventory.
- The planned contribution margins will be slightly higher in absolute terms and per unit for this item, because the lower standard cost per unit will also be applied.
- The planned activities of the cost centers directly involved increases. There will be more proportional manufacturing costs which in turn lowers the previously planned unit fixed costs, if no additional personnel must be employed.
- The overall effect of the factors mentioned also improves the budgeted result.

The simulation model automatically performs these calculations in all worksheets and shows the consequences up to the (internal) balance sheet. It helps shorten and professionalize the planning process.

However, planners must check in the individual plans whether adjustments are necessary because of the quantity change:

- Increasing planned activities can lead to a higher demand for staff or machinery. Such a requirement can be seen in the sheet "Costcenterplan" in the column "Capacity bottleneck personnel". In the same sheet, the number of planned FTE's must be adjusted as a consequence (see Sect. 4.5.2).
- The stock of semi-finished products required for increased planned production does not exist, which is why these production quantities need to be increased and additional personnel provided in the performing cost centers. The check is carried out in the Inventory draft plan (sheet "Stockplan") and again in "Capacity bottleneck personnel."
- The change in raw material stocks also needs to be monitored. If their range targets (safety stocks) is not reached anymore, higher-order quantities must be entered in the sheet "Purchaseplan."
- Finally, it must be monitored as to whether the maximum inventory level targets for semi-finished and finished goods are met, as higher inventories tie up more capital.

These "if-then examples" are a further indication that a fully automatic simulation model is not enough for integrated planning and control. Consequences of managerial decisions must be entered in the simulation model and thus interrupt the planning automation once more. But these decisions are also prerequisites for holistic planning.

4.9 Planned Earnings

According to our current state of knowledge, multilevel and multidimensional contribution margin accounting is best suited for the planning of results from individual products to the entire company and thus for providing managers with decision-relevant insights. One of the most important reasons for this is that in real contribution accounting there are no fixed cost allocations. All revenue and cost components are recorded and displayed where they can be directly influenced.

4.9.1 Stepwise Contribution Margin Accounting

Contribution margin accounting should show what monetary contribution a product unit, all units of an item, or—aggregated even higher—a product group makes to cover the costs of the (fixed) structures and to make a profit. Contribution margin I is defined internationally as (CWB 2010, p. 74):

+	Net proceeds	Revenue to net proceeds planning	4.3
–	Proportional product costs	Product calculation	4.8.1
=	**Contribution margin I (CM I)**		
–	Fixed costs of all cost centers	Cost center plans	4.7
=	Operating result (EBIT)		

To be precise, CM I is not a margin but the absolute amount available to cover all fixed costs plus the operating profit. But as the technical term "Contribution margin" is widely used, it will also be used here.

In contrast to product calculation, which is based on the quantities to be produced, contribution accounting starts from the market and thus from the quantities sold. The proportional standard cost of an item (see Figs. 4.57 and 4.58) is deducted from the net proceeds (see Fig. 4.17). The standard value of one unit is taken from the finished goods or merchandise inventory. Incoming goods were also valued at standard. If this procedure is carried out for the entire range of products, all proportional product costs are first put into inventory after the production process and are then withdrawn from there when the goods are sold. As a result, all fixed costs remain in the cost centers. As mentioned above, these are not allocated to the produced items, but are combined into meaningful fixed cost blocks.

Figure 4.62 shows the origination of the contribution and of the operating result (for the whole company) in the value flow for a two-level production process.

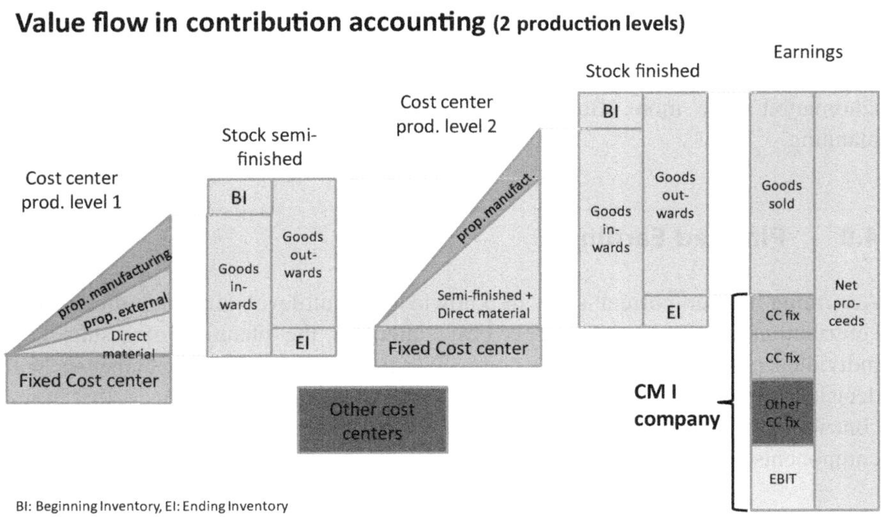

Fig. 4.62 Value flow in contribution accounting

- The proportional manufacturing costs for production level 1 originate from the cost centers (summarized across all produced items).
- In addition, there are direct material costs and any proportional external activity costs (documented in the Bills of Material).
- The sum of these is the value of the semi-finished products to be produced in production level 1. These products are sent to the semi-finished goods warehouse at the planned proportional cost of goods manufactured.
- In production level 2, the semi-finished products and any other raw materials are taken from stock (direct material including the product costs from level 1). Further processing generates further proportional manufacturing costs, so that finished products go to the finished goods warehouse at the proportional planned product cost rate.
- From an accounting point of view, all proportional planned product costs "land" in the two warehouses.
- By definition all other cost center costs are also fixed costs; these remain in the production cost centers.
- For space reasons, the raw material warehouse is not listed, but only the references in the blocks "direct material" of the two production levels. The inflows and outflows of merchandise are included in the movements in the finished goods inventory.
- In contribution accounting the net revenues to be achieved are compared with the planned stock withdrawals for the units to be sold, which results in the CM I of the entire company.
- The contribution must be enough to cover all remaining fixed cost and to achieve an operating result (EBIT) in line with the market.
- The final inventory remaining in the warehouses is also valued at standard cost.

For management support, this generally valid structure must be extended and adapted to the real structure and marketing dimensions of a company. This is done by grouping the cost centers as they can be uniquely assigned to the different CM levels (Fig. 4.63).

Stepwise Contribution Accounting in the Example Company

To determine the planned CM I of item 101060 (4.0 cm, 4-ring book with film), the data from net revenue planning (sheet "Itemrevenue") is merged with the standard cost of item 101060 from Fig. 4.59.

Note that a distinction is made between planned CM I and CM I after deduction of sales commissions. Commissions to sales representatives are usually treated together with the planning of net proceeds (see Sect. 4.3.2). Ringbook Ltd. uses a benefit commission system. This requires knowledge of Plan-CM I. For this reason, the explanation of the sales deduction through commission can only be addressed here (Fig. 4.64).

Benefit Commission

In many companies, the income of salespeople consists partly of a fixed amount and partly of a commission. According to our surveys, the commission is still calculated in most companies as a percentage of the invoiced (net) turnover (i.e., net sales). This has the serious disadvantage that sellers focus on maximizing sales and ignore the profitability aspect. A simple way to increase sales is to grant higher discounts or other sales deductions, such as cash discounts, subsequent bonus payments, or refunds based on the sales generated by the customer. Free delivery or free samples can also be promised, as well as the manufacture of customer-specific tools without invoicing the resulting tool costs. All these items reduce net revenue and thus also

	Contribution margin I (CM I)	Purpose: product control, CM-objectives of sales
-	Fixed distribution costs	Sales and Marketing Cost Centers enable Sales
=	Sales CM	Achievement of the overall sales targets
-	Fixed production costs	All fixed cost center costs (of the plant)
-	Possible project costs	Projects that run for the entire company
-	Fixed cost of the support areas	All fixed cost center costs (of the support areas)
-	Fixed administration costs	All fixed cost center costs (remaining cost centers)
=	Operating result (EBIT)	Earnings Before Interest and Taxes

Fig. 4.63 Rough structure of stepwise contribution accounting

Year	Sales rep	PG#	PR#	Planned sales quantity	Gross revenue planned	Avg. discounts	Net sales planned year	Prop. cost / unit	Prop. cost volume	Planned CM I	CMI / unit	Sales commis-sion	CM I after commis-sion	CM I as % of net sales
2011	201	2	2	619	2,600	19.75%	2,087	2.1157	1,310	777	1.25	16	761	36.49%
2011	202	2	2	82,069	344,690	19.75%	276,628	2.1157	173,635	102,994	1.25	2,060	100,934	36.49%

Fig. 4.64 Determination of planned CM I of product 101,060

the contribution margin and the overall result. In addition, in the medium term they lead to a reduction in price levels (especially in saturated markets), which in turn reduces overall profitability (Fig. 4.65).

It is more profitable to reward the salespeople for the residual amount that the company retains after deducting all sales deductions and the proportional standard product costs of the products and services sold. This is CM I. If from the net proceeds only the standard cost of the sold units is deducted, the resulting contribution shows what the representative can directly influence himself (except his own fixed costs).

CM I per article			Planned year:	**2011**					
Itemnr.	Planned sales quantity	Gross revenue planned	Net sales planned year	Prop. cost volume	Planned CM I	Sales commis-sions	CM I after commissions	CMI/ unit after comm.	CM I as % of net sales
105010	138,023	496,884	398,771	135,288	263,483	5,270	258,213	1.87	64.8%
105020	82,276	279,740	224,503	73,990	150,513	3,010	147,503	1.79	65.7%
105030	70,527	268,003	215,084	72,100	142,984	2,860	140,124	1.99	65.1%
105040	3,808	13,709	11,002	3,868	7,134	143	6,991	1.84	63.5%
105050	99,534	487,719	391,415	132,165	259,250	5,185	254,065	2.55	64.9%
105060	15,484	71,226	57,162	19,805	37,357	747	36,610	2.36	64.0%
105070	19,894	97,483	78,234	26,899	51,335	1,027	50,309	2.53	64.3%
105080	31,952	146,979	117,957	39,732	78,226	1,565	76,661	2.40	65.0%
101010	47,496	151,986	121,975	67,533	54,442	1,089	53,353	1.12	43.7%
101020	91,276	273,828	219,758	117,483	102,275	2,045	100,229	1.10	45.6%
101030	30,920	111,312	89,333	45,306	44,027	881	43,146	1.40	48.3%
101040	60,055	210,191	168,687	80,191	88,496	1,770	86,726	1.44	51.4%
101050	38,312	168,571	135,285	86,035	49,250	985	48,265	1.26	35.7%
101060	82,688	347,290	278,715	174,944	103,771	2,075	101,695	1.23	36.5%
101070	116,778	513,823	412,365	261,936	150,428	3,009	147,420	1.26	35.7%
101080	2,476	10,401	8,347	5,692	2,655	53	2,602	1.05	31.2%
105090	85,833	472,081	378,865	145,418	233,447	4,669	228,778	2.67	60.4%
105100	5,417	29,793	23,910	8,876	15,034	301	14,733	2.72	61.6%
105110	150,950	830,226	666,292	256,769	409,523	8,190	401,333	2.66	60.2%
105120	55,300	304,150	244,093	91,336	152,757	3,055	149,702	2.71	61.3%
101090	112,242	628,555	504,442	256,413	248,029	4,961	243,068	2.17	48.2%
101100	80,333	449,867	361,037	154,281	206,756	4,135	202,621	2.52	56.1%
101110	7,690	43,064	34,561	15,961	18,600	372	18,228	2.37	52.7%
101120	18,735	104,914	84,198	35,886	48,312	966	47,346	2.53	56.2%
103000	113,000	768,400	616,674	159,519	457,155	9,143	448,012	3.96	72.6%
104000	106,000	720,800	578,473	339,588	238,885	4,778	234,107	2.21	40.5%
120010	5,718	142,938	120,437	77,186	43,250	865	42,385	7.41	35.2%
120020	830	20,761	17,493	11,377	6,116	122	5,994	7.22	34.3%
120030	161	4,633	3,904	2,292	1,611	32	1,579	9.78	40.5%
120040	2,623	76,601	64,543	37,776	26,767	535	26,231	10.00	40.6%
120050	1,322	19,033	16,037	10,045	5,992	120	5,872	4.44	36.6%
120060	3,410	49,109	41,378	25,918	15,460	309	15,150	4.44	36.6%
120070	1,019	14,674	12,364	7,745	4,620	92	4,527	4.44	36.6%
120080	1,329	52,633	44,348	32,696	11,651	233	11,418	8.59	25.7%
120090	525	20,777	17,506	12,907	4,599	92	4,507	8.59	25.7%
120100	326	12,924	10,889	8,028	2,861	57	2,804	8.59	25.7%
120110	581	23,020	19,396	14,300	5,096	102	4,994	8.59	25.7%
120200	4,655	5,586	4,706	3,258	1,448	29	1,419	0.30	30.2%
Totale	1,689,500	8,443,683	6,794,141	3,050,546	3,743,595	74,872	3,668,723		54.0%

Fig. 4.65 Planned CM I after sales commissions

The seller recognizes which (residual) benefit he is generating for the company. All variances that occur in purchasing, production, or cost centers will be listed in lower levels of contribution accounting. Thus, for the benefit of the company, bonuses for sales people should be determined based on realized absolute contribution. This procedure is called benefit commissioning. Further descriptions and calculation examples can be found in *Benefit Commission* (Rieder 2012, available free at https://en.management-control.eu).

In the example company Ringbook Ltd., a simple form of benefit commissioning is utilized. Sales representatives receive 2% of the CM I they generate as part of their gross wages, which is considered in the simulation model in both the planned and the actual calculations. As a result, the "CM I after commissions"results. This figure shows the contribution of an item to fixed cost and profit recovery after deduction of sales commissions and standard product cost from the net proceeds.

Net revenue planned, standard cost of products sold as well as CM I before and after sales commissions can be found in sheet "CMplanitems".

Contribution Margin Levels/Deduction of Fixed Cost Blocks

The next step is to determine whether the sum of all CM I will be enough to cover all fixed costs and to generate an operating profit in line with the objective. Because results are presented here in the product dimension and according to product groups, CM I (after commissions) is aggregated by product group.

The fixed costs from the cost centers are subsequently subtracted, step by step (hence the name stepwise contribution accounting). In the example case (see Fig. 4.49 in Sect. 4.7.8), the cost centers sales promotion finished goods (101) and sales promotion merchandise (102) exist. Their costs can be deducted directly from the CM I for the range totals of finished goods and merchandise because the purpose of these two cost centers is to pursue sales promotion for the product groups assigned to them and thus to support the achievement of the planned CM. Note that these fixed costs can neither be allocated to the individual product groups nor to the individual items according to their cause, as they are incurred for all products in the respective product range. As an interim result, the product range contribution is created, for which the sales promotion specialists and the sales staff are jointly responsible.

Next, the fixed cost block of the remaining selling costs is deducted from the sum of the product range CMs. For this purpose, the cost center costs of all remaining sales functions (Fig. 4.56) are summarized. These fixed sales costs can only be clearly assigned to the total sum of all product range CMs, since the sales representatives sell all products and the office staff and sales management also take care of all products. The result is the sales-CM. This is one of the financial objectives of the sales manager, since he controls all the above figures except standard product cost.

The final levels are the fixed cost of production (which can only be clearly linked to the company's finished goods) and other necessary corporate functions. The latter can only be appropriately shown in the total column of the company, since the work done in these departments is for all product groups and ranges.

Stepwise contribution accounting Cost of sales method

2011

PG-Nr. / Product group	Total Ringbook Ltd.	Subtotal Finished goods	1 2Ring normal (stock)	2 4Ring normal (stock)	3 2Ring special designs	4 4Ring special designs	5 2Ring special formats	6 4Ring special formats	7 Merchandise
CM I after sales commissions	3,668,723	3,541,841	970,476	583,436	794,546	511,263	448,012	234,107	126,882
fixed cost of product ranges	311,730	158,640							153,090
Product range CM	3,356,993	3,383,201							-26,208
Fixed cost sales organization									
100 Sales mgmt. & office	543,082								
151 Eastern Switzerland	120,113								
152 Western Switzerland	91,960								
153 Business clients (direct)	105,880								
Sales- CM	2,495,958								
Fixed cost of production	995,112								
200 Plant mgmt. & work scheduling		210,965							
220 Stamping		93,373							
231 Wire rolling		31,565							
232 Wire bending & forming		281,795							
240 Cardboarding		61,316							
245 Personnel pool 240-260		241,346							
250 Assembly		48,251							
260 Film welding		26,501							
Other fixed cost	1,299,788								
210 Procurement & warehouse	182,155								
320 Buildings & maintenance	149,649								
330 Repair center	11,445								
340 Energy center	27,278								
300 IT	269,825								
900 Corp. Mgmt. & administration	659,437								
EBIT	201,058								

Fig. 4.66 Stepwise planned contribution accounting in the product dimension

With the calculation of EBIT contribution accounting ends. This becomes the profit target of the responsible managing director, provided that the presented annual plan is approved for implementation by senior management. All variables the managing director can influence together with his managers are included in the system. They form the yardstick for evaluating the results achieved (Fig. 4.66).

With this stepwise contribution accounting, the planned result can be determined unambiguously and without making any arbitrary allocations. It is also consistent with the income statement, insofar as the same valuation approaches are used and if inventories are valued at standard (see Sect. 4.10.1).

4.9.2 Multidimensional Presentation of Contribution Margins

Section 4.9.1 described the presentation of contribution accounting in the product dimension. It focused on the contribution of a single item—or aggregated of a product group—to cover the fixed cost. Accordingly, the fixed cost totals were allocated to the product groups and ranges, insofar as they could be clearly assigned without making allocations.

In many companies, it is evident that market cultivation happens in different dimensions, e.g.,

- By product groups through sales promotion.
- By regions or sales territories through the company's own sales representatives.
- According to sales channels through direct sales or sales via (intermediate) dealers and increasingly via online sales.

Additionally,

- If a company operates internationally it needs to know how successful its products are in the various countries.
- For strategic questions, further evaluations according to strategic business areas are necessary.

Therefore, an integrated planning and control system should be designed in such a way that the profitability analysis can be created in each of the dimensions described. This supposes that:

- Planning is carried out at the lowest possible level (here per sales area and product group with statistical distribution to the individual items).
- For real sales, the evaluations can be summarized starting from the individual billing line, since the bill to the customer contains all the relevant evaluation dimensions or has the data stored in the ERP.
- The product costs of all items are available so that they can be assigned to the net proceeds by dimension.

If the net sales, net revenues and the standard cost of the items can be aggregated from the customer and from the item sold (bottom-up), a step-by-step contribution accounting can also be created in the dimensions described. When only full product costs per unit are available this multidimensional analysis cannot be accurately achieved since period-related fixed costs are included in the full cost of a produced unit. If, due to higher sales volumes in a certain country or sales channel, the total production volume increases without increasing the fixed costs of production, the latter are allocated to more units, which also results in lower product costs per unit in all other countries and thus in an automatic improvement of their profit without their involvement.

Contribution Margins in the Sales Territories
If the starting table in sheet "CMplanitems" with the data on the planned gross and net sales and contribution margins is summarized by sales regions instead of by items, the CM I per sales representative becomes visible (Fig. 4.67).

Since all items are sold in each sales region, adding up the sales volumes or determining an average price does not bring any additional knowledge. Management-relevant information is the CM I volume per sales area and the overall discount granted in these areas.

CM I per sales region Plan: **2011**

Sales region	Sales representative	Gross revenue	Avg. discounts	Net revenue	Prop. cost of sales	CM I plan	Sales commission	CM I plan after commission
201	Bauer	2,629,125	19.3%	2,120,783	917,529	1,203,254	24,065	1,179,189
202	App	2,911,736	19.5%	2,343,575	1,063,405	1,280,171	25,603	1,254,567
203	Sahli	683,673	19.7%	548,773	236,785	311,988	6,240	305,748
204	King (SM)	2,219,149	19.7%	1,781,010	832,828	948,182	18,964	929,219
	Totals	8,443,683	19.5%	6,794,141	3,050,546	3,743,595	74,872	3,668,723

Fig. 4.67 CM I plan after commissions per sales region

In this dimension, the fixed costs of the sales areas (personal number 201–204) are deducted first from CM I, since these can be clearly assigned to the respective area. Fixed sales area costs do not appear in cost center 204. This is since the costs of sales manager King as well as those of the internal sales office are incurred for the entire company and thus also for the other sales areas. Furthermore, the costs of sales promotion have fallen one CM level because, although they can clearly be allocated to the respective product range, they cannot be allocated to a single sales region. For this reason, the CM level after deduction of the sales territory fixed costs is called "sales region CM."

In a multistep and multidimensional contribution analysis, only the controllable fixed costs that can be uniquely assigned to a level are deducted. This has the consequence that in each dimension other amounts are to be subtracted. The example shows a product range CM total of 3,356,993 (Fig. 4.66) and a sales region CM total of 3,350,771 (Fig. 4.68). We therefore recommend not numbering the CM levels consecutively but giving them a name that speaks for the respective company structure. The term "CM I" is applied here because this definition is used internationally (see Sect. 4.9.1). The sales CM is the same in the two presented dimensions as all controllable fixed cost of the complete sales function is included at this level.

4.9.3 Two-Dimensional Contribution-Margin Targets

In the sections on management by objectives (Sect. 1.2) and the integrated management system IMS (Sect. 2.1), the importance of personal annual objectives was emphasized. This also applies to a company with multidimensional market cultivation. However, it should be noted that it is advantageous for an area manager in sales to coordinate his planning with the plans of the sales promoters so that the planned sales promotion campaigns can be placed correctly in sales talks with customers.

As a result, while product group managers and regional managers should each have their own CM targets, their achievement also depends on good coordination. Thus, contribution margin responsibility arises in two dimensions, on the one hand according to product groups after deduction of the product group (or range) fixed

CM's in steps

	2011	Dimension sales regions				
	Region	201	202	203	204	299
Sales region CM	Total Ringbook Ltd.	Eastern Switzerland	Western Switzerland	Business clients (direct)	Sales mgmt. & office	Online shop
CM I after sales commissions	3,668,723	1,179,189	1,254,567	305,748	929,219	-
Cost center number sales region		151	152	153	100	-
Fixed cost of sales regions	317,953	120,113	91,960	105,880	-	
Sales region CM	3,350,771	1,059,076	1,162,607	199,868	929,219	-
Fixed cost of sales promo & -mgmt.	854,812					
101 Sales promotion finished goods	158,640					
102 Sales promotion merchandise	153,090					
100 Sales mgmt. & office	543,082					
Sales CM	2,495,958					
Fixed cost of production	995,112					
200 Plant mgmt. & work scheduling	210,965					
220 Stamping	93,373					
231 Wire rolling	31,565					
232 Wire bending & forming	281,795					
240 Cardboarding	61,316					
245 Personnel pool 240-260	241,346					
250 Assembly	48,251					
260 Film welding	26,501					
Other fixed cost	1,299,788					
210 Procurement & warehouse	182,155					
320 Buildings & maintenance	149,649					
330 Repair center	11,445					
340 Energy center	27,278					
300 IT	269,825					
900 Corp. Mgmt. & administration	659,437					
EBIT	201,058					

Fig. 4.68 Stepwise Contribution accounting by sales region

costs and, on the other hand, according to sales regions and after deduction of the fixed costs of the respective area manager (Fig. 4.69).

The agreement of the two dimensions with the stepwise contribution accounting results again in the CM sales, which is shown after deduction of all fixed costs of the complete sales organization (2,495,958). The product range CM total corresponds to that in Fig. 4.68; the area CM total to that in Fig. 4.66.

These CM-objectives were structured according to the structures of the example company. In a specific application case, the effective structures of the company to be depicted must be considered (and not those from a textbook and any terms recommended therein). Accordingly, suitable names should be assigned in each company for their respective CM-objectives, so that those responsible can easily orient themselves.

PG	Product groups ↓	Sales regions → 201 Eastern Switzerland	202 Western Switzerland	203 Business clients (direct)	204 Export	CM I product-groups	Fix cost sales promotion	CM product ranges
1	2Ring normal (stock)	654,231	147,886	31,313	137,045	970,476		
2	4Ring normal (stock)	181,999	143,317	31,527	226,592	583,436		
3	2Ring special designs	32,382	388,219	139,415	234,530	794,546		
4	4Ring special designs	26,720	178,690	78,190	227,663	511,263		
5	2Ring special formats (stock)	111,012	218,059	15,859	103,082	448,012		
6	4Ring special formats (stock)	92,759	132,513	8,834	-	234,107		
	Total finished goods	1,099,103	1,208,686	305,139	928,914	3,541,841	158,640	3,383,201
7	Merchandise	80,086	45,882	610	305	126,882	153,090	-26,208
	CM I sales region	1,179,189	1,254,567	305,748	929,219	**3,668,723**	311,730	**3,356,993**
	Fixed cost sales regions	120,113	91,960	105,880		317,953		
	CM sales regions	1,059,076	1,162,607	199,868	929,219	**3,350,770**		
	Fixed cost sales management & -administration							543,082
	CM sales							2,495,958

Fig. 4.69 CM responsibility "crossed over"

4.10 Compacting for the Planned Income Statement and the Balance Sheet

The contribution margin calculation in Sect. 4.9.1 is condensed here into the **planned profit and loss statement** and, including changes in inventories, into the **budgeted balance sheet.**

4.10.1 Planned Income Statement According to the Total Cost Method

The complete budget, including contribution accounting, was presented according to the cost of sales method (COSM), because this is more in line with the way a manager thinks (from the market into the company). In COSM the costs of sales and non-sales-related costs are deducted from net proceeds to determine EBIT. To determine the cost of sales, the product costs per sales unit must first be known. This means that cost/activity accounting is a prerequisite for using COSM in the manufacturing or service company.

The cost of sales method is the usual presentation form of the P&L in English-speaking countries. In many European countries, especially in the German-speaking ones, the total cost method (TCM) is still primarily used. In the TCM, the expenses for *total* production are compared (on an accrual basis) with the realized net sales, which corresponds in the example with the "produced value." To make the cost of production consistent with net sales (sales quantity does not correspond to the production quantity), cost of production must be adjusted. This is done by adding or subtracting the inventory changes of the semi-finished and finished goods inventories. These also include (proportional) manufacturing costs, which are either included in the items still in inventory or, if more was sold than produced, were included in the previous year's inventories.

In the TCM, all consumption of raw materials and merchandise is subtracted from the value produced (these were taken from the warehouse), resulting in the gross profit. The latter indicates how much money remains to cover all personnel and material costs as well as the profit in the plan. Gross profit is often mistakenly referred to as value added. This use of the term is incorrect because cost types 4–14 (as depicted in Fig. 4.70) also flow outside the company and are not available to pay staff, maintain assets (depreciation), or earn a profit (these three elements are the value added). It can also be seen from the example that in the TCM expense types are deducted from the gross profit, while in the cost of sales method cost center costs are deducted from CM.

The cash flow before interest and taxes (CFBIT) is the balance of all inflows and outflows that have their offsetting item in the balance sheet in the accounts of net current assets (cash and cash equivalents, accounts receivable, inventories, less bank

Planned internal income statement		**Total cost method**	
	Cost_type_desc	Source / comments	**2011**
	Net revenue	acc. CM I plan	6,794,141
	Inventory change finished goods	at planned prop. cost	50,249
	Inventory change semi-finished	acc. planned stock development	-1,955
	Change in assets under construction	acc. project plans	33,866
	produced value	Total	6,876,300
	Raw material consumption	see planned purchases	665,307
	Merchandise consumption	see planned purchases	243,530
	Gross profit		5,967,462
1	Personnel costs	see cost type plan	4,802,516
2	Sales commissions	see contribution margins planned	74,872
3	Purchasing & shipping costs	see cost type plan	20,000
4	Advertisement	see cost type plan	110,000
5	Office supplies	see cost type plan	13,730
6	Auxiliary and operating materials	see cost type plan	52,270
7	Telephone, communication	see cost type plan	34,860
9	El. energy, water, fuel oil	see cost type plan	67,800
8	Cleaning & conserving supplies	see cost type plan	4,080
10	Rent	see cost type plan	30,000
12	External maintenance & repair	see cost type plan	222,575
13	Other expense, non-activated project costs	see cost type plan	82,860
14	Software (Licenses & maintenance)	see cost type plan	24,000
40	Internal clearing (personnel for other CC)	see cost type plan	-
	Creation of other new provisions (not attributable to operations (see balance)		-
	Total cost center costs (cash out)		5,539,563
	CFBIT Cashflow Before Interest and Taxes		427,900
31	Planned imputed depreciation	Invest&depr(column u)	226,842
	EBIT		201,058

Fig. 4.70 Planned income statement

liabilities, accounts payable, and any short-term provisions). CFBIT thus indicates how much cash or near money should result from the planned business.

Methodically one should note that in this operational view, the material-related items (material consumption and stock changes) are always taken from the planned purchasing data and from planned inventory management (sheet "Stockplan"). These items are valued at the planned purchase prices and at standard cost of goods to manufacture. Thus, the starting point is always the planned material consumption. Valuation adjustments for financial accounting purposes are excluded.

The EBIT of the income statement according to the TCM corresponds to that of stepwise contribution accounting (201,058). The CFBIT could also be shown in the CM accounts if imputed depreciation was not planned directly in the respective cost centers as in the model but instead listed as a total amount.

4.10.2 Internal Budgeted Balance Sheet as the Completion of Planning

To date, the planning process has not yet addressed the initial situation, i.e., the opening balance at the beginning of the planned year 2011. The following two figures illustrate how—from an operational (management) point of view—the opening balance sheet is to be translated into the planned closing balance sheet.

First, the opening balance sheet must be revalued or supplemented in a way that is relevant to management:

- The items marked in yellow (cash and cash equivalents, accounts receivable, accounts payable, bank debt, assets under construction/ projects not yet completed, provisions, and share capital/reserves) can be taken from the financial accounting records (closing balance of the previous year).
- The quantity-based material stocks are valued with the planned purchase prices of the plan year, so that managers find the same valuation approach in the opening stocks as in the entire planned calculation. The stock quantity at opening is recorded item by item in the sheet "Openingbalance."
- Fixed assets are valued at replacement values (RepV) to give management a better overview of the fixed assets required to implement the plan. The procedure for determining the replacement value per asset was explained in Sect. 4.7.7. The sum of the RepV estimated for the beginning of the planned year (2,791,000) is included in the sheet "Openingbalance." The difference to the residual asset value (according to financial accounting) is calculated (541,000) and shown as an adjustment item in equity. In fact, this difference is the balance of the over-amortization of previous years compared to the RepV determined as the starting point.
- Leased assets (financial lease not operating lease) also belong in the management-relevant balance sheet. Whether assets are financed with equity, loans, or a leasing contract is decided by the owners or top management and implemented by the CFO. For the manager, the asset used in his area, e.g., a service vehicle or a

computer system, counts. From management's point of view, the residual replacement value of these assets corresponds to the invested operating assets. The cost of these assets is the imputed depreciation (plus maintenance). From the point of view of the cost center manager, the financing of the asset is a variable he cannot influence.

- Taking these initial value adjustments into account, the result is higher operating assets (4,415,854) than in financial accounting, which leads to a lower return on investment than in the accounting-based calculation if the planned EBIT remains unchanged. Even if the RepV is estimated, this results in a more realistic value for the assets required for implementation of the plan (Fig. 4.71).

Opening balance (internal view)

	PR#	Opening	
Assets			
Liquid assets		210,100	
Accounts receivable		1,001,514	
Inventory:			
- Raw-/operating material	3	68,400	at planned purchase prices 2011
- Merchandise	6	20,516	at planned purchase prices 2011
- Semi-finished goods	1	176,297	at standard (prop.) production cost 2011
- Finished goods	2	148,028	at standard (prop.) production cost 2011
Current assets		1,624,854	
fixed assets		2,791,000	at replacement value 01/01/2011
Assets under construction / Projects		-	
Total fixed assets		2,791,000	
Balance sum		4,415,854	
Liabilities			
Accounts payable		179,940	
Bank account		1,171,542	
Short-term provisions		250,000	
Current liabilities		1,601,482	
Long term loan		800,000	
Long-term liabilities		800,000	
Replacement value adjustments		541,000	
Reserves		473,372	
Share capital		1,000,000	
Equity		2,014,372	
Balance sum		4,415,854	
Net sales previous year		6,227,056	
Fixed assets financial Accounting		2,250,000	fixed assets 12/31/2010 (financial accounting)
Fixed assets Replacement Value		2,791,000	
Replacement value adjustments		541,000	

Fig. 4.71. Initial balance sheet and operating assets at the beginning of the planned year

To reconcile the opening balance sheet with the closing balance sheet, all transactions are summarized in two columns:

- The **Operation column** shows the effects of the income statement and inventory changes on the balance sheet (management view).
- The **money flow column contains** the postings not affecting income (primarily incoming payments from receivables and payments to suppliers as well as banking transactions). This column thus reflects those transactions which are usually only of interest to the accounting department and which influence liquidity.

In order not to complicate the example in the accounting and closing area too much, various planning assumptions were made in the lower part of Fig. 4.72. These enable the automated calculation of balance sheet items; otherwise, they must be entered by the user of the simulation model (on the budgeted balance sheet). These include assumptions regarding:

- Change in provisions (accrued liabilities).
- Average number of days between billing and incoming payment (debtor days).
- Average number of days between invoice receipt and outgoing payment (creditor days).
- Change in loan amounts and firm loans.
- The account liquid funds is left unchanged on the assumption that all cash movements are settled via the bank account.
- Expected average interest rate for interest-bearing liabilities.
- Interest calculation is based on debt at beginning of year.
- Local tax burden as a percentage of profit before tax.
- Retention of the annual profit, increasing the equity base. In any case, a distribution could only be determined by the company owners after the end of the actual year.

For managers, the plan data for the current year is always relevant for the target to actual comparison (target orientation). This will require some revaluation when preparing next year's budgeted balance sheet. The procedure is described in Sect. 8.1.

4.11 Simulation in the Annual Planning Process

With the presentation of the expected final balance sheet, always from a management's point of view, the cycle of quantity, performance, and finance-related integrated annual planning is closed.

Planned balance sheet (internal)

	PG#	Opening balance 01/01/2011	Operation	Money flow	**Planned balance 12/31/2011**
Assets					
Liquid assets		210,100	-		210,100
Accounts receivable		1,001,514	6,794,141	-6,539,689	1,255,967
Inventory:					
- Raw-/operating material	3	68,400	-665,307	672,160	75,253
- Merchandise	6	20,516	-243,530	239,288	16,274
- Semi-finished goods	1	176,297	-1,955	-	174,341
- Finished goods	2	148,028	50,249	-	198,276
Current assets		1,624,854	5,933,597	-5,628,241	1,930,211
fixed assets		2,791,000	-226,842	221,000	2,785,158
Changes replacement value			-		-
Assets under constr. / Projects		-	33,866	107,500	141,366
Total fixed assets		2,791,000	-192,976	328,500	2,926,524
Balance sum		4,415,854	5,740,621	-5,299,741	4,856,735
Liabilities					
Accounts payable		179,940	662,175	-637,566	204,549
Bank account		1,171,542	4,802,516	-4,363,597	1,610,461
Provisions for sales commission		-	74,872		74,872
other short-term provisions		250,000	-	*-179,504*	70,496
Current liabilities		1,601,482	5,539,563	-5,180,667	1,960,378
Long term loan		800,000			800,000
Long-term liabilities		800,000	-	-	800,000
EBIT			201,058	-201,058	-
Interest				*98,577*	
EBT				*102,481*	
deferred tax liabilities				*20,496*	
Annual profit				*81,985*	81,985
Replacement value adjustments		541,000			541,000
Reserves		473,372			473,372
Share capital		1,000,000			1,000,000
Equity		2,014,372	-	81,985	2,096,357
Balance sum		4,415,854	5,740,621	-5,299,741	4,856,735
Net revenue		6,794,141			
Creation of other new provisions					
Dissolution of other new provisions				200,000	
Debtor days (previous year/planned)		53		58	
Inflow accounts payable				2,048,197	
Creditor days				30	
Accounts payable payed				1,877,514	
Change of long term loan				0	
Interest on loan and opening balance bank credit			5%	1,971,542	
Tax rate			20%		

Fig. 4.72. From the opening to the closing balance sheet of the planned year

The presented planning model shows that:

- Thinking from the market into the company makes sense.
- The units to be sold form the basis for production planning.
- Planning quantities without bills of material and work plans does not allow integrated requirements planning.
- Inventory planning needs to take place at the individual item level, so that during production supply bottlenecks or waiting times can be avoided.
- It is necessary to plan material requirements and capacity requirements in order for the necessary purchases and capacities to be made available in the cost centers.
- Costs are the consequence of activities, which is why performance planning is always in the foreground.
- Projects also must be planned in terms of quantities and activities to integrate them into the consolidated view.
- Estimated replacement values provide managers a more realistic basis for determining the necessary operating assets and imputed depreciation.
- The planning system cannot be a fully automated simulation model, because various decisions of the managers responsible for implementation must be recorded and remain adaptable while planning is still in progress.

With annual planning at all levels, from the customer to the product, the material and the cost centers/employees, the yardsticks for assessing the implementation success, and for improving the cost position are built at the lowest level to be controlled.

Integrated annual planning is challenging, complex, and labor intensive. Nevertheless, it is worth investing in the continuous improvement of this process. All managers want to win measurable objectives for themselves and their employees. These goals permit the short-term traceability of the success of one's own efforts and thus help generate a sustainable competitive advantage for a company relative to its less integrated competitors.

Recording Services, Cost, and Revenue 5

Work in companies is triggered by placing an order. The orders released for execution, whether in sales or in production/activity creation usually do not correspond to plan because customers have different requirements or because different production quantities and dates are required due to market demand and inventory changes. The adjustment to short-term changes was defined in Sect. 1.4 as tactical planning and control, or disposition for short. This short-term planning and scheduling work must also ensure that it is possible to determine the actual monthly and annual results achieved and that comparisons can be made between plan and actual. For this purpose, the services rendered, costs, and revenues as well as inventories need to be recorded in a process- and structure-oriented manner compatible with the plans. How to design a system to accomplish this is the subject of this chapter.

5.1 Performances

In production, issuing a production order leads to material staging and withdrawal, to processing in the cost centers, and to goods flowing to the semi-finished or finished products warehouse. Ordering takes place with production orders or project orders.

5.1.1 Production Orders

In Sect. 4.4.1 concerning the production plan, the material requirements planning and the BOM explosion for product item 101060 (4-ring book, 4 cm spine width, plasticized) were described as in Fig. 5.1.

Since the ordering behavior of customers does not follow the planning calendar, it needs to be decided whether the production quantity released should differ from the lot size quantity defined in the yearly plan. This means that inventory levels also need to be considered.

L. Rieder, R. Lawson, *Management Control with Integrated Planning*, Management for Professionals, https://doi.org/10.1007/978-3-030-48302-9_5

Material requirements plan finished good

Year	Itemnr.	Description	Planned sales	Planned production	Planned lots	Planned lot size
2011	101060	4ring 4 cm plasticized	82,688	85,800	11	7,800

Bill of materials for item 101060

Year	Itemnr 2	Description	Type	Quantity unit	preset quantity / unit	setup units per lot	Scrap / lot	Gross requirement per Lot	Gross requirement per Year
2011	32	4.0 cm-envelope	SG	piece	1	10	50	7,860	86,460
2011	23	4-Ring-mechanism 4cm	SG	piece	1	10	50	7,860	86,460
2011	2	Film	Raw	Running meter	0.44	10	50	3,458	38,042

Fig. 5.1 Material requirements calculation and BOM explosion for item 101060 in plan year 2011

Due to strong demand it is necessary for Ringbook Ltd. to change month 3's production order for item 101060. The production planning and scheduling department decides to increase the lot to be released for production by 3000 pieces from the planned lot size of 7800 pieces to 10,800 pieces.

This again is a **deliberate interruption of automated planning**. This intervention must be possible, since the readiness to deliver to the customer must always be ensured and, on the other hand, inventories should remain as low as possible.

The initial data for placing the production order is as follows:

Year	Itemnr.	Month	Porderrnr	Description	Planned production (year)	Planned lots	Planned lot size	**Adapted production quantity**	Dispatched lot
2011	101060	3	**90**	4ring 4 cm plasticized	85,800	11	7,800	**3,000**	10,800

For the sake of simplicity, only "year" and "month" are used here. In a real application complete date specification are required, i.e.:

- Creation/release date of the order
- Planned (and scheduled) start date in production
- Planned end date (stock receipt of good units)

These entries are necessary to determine the staging dates for the material in the warehouse and the capacity commitment in the cost centers. In addition, this data also serves to provide key figures for assessing the degree of adherence to production schedules.

5.1.2 Order-Specific Bills of Material and Work Plans

The bill of materials for products were defined in Sect. 4.4.1, and preset quantities were set during annual planning. This was also done for the work plans together with

Bill of materials for item 101060 in production order 90

Year	Itemnr 2	Description	Input units	Preset quantity / unit	Standard cost / purchase price	Quantity from warehouse	Precalc. material cost for raw & SG
2011	32	4.0 cm-envelope	10,860	1	0.3181	10,860	3,454.57
2011	23	4-Ring-mechanism 4cm	10,860	1	0.6471	10,860	7,027.51
2011	2	Film	10,860	0.44	0.2000	4,778	955.68
							11,437.75

Fig. 5.2 Order-specific BOM (sheet "Actualmaterial," production order 90)

Year	Itemnr	Month	Description	Dispatched lot	CCnr	Description	Standard time /unit	Setup-time (in RFU) per lot	Capacity required / position (in RFU)	Standard prop. cost-rate	Standard prop. manufac-turing cost
2011	101060	3	4ring 4 cm plasticized	10,800	250	Assembly	1.00	120	10,920	0.78979	8,624.55
2011	101060	3	4ring 4 cm plasticized	10,800	260	Film welding	1.00	20	10,820	0.25185	2,725.04
											11,349.58

Fig. 5.3 Order-specific work plan for production order 90

the allowed times per process and the setup times, discussed in Sect. 4.5.4. Since the production quantity ordered (lot size) can differ from that in the annual plan, the material and working time specifications must be recalculated for each production order to be released. Using order 90 as an example, one can see that the requirements for setup and scrap per lot as well as the specified quantities per item are copied unchanged (these are the target values).

The planned purchase prices are also copied from the annual plan as price variances in Purchasing should not be included in the preliminary and final costing of an order. This is required so that the person responsible for the order can later understand which variances (efficiency changes) have arisen due to consumption other than planned and which are due to purchase prices other than planned. The semi-finished products to be used (envelope and mechanisms) were also taken from the annual article master and thus from the standard cost estimates in the purchase-price column with their planned values. The planned costs per unit of semi-finished products include the planned proportional manufacturing costs. The last column therefore contains the standard values for direct material in relation to the quantity to be produced in this production order. Since the semi-finished and finished product inventories are always valued at standard, there is no difference in value between goods outwards and the consumption in the production order (Fig. 5.2).

Foil welding and assembly for item 101060 were taken from the "Workplans" sheet. Standard (allowed) times were multiplied by the production quantity to be dispatched and the planned setup times were added to them. This results in the performance specifications for production order 90. With this information the requirements for the production order are set and can be released for production. The recording of actual consumptions is discussed in Sect. 5.1.4 (Fig. 5.3).

5.1.3 Plan and Preliminary Calculation, Lot Size Optimization

For item 101090 the planned quantity was 112,310 good units (sheet "Productionplan"). With 11 equal lots planned per year this corresponds to 10,210 unit lots. This added up to 23,234 proportional standard product costs. These included 173 in setup costs (see Fig. 4.59).

For both planning and actual purposes, every good unit delivered to stock is valued at the standard valuation rate of 2.2845 (23,324/10,210 = 2.2845) (Fig. 5.4).

In this production order 11,010 units were ordered due to robust market demand, an increase of 800 units. Multiplied by the standard of 2.2845, 11,010 units were stored in stock (or inventory) after completion of the order, which corresponds to a value of 25,152. From this 1827.57 (800 × 2.2845 = 1827.57) is the result of the higher quantity delivered to stock. The remaining difference of 13.58 is for the overcharged setup and scrap costs. This can be verified by comparing the 800 units of additional quantity with the planned quantity of 10,210 (= 7.84%) and multiplying this percentage by the planned setup cost of 172.36. The resulting 13.58 is the **lot size variance** between the standard cost calculation estimate and the preliminary cost of order 118.

The formula for determining the lot size variance is as follows:

$$\text{Lot size variance} = \text{Plan setup costs}/\text{Plan lot size} \times (\text{Actual lot size} - \text{Plan lot size})$$

In Sect. 1.5 it was explained why, from a management point of view and to simplify value-based inventory management, all inventory in- and outflows should be valued at standard throughout the year, as implemented in the example.

Proof for itemnr.:	101090			Of which setup cost		
Yearly planning	Units to produce (sheet Production-plan)	Standard cost from sheet Yearlyitems	Prop. cost of planned production	Direct material from sheet directmatcalc	Manufacturing from sheet Capacityplan	Total
Planned per lot	10,210	2.2845	23,324.42	73.55	99.81	173.36
Production order 118	Dispatched lot	Valuation at standard	Precalc. inventory entry			
net units to produce = stock entry actual	11,010	2.2845	25,152.00			
Precalculation production order 118	Input quantity incl. setup		Prop. cost			
Raw mat. & SG from inventory (Actualmaterial)		11,070	13,570.08			
Precalculated manufacturing cost (Actualmanufcost)						
Assembly		11,130	8,790.40			
Total precalculation			25,138.41			
- Extra units compared to plan (Productionorders)	800.00	2.2845	-1,827.57			
Too much setup cost in stock entry (lot-size variance)			13.58			
= again plan-calculation			23,324.42			
Lot size increase compared to paln-calculation		7.84%		5.76	7.82	13.58

Lot size variance is thus always the difference between plan-calculation and precalculation.

Fig. 5.4 Plan-calculation of item 101090 and pre-calculation of production order 118

The **plan-calculation** is used in annual planning to determine the proportional plan product costs. This is the yardstick for the entire plan year. All inventory movements are valued throughout the year at standard, including the units delivered to inventory from the production order.

Preliminary costing or **pre-calculation** is the cost yardstick for the actual implementation of production order 118. The person responsible for the order works ensures that actual consumption does not exceed planned quantities and times from the plan-calculation.

This standards-based approach has several advantages:

- The value-based inventory valuation always runs synchronously with the inventory quantities. Variances in the production orders are not represented in the valuation of stocks during the year.
- Stock withdrawals for sales are valued at standard throughout the year. This is correct because the salespersons are not responsible for variances that occurred in the production area.
- For their part, production managers are not responsible for variances between planned and actual purchase prices during the year. The differences are to be disclosed as purchase price variances (see Sect. 5.3.2).
- It is possible to automatically calculate the lot size variance per order between plan-calculation and pre-calculation. A positive lot size variance can be interpreted as a gain in efficiency compared to the plan. These amounts are later required for the variance statement in Profitability Analysis.

It is often argued that the determination of lot size variances is too complex and that it is more important to know the "true" post-calculated product costs during the year and to evaluate the stock receipts accordingly:

- However, as Sect. 4.8.2 showed, the "real" recalculated costs of a production order cannot be determined because fixed cost allocations and thus also allocations of variances would be necessary (see Sect. 4.7.1).
- If variances were to be included in a pre- or post-calculation of an order, more or less every material slip would present another cost per unit as the respective rates would have to be adapted to the valuation principle used (e.g., first in—first out or weighted average). The proportional cost rate would also have to be adapted every time when actual costs in the manufacturing centers did not correspond to the rates in the previous order. As a result, the person responsible for the order would no longer be able to compare the actual cost with the plan as the applied rates would change all the time.
- If the management accounting system is installed as described with annual plan calculations and precalculated order costs, calculation of lot size variances occurs automatically (see derivation above and sheet "Completemessage," column "Lot size variance").

Lot Size Variances and Stocks

The management relevance of lot size variance is that it helps to evaluate productivity gains (or losses) versus plan. If the 13.58 positive lot size variance is considered at an assumed 5% interest costs, it can be deduced that 272 (13.58/5 × 100) more stock could be financed for 1 year, which corresponds to about 119 (272/2.2845 planned proportional costs) units of this item. This can be used as a reference value for the evaluation of lot size changes in comparison to stock levels. In other words: Is it worthwhile to release smaller batches to comply with the inventory targets in the warehouse?

The model below shows that the combined consideration of setup and interest costs can lead to an optimal (planned) lot size. The impact of the sum of setup and interest costs on unit costs is considered. The following basic assumptions are made:

- Planned production quantity of the year: 1200 units, since a monthly sales volume of 100 pieces is estimated.
- Proportional standard manufacturing cost per unit (without setup): 2.00
- Setup cost per lot: 20.00
- Interest costs: 5% of the average inventory value of the year (including setup)

In the scenario with setup cost of 20.00 per lot, having two production lots proves to be optimal. If the setup cost is doubled to 40.00, the optimum shifts to 1 lot. If the interest rate is increased to 10%, the optimum (not shown in Fig. 5.5) shifts back to 2 lots per year.

Higher setup cost in proportion to proportional product cost argues for a small number of lots, while the interest costs associated with larger inventories argue for a larger number of lots (see Sect. 4.4.3). Production management should make use of a model such as this for annual planning and the determination of lot sizes, as considerable cost savings are possible.

5.1.4 Release of Orders and Notification of Completion

During the execution of a released production order, the material items drawn from inventory as well as the performances executed in the single processes must be recorded for each step. For production scheduling, it should be possible to track where the order currently is in the process flow, whether delays can be foreseen, how much material was really consumed, how much work was consumed for the individual work plan items and, finally, how many good units were delivered to the warehouse.

In order to do this for each work plan position the following data must be entered in the system:

- Production order number
- Workplan position
- Start and end date per position

Lot sizes, setup cost and interest

Standard-prop.cost /unit without setup	2.00
Prop. setup cost/lot	20.00
Interest rate p.a.	5%

Production volume p.a.	1,200	1,200	1,200	1,200	1,200	1,200
Number ot lots p.a	1	2	3	4	5	6
Inventory entry per lot	1,200	600	400	300	240	200
Monthly sales quantity	-100	-100	-100	-100	-100	-100
Total setup cost	20	40	60	80	100	120
Setup cost / unit	0.0167	0.0333	0.0500	0.0667	0.0833	0.1000
Average inventory in units	550	250	150	100	70	50
Average inventory value incl. setup	1,120	540	360	280	240	220
Interest p.a.	56.00	27.00	18.00	14.00	12.00	11.00
Sum setup cost plus interest	76.00	67.00	78.00	94.00	112.00	131.00
Sum setup cost plus interest per unit	0.0633	0.0558	0.0650	0.0783	0.0933	0.1092

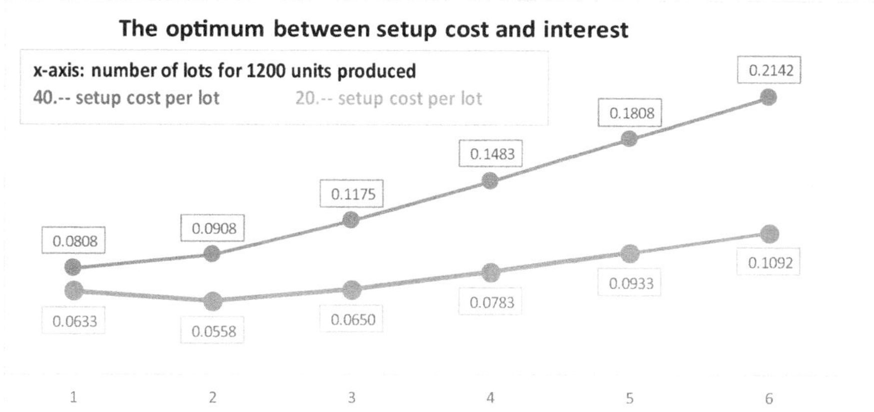

Fig. 5.5 The optimum between setup and interest costs

- Actual time or RFU consumption
- Actual material procurement from stock, item number, quantity, date, possibly also return deliveries of surplus material or subsequent consumptions

The data in Fig. 5.6 is transferred to the production department to start the production order.

These are the general specifications for the production order as well as the order-specific BOM and work plan. All data elements already defined in the annual planning can be transferred automatically. Any market-specific adjustment of the order quantity (see Sect. 5.1.1) is also reflected. This is the same data required for pre-calculation.

Pordernr.	Year	Month	Itemnr	Dispatched lot
90	2011	3	101060	10,800

Order-specific bill of materials

Pordernr.	Itemnr	Month	Input quantity	Input-itemnr	Description	Preset quantity /unit	Precalculated withdrawal from inventory
90	101060	3	10,860	32	4.0 cm-envelope	1.0000	10,860
90	101060	3	10,860	23	4-Ring-mechanism 4cm	1.0000	10,860
90	101060	3	10,860	2	Film	0.4400	4,778

Order-specific work plan

Pordernr.	Itemnr	Month	Dispatched lot	CCnr serving	description	Setup time / lot	Allowed time/unit
90	101060	3	10,800	250	Assembly	120	1.0000
90	101060	3	10,800	260	Film welding	20	1.0000

Fig. 5.6 Data template for manufacturing

As production progresses, real consumption and performance must be recorded:

- Actual consumption by material item (which can include several entry items if subsequent procurements or return deliveries of input material become necessary). This recording is carried out by means of material procurement slips, so that there is a document available for the tracking of stock levels. The data is entered in the sheet "Actualmaterial."
- Activity performed by the processing cost center per work plan item. This takes place in the sheet "Actualprodtime". If possible the respective data is acquired with a Factory Data Collection (FDC) system.
- Number of good units delivered to stock. Several entries are also possible here, since the finished parts of a production order can go to stock in several deliveries (depending on the capacity of the transport containers or on the necessity to know the stock of the good parts at any time up to date). Partial completion notifications also mean that the stock of goods in production WIP can be reduced promptly and, at the same time, inventories can be increased, which is particularly important for the annual financial statements. Entry is made in sheet "Completemessages."
- In the sheet "Completemessages" it is necessary to specify whether it is a partial (t) or complete (k) completion of the order. Only when the order is finished completely it can be deleted from WIP and open production orders.

The actual data as in Fig. 5.7 is entered for production order 90.

In this example, the standard quantities and times from the pre-calculation were transferred as actual quantities and actual activities. This means that the order was produced exactly as planned. If procurements, activities, and quantities deviate from

Actual material consumption

Pordernr.	Itemnr	Year	Month	Input item	Quantity consumed
90	32	2011	3	4.0 cm-envelope	10,860
90	23	2011	3	4-Ring-mechanism 4cm	10,860
90	2	2011	3	Film	4,778

Actual performance of cost centers

Pordernr.		Year	Month	CCnr serving	Acutal consumption
90		2011	3	250	10,920
90		2011	3	260	10,820

Good units produced

Pordernr.	Year	Month	t or k	Quantity delivered
90	2011	3	t	6,000
90	2011	3	k	4,800

t = partially finished
k = completely finished

Fig. 5.7 Actual data for posting and analyzing production order 90

pre-calculation, variances arise that are discussed in the section on the target to actual comparison (Sect. 6.1):

- Actual quantity of material results in a material quantity variance
- Actual consumption of cost center activity results in a working time variance
- Good units delivered to stock results in a yield variance

5.1.5 Cost Center Performance

With the preparation of the production order data, the actual services of the cost centers directly involved in the production process (CCnr 220–260) are also recorded. The sheet "Actualprodtime" contains the target times and the actual times performed for each work plan position. For the assembly cost center alone, this amounts to more than 170 records per year. To stay manageable the individual transaction data per month are summarized in Fig. 5.8. The actual activity and the activity level of the cost center are shown.

To keep the simulation model accessible the seized number of variances has been kept small. With one exception the confirmed actual times correspond to the standard times. The exception concerns production order 112 for item 101090. The tolerances were not observed due to the incorrect setting of the assembly equipment. Therefore, the order had to be restarted after 1000 units. This led to a corresponding replenishment of direct material and semi-finished goods as well as to 1000 extra-minutes in assembly. The value-related consequences of this "false start" are quantified in the section on the target/actual comparison (Sect. 6.1).

5.1.5.1 Downtimes in Production

Machines and equipment sometimes are not available for production due to maintenance or repair work. During the time required for this, the employees do not work

Planned and actual activity of cost center assembly 2011

Serving CC	Month	Actual time factory data	Planned activity	Activity level
250	1	141,995	118,516	119.8%
250	2	126,310	118,516	106.6%
250	3	115,325	118,516	97.3%
250	4	133,530	118,516	112.7%
250	5	104,895	118,516	88.5%
250	6	133,215	118,516	112.4%
250	7	-		0.0%
250	8	144,990	118,516	122.3%
250	9	96,370	118,516	81.3%
250	10	147,365	118,516	124.3%
250	11	100,314	118,516	84.6%
250	12	109,703	118,516	92.6%
		1,354,016	1,303,679	103.9%

Fig. 5.8 Determination of the actual activity level based on completed manufacturing orders

on production orders but on the performance readiness of the cost center. Although time is consumed, there is no cost center activity. These standstill times were planned in cost center planning (sheet "Costcenterplan"). During work, however, they should be measured and commented on per incident in the respective cost center by means of the Factory Data Collection (FDC) system. The reduction of downtimes should be pursued in the cost centers because by doing so manufacturing efficiency can be increased and total costs can be lowered.

5.1.5.2 Internal Services Provided (ISP)

According to the definition given in Sect. 4.5.5, a genuine internal exchange of services exists if:

- The service recipient can decide whether and how much service it wants to receive from the servicing cost center, or
- It is automatic that the activity input is dependent on the actual activity level of the receiving cost center, and
- The performing cost center must plan proportional costs directly caused by the performed activity.

In the example, the cost centers Personnel Pool (245), Maintenance and Repairs (330), Energy Center (340), and IT (300) perform such activities to be charged with their proportional planned cost rate to the receiving cost centers. These services must be gathered monthly for each receiving cost center on an accrual basis.

Figure 5.9 contains all services rendered by ISP cost centers for assembly (CCnr 250) aggregated by month. In the specific application, it is important that the service providers note the work they have performed in a comment column for each entry. The beneficiary must in fact be able to intervene, if he considers that the hours

Year	Month	CCnr serving	Description	RFU	Activity type	Description	CCnr receiving	Description	Actual delivery from serving CC
2011	1	245	Personnel pool 240-260	Pmin	23	Personnel pool services	250	Assembly	141,995
2011	2	245	Personnel pool 240-260	Pmin	23	Personnel pool services	250	Assembly	126,310
2011	3	245	Personnel pool 240-260	Pmin	23	Personnel pool services	250	Assembly	115,325
2011	4	245	Personnel pool 240-260	Pmin	23	Personnel pool services	250	Assembly	133,530
2011	5	245	Personnel pool 240-260	Pmin	23	Personnel pool services	250	Assembly	104,895
2011	6	245	Personnel pool 240-260	Pmin	23	Personnel pool services	250	Assembly	133,215
2011	8	245	Personnel pool 240-260	Pmin	23	Personnel pool services	250	Assembly	144,990
2011	9	245	Personnel pool 240-260	Pmin	23	Personnel pool services	250	Assembly	96,370
2011	10	245	Personnel pool 240-260	Pmin	23	Personnel pool services	250	Assembly	147,365
2011	11	245	Personnel pool 240-260	Pmin	23	Personnel pool services	250	Assembly	100,314
2011	12	245	Personnel pool 240-260	Pmin	23	Personnel pool services	250	Assembly	109,703
2011	1	330	Repair center	Phours	22	Maintenance & repair services	250	Assembly	28
2011	2	330	Repair center	Phours	22	Maintenance & repair services	250	Assembly	28
2011	3	330	Repair center	Phours	22	Maintenance & repair services	250	Assembly	28
2011	4	330	Repair center	Phours	22	Maintenance & repair services	250	Assembly	28
2011	5	330	Repair center	Phours	22	Maintenance & repair services	250	Assembly	28
2011	6	330	Repair center	Phours	22	Maintenance & repair services	250	Assembly	28
2011	8	330	Repair center	Phours	22	Maintenance & repair services	250	Assembly	28
2011	9	330	Repair center	Phours	22	Maintenance & repair services	250	Assembly	28
2011	10	330	Repair center	Phours	22	Maintenance & repair services	250	Assembly	28
2011	11	330	Repair center	Phours	22	Maintenance & repair services	250	Assembly	28
2011	12	330	Repair center	Phours	22	Maintenance & repair services	250	Assembly	28
2011	1	340	Energy center	kWh	21	internal energy consumption	250	Assembly	4,794
2011	2	340	Energy center	kWh	21	internal energy consumption	250	Assembly	4,292
2011	3	340	Energy center	kWh	21	internal energy consumption	250	Assembly	3,940
2011	4	340	Energy center	kWh	21	internal energy consumption	250	Assembly	4,523
2011	5	340	Energy center	kWh	21	internal energy consumption	250	Assembly	3,607
2011	6	340	Energy center	kWh	21	internal energy consumption	250	Assembly	4,513
2011	7	340	Energy center	kWh	21	internal energy consumption	250	Assembly	250
2011	8	340	Energy center	kWh	21	internal energy consumption	250	Assembly	4,890
2011	9	340	Energy center	kWh	21	internal energy consumption	250	Assembly	3,334
2011	10	340	Energy center	kWh	21	internal energy consumption	250	Assembly	4,966
2011	11	340	Energy center	kWh	21	internal energy consumption	250	Assembly	3,460
2011	12	340	Energy center	kWh	21	internal energy consumption	250	Assembly	3,761

Fig. 5.9 List of internal services performed for the assembly cost center in 2011

reported do not correspond to reality or that there was no reason to provide this service.

There are two ways to measure the performance of the Personnel Pool:

- The activity received is calculated based on the specifications in the annual plan (actual activity of the receiving cost center (250) × personnel multiplier (activity-dependent), see sheet "ISPplan").
- An existing electronic FDC enables the transfer of the working times recorded by the individual employees of the pool to the assembly cost center.

In both cases, an explanatory comment is not necessary, since the mechanism has already been defined in cost center planning. However, because the example company has not yet set up an automated FDC, the actual times provided by the personnel pool are determined depending on the actual activities of the receiving cost centers (for details, see sheet "ActualISP").

In most companies there are no instruments for measuring actual energy consumption installed directly on the machines. The energy costs can then only be charged to the individual cost centers using the technical determination of the electricity consumption per operating hour. The necessary consumption data for each receiving cost center were also stored in the sheet "ISPplan." The related kWh can be found in the second last column of Fig. 4.30.

The hours spent on maintenance and repairs were recorded manually and transferred to the sheet "ActualISP." The same applies to the ISP of the IT cost center for the projects.

5.1.5.3 Time Consumption for Internal Tasks

In many companies the proportion of working time for internal tasks of the total hours worked is steadily increasing for a variety of reasons (see Sect. 4.5.5). An instrument to control this development, and thereby achieve a better cost position in comparison to the competition, is the recording and analysis of the time required to carry out internal tasks. For this purpose, the most important groups of internal tasks are defined and assigned an activity type number for easier entry. Practice shows that in medium-sized companies 10–20 activity types are enough to make the essential positions of internal tasks comparable across cost centers.

During planning, cost center managers are asked to estimate, together with their employees, how many hours per year they work in the various activity types. This estimate should not be based on the planned presence time of a year (net hours available per year and employee, see Sect. 4.5.2) but should record the hourly consumption based on an activity analysis (Fig. 5.10).

The verification of these estimates should also be possible via performance data recording (FDC) in the area of internal tasks. In 2011, however, an FDC could not yet be introduced due to other projects considered more urgent. In the absence of actual data, the planned times for 2011 are also regarded as actual times for 2011 and analyzed later.

The importance of this analysis becomes apparent when the personnel structure of the sample company is viewed (see sheet "Costcenterplan"):

- Planned full-time positions 2011: 55.2

Year	CCnr	Description	Ativity type		Actual min. / hours
2011	200	Plant mgmt. & work scheduling	7	give IT-support	300
2011	200	Plant mgmt. & work scheduling	20	other non product linked tasks	200
2011	200	Plant mgmt. & work scheduling	1	plan, organize, manage, care	1,700
2011	200	Plant mgmt. & work scheduling	4	Education (further and on the job)	200
2011	200	Plant mgmt. & work scheduling	6	administrative tasks	1,000
					3,400

Fig. 5.10 Recording the actual working hours of the plant management cost center (all internal tasks)

- Those working directly on production orders: 28.2
- 27 (55.2 − 28.2) people work on internal tasks, which corresponds to about 49% of the total working time.

The fact that the proportion of employees working directly on the product is often less than 50% of the total workforce is partly due to the fact that automation in the production areas is constantly advancing. This development is often noticeable in both production and service companies, both large and small.

In many places, it is required that the recording of presence time be extended to all employees, including management personnel and so-called knowledge workers, to correctly account for overtime and vacation credits and to avoid burnout cases. From the point of view of integral management, however, it is more important that knowledge workers record the hours they worked on various tasks.

5.2 Actual Cost

Utilizing pre- and post-calculation of production orders, by charging for the proportional cost of internal services a significant part of period costs has already arrived at their appropriate destination, be it the warehouse, the orders, or the cost centers. Still missing are the costts that are directly addressable to the cost centers. They also must be integrated into the overall system.

The necessary data is provided by the following systems:

- Materials management including ordering, purchasing, and inventory management
- Accounts payable accounting with all external invoices for goods and services and the associated payment process
- Payroll accounting including accounting for social insurance programs
- Asset accounting with investments and imputed depreciation
- Internal cost clearances between cost centers (reassigned primary costs)

This is about recording primary costs. They are assigned either to the manufactured items or to the cost centers and projects according to the principle of direct cost recording (see Sect. 4.7.1).

5.2.1 Actual Primary Costs

In Sect. 4.7.2 primary costs were defined as consumptions of factors that originate outside the company. They are first recorded based on the invoices in one of the accounting systems listed above (with the invoice receipt still without cost effect) and only become costs (factor consumption) when they are withdrawn from the warehouse, consumed from the workforce, or utilize the asset inventory. It is to be specified (account assignment), whether the consumption is for a production order, a

Year	CCnr	Month	Description	Cost type	Description	Actual primary cost
2011	250	1	Assembly	5	Office supplies	73
2011	250	1	Assembly	6	Auxiliary and operating materials	733
2011	250	1	Assembly	12	External maintenance & repair	2,617
2011	250	1	Assembly	13	Other expense, non-activated project costs	1,000
2011	250	1	Assembly	31	Imputed depreciation	1,333
						5,757

Fig. 5.11 Primary assembly costs in January (CC 250)

Year	CCnr	Month	Description	Cost type	Description	Actual primary costs
2011	100	1	Sales mgmt. &	1	Personnel costs	35562
2011	100	1	Sales mgmt. &	4	Advertisement	2500
2011	100	1	Sales mgmt. &	5	Office supplies	300
2011	100	1	Sales mgmt. &	6	Auxiliary and operating materials	207
2011	100	1	Sales mgmt. &	7	Telephone, communication	1,200
2011	100	1	Sales mgmt. &	12	External maintenance & repair	300
2011	100	1	Sales mgmt. &	13	Other expense, non-activated project costs	950
2011	100	1	Sales mgmt. &	31	Imputed depreciation	1,000
						42,019

Fig. 5.12 Primary costs of sales management and its office in January

project, or a cost center. This specification leads to the assignment of the costs to their primary consumer (product, project, cost center).

From a management perspective, and to take responsibility for costs incurred, it is of fundamental importance that each primary cost item be assigned to the point where it can be clearly addressed as a **direct cost** (Sect. 4.7.1). A high quality of account assignment is critical to the accuracy of the management accounting system.

In the simple case, such as for the Assembly cost center, there are only five primary cost types that the cost center manager must have "under control" because he is also responsible for their consumption (except for the month of January) (Fig. 5.11).

If a cost center receives more external inputs of different types, the number of cost types for which the cost center manager is responsible also increases (as in the case below for the head of sales management and the sales office) (Fig. 5.12).

In the examples, only the totals per cost type and month are entered. In practice, the responsible manager must be able to access any cost document or voucher. This is important because it is only on the individual document that he can see for which external services the bill was written (proof of actual costs). All primary cost items recorded in the year under review can be found in the sheet "Actualprimarycosts."

Year	Receiving CC	Month	Description receiver	Sender	Cost type	Description	Personnel multiplier (Pmin/unit)	Actual activity	Planned presence rate	Primary cost charged
2011	231	1	Wire rolling	232	40	Internal clearing (personnel for other CC)	0.0375	457000	0.8112	13,902
2011	231	2	Wire rolling	232	40	Internal clearing (personnel for other CC)	0.0375	457000	0.8112	13,902
2011	231	3	Wire rolling	232	40	Internal clearing (personnel for other CC)	0.0375	457000	0.8112	13,902
2011	231	4	Wire rolling	232	40	Internal clearing (personnel for other CC)	0.0375	457000	0.8112	13,902
2011	231	5	Wire rolling	232	40	Internal clearing (personnel for other CC)	0.0375	467900	0.8112	14,233
2011	231	6	Wire rolling	232	40	Internal clearing (personnel for other CC)	0.0375	467900	0.8112	14,233
2011	231	7	Wire rolling	232	40	Internal clearing (personnel for other CC)	0.0375	0	0.8112	-
2011	231	8	Wire rolling	232	40	Internal clearing (personnel for other CC)	0.0375	467900	0.8112	14,233
2011	231	9	Wire rolling	232	40	Internal clearing (personnel for other CC)	0.0375	480200	0.8112	14,607
2011	231	10	Wire rolling	232	40	Internal clearing (personnel for other CC)	0.0375	480200	0.8112	14,607
2011	231	11	Wire rolling	232	40	Internal clearing (personnel for other CC)	0.0375	491100	0.8112	14,939
2011	231	12	Wire rolling	232	40	Internal clearing (personnel for other CC)	0.0375	457000	0.8112	13,902
										156,362

Fig. 5.13 Internal clearings between cost centers 232 and 231 in 2011

5.2.2 Actual Internal Clearance

The loading of the automatic wire rolling machines as well as the monitoring of the efficient functioning of the machines in cost center (CC) 231 is conducted by employees of CC 232. Therefore, as described in Sect. 4.7.5, an internal clearing based on the personnel minutes worked for 231 is necessary (although cost responsibility remains with the manager of CC 232). The procurement of personnel performance depends on the actual production in CC 231. Therefore, only the corresponding personnel cost is to be passed from CC 232 to CC 231, not the planned cost-center-rate. Since there is no electronic PDC, the actual activity of CC 231 is multiplied by the personnel multiplier and the presence rate per minute of CC 232. Possible further internal billings were described in Sect. 4.7.5 but in this example there are no other settlements of this type (Fig. 5.13).

5.2.3 Actual Cost of Internal Services

The internal services provided are only charged to the receivers at the planned proportional cost rate (as described in Fig. 5.1, Sect. 5.1.5.2). The actual cost is calculated by multiplying the proportional plan cost rate by the amount of services actually consumed in a month. The instrument to measure the actual performances is again the PDC. These are the kWh according to the technical specifications and the worked hours of the other ISP-Cost centers. The costs charged monthly as ISPs can be found in the last column of Fig. 5.6. Due to the large number of ISP positions, only the loads for the receiving cost center 250 are shown (Fig. 5.14).

Description	RFU	Activity type	Description	CCnr receiving	Description	Actual delivery from serving CC	Prop. cost-rate	ISP charged to receiving CC
Personnel pool 240-260	Pmin	23	Personnel pool services	250	Assembly	141,995	0.7580	107,632
Personnel pool 240-260	Pmin	23	Personnel pool services	250	Assembly	126,310	0.7580	95,742
Personnel pool 240-260	Pmin	23	Personnel pool services	250	Assembly	115,325	0.7580	87,416
Personnel pool 240-260	Pmin	23	Personnel pool services	250	Assembly	133,530	0.7580	101,215
Personnel pool 240-260	Pmin	23	Personnel pool services	250	Assembly	104,895	0.7580	79,510
Personnel pool 240-260	Pmin	23	Personnel pool services	250	Assembly	133,215	0.7580	100,976
Personnel pool 240-260	Pmin	23	Personnel pool services	250	Assembly	144,990	0.7580	109,902
Personnel pool 240-260	Pmin	23	Personnel pool services	250	Assembly	96,370	0.7580	73,048
Personnel pool 240-260	Pmin	23	Personnel pool services	250	Assembly	147,365	0.7580	111,702
Personnel pool 240-260	Pmin	23	Personnel pool services	250	Assembly	100,314	0.7580	76,038
Personnel pool 240-260	Pmin	23	Personnel pool services	250	Assembly	109,703	0.7580	83,154
Repair center	Phours	22	Maintenance & repair services	250	Assembly	28	38.9488	1,091
Repair center	Phours	22	Maintenance & repair services	250	Assembly	28	38.9488	1,091
Repair center	Phours	22	Maintenance & repair services	250	Assembly	28	38.9488	1,091
Repair center	Phours	22	Maintenance & repair services	250	Assembly	28	38.9488	1,091
Repair center	Phours	22	Maintenance & repair services	250	Assembly	28	38.9488	1,091
Repair center	Phours	22	Maintenance & repair services	250	Assembly	28	38.9488	1,091
Repair center	Phours	22	Maintenance & repair services	250	Assembly	28	38.9488	1,091
Repair center	Phours	22	Maintenance & repair services	250	Assembly	28	38.9488	1,091
Repair center	Phours	22	Maintenance & repair services	250	Assembly	28	38.9488	1,091
Repair center	Phours	22	Maintenance & repair services	250	Assembly	28	38.9488	1,091
Repair center	Phours	22	Maintenance & repair services	250	Assembly	28	38.9488	1,091
Energy center	kWh	21	internal energy consumption	250	Assembly	4,794	0.2000	959
Energy center	kWh	21	internal energy consumption	250	Assembly	4,292	0.2000	858
Energy center	kWh	21	internal energy consumption	250	Assembly	3,940	0.2000	788
Energy center	kWh	21	internal energy consumption	250	Assembly	4,523	0.2000	905
Energy center	kWh	21	internal energy consumption	250	Assembly	3,607	0.2000	721
Energy center	kWh	21	internal energy consumption	250	Assembly	4,513	0.2000	903
Energy center	kWh	21	internal energy consumption	250	Assembly	250	0.2000	50
Energy center	kWh	21	internal energy consumption	250	Assembly	4,890	0.2000	978
Energy center	kWh	21	internal energy consumption	250	Assembly	3,334	0.2000	667
Energy center	kWh	21	internal energy consumption	250	Assembly	4,966	0.2000	993
Energy center	kWh	21	internal energy consumption	250	Assembly	3,460	0.2000	692
Energy center	kWh	21	internal energy consumption	250	Assembly	3,761	0.2000	752
								1,047,597

Fig. 5.14 Monthly ISP's charged to the assembly cost center (250)

5.3 Actual Inventories

Inventory management functions the same way for all types of inventory, i.e., for raw materials, merchandise, semi-finished and finished goods. Figure 5.15 gives an overview of the aggregated inventory intakes and outflows in actual quantities for 2011.

From left to right, the columns provide an overview of how physical stocks were built up and reduced by purchasing, production (basis is production orders), and sales (based on deliveries and billing documents). The last column shows the change in quantity compared to the opening inventory. The details are explained in the following subsections.

Year	Itemnr	Description	Opening inventory = ending prev. year	Goods inwards from procurement	Goods outwards to production	Goods inwards from production	Goods outwards to sales	Outwards to projects	Final inventory	Change - = reduction
2011	1	Cardboard	40,000	350,000	355,218	-	-	-	34,782	-5,218
2011	2	Film	50,000	440,000	443,716	-	-	-	46,284	-3,716
2011	3	Wire	2,000,000	94,500,000	95,726,000	-	-	-	774,000	-1,226,000
2011	4	Sheet metal	10,000	25,000	24,958	-	-	-	10,042	42
2011	5	Consumables (Set)	200,000	2,020,000	2,196,320	-	-	200	23,480	-176,520
2011	6	Welding consumables (Set)	80,000	670,000	718,540	-	-	-	31,460	-48,540
2011	11	Base plate 4Ring	90,000	-	874,200	816,200	-	-	32,000	-58,000
2011	12	Base plate 2Ring	110,000	-	894,600	881,100	-	-	96,500	-13,500
2011	13	7.5 cm-brackets	120,000	-	3,433,000	3,345,400	-	-	32,400	-87,600
2011	14	4.0 cm-brackets	75,000	-	1,853,000	1,793,700	-	-	15,700	-59,300
2011	21	4-Ring-mechanism 7.5	30,000	-	489,070	499,000	-	200	39,730	9,730
2011	22	2-Ring-mechanism 7.5	30,000	-	725,650	718,500	-	-	22,850	-7,150
2011	23	4-Ring-mechanism 4cm	30,000	-	382,760	375,200	-	100	22,340	-7,660
2011	24	2-Ring-mechanism 4 cm	30,000	-	186,310	176,100	-	200	19,590	-10,410
2011	31	7.5 cm-envelope	100,000	-	973,160	924,000	-	200	50,640	-49,360
2011	32	4.0 cm-envelope	50,000	-	569,070	553,800	-	200	34,530	-15,470
2011	101010	4ring 7.5 back glued	4,000	-	-	53,800	49,000	-	8,800	4,800
2011	101020	4ring 4 cm back glued	4,000	-	-	96,800	94,000	-	6,800	2,800
2011	101030	4 ring 7.5 back welded	5,000	-	-	28,500	30,000	-	3,500	-1,500
2011	101040	4ring 4 cm back welded	4,000	-	-	66,500	59,400	-	11,100	7,100
2011	101050	4ring 7.5 plasticized	4,000	-	-	36,000	37,000	-	3,000	-1,000
2011	101060	4ring 4 cm plasticized	4,000	-	-	98,800	85,600	-	17,200	13,200
2011	101070	4 ring 7.5 plasticized	6,000	-	-	130,000	119,000	-	17,000	11,000
2011	101080	4ring 4 cm plasticized	2,000	-	-	6,300	2,400	-	5,900	3,900
2011	101090	4ring 7.5 special design	-	-	-	113,350	113,250	-	100	100
2011	101100	4ring 4 cm special design	-	-	-	82,100	82,000	-	100	100
2011	101110	4ring 7.5 special design	-	-	-	7,500	7,400	-	100	100
2011	101120	4ring 4 cm special design	-	-	-	30,200	20,800	-	9,400	9,400
2011	103000	2ring special format A5 7.5	8,000	-	-	124,300	116,300	-	16,000	8,000
2011	104000	4ring special format A3 7.5	7,000	-	-	116,600	110,300	-	13,300	6,300
2011	105010	2ring 7.5 back glued	10,000	-	-	149,800	126,500	-	33,300	23,300
2011	105020	2ring 4 cm back glued	11,000	-	-	78,000	85,000	-	4,000	-7,000
2011	105030	2ring 7.5 back welded	7,500	-	-	70,800	75,000	-	3,300	-4,200
2011	105040	2ring 4 cm back welded	1,200	-	-	6,500	7,000	-	700	-500
2011	105050	2ring 7.5 plasticized	8,000	-	-	99,600	102,600	-	5,000	-3,000
2011	105060	2ring 4 cm plasticized	5,000	-	-	11,600	15,400	-	1,200	-3,800
2011	105070	2ring 7.5 plasticized	3,500	-	-	18,000	20,300	-	1,200	-2,300
2011	105080	2ring 4 cm plasticized	4,000	-	-	27,000	31,000	-	-	-4,000
2011	105090	2ring 7.5 special design	-	-	-	88,010	87,900	-	110	110
2011	105100	2ring 4 cm special design	-	-	-	5,500	5,400	-	100	100
2011	105110	2ring 7.5 special design	-	-	-	156,700	156,400	-	300	300
2011	105120	2ring 4 cm special design	-	-	-	54,070	53,800	-	270	270
2011	120010	Index A-Z	120	6,000	-	-	5,770	-	350	230
2011	120020	Index A-Z	120	1,900	-	-	1,780	-	240	120
2011	120030	Index 1-31	100	1,400	-	-	1,220	-	280	180
2011	120040	Index 1-31	100	2,900	-	-	2,770	-	230	130
2011	120050	Transparent envelopes	200	1,470	-	-	1,430	-	240	40
2011	120060	Transparent envelopes	200	2,600	-	-	2,030	-	770	570
2011	120070	Transparent envelopes	200	1,400	-	-	1,190	-	410	210
2011	120080	Follow-up file 1-31	80	1,800	-	-	1,710	-	170	90
2011	120090	Follow-up file A-Z	80	1,450	-	-	1,310	-	220	140
2011	120100	Follow-up file 1-31	80	1,200	-	-	1,090	-	190	110
2011	120110	Follow-up file A-Z	80	1,900	-	-	1,640	-	340	260
2011	120200	Archive boxes	2,800	5,000	-	-	5,700	-	2,100	-700

Fig. 5.15 Actual inventory changes—annual view for 2011

5.3.1 Actual Purchases

In the management-oriented planning and control system, all inventories are always valued at planned standard prices or costs. In Purchasing, it is thus possible to see which variances have arisen in relation to the planned purchase prices. The disclosure of price variances enables several findings to be made:

Year	Itemnr	Description	QU	PR#	Standard purchase price	Month	Quantity bought	Actual price	Purchase value at standard	Purchase price variance
Raw material and merchandise										
2011	120080	Follow-up file 1-31	unit	6	24.60	7	450	25.6000	11,520.00	-450.00
2011	120090	Follow-up file A-Z	unit	6	24.60	7	300	25.6000	7,680.00	-300.00
2011	120100	Follow-up file 1-31	unit	6	24.60	7	300	25.6000	7,680.00	-300.00
2011	120110	Follow-up file A-Z	unit	6	24.60	7	400	25.6000	10,240.00	-400.00
2011	120080	Follow-up file 1-31	unit	6	24.60	10	450	25.6000	11,520.00	-450.00
2011	120090	Follow-up file A-Z	unit	6	24.60	10	300	25.6000	7,680.00	-300.00
2011	120100	Follow-up file 1-31	unit	6	24.60	10	300	25.6000	7,680.00	-300.00
2011	120110	Follow-up file A-Z	unit	6	24.60	10	400	25.6000	10,240.00	-400.00
2011	120200	Archive boxes	unit	6	0.70	10	1,500	0.7200	1,080.00	-30.00
2011	1	Cardboard	sqm	3	0.28	1	87,500	0.2600	22,750.00	1,750.00
2011	3	Wire	g	3	0.00	1	24,500,000	0.0019	46,550.00	2,450.00
2011	4	Sheet metal	sqm	3	2.00	1	6,250	1.8500	11,562.50	937.50
2011	1	Cardboard	sqm	3	0.28	4	87,500	0.2600	22,750.00	1,750.00
2011	4	Sheet metal	sqm	3	2.00	4	6,250	1.9500	12,187.50	312.50
2011	1	Cardboard	sqm	3	0.28	7	87,500	0.2600	22,750.00	1,750.00
2011	2	Film	runningm	3	0.20	7	110,000	0.2200	24,200.00	-2,200.00
2011	3	Wire	g	3	0.00	7	22,500,000	0.0021	47,250.00	-2,250.00
2011	4	Sheet metal	sqm	3	2.00	7	6,250	2.0500	12,812.50	-312.50
2011	1	Cardboard	sqm	3	0.28	10	87,500	0.2600	22,750.00	1,750.00
2011	2	Film	runningm	3	0.20	10	110,000	0.2200	24,200.00	-2,200.00
2011	3	Wire	g	3	0.00	10	22,500,000	0.0023	51,750.00	-6,750.00
2011	4	Sheet metal	sqm	3	2.00	10	6,250	2.2000	13,750.00	-1,250.00
			Total purchase price variances in contribution accounting and P&L							-7,192.50
			of which merchandise							-2,930.00
			of which raw material							-4,262.50

Fig. 5.16 Origin of purchase price variances in the actual year

- The information serves procurement agents in further negotiations.
- The price variances can be shown by period in the month of purchase, not consumption, resulting in recognition of the variances in profit and loss statements according to the period incurred.
- Purchasing management is responsible for the purchase price variances, so the amounts must also be displayed there.
- Production always gets raw materials at planned (standard) prices from the warehouse. Due to this, price variances do not distort the analysis of production variances (differentiation between price and quantity effects).
- The sales department also receives merchandise, semi-finished, and finished products at proportional standard costs since it is not responsible for variances in purchasing or in production.
- The procurement staff is the first to learn about higher or lower purchase prices. Hence, they are able to be the quickest to inform the sales force that (if the market situation permits) adjustments to the selling prices will be necessary (resulting in a gain of time).

Figure 5.16 contains only those purchases during the year for which purchase price variances have arisen (details can be found in the sheet "Actualpurchases"). The sum of all price variances shows that in 2011, total purchases were 7192.5 more expensive than planned. In contribution accounting 4262.5 of these were for raw materials and 2930 for merchandise. In the case of merchandise, it is possible to address the variance to the individual sales item. This is not the case for raw materials, since a purchased item is used for a variety of semi-finished and finished products. The total sum of price variances will also appear in the P&L statement as total material consumption of the year includes both the standard consumption and the variances.

5.3.2 Consumption of Raw Materials, Semi-finished and Finished Goods and Work in Progress

In the simulation model all inventory movements for the actual year are condensed into one monthly figure per item. This makes the table too extensive to be displayed here (see sheets "Actualstock" and "Actualstockmonth"). But the detailed table is important for control because it is necessary to ensure that the availability of the items required for production and sales is always guaranteed and that the safety stocks of those items with a small number of scheduled lots per year are maintained.

Figure 5.17 is the continuation of Fig. 5.15 in terms of value. It can be used for the actual year per item and in total as it contains:

- The total value of changes in inventories of raw materials, merchandise, semi-finished and finished goods for the purposes of preparing the balance sheet and income statement (see Fig. 5.18).
- Consumption values for raw materials and merchandise.
- The proportional standard product cost of sold and manufactured product units. This information is required for creating the contribution accounting and internal income statement.

Here too, inventories will be systematically valued at planned proportional product cost, since the variances are shown separately in Profitability Analysis and no fixed period costs are allocated to the cost of goods manufactured.

Work in Process (WIP)

The production orders not yet completed at the end of a period (such as the end of a year) form the stock of goods in production, WIP. All finished good pieces in the production order are delivered to the semi-finished or finished goods warehouse by means of a partial completion message (valued at planned proportional product costs). The costs of raw materials or semi-finished products that have already been procured, as well as the production activities previously performed for the order (valued at projected planned cost rates) remain on the production order that has not yet been completed. The variances that have occurred so far are also included in the accumulated order costs, as the full extent of the variances can only be determined once the order has been definitively concluded.

Year	Itemnr	Description	Values					
			Standard prop. cost / unit	End value at standard- cost	Value change inventory	Raw material & SG- con- sumption	Standard cost sold units	Standard cost produced units
2011	1	Cardboard	0.2800	9,739	-1,461	99,461		
2011	2	Film	0.2000	9,257	-743	88,743		
2011	3	Wire	0.0020	1,548	-2,452	191,452		
2011	4	Sheet metal	2.0000	20,084	84	49,916		
2011	5	Consumables (Set)	0.1000	2,348	-17,652	219,652		
2011	6	Welding consumables (Set)	0.0400	1,258	-1,942	28,742		
2011	11	Base plate 4Ring	0.2730	8,737	-15,837	-		222,860
2011	12	Base plate 2Ring	0.1474	14,228	-1,990	-		129,909
2011	13	7.5 cm-brackets	0.1151	3,729	-10,083	-		385,070
2011	14	4.0 cm-brackets	0.0935	1,468	-5,545	-		167,727
2011	21	4-Ring-mechanism 7.5	0.7335	29,140	7,137	-		365,998
2011	22	2-Ring-mechanism 7.5	0.3776	8,629	-2,700	-		271,340
2011	23	4-Ring-mechanism 4cm	0.6471	14,456	-4,957	-		242,785
2011	24	2-Ring-mechanism 4 cm	0.3345	6,552	-3,482	-		58,898
2011	31	7.5 cm-envelope	0.3599	18,228	-17,767	-		332,589
2011	32	4.0 cm-envelope	0.3181	10,984	-4,921	-		176,159
2011	101010	4ring 7.5 back glued	1.4219	12,513	6,825	-	69,672	76,497
2011	101020	4ring 4 cm back glued	1.2871	8,752	3,604	-	120,990	124,594
2011	101030	4 ring 7.5 back welded	1.4653	5,128	-2,198	-	43,958	41,760
2011	101040	4ring 4 cm back welded	1.3353	14,822	9,481	-	79,317	88,798
2011	101050	4ring 7.5 plasticized	2.2457	6,737	-2,246	-	83,090	80,844
2011	101060	4ring 4 cm plasticized	2.1157	36,390	27,927	-	181,105	209,033
2011	101070	4 ring 7.5 plasticized	2.2430	38,132	24,673	-	266,921	291,594
2011	101080	4ring 4 cm plasticized	2.2986	13,562	8,964	-	5,517	14,481
2011	101090	4ring 7.5 special design	2.2845	228	228	-	258,716	258,944
2011	101100	4ring 4 cm special design	1.9205	192	192	-	157,482	157,674
2011	101110	4ring 7.5 special design	2.0756	208	208	-	15,359	15,567
2011	101120	4ring 4 cm special design	1.9155	18,005	18,005	-	39,842	57,847
2011	103000	2ring special format A5 7.5	1.4117	22,587	11,293	-	164,177	175,470
2011	104000	4ring special format A3 7.5	3.2037	42,609	20,183	-	353,364	373,547
2011	105010	2ring 7.5 back glued	0.9802	32,640	22,838	-	123,993	146,831
2011	105020	2ring 4 cm back glued	0.8993	3,597	-6,295	-	76,439	70,144
2011	105030	2ring 7.5 back welded	1.0223	3,374	-4,294	-	76,673	72,379
2011	105040	2ring 4 cm back welded	1.0158	711	-508	-	7,110	6,602
2011	105050	2ring 7.5 plasticized	1.3278	6,639	-3,983	-	136,235	132,252
2011	105060	2ring 4 cm plasticized	1.2791	1,535	-4,860	-	19,698	14,837
2011	105070	2ring 7.5 plasticized	1.3521	1,622	-3,110	-	27,447	24,337
2011	105080	2ring 4 cm plasticized	1.2435	-	-4,974	-	38,548	33,574
2011	105090	2ring 7.5 special design	1.6942	186	186	-	148,920	149,107
2011	105100	2ring 4 cm special design	1.6386	164	164	-	8,848	9,012
2011	105110	2ring 7.5 special design	1.7010	510	510	-	266,039	266,549
2011	105120	2ring 4 cm special design	1.6517	446	446	-	88,859	89,305
2011	120010	Index A-Z	13.5000	4,725	3,105	77,895	77,895	-
2011	120020	Index A-Z	13.7000	3,288	1,644	24,386	24,386	-
2011	120030	Index 1-31	14.2000	3,976	2,556	17,324	17,324	-
2011	120040	Index 1-31	14.4000	3,312	1,872	39,888	39,888	-
2011	120050	Transparent envelopes	7.6000	1,824	304	10,868	10,868	-
2011	120060	Transparent envelopes	7.6000	5,852	4,332	15,428	15,428	-
2011	120070	Transparent envelopes	7.6000	3,116	1,596	9,044	9,044	-
2011	120080	Follow-up file 1-31	24.6000	4,182	2,214	42,066	42,066	-
2011	120090	Follow-up file A-Z	24.6000	5,412	3,444	32,226	32,226	-
2011	120100	Follow-up file 1-31	24.6000	4,674	2,706	26,814	26,814	-
2011	120110	Follow-up file A-Z	24.6000	8,364	6,396	40,344	40,344	-
2011	120200	Archive boxes	0.7000	1,470	-490	3,990	3,990	-
				481,871	68,630	1,018,239	3,198,592	5,334,915

Fig. 5.17 The values of inventory development

Fig. 5.18 Total inventory changes end of 2011

Inventory changes at prop. standard cost	
at planned purchase prices as per 12/31/2011	
Raw material	-24,166
Semi-finished goods	-60,145
Finished goods	123,262
Merchandise	29,679
Total	68,630

Year	Production order nr	Itemnr	Description	Month	Planned prod. p.a.	Planned lots p.a.	Planned per lot	Quantity adaption	Dispatched lot
2011	274	105010	2ring 7.5 back glued	12	139,800	6	23,300		23,300

Year	Production order nr	Itemnr	Description	Month	Planned lots p.a.	Input quantity	Input itemnr	Description	Preset quantity	Standard-prop. cost or purchase price	Precal-culated withdrawal from inventor
2011	274	105010	2ring 7.5 back glued	12	6	23,350	31	7.5 cm-envelope	1.0000	0.3599	23,350
2011	274	105010	2ring 7.5 back glued	12	6	23,350	22	2-Ring-mechanism 7.5	1.0000	0.3776	23,350

Fig. 5.19 Actual withdrawals of semifinished items for order 274 (WIP)

Proof of work in progress, order 274			Itemnr	**105010**
as per 12/31/2011			Lot size	23,330
			Partly complete message	10,000
Material received for order			Sheet "Actualmaterial"	17,222.80
	Minutes	Prop. rate		
Cost center activities (CC 250)	3,120	0.7898		2,464.16
	units	prop. rate		
Partly completion at year end	10,000	0.980182		-9,801.82
Value work in progress				9,885.14

Fig. 5.20 Proof of work in progress

In the simulation model, production order 274 was only partially completed at the end of the year.

23,300 pieces were ordered (sheet "Productionorders"). Of these, 10,000 had been completed by the end of 2011 and delivered to stock at the end of the year at the standard rate of 0.9802 (9802 in absolute terms) (indicator "*t*", see order 274 in the sheet "Completemessages") (Fig. 5.19).

At the end of the year all the raw material plus the semi-finished products to be used had already been purchased (envelopes and 2-ring mechanisms). The raw material for the remaining 13,300 units to be produced was stored in the production hall. In addition, the setup times and the scrap material for the entire order had already been consumed but were not included in the stock receipt (only 10,000 good items had been reported by then).

Figure 5.20 shows how the value of 9885 for WIP at year-end is calculated. This item will be reflected in the income statement and in the operating balance sheet as of

Sales order nr	Cust nr	Order date	Due date	Delivery date = billing date	Itemnr	Sales quantity	Month	Year	PG#	PR#	Cust group	Sales region	Sales chan-nel	Item dis-count	Invoice dis-count	List price	Gross revenue	Net sales / position
81	120	2011-03-28	2011-04-04	2011-04-04	105010	200	4	2011	1	2	1	201	1	14%	0%	3.60	720	619
81	120	2011-03-28	2011-04-04	2011-04-04	105010	300	4	2011	1	2	1	201	1	14%	0%	3.60	1,080	929
82	120	2011-03-31	2011-04-05	2011-04-05	101040	600	4	2011	2	2	1	201	1	14%	0%	3.50	2,100	1,806
82	120	2011-03-31	2011-04-05	2011-04-05	101040	600	4	2011	2	2	1	201	1	14%	0%	3.50	2,100	1,806
82	120	2011-03-31	2011-04-05	2011-04-05	120100	150	4	2011	7	6	1	201	1	10%	0%	39.60	5,940	5,346
83	390	2011-04-22	2011-04-30	2011-04-30	120040	500	4	2011	7	6	3	203	2	10%	5%	29.20	14,600	12,410
84	360	2011-04-07	2011-04-09	2011-04-10	105030	400	4	2011	1	2	5	201	2	0%	15%	3.80	1,520	1,292
87	390	2011-04-06	2011-04-18	2011-04-18	101050	2000	4	2011	2	2	3	203	2	14%	5%	4.40	8,800	7,128
87	390	2011-04-06	2011-04-18	2011-04-18	101070	1000	4	2011	2	2	3	203	2	14%	5%	4.40	4,400	3,564
89	330	2011-04-19	2011-04-19	2011-04-19	101080	500	4	2011	2	2	3	201	1	14%	5%	4.20	2,100	1,701
92	400	2011-04-01	2011-04-12	2011-04-20	105090	9000	4	2011	3	2	6	204	2	0%	28%	5.50	49,500	35,640
93	190	2011-04-20	2011-04-21	2011-04-21	105050	4000	4	2011	1	2	2	201	1	19%	5%	4.90	19,600	14,896
93	190	2011-04-20	2011-04-21	2011-04-21	120060	200	4	2011	7	6	2	201	1	14%	5%	14.40	2,880	2,333
94	300	2011-04-01	2011-04-20	2011-04-21	103000	8000	4	2011	5	2	4	202	2	10%	5%	6.80	54,400	46,240

Fig. 5.21 Extract from the file of invoiced items (sheet "Actualsales")

December 31, 2011. No unfinished orders are foreseen in the simulation model in subsequent years.

5.4 Actual Sales and Net Revenue

The data source for revenue determination is billing. Management wants to be able to analyze the sales achieved along various dimensions. Due to this multidimensionality the analysis must always start from the individual billing line (see Sect. 1.8). This is the only place where all information is available. Here in the text only a small section of the billings can be presented (see sheet "Actualsales" for all records).

The basic billing file is structured so that the analysis can answer the following questions:

- **For whom** (customer)?
- **By whom** (sales representative/sales area)?
- Via which **sales channel?**
- **When** (delivery date = billing date)?
- **What** (item)?
- From **which product group?**
- From **which assortment?**
- **How much** (quantity)?
- At which **price** (gross minus all discounts and deductions) bought? (Fig. 5.21)

Order date and delivery date are also saved in the table to assess adherence to delivery dates and the amount of processing time. The discounts granted (see Sect. 4.3.2) are taken from the sheets "Salesstructure" and "Itemdiscount" (salespersons cannot grant individual discounts).

Evaluation of the sales generated, based on the individual billing items, is of great value for sales management. The analysis generates information regarding:

- Customer profitability (identification of A, B, and C customers)

- Period view (identification of those months in which peak sales of the various items occur)
- Change in order sizes over time (number of items per order and change in average order quantities)
- Assessment of advertising effects (change in sales due to advertising or sales promotion efforts)
- Changes in sales quantities to assess strategy implementation.

5.5 Actual Result

As described for planning in Sect. 4.9, the realized revenues and costs are combined in the contribution account presentation. The transfer to the internal income statement and balance sheet is discussed in Sect. 6.4.

5.5.1 Contribution Margin I Realized

To prepare the contribution steps the actual CM I's are condensed by product group. The results for the month of December and for the whole year 2011 are shown in Fig. 5.22. The net revenues data was taken from the sheet "Actualsales." The standard proportional cost of the units sold came from the sheet "ActualCMitems."

Year	Month	PG#	Actual sales	Gross revenue actual	Net revenue actual	Standard prop. cost actual units	CM I standard actual units	Sales com-missions actual	CM I actual after com-mission
2011	12	1	33,000	148,200	114,564	39,962	74,602	1,492	73,110
2011	12	2	42500	170,800	127,660	79,385	48,275	965	47,309
2011	12	3	13500	74,250	61,540	22,810	38,729	775	37,955
2011	12	4	35600	199,360	155,602	78,654	76,948	1,539	75,409
2011	12	5	17000	115,600	86,496	23,998	62,498	1,250	61,248
2011	12	6	23200	157,760	136,476	74,325	62,151	1,243	60,908
2011	12	7	1,710	59,130	49,747	35,711	14,036	281	13,756
			166,510	925,100	732,084	354,845	377,239	7,545	369,694

Year	Month 1- ?	PG#	Actual sales	Gross revenue actual	Net revenue actual	Standard prop. cost actual units	CM I standard actual units	Sales com-missions actual	CM I actual after com-mission
2011	12	1	462800	1,870,250	1,500,219	506,143	994,076	19,882	974,194
2011	12	2	476400	1,810,700	1,424,775	850,570	574,205	11,484	562,721
2011	12	3	303500	1,669,250	1,362,900	512,666	850,234	17,005	833,229
2011	12	4	223450	1,251,320	983,150	471,399	511,751	10,235	501,516
2011	12	5	116300	790,840	644,694	164,177	480,517	9,610	470,907
2011	12	6	110300	750,040	638,928	353,364	285,564	5,711	279,853
2011	12	7	27640	606,148	495,490	340,273	155,217	3,104	152,113
			1,720,390	8,748,548	7,050,157	3,198,592	3,851,565	77,031	3,774,533

Fig. 5.22 CM I actual per product group for December and the whole year (sheet "ActualCMitems")

As in the planning process, the standard proportional product cost is deducted from net revenue; from the resulting CM I the 2% for sales commission is deducted.

CM I Actual after commissions thus shows how much a product group contributes to cover fixed costs and profit. All variances in purchasing, production, cost centers, and projects are not considered yet as they are not in the responsibility of the salespeople.

5.5.2 Actual Stepwise Contribution Accounting

Stepwise contribution accounting, shown in Fig. 5.23, starts with CM I after commissions. (Note that in that exhibit the two ranges "finished goods" and "merchandise" are condensed.) In subsequent contribution margin steps, only the fixed costs remaining in the cost centers are deducted. The contribution levels are created in the same structure as described in Sect. 4.9.1.

The presented actual EBIT is still too high because the variances from purchasing and production are not yet deducted. The final actual EBIT is calculated in Sect. 6.3.

	Productgroups / ranges	Total Ringbook Ltd.			Finished goods			Merchandise		
Year	2011	Plan	Actual	Variance	Plan	Actual	Variance	Plan	Actual	Variance
	CM I after commissions	3,668,723	3,774,533	105,810	3,541,841	3,622,421	80,579	126,882	152,113	25,231
	Fixed cost product ranges	311,730	310,524	1,206	158,640	159,381	-741	153,090	151,143	1,947
	Product range CM	3,356,993	3,464,009	107,016	3,383,201	3,463,039	79,838	-26,208	970	27,178
	Fixed cost sales organization	861,035	868,373	-7,338						
100	Sales mgmt. & office	543,082	550,530	-7,448						
151	Eastern Switzerland	120,113	120,076	37						
152	Western Switzerland	91,960	91,923	37						
153	Business clients (direct)	105,880	105,843	37						
	Sales CM	2,495,958	2,595,637	99,679						
	Fixed cost of production	995,112	982,329	12,783	995,112	982,329	12,783			
200	Plant mgmt. & work scheduling				210,965	216,421	-5,457			
220	Stamping				93,373	93,726	-353			
231	Wire rolling				31,565	26,734	4,831			
232	Wire bending & forming				281,795	280,876	919			
240	Cardboarding				61,316	60,555	761			
245	Personnelpool 240-260				241,346	241,686	-340			
250	Assembly				48,251	42,861	5,390			
260	Film welding				26,501	19,470	7,031			
	Other fixed cost	1,299,788	1,313,185	-13,397						
210	Procurement & warehouse	182,155	192,251	-10,097						
320	Buildings & maintenance	149,649	148,294	1,355						
330	Repair center	11,445	15,736	-4,291						
340	Energy center	27,278	16,617	10,661						
300	IT	269,825	265,505	4,320						
900	Corp. mgmt. & administration	659,437	674,782	-15,345						
	EBIT	201,058	294,374	93,316						

Fig. 5.23 Stepwise CM calculation plan and actual (still without variances)

Comparison of Plans and Targets to Actuals 6

In this chapter we "harvest." Chapters 4 and 5 were devoted to the annual planning process and the recording of real events. According to the management cycle (Sect. 1.2.1), the plan and actual data form the prerequisite for plan to actual and target to actual comparisons. These comparisons show variances, and these are intended to help responsible managers find, decide, and implement corrective actions so that they and thus the entire company can achieve their objectives despite any disruptions. This chapter is devoted to the determination and interpretation of such variances and the transfer of the results to the operating income statement and the operating balance sheet.

6.1 Production Orders and Purchasing

One of the results of the annual planning process was the determination of how many units are to be produced per item and in how many lots (if possible of the same size). Sections 5.1.1 through 5.1.4 described how production orders are developed starting from the plan and from more current sales expectations or from incoming orders. It was also pointed out that a firm production order can receive an adjusted BOM or an adjusted work plan (planning adjustments). As a result, the production order to be released for production must also be recalculated. The **pre-calculation** results in the target cost of the production order that could be achieved if production were to proceed optimally. As a result, variances can occur between the planned cost and the pre-calculation as well as between the pre-calculation and the **actual cost of the accomplished production order.** The various causes of variance should be quantified since they indicate where costs have been saved or exceeded.

Variances between planned and pre-calculated cost can result from:

(a) The lot size to be ordered differing from the planned lot size (larger or smaller orders) = **lot size variance**, and

L. Rieder, R. Lawson, *Management Control with Integrated Planning*, Management for Professionals, https://doi.org/10.1007/978-3-030-48302-9_6

(b) Capacity bottlenecks requiring an adjustment of the routings (production on other machines) and therefore possibly also the use of other materials (BOM) = **process or routing variance.**

Variances between pre-calculation and post-calculation can result from:

(c) Higher or lower actual material consumption than in the pre-calculation (setup work and/or scrap) = **material quantity variance**
(d) More or less activity consumption in the manufacturing cost centers during setup or production than in the pre-calculation = **working time variance**
(e) Short-term change of the machines/cost centers used *after* pre-calculation = **process or routing variance**, and
(f) Better or worse yield from the process (= more or less good units delivered to stock than in the pre-calculation) = **yield variance**.

Regarding a:

Of the 274 production orders in the example, the approved batch size deviated from the planned batch size in 50 cases (see sheet "Completemessages"). Of these, smaller actual lot sizes than the planned lot sizes were released in 12 cases, which led to lot size variances of –331 (too little setup and scrap cost charged to stock). Because of sales growth in the year under review, the actual lot size was increased in 38 cases compared to plan, which enabled a total of 3567 savings in setup/scrap cost. Adjustment of the released lots to the actual demand thus led to savings of 3236 in total (see sheet "Completemessages", column "lot size variances"). Whether these cost savings were factually realized can only be assessed after analyzing all other variances.

Note: The total 3263 positive lot size variance (in Fig. 6.3) would finance an additional stock of 65,260 for 1 year at 5% imputed interest (3263 × 5% * 100). Figure 5.18 shows that total stocks had risen by around 68,600 by the end of 2011. Sales growth led to larger batches, which enabled the positive lot size variances. These almost covered the interest cost of the higher inventory.

Regarding b:

Since no substitute cost centers have been included in the model that could take over a processing order for another cost center, there can be no process variances. Should process deviations occur in the real world, the production planning department or production management is responsible for this. By adapting the production orders to be released, they try to make optimum use of the available equipment so that, on the one hand, the specified completion dates are met, and, on the other hand, no orders must be interrupted (in order to avoid double setup cost).

Regarding c and d:

Production order 112 could not be executed according to pre-calculation. After the production of 1000 of the 10,200 pieces ordered, it was determined that the assembly equipment was not set correctly, which meant that the quality specifications were missed. As a result, 1000 additional units each of the semi-finished products envelope (31) and mechanism (21) had to be fetched from the warehouse. This led to material quantity variances of –360 and –733, a total of –1093 (see sheet "Actualmaterial").

Since the assembly work had to be restarted, 1000 min. more were consumed during assembly, which resulted in a working time variance of –790 (see sheet "Actualprodtime") (Fig. 6.1).

Regarding e:

If the decision to carry out an operation in a cost center other than that specified in the order release is taken during the execution of a production order, a process variance arises. In this case, the reported actual activities of the planned cost center will be zero, while the executing cost center will enter its own work activity.

Regarding f:

It is also possible that the number of good pieces delivered to stock differs from that in the pre-calculation because less or more scrap or setup material was accumulated than planned. This results in a yield variance as shown in the example of production order 116. The 40 good units, which could be added to stock in addition to the specification of 10,210 pieces, represent —valued at proportional standard cost—an increase in value of 91.38 (Fig. 6.2).

The production order variances can only be calculated when an order has been definitively confirmed as completed, since the entry of actual activities and material consumption as well as warehouse receipts (good items) is only complete then (see also the example work in progress in Sect. 5.3.2).

The **purchase price variances** that actually occurred in the year are displayed together with the production order variances, because both variance groups refer to the consumption and procurement of raw materials, merchandise, and semi-finished or finished products, and thus also determine the inventory values to be displayed. The origin of purchase price variances (–7192) is listed in detail in Sect. 5.3.1.

If **all variances arising in purchasing and production** are combined, the total overview of the product and procurement-related variances from the stock receipt results. The latter was consistently valued throughout the year at planned proportional product costs or at standard purchase prices (Fig. 6.3).

Since all variances per production order were calculated in the simulation model, they can be added up for each variance type and assigned to the product groups. Because the raw materials are used in all product groups, the raw material price variances can only be assigned to the complete range "finished good." The total of –5749 must be incorporated in the stepwise contribution accounting to arrive at the correct annual operating result (see Sect. 5.5.2). This total indicates how much the goods inward to the warehouse differed from the standards of the annual plan.

When transferring to the income statement and balance sheet, only the purchase price variances will have to be included, because these represent the difference in

Itemnr	101090	Month	1											
Production order nr	Description	Dispatched lot size	Need for setup & scra	Input-quantity	Itemnr 2	description input item	Preset quantity	Standard prop. cost /unit	Precalculated withdrawal from	Precalculated direct material cost	Actual consumption (stock pickslips)	Actual direct material cost	Material quantity variance (units)	Material quantity variance (value)
112	4ring 7.5 special design	10,210	60	10,270	7	7.5 cm-envelope	1.0000	0.36	10,270	3,697	11,270	4,057	-1,000	-360
112	4ring 7.5 special design	10,210	60	10,270	21	4-Ring-mechan.	1.0000	0.73	10,270	7,533	11,270	8,266	-1,000	-733
														-1,093
Prod. order nr	Description	Dispatched lot size	Setup / lot	Serving cost center			Allowed time	Plan-prop.-rate	Precalculated activities	Precalc. Manufacturing cost	Actual time worked	Prop. manuf. actual	Time difference	Working time variance
112	4ring 7.5 special design	10,210	120	Assembly			1.0000	0.7898	10,330	8,158	11,330	8,948	-1,000	-790
112	4ring 7.5 special design	10,210	20	Film welding			1.0000	0.2519	10,230	2,576	10,230	2,576	-	-
														-790
													Total order 112	**-1,883**

Fig. 6.1 Material quantity and working time variances in production order 112

Year	Prod. order nr	Itemnr	Description	Dispatched lot size	stock-entry actual	Standard-prop. cost/unit	Goods inwards value	Direct material in order	Manufacturing in order	Order total precalc.	Yield variance
2011	116	101090	4ring 7.5 special design	10,020	10,250	2.2845	23,416	12,589	10,735	23,324	**91.38**

Fig. 6.2 Better yield than pre-calculated

Variances	Total Ringbook Ltd.	Subtotal finished goods	2Ring normal (inventory)	4Ring normal (inventory)	2Ring special designs	4Ring special designs	2Ring special formats (inventory)	Semi-finished	Merchandise
Purchase price	-7,192	-4,262							-2,930
Material quantity	-1,093	-1,093	-	-	-	-1,093	-		
Working time	-790	-790	-	-790	-	-	-	-	-
Lot-size	3,236	3,236	267	1,668	1,135	82	0	84	-
Yield	91	91	-	-	-	91	-		-
Sum purchase & orders	-5,749	-2,819	267	879	1,135	-920	0		-2,930

Fig. 6.3 All purchase and production order-related variances compared to standards

expense in procurement compared to the stock received from purchasing at planned prices.

The variances in the production orders are only recognizable in management accounting, since only there can all production orders are analyzed individually. The stock receipt is always valued at proportional standard product cost.

In the example company corporate management can conclude that the result of production deteriorated a little due to isolated variances in material quantities and working hours. These variances were more than offset by the savings achieved in setup costs (larger batches) and by a favorable yield variance. Production and procurement have thus achieved a small increase in productivity compared to the plan.

6.2 Cost Centers

In Sect. 5.2 the actual costs of the cost centers were prepared. They included:

- Primary costs (material consumption, supplier invoices, imputed depreciation, personnel costs)
- (Internal) clearances from one cost center to another
- The charges from internal services provided (ISP)

These cost center costs must be compared with the plan to determine whether the cost center manager has succeeded in adhering to his budget. However, if the actual costs are based on an activity level different than planned, a simple plan to actual comparison makes no sense. To create comparability, the plan costs of the actual activity level must be calculated. This is done with the help of the flexible budget.

6.2.1 Flexible Budgeting

Cost splitting was used in cost center planning to define the proportional planned costs that are directly caused by the activities procured from the products or other cost centers. The illustration with the example of the stamping department is repeated in Fig. 6.4 (see Sect. 4.7.8).

If the actual activity level is smaller than the planned level, i.e., due to a lack of orders, the total cost of the cost center should be reduced by the corresponding proportional cost of this cost center. If the actual activity level exceeds the plan, the budget may rise by the change in proportional stamping costs. Since the planned fixed costs represent the organizational and capacity structure of the cost center, it should not change when activity level adjustments occur.

Here the term "flexible budget" is used, because it is frequently used in American cost accounting literature. In German-speaking countries the respective term is "Sollkosten," meaning "**should-be cost.**" This term is better as it quantifies the cost target that should be met based on consideration of the planned cost (budget) *and* the actual work performed (actual activity level). The yearly budget of the cost center (which was released at the beginning of the year) is not changed but the cost target is adjusted to the work performed.

The **flexible budget** (planned fixed costs + actual activity x projected plan cost rate) shows the cost center manager what cost should have been incurred if the actual

	Cost center		220 Stampimg		
	Manager:	Vogel			
	Number of shifts	1			
	RFU reference factor unit	Pmin			
	Planned FTE's	Mgmt.	0.3		
		Operation	3.7		
	Normal capacity employees	408,000			
	Installed machines:		4		
	Annual capacity per machine & shift:		108,960		
	Personnel multiplier (Pmin/ unit)		1		
	Planned activity including setup	338,855			
Nr.	Cost type	Planned amount	Propor-tional	Fixed	Consump-tion / RFU
1	Personnel costs	337,560	280,353	57,207	0.8274
5	Office supplies	440	-	440	
6	Auxiliary and operating materials	12,980	10,166	2,814	0.0300
12	External maintenance & repair	17,500	11,182	6,318	0.0330
13	Other expense	4,800	1,017	3,783	0.0030
31	Imputed depreciation	13,063		13,063	
	Total primary costs	386,343	302,717	83,626	
21	ISP energy	536	136	400	0.0004
22	ISP int. Repair & maintenance	9347		9348	
	Total controllable cost	396,226	302,853	93,374	
	Prop. planned cost-rate		0.8938		

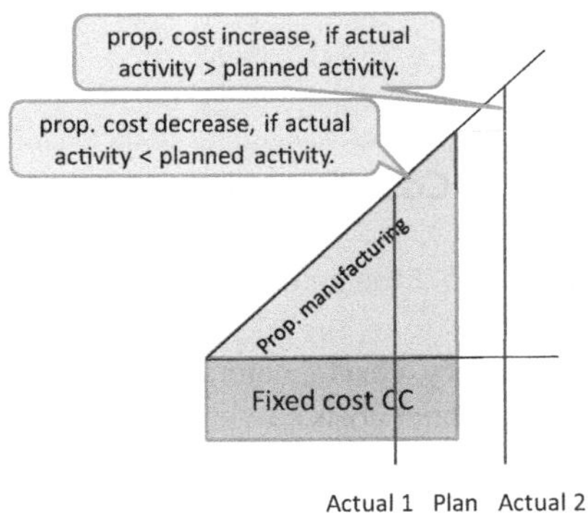

Fig. 6.4 Cost plan of the Stamping cost center

	Stamping	Act. year 2011	220	0			7	Company holiday: July	
	Please choose CC, year, month	Month 12		December				January -	December
	Planned activity year:	338,855		Plan	Actual	Level	Plan	Actual	Level
	Activity and activity level			30,805	30,805	100.00%	338,855	338,855	100.00%
RFU:	Pmin	Plan (year)		Month	12		YTD / cumulated		
Cost type	Cost type description	Propor-tional	Planned fix	Flexible budget	Actual	Spending variance	Flexible budget	Actual	Spending variance
40	Internal clearing (personnel for other CC)	-	-	-	-	-	-	-	-
40	Internal clearing (personnel for other CC)	-	-	-	-	-	-	-	-
1	Personnel costs	280,353	57,207	30,254	29,592	662	337,560	341,277	-3,717
3	Purchasing & shipping costs	-	-	-	-	-	-	-	-
4	Advertisement	-	-	-	-	-	-	-	-
5	Office supplies	-	440	37	37	-	440	403	37
6	Auxiliary and operating materials	10,166	2,814	1,159	1,082	77	12,980	11,898	1,082
7	Telephone, communication	-	-	-	-	-	-	-	-
9	El. energy, water, fuel oil	-	-	-	-	-	-	-	-
8	Cleaning & conserving supplies	-	-	-	-	-	-	-	-
10	Rent	-	-	-	-	-	-	-	-
12	External maintenance & repair	11,182	6,318	1,543	1,458	85	17,500	16,042	1,458
13	Other expense, non-activated project costs	1,017	3,783	408	400	8	4,800	4,400	400
14	Software (Licenses & maintenance)	-	-	-	-	-	-	-	-
21	ISP Energy provided	136	400	46	46	-0	536	537	-2
22	ISP Repair center	-	9,348	779	857	-78	9,348	8,958	389
23	ISP Service provisions from personnel pool	-	-	-	-	-	-	-	-
		302,853	80,311	34,225	33,472	753	383,163	383,516	-353
31	Imputed depreciation	-	13,063	1,089	1,089	-	13,063	13,063	-
		302,853	93,373	35,313	34,560	753	396,226	396,579	-353
			396,226				*396,226*	93,726	
	Planned CC-rate prop.		0.8938		27,532	<-- For orders or CC's -->		302,853	

Fig. 6.5 Target to actual comparison for the reported month and year-to-date (YTD) of cost center

activity had occurred. This makes it **a suitable basis for comparison.** The flexible budget shows the allowed cost for the actual level of activity!

Figure 6.5 illustrates how the flexible budget for a specific month or year is calculated. The should-be cost mechanism has the advantage that it greatly simplifies cost center planning. It is **sufficient to prepare the cost center planning for the entire year** and then divide the plan values by the number of operating months (see Sect. 4.7.8). Because the planned cost is adjusted monthly to the actual performance level, the comparison scale is automatically calculated correctly, regardless of how many working days are incurred in a specific month.

6.2.2 Target to Actual Comparison in the Cost Center

The system automatically calculates the target costs by cost element, using the plan data above and the actual activity levels of the months and cumulated for the entire year. These levels come from the sheet "Actualprodtime." Actual costs are the totals per cost type from the sheets "Actualprimarycosts," "ActualISP," and "Actualclearance." The variance column results from the difference between should-be cost and actual cost. The formula is as written to reflect whether the deviation improves (+) or worsens (–) the overall result of the company.

Usually there are no variances in "imputed depreciation" as the investments of the planned year are already included in the statement of changes in fixed assets (sheet "Invest&depr"). If unplanned investments are made during the fiscal year, the (partial year) depreciation resulting from the additional investment is added to the actual column.

The columns proportional and planned fixed costs of the annual plan no longer need to be displayed in the real application, since the cost center manager always has the plan available as a comparison. They are shown here so that it is easier to see how the should-be cost is calculated.

In the month of December, the cost center manager for the stamping shop succeeded in keeping his actual cost lower than the flexible budget. In relation to the complete year 2011, the should-be costs were exceeded by 353, which is less than one one-thousandth of his target. A glance at the variance columns shows that this positive result is mainly the consequence of having the costs for auxiliary material and external repair well under control.

The difference between target and actual costs is called the **spending variance.** It indicates whether more or less than the should-be costs were consumed in the period under consideration. The spending variance has the character of fixed costs because it is assumed that processes will remain constant throughout the year and that planned cost rates will therefore remain the same. If variances arise between target and actual, this is due to changes in the structural costs.

This presented methodology can also be used for all other cost centers working directly on the product as well as for the ISP cost centers. In the pure fixed cost centers, the target to actual comparison corresponds to a plan to actual comparison because no proportional costs are planned in these cost centers (see the cost center plans in Sect. 4.7.8).

The **cost objective of every cost center manager** is to **adhere to his should-be costs**. If no proportional cost was planned, the target corresponds to the planned costs.

The target-to-actual comparison also includes an overview of the planned and consumed times for internal tasks. Due to the lack of an extensive FDC system, this information is only available as estimates and as notes at the annual level (see sheets "Internaltaskplan" and "Actualinternaltasks"). Actual electricity consumption can only be compared with planned consumption if measuring devices are installed on each machine or per cost center and consumption is captured monthly.

In many schools and in older textbooks it is recommended to show the **activity variance** as an important indicator for the cost center manager (see, e.g., Fässler et al. 1980, p. 49). In our opinion, however, the activity variance has no place in management accounting. This is because it is based on the fixed costs charged by allocation to a cost center and is therefore a misleading figure.

For example, if the planned fixed costs of the stamping cost center of 93,373 were divided by the planned activity level of 338,855 minutes, this would result in a fixed cost allocation rate of 0.2756. This allocation would be passed on to the manufactured products and thus to inventory with every minute worked in the stamping cost center. If the actual activity were to increase to 120%, $406{,}626 \times 0.2756 = 104{,}747$ in fixed costs would be charged to inventory, although in reality only the planned 93,373 plus the spending variance of 353 (total 93,726 fixed costs) were incurred.

A cost center manager should be responsible for the cost of his center, but it would be illogical to make the costs of the manufactured products dependent on the activity level of that cost center. In the proposed accounting for management only proportional manufacturing costs are passed on. This is also the case for goods going in and out of the warehouse. The performance measurement is driven by BOMs and work plans. These usually do not change depending on the employment situation.

6.3 Analysis of Actual Profitability

After all post-calculations of the production orders and all cost center target to actual comparisons as well as the net revenues of a reporting period are known, the results from operations (here EBIT) can be determined.

6.3.1 Stepwise Contribution Accounting in the Product Dimension

To generate the overall view, we start with Fig. 5.23 in Sect. 5.5.2. The already mentioned variances of production (see Fig. 6.3) as well as the columns for the variances must be incorporated. CM I after sales commissions again serves as the starting line. The Plan, Actual, and Variance columns are displayed for both the company total and the two product ranges Finished Goods and Merchandise. Since in CM I after commissions all proportional standard product costs of the products sold are already included, the remaining fixed costs plus the spending variances remain in the cost centers. For this purpose, the actual costs for the entire year per cost center are summarized in the sheet "CCtotals."

The actual amounts (in column "Actual") contain the planned fixed costs plus the spending variances. The cost centers are grouped according to areas of responsibility and listed in the stepwise contribution accounting (sheet "ActualstepwiseCM") with their planned fixed costs and the actual amount. The spending variances (- sign = unfavorable variance for the overall result) appear in the "Variance" column.

The formula Should-be cost – Actual cost = Spending variance mentioned in Sect. 6.2.2 applies to all cost centers. The origin of the values can be traced in the sheets "CCtotals" and "CCtargettoactual" for each cost center individually by month and cumulatively (Fig. 6.6).

In comparison to Sect. 5.5.2, Fig. 5.23, the correct EBIT is presented here, as are all variances related to purchasing and production orders. In Fig. 6.3 in Sect. 6.1 the purchase and production order variances were shown by product group; here they are condensed according to product ranges.

6.3.2 Actual Contribution Margins per Sales Area

Since the complete data preparation of sales, proportional production costs, and cost center costs always takes place bottom-up, i.e., comes from the individual

Year	Productgroups / ranges 2011	Total Ringbook Ltd. Plan	Actual	Variance	Finished goods Plan	Actual	Variance	Merchandise Plan	Actual	Variance
	CM I after commissions	3,668,723	3,774,533	105,810	3,541,841	3,622,421	80,579	126,882	152,113	25,231
	Fixed cost product ranges	311,730	310,524	1,206	158,640	159,381	-741	153,090	151,143	1,947
	Product range CM	3,356,993	3,464,009	107,016	3,383,201	3,463,039	79,838	-26,208	970	27,178
	Fixed cost sales organization	861,035	868,373	-7,338						
100	Sales mgmt. & office	543,082	550,530	-7,448						
151	Eastern Switzerland	120,113	120,076	37						
152	Western Switzerland	91,960	91,923	37						
153	Business clients (direct)	105,880	105,843	37						
	Sales CM	2,495,958	2,595,637	99,679						
	Purchase price variances		-7,192	-		-4,262			-2,930	
	Material quantity variances		-1,093	-		-1,093				
	Worktime variances		-790			-790				
	Lot-size variances		3,236	-		3,236				
	Yield variances		91	-		91				
	Sum order & purchase variances		-5,749			-2,819			-2,930	
	Fixed cost of production	995,112	982,329	12,783	995,112	982,329	12,783			
200	Plant mgmt. & work scheduling				210,965	216,421	-5,457			
220	Stamping				93,373	93,726	-353			
231	Wire rolling				31,565	26,734	4,831			
232	Wire bending & forming				281,795	280,876	919			
240	Cardboarding				61,316	60,555	761			
245	Personnelpool 240-260				241,346	241,686	-340			
250	Assembly				48,251	42,861	5,390			
260	Film welding				26,501	19,470	7,031			
	Other fixed cost	1,299,788	1,313,185	-13,397						
210	Procurement & warehouse	182,155	192,251	-10,097						
320	Buildings & maintenance	149,649	148,294	1,355						
330	Repair center	11,445	15,736	-4,291						
340	Energy center	27,278	16,617	10,661						
300	IT	269,825	265,505	4,320						
900	Corp. mgmt. & administration	659,437	674,782	-15,345						
	EBIT	201,058	294,374	93,316						

Fig. 6.6 Stepwise contribution accounting plan and actual of the reporting year (product dimension)

Year	Sales rep	CCnr	Sales region	Gross revenue actual	Net revenue actual	CM I standard actual	Sales com-missions	CM I after commission	Actual cost own CC	CM sales region
2011	201	151	Eastern Switzerland	2,582,088	2,063,504	1,170,406	23,408	1,146,998	120,076	1,026,922
2011	202	152	Western Switzerland	3,103,968	2,690,213	1,563,081	31,262	1,531,820	91,923	1,439,896
2011	203	153	Business clients (direct)	742,952	626,371	352,265	7,045	345,220	105,843	239,377
2011	204	100	Sales mgmt. & office	2,319,540	1,670,069	765,812	15,316	750,496		750,496
			Total	8,748,548	7,050,157	3,851,565	77,031	3,774,533	317,843	3,456,691
2011			Fixed cost of product range		101	Finished goods				159,381
2011					102	Merchandise				151,143
2011			Sales mgmt. & office		100					550,530
			Sales- CM							2,595,637

Fig. 6.7 Sales region contributions for 2011

transaction, contribution accounting can also be created multidimensionally. For space reasons, only the actual values are displayed in Fig. 6.7.

The last column shows the contribution margins for the year generated in the individual sales regions. For this purpose, the proportional standard cost of sales was deducted from the net sales revenue. This resulted in the "CM I standard actual" per sales area serving as the basis for commissions calculation.

Each sales representative is also responsible for his own cost center's cost. The achievement of his objectives can thus be assessed by comparing the realized sales territory CM with the planned one. The representative himself can influence all elements entering the sales area CM, provided that only the standard proportional costs of the units he sold are deducted from net sales. The cost of the sales promotion cost centers is deducted here only after the total of the area CM because each of these cost centers work for all sales areas.

No fixed costs were allocated to exports because the sales manager also oversees this area. If necessary, an export cost center can be defined if it later has its own employees and the manager wants to show the travel expenses and other costs that can be directly assigned to the export. The sale CM of 2,595,637 is the same as that in Fig. 5.21.

6.3.3 Summary and Interpretation of the Target to Actual Comparison

A waterfall chart shows the top management of Ringbook Ltd. which factors have led to an improvement in EBIT in 2011 compared to plan (Fig. 6.8).

If the figures aggregated in the graph for the entire target to actual comparison are analyzed, various conclusions can be drawn, and a causal analysis performed. It indicates:

- The operating result (EBIT) achieved was around 1.4 times the planned amount.
- This was mainly attributable to revenue increases, which are shown in Fig. 5.22 (Sect. 5.5.1) with gross and net revenues as well as CM I realized per product group.

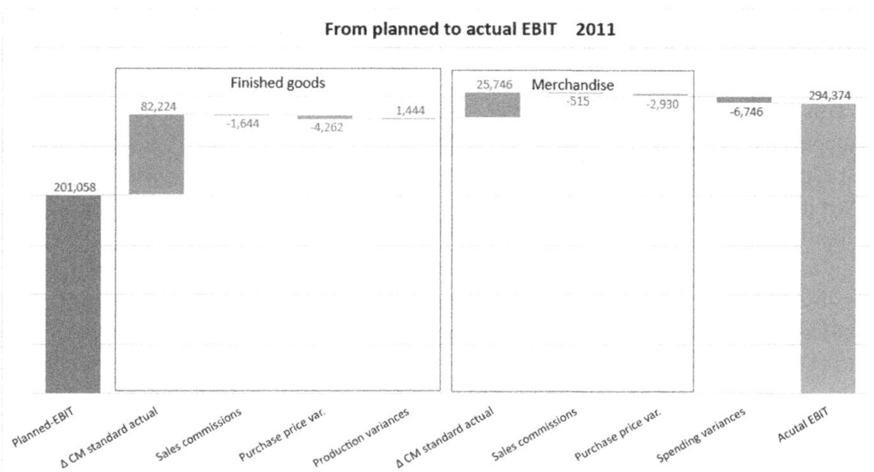

Fig. 6.8 Factors for the improvement of EBIT compared to plan

- Detailed stepwise contribution accounting shows in the simulation model that roughly 82,000 of this increase in CM I after commissions came from the range "Finished goods." Two-ring product groups and the special four-ring formats were the main contributors to this success.
- Merchandise also sold better than planned. CM I after commissions was around 25,000 higher. This corresponds to an increase of around 20% over plan. The product range now shows a positive CM of around 1000. With this the sales promotion costs clearly attributable to the merchandise are covered.
- The production of own products has its orders and processes very well under control. Compared to the plan, production was able to underspend the pre-calculated costs of all orders by 1444. This is primarily a result of the positive lot size variances (3236). The plan calculations were underspent by this amount.
- The column "Value of inventory change" in the sheet "Actualstock" shows that inventories of semi-finished goods decreased by approximately 60,000 and inventories of finished goods increased by approximately 123,000. The good thing is that this improved the supply capability, as the company had difficulties in its ability to deliver on time.
- Purchase price variances for raw materials and merchandise (–4262 – 2930 = –7192) do not impact the result very much, as they amount to only 0.7% of the total material consumption.
- The cost centers have almost been able to meet their should-be costs. Overall, there was a negative spending variance of 6746 that had a direct impact on earnings. The main causes of the negative spending variances were the cost centers Sales, Warehouse and Purchasing as well as Administration and Management.
- Even if only minor variances occur in a production order or in a cost center, they are still important for the responsible manager. They are an indication of how well a company succeeds in improving productivity or efficiency and thus improving its cost position in relation to its competitors.

This short analysis describes the view of top operational executives. Every manager should deepen the analysis in his area of responsibility, be it in a certain cost type in his cost center or in the details of parts lists and work plans/processes or down to the individual document because improvement potentials are often hidden in the details.

In the simulation model integration has been expanded to such an extent that it is possible to carry out quantitative, performance, and value analyses down to a very detailed level. We note that while in the example presented here cost variances do not "carry much weight," only a few such variances were "built in" in order not to overload the model in the first reporting year, and results may be much different for a company in actual practice.

6.4 Transfer to the Actual Internal Income Statement and Balance Sheet

6.4.1 Income Statement/Projects

The operating income statement for the year under review is prepared in the same way as in planning (Sect. 4.10.1). It is again presented according to the total cost method. The plan values were transferred to the Plan year column. The revenue and expense type totals summarized for the actual year are taken from the following tables (Fig. 6.9):

- Net sales from "ActualCMitems" or "Salesstatistics"
- Value changes in inventories of semi-finished and finished goods, as well as consumption of raw materials and merchandise from the sheet "Actualstock"

				Plan 2011	Actual 2011	Difference
60	Net revenue		PR#	6,794,141	7,050,157	256,016
61	Inventory change finished goods	+/-	2	50,249	123,262	73,013
62	Inventory change semi-finished		1	-1,955	-60,145	-58,190
63	Work in progress WIP (at year end)				9,885	9,885
64	Change in assets under construction			33,866	36,551	2,685
	Produced value	=		6,876,300	7,159,709	283,409
	Raw material consumption	-	3	665,307	677,966	12,658
	Purchase price variances	-			7,192	7,192
	Merchandise consumption	-	6	243,530	340,273	96,743
	Gross profit	=		5,967,462	6,134,278	166,816
1	Personnel costs	-		4,802,516	4,909,599	-107,083
2	Sales commissions	-		74,872	77,031	-2,159
3	Purchasing & shipping costs	-		20,000	20,004	-4
4	Advertisement	-		110,000	110,000	-
5	Office supplies	-		13,730	12,623	1,108
6	Auxiliary and operating materials	-		52,270	48,121	4,149
7	Telephone, communication	-		34,860	34,722	138
9	El. energy, water, fuel oil	-		67,800	60,100	7,700
8	Cleaning & conserving supplies	-		4,080	3,740	340
10	Rent	-		30,000	30,000	-
12	External maintenance & repair	-		222,575	205,385	17,190
13	Other expense, non-activated project costs	-		82,860	77,738	5,122
14	Software (Licenses & maintenance)	-		24,000	24,000	-
	Creation of other new provisions			-	-	-
	Total cash out costs			5,539,563	5,613,063	-73,500
	CFBIT Cash Flow Bef.Interest & Taxes	=		427,900	521,215	93,316
31	Imputed depreciation	-		226,842	226,842	-
	EBIT	=		201,058	294,374	93,316

Fig. 6.9 Internal income statement for the year under review

- Purchase price variances from sheet "Actualpurchases"
- All primary costs of cost types 1–14 from sheet "Costtypesactual"
- Imputed depreciation from the statement of changes in fixed assets in "Invest&depr"
- Change in work in progress from sheet "ProofWIP"
- Change in the value of assets under construction and projects from sheet "Actualprojects"

Except for purchase price variances, all order-related variances from the stepwise contribution accounting are no longer visible in the income statement. This is because the direct material consumption is valued at planned purchase prices (hence the correction for purchase price variances) whereas the other primary costs are always valued with the amounts actually paid to the suppliers. From the totals of the individual expense types, it is no longer possible to determine which part is directly activity-dependent and which represents structural costs. Proof that personnel costs and sales commissions are accrued and include all social deductions requires a separate section (see Sect. 6.6).

The income statement is required for the derivation of the balance sheet and for external reporting. For the responsible managers, however, it means "information destruction" since all details about sales, production, cost centers, and inventories are reduced to a single column.

Projects and Assets Under Construction

The (internal) projects are not explicitly shown in contribution accounting for the following reasons:

- If a project is opened and completed in the same year, then its cost appears either directly in the cost center (material purchases and/or cost center activities) or on a project order, which in turn is debited to a cost center.
- Projects only are activated or charged to the annual accounts via a cost center after project completion (see Sect. 4.6.2).

In the first case, the project costs to be charged to the year under review are included in the cost center costs. In the second case, a project is not recognized in profit or loss until the year following completion and capitalization (at the end of the year of the project completion) of the project via imputed depreciation. At the end of the year, it is shown in the operating balance sheet at cost as an asset under construction.

In Sect. 4.6.2 the planning for the two projects "automatic material positioning" and "onlineshop setup" was presented. The sheet "Actualprojects" contains all the material and internal services provided for the projects as well as the target to actual comparison of the projects (Fig. 6.10).

Both projects were successfully completed by the end of 2011. The accrued values (actual investment) in the actual "Total project" column are therefore included in the final balance sheet at the end of 2011 in the line "Assets under

Comparison plan to actual

Year	Pro-jectnr	Description	Kickoff Plan	Kickoff Actual	Kickoff Decision	Milestone_1 Plan	Milestone_1 Actual	Milestone_1 Decision	Milestone 2 Plan	Milestone 2 Actual	Milestone 2 Decision
2011	1	Automatic material positioning	2011-05-08		go	2011-10-31	2011-11-02	go	2011-11-30	2011-10-28	go
2011	2	Installation online shop	2011-01-31		go	2011-04-30	2011-05-05	go	2011-08-31	2011-08-29	go

Year / Jahr				Material consumption			ISP from cost centers			Purchases for project			Total project		
				Budget	Actual	Variance	Budget	Actual	Variance	Budget	Actual	Variance	Budget	Actual	Variance
2011	1	Automatic material positioning	P	369	434	-65	6,515	6,515	-	50,500	50,500	-	57,384	57,449	-65
2012	3	*for test only*													
2011	2	Installation online shop	P	0	0	0	26,981	29,602	-2,620	57,000	57,000	-	83,981	86,602	-2,620
		Total projects		369	434	-65	33,496	36,117	-2,620	107,500	107,500	-	141,366	144,051	-2,685

Fig. 6.10 Actual consumption and investments for the projects completed in the year under review

construction/projects." In the income statement at the end of 2011, the material purchases for the projects (434) and the services provided by the cost centers Repairs and Maintenance and IT (36,117), totaling 36,551, must be shown in the line "change in assets under construction," because they represent a value generated in the reporting period and are therefore recognized in profit or loss (reduction of expenses).

6.4.2 Internal Balance Sheet

The same procedure as in planning (Sect. 4.10.2) is also used to derive the internal balance sheet:

- The starting point is the opening balance as at 1/1/2011.
- The operation column shows the reflection of the income statement in the balance sheet accounts down to EBIT (294,374). This also includes the changes in inventories resulting from the business realized in 2011 (including raw materials and merchandise, inventories of semi-finished and finished goods, work in progress).
- In the operation column, the change in the account for assets under construction/ projects is also reflected. All materials previously procured from the warehouse for projects or new plants as well as ISP services (own contributions) are included. These assets are capitalized and amortized only following the completion of the project. This procedure enables the project manager to monitor all positions in the projects target to actual comparison until project completion (Fig. 6.11).
- The money flow column includes the cash flows from nonoperating activities:
  - Incoming payments (from debtors), which can be adjusted based on the actual payment behavior of customers (see debtor days in Sect. 4.10.2).
  - Outgoing payments (personnel payments, supplier payments including investments, payback of provisions, possible changes in loans, external interest), also adaptable here via creditor days (Sect. 4.10.2).
  - The newly formed provisions (sales commissions paid in the following year and expected income taxes), as well as the reduction of existing provisions.
  - The determination of the annual profit from an operational point of view.

Balance sheet (actual)					2011
Assets	PR#	Opening balance 01/01/2011	Operation	Money flow	Internal balance 12/31/2011
Liquid assets		210,100	-	-	210,100
Accounts receivable		1,001,514	7,050,157	-6,866,286	1,185,385
Inventory:					
- Raw-/operating material	3	68,400	-685,158	658,063	41,304
- WIP Work in progress			9,885		9,885
- Merchandise	6	20,516	-340,273	372,882	53,125
- Semi-finished goods	1	176,297	-60,145		116,152
- Finished goods	2	148,028	123,262		271,290
Current assets		1,624,854	6,097,728	-5,835,341	1,887,241
Fixed assets		2,791,000	-226,842	221,000	2,785,158
Changes replacement value			-		-
Assets under constr. / projects			36,551	107,500	144,051
Total fixed assets		2,791,000	-190,291	328,500	2,929,209
Balance sum		4,415,854	5,907,437	-5,506,841	4,816,450
Liabilities					
Accounts payable		179,940	626,432	-625,888	180,485
Bank account		1,171,542	4,802,516	-4,582,377	1,391,681
Provisions for sales commission		-	77,031		77,031
Time bonus for employees			107,083	-	107,083
Other short term provisions		250,000	-	*-160,841*	89,159
Current liabilities		1,601,482	5,613,063	-5,369,105	1,845,440
Long term loan		800,000		-	800,000
Long-term liabilities		800,000	-	-	800,000
EBIT			294,374	-294,374	-
Interest				*98,577*	
EBT				*195,796*	
Deferred tax liabilities				*39,159*	
Annual profit				*156,637*	156,637
Replacement value adjustments		541,000	-		541,000
Reserves/profit carried forward		473,372			473,372
Share capital		1,000,000			1,000,000
Equity		2,014,372	-		2,171,010
Balance sum		4,415,854	5,907,437	-5,506,841	4,816,450
Net revenue		6,794,141			7,050,157
Checksums		-	-	-	-

Financing / definancing			
Creation of other new provisions			-
Dissolution of other provisions			200,000
Debtor days	53		53
Inflow accounts payable			2,165,817
Creditor days			30
Accounts payable payed			1,985,332
Change of long term loan			0
Interest on loan and opening balance bank credit		5%	1,971,542
Tax rate (income tax)		20%	

Fig. 6.11 Closing internal balance 2011

Adding from left to right results in the closing balance sheet for the year. For Ringbook Ltd. the distribution of profit is not anticipated; it is assumed that the annual profit will be added to the reserves or to the profit carried forward. To determine from an operational point of view how much annual net profit was generated, the interests payable and the expected income taxes must be subtracted from EBIT.

For the estimation of interest and tax expense the following deduction items are created in the simulation model:

- External interest: These are calculated from the opening balance of the bank account and the loans (5%) in a simplified way and in the same way as for the plan (Sect. 4.10.2).
- Income taxes: The assumption is that 20% of the profit before tax will have to be transferred to the government (this percentage can be adjusted).
- The account "provision for time bonuses for employees" is dealt with in Sect. 6.5.

These simplifications are considered justifiable in the example because they show operational management in a clear way how much money is earned for the lenders, the state, and the owners. Additionally, the allocation to reserves and the dividends to the owners will be determined on the basis of the published closing balance sheet and income statement.

Of course, the positive picture for 2011 also emerges from the analysis of the operating income statement and the balance sheet: Current assets increased due to sales growth and also to increases in inventories of finished products. Fixed assets, valued at RepV, increased primarily due to the capitalized projects. Both factors led to a somewhat lower asset turnover rate. However, this was more than offset by the increase in return on sales, which led to a higher ROI on total assets. As a result, the equity ratio also rose, which corresponds to an increase in stability (as mentioned above, the items after the EBIT are not yet included). The development of the different financial key ratios is shown in Sect. 8.2, Fig. 8.3, for the whole time-range (5 years) of the simulation model.

6.5 Harmonization of Actual Personnel Costs in Particular

In the integrated planning and control system presented up to now, only the cost-type "personnel costs" was planned and charged in the planned to actual comparison. The intention here is to present cost center managers only those costs for which they can actually take responsibility and leave out cost types that are dependent on gross salary. The basic data for this computation is the planned and used working times of the respective employees and the markup rate including all social welfare and nonwage labor costs dependent on the wage total.

In addition to the actual wage, personnel costs include many other types of expenses, most of which are dependent on the wage amount. For example, in

Switzerland the following positions are considered because they are paid in full or in part by the employer:

- Old-age and survivors' insurance (state pension and widow's or orphan's pension), including levy for the administration of these insurance policies
- Family equalization fund and child allowances
- Unemployment and disability insurance
- Private pension insurance
- Accident and possible daily sickness benefit insurance
- Financial contributions to professional associations

We note that many of these are common throughout the world. All these levies are regulated by law or by employment contracts; the cost center manager cannot change or circumvent these specifications. Similarly, employees' rights to holidays and paid vacations are predetermined by law or employment contract. The cost center manager is therefore helped if he does not have to worry about these details but can plan and monitor the personnel costs of his area as an entity.

To control personnel costs, the cost center manager must know the cost of "one hour been there" of his employees. Whether the person has worked on the product, completed internal tasks or "waited for work", does not matter for the time being. Therefore, the proposed system works based on hourly presence rates. From presence time recording it is known how many hours an employee has worked. This figure, multiplied by the planned hourly presence rate, gives the personnel costs.

The planned presence hour rate can be calculated per employee, see sheet "Personnelcosts." If, for reasons of secrecy, the payroll total of individuals should not be recognizable, an average planned presence rate per cost center can also be determined and applied to debit the cost center. This procedure also helps when personnel pools are set up for jumpers or for a larger group of employees who perform homogeneous work (see cost center 245 Personnel pool).

If shift or weekend work is planned, the bonuses due for employees, including social benefits, should also be included in the planned personnel costs, so that a weighted planned presence rate is created for all shifts. From a business point of view, it does not make sense to charge higher personnel costs to an order that was produced on a Sunday than to one that was carried out during normal daily working hours. If the highly urgent order had been dispatched for a usual workday, one or more other orders would have had to be produced on Sunday.

By working with presence time recording and planned presence rates, the cost center manager can concentrate on controlling employee deployment because he knows that the planned presence rate in his cost center will remain the same throughout the year. Minor deviations remain in the wage and salary administration and are transferred from there to the overall result.

Another advantage of working with planned and actual presence times is that the respective cost center receives the actual hours worked each month, multiplied by the planned record, as **actual personnel costs** that correspond to the actual consumption regardless of the wages paid out.

Without any further effort, the data is also generated to maintain a monthly, independent **working time account** for each employee. The planned presence time for a month results from the work calendar and the employment contract, the actual (presence) time from time recording. If more hours were worked than planned, the account for personnel cost provisions automatically increases; if less work is done, the balance is automatically reduced. On the one hand, this facilitates the reconciliation between financial accounting and management accounting and, on the other hand, the adjustment of provisions on an accrual basis.

Personnel expenses also include the commissions for salespeople. Although they are listed in the model as a separate cost type, the total amount also includes the planned nonwage charges (16%). The personnel costs are shown as follows in the simulation model:

(a) Nonwage labor costs
In addition to the gross wage agreed with an employee, the employer must pay (in Switzerland) approximately 16% social security contributions. In any specific case, this percentage may vary slightly if the employer provides more or less private-sector benefits to its employees.

Non wage labor costs for the employer	
Public rent and insurance for orphans, survivors, disability an unemployment	7.856%
Private pension insurance	4.800%
Private accident and health insurance	3.344%
Percentage of total non-wage labor costs for the employer (from salary)	16.000%

Deductions to be paid by the employee are deduced from the gross salary and are not presented in management accounting.

(b) Personnel costs
The gross wage agreed for the planned year (including expected shift or standard overtime bonuses) is entered in the sheet “Personnelcosts” for each employee. Furthermore, the level of employment must be stated in full-time equivalents and it is to be noted whether or not time credits are carried over into the following year. Senior executives receive their salary as a fixed amount, regardless of the hours worked (entry “no” in the column “Time bonus forwarded?”).

The sheet “Workingtime” shows the net working days for each plan year after deduction of public holidays, absences due to illness, military service or other unpaid absences and after deduction of contractually guaranteed vacation days. Since the structure of the employees of a cost center can result in different planned presence times, the sheet “Costcenterplan” provides for adjustment of the annual working times.

(c) Plan presence time and plan presence rate
Based on the above information, the system calculates the planned presence time per year per employee in hours (1700) or minutes (102,000). The planned presence rate is calculated by dividing the total personnel costs (gross wage +

nonwage labor costs) by the planned attendance time (column Planned presence time min p.a.). This rate was already used in cost center planning for the split into proportional and fixed personnel costs and was also used in the cost center target to actual comparison.

(d) Actual presence time and provision for time credits
The actual presence time is recorded via the recording of presence time. The resulting hour totals can be found in the column "Actual presence time." The system uses this to calculate the change in the time credit of each employee. Multiplication by the planned presence time rate results in the value in the "Provision for time bonus" column. The total change in provisions (107,083) should be shown in the balance sheet as a liability to employees and social security (see the corresponding account in Fig. 6.11).

(e) Reversal of provisions
The balance of time credits is usually determined by employees themselves. Either they compensate for working too many hours in the following period or they work more hours in a later month to compensate for a deficiency in hours worked. An employee may also be paid a larger amount as wages for excess hours worked. For the example company this is the case for six people (marked in red in the column "payout of time bonus"). These amounts (a total of 25,026) will be paid out in 2012, which is reflected in the 1/1/2012 balance sheet.

(f) Personnel data
The following employee data is entered in the sheet "Personnelcosts": name, personnel number, degree of employment, cost center affiliation, gross total annual wage. The information should be updated each year as staff changes and other changes occur. From this worksheet other worksheets import this original data.

Figure 6.12 shows the planned personnel costs of all employees including social benefits (planned total 4,802,516). The change in the time credit in hours and value is also displayed for each person. The actual total personnel costs for the year under review amount to 4,909,599 (+107,083, see P+L). If the 16% nonwage labor costs are deducted, the gross wages from the pay slips remain (4,140,100) plus the change in the value of time credits per employee at the end of the year.

This proof shows that:

- It is sufficient to show the cost center manager personnel costs in a single line in the target to actual comparison.
- Since actual personnel costs are always calculated by multiplying the actual working times performed in a month by the planned presence rate, the cost center manager has the guarantee that the actual consumption by his cost center is shown on an accrual basis. In most companies today, the balance of the paid out payroll is debited to the cost center, which does not correspond to the period-based consumption in the case of a fixed gross wage.

Year	Empl nr.	Last name	In CC	Employment rate in%	Time bonus forwarded?	Planned presence time (min. p.a.)	Planned presence time (hours p.a.)	Personnel cost p.a.	Presence time-rate /min.	Actual presence time	Change of time bonus account (hours)	Provision for time bonus	Actual personnel cost	Payout of time bonus	Revaluation on difference to following year
2011	1005	Vogel	220	100%		102,000	1,700	107,880	1.0576	1,716	16.00	1,015	108,895		4.76
2011	1006	Vögl	220	100%		102,000	1,700	83,520	0.82	1,720	20.00	983	84,503		4.60
2011	1007	Vanderhaas	220	100%		102,000	1,700	73,080	0.72	1,720	20.00	860	73,940		4.03
2011	1008	Voigt	220	100%		102,000	1,700	73,080	0.72	1,720	20.00	860	73,940		4.03
2011	1009	Berger	232	90%		91,800	1,530	114,840	1.25	1,720	190.00	14,261	129,101		66.80
2011	1010	Bilfinger	232	100%		102,000	1,700	75,400	0.74	1,712	12.00	532	75,932		2.49
2011	1011	Burstaller	232	100%		102,000	1,700	75,400	0.74	1,720	20.00	887	76,287		4.15
2011	1012	Bentivoglio	232	100%		102,000	1,700	75,400	0.74	1,720	20.00	887	76,287		4.15
2011	1013	Berenzi	232	100%		102,000	1,700	75,400	0.74	1,720	20.00	887	76,287		4.15
2011	1014	Blatter	232	100%		102,000	1,700	75,400	0.74	1,680	-20.00	-887	74,513		-4.15
2011	1015	Bucher	232	50%		51,000	850	37,700	0.74	704	-146.00	-6,476	31,224		-30.33
2011	1016	Toscano	245	100%		102,000	1,700	104,400	1.02	1,720	20.00	1,228	105,628		5.75
2011	1017	Waberer	245	100%		102,000	1,700	73,080	0.72	1,720	20.00	860	73,940		4.03
2011	1037	Wachtel	245	100%		102,000	1,700	73,080	0.72	1,720	20.00	860	73,940		4.03
2011	1038	Wanisch	245	100%		102,000	1,700	73,080	0.72	1,720	20.00	860	73,940		4.03
2011	1039	Wartmann	245	100%		102,000	1,700	73,080	0.72	1,768	68.00	2,923	76,003		13.69
2011	1040	Weber	245	100%		102,000	1,700	73,080	0.72	1,800	100.00	4,299	77,379	p	-
2011	1041	Weh	245	100%		102,000	1,700	73,080	0.72	1,800	100.00	4,299	77,379	p	-
2011	1042	Weibel	245	100%		102,000	1,700	73,080	0.72	1,800	100.00	4,299	77,379	p	-
2011	1043	Weickert	245	100%		102,000	1,700	71,920	0.71	1,800	100.00	4,231	76,151		19.82
2011	1044	Weiler	245	100%		102,000	1,700	71,920	0.71	1,784	84.00	3,554	75,474	p	-
2011	1045	Werner	245	100%		102,000	1,700	71,920	0.71	1,784	84.00	3,554	75,474	p	-
2011	1046	Wichtl	245	100%		102,000	1,700	71,920	0.71	1,752	52.00	2,200	74,120		10.30
2011	1047	Wilhelm	245	100%		102,000	1,700	121,800	1.19	1,752	52.00	3,726	125,526		17.45
2011	1018	Winzenried	245	100%		102,000	1,700	71,920	0.71	1,752	52.00	2,200	74,120		10.30
2011	1019	Witzig	245	100%		102,000	1,700	71,920	0.71	1,752	52.00	2,200	74,120		10.30
2011	1020	Wohlauf	245	100%		102,000	1,700	71,920	0.71	1,752	52.00	2,200	74,120		10.30
2011	1021	Wolter	245	100%		102,000	1,700	71,920	0.71	1,768	68.00	2,877	74,797		13.47
2011	1022	Wörgötter	245	100%		102,000	1,700	71,920	0.71	1,760	60.00	2,538	74,458		11.89
2011	1023	Worth	245	100%		102,000	1,700	71,920	0.71	1,704	4.00	169	72,089		0.79
2011	1024	Wurm	245	100%		102,000	1,700	71,920	0.71	1,704	4.00	169	72,089		0.79
2011	1025	D'Agostinho	245	50%		51,000	850	35,960	0.7051	880	30.00	1,269	37,229		5.94
2011	1026	Womberger	245	100%		102,000	1,700	97,440	0.96	1,760	60.00	3,439	100,879		16.11
2011	1027	Temmel	330	100%		102,000	1,700	64,496	0.63	1,704	4.00	152	64,648		0.71
2011	1028	Fichter	200	100%		102,000	1,700	116,000	1.14	1,720	20.00	1,365	117,365		6.39
2011	1029	Fantelli	200	100%		102,000	1,700	81,200	0.80	1,800	100.00	4,776	85,976		22.37
2011	1030	Grantl	210	100%		102,000	1,700	87,000	0.85	1,832	132.00	6,755	93,755		31.64
2011	1031	Grimaldi	210	100%		102,000	1,700	52,200	0.51	1,832	132.00	4,053	56,253		18.98
2011	1032	Huber	320	100%		102,000	1,700	52,200	0.51	1,752	52.00	1,597	53,797		7.48
2011	1033	Stelker	300	100%		102,000	1,700	116,000	1.14	1,752	52.00	3,548	119,548		16.62
2011	1034	Stöger	300	90%		91,800	1,530	69,600	0.76	1,582	52.00	2,365	71,965		11.08
2011	1035	Stadelmann	300	50%		51,000	850	37,120	0.73	836	-14.00	-611	36,509		-2.86
2011	1036	Hofmann	900	100%	no	102,000	1,700	255,200	2.50	1,832	132.00	-	255,200		-
2011	1048	Holbeck	900	100%		102,000	1,700	69,600	0.68	1,772	72.00	2,948	72,548		13.81
2011	1050	Hemmer	900	100%		102,000	1,700	69,600	0.68	1,751	51.00	2,088	71,688		9.78
2011	1052	Hinder	900	100%		102,000	1,700	81,200	0.80	1,776	76.00	3,630	84,830		17.00
2011	1054	Houillemer	900	100%		102,000	1,700	92,800	0.91	1,792	92.00	5,022	97,822	p	-
2011	1056	Habedieehre	900	100%		102,000	1,700	58,000	0.57	1,752	52.00	1,774	59,774		8.31
2011	1058	Küng (VL)	100	100%	no	102,000	1,700	220,400	2.16	1,812	112.00	-	220,400		-
2011	1060	Kalberer	100	100%		102,000	1,700	92,800	0.91	1,732	32.00	1,747	94,547		8.18
2011	1062	Koschnitz	100	100%		102,000	1,700	81,200	0.80	1,756	56.00	2,675	83,875		12.53
2011	1064	Keygun	100	100%		102,000	1,700	69,600	0.68	1,792	92.00	3,767	73,367		17.64
2011	1066	Luginbühl	101	100%		102,000	1,700	110,200	1.08	1,712	12.00	778	110,978		3.64
2011	1068	Vonäsch	102	90%		91,800	1,530	104,400	1.14	1,502	-28.00	-1,911	102,489		-8.95
2011	1070	Bauer	151	100%	no	102,000	1,700	111,360	1.09	1,712	12.00	-	111,360		-
2011	1072	App	152	100%	no	102,000	1,700	83,520	0.82	1,712	12.00	-	83,520		-
2011	1074	Sahli	153	100%	no	102,000	1,700	97,440	0.96	1,712	12.00	-	97,440		-
								4,802,516	Total time bonus gross			114,280			418
									To pay out (gross)			25,026			

Proof

+	Personnel costs according to P&L		4,916,796	Of which gross time bonus	114,280
-	Non-wage labor costs for the employer	16%	678,179	Social welfare cost in time bonus	15,763
=	Gross salalries of the employees		4,238,617	Gross salaries in time bonus	98,517
-	Gross salary ins sheet "Personnelcosts"		4,140,100		
=	Is again the provision for time bonus		98,517		

Fig. 6.12 Actual personnel costs (including nonwage labor costs) for 2011 (time credits to be paid in cash in 2012 are marked in red)

- If, as in the example company, there are company holidays in the month of July, no personnel costs are incurred in the corresponding cost centers, since no hours were consumed. Of course, the salary is paid in July in accordance with the contract (possibly including a pro-rata 13th monthly salary).
- If the rate for wage dependent social costs is set correctly, these costs are included in the cost centers actual costs based on consumption.
- When and in what amounts these levies are paid out to the social security organizations is important for cash account balances but has nothing to do with accrued costs and therefore with accounting for management.
- The total amounts appearing in cost accounting are exactly the same as those that must ultimately be paid to the social insurance agencies.
- Small valuation differences can arise if time credits are "inherited" beyond the annual limits. The year 2011 will have a net of 212.5 presence days of 8 h (1700 h), while the year 2012 will have one more day (1708 h). The presence hour-rate for 2012 is thus slightly lower than that for 2011—with the gross wage remaining the same. These differences are calculated based on the change in the time credit in the last column of the sheet "Personnelcosts." These are a total of 418 monetary units, see also the last column in Fig. 6.12. Although they are not large, they are presented so that the provision in the balance sheet is calculated correctly. (See the formula for calculating the provision for time credits in the cash flow column in the balance sheets).

The same rules apply to the sales commissions. The 2% commission from CM I Standard applicable to 2011 also includes 16% nonwage labor costs. However, the total amount (77,031) is posted directly to provisions in the balance sheet since it is not paid out until the following year.

Conclusion Regarding Personnel Costs

The methodology described and contained in the model, i.e., depicting personnel costs in the cost centers using only one cost type, greatly increases the understandability of the cost center target to actual comparisons and enables performance-based control. Since the presence times in many countries must be recorded anyway, there is no additional recording effort. The periodical mapping is "only" a question of programming. Since only the gross wages per employee and year are recorded in the simulation model for reasons of simplification, wage adjustments during the year cannot be depicted in the model.

6.6 Transformation to the External Income Statement and Balance Sheet

Until now all deliberations focused on accounting for management with integrated planning and control. The focus has always been on the question of which data, quantities, and valuation approaches are necessary so that managers at all levels can properly manage their units.

Here we show how the management-oriented actual data of the internal income statement and balance sheet can be transferred to the statements required under commercial and tax law with relatively little effort and how the reporting requirements contained in accounting standards such as IFRS (International Financial Reporting Standards), US GAAP or Swiss GAAP FER can be complied with.

In management accounting, the central elements are activities, consumption, and performance as well as the comparison between plan and actual. This means that all items of the company income statement and balance sheet must also appear in the external reporting. What differs from the operational view, however, are the valuation approaches recommended or even prescribed by law or accounting standards.

Expense / Income Item	Operating Treatment	Treatment under Commercial Law
Losses on receivables (incurred)	If these cause a significant reduction in the revenue for a business, they should be planned as standard revenue reduction and deducted in the reports. Their effective amount is usually not known until after the end of the reporting period.	Deducted in accordance with commercial and tax law requirements; often resulting in the postponement of tax payments.
Warranty provisions	If regular replacement deliveries or remuneration are to be made it is advisable to deduct a standard sales deduction for both plan and actual in the operational system.	Deducted in accordance with commercial and tax law requirements; often resulting the postponement of tax payments.
Provisions for litigation risks	Rarely considered since they are only indirectly the consequence of the operational processes; often only known after the end of the reporting period.	Deducted in accordance with commercial and tax law requirements.
Income from investments	Only to be considered in the group-wide view, if the operational management (System 3) also manages the subsidiaries (complete contribution margin across all companies).	Includes dividends and other distributions by subsidiaries.
Income and expenses from financial investments	Management is assessed based on EBIT because it cannot directly influence the financing structure. Therefore, these are not shown.	Reported in conformance with accounting and legal requirement.
Other operating expense and income	Included in cost center plans only to the extent they are truly operational items.	Reported in conformance with accounting and legal requirement.
Extraordinary transactions	Included in cost center plans only to the extent they are truly operational items. This applies in particular to supplements from previous financial years.	Reported in conformance with accounting and legal requirement.

Fig. 6.13 Expense and income items without direct link to operations

6.6.1 Items to Be Added

In the model presented, some items that are usually found in commercial and tax financial statements were not mentioned. Examples are shown in Fig. 6.13.

6.6.2 Valuation of Inventories at Full Production Cost

The valuation of inventories always gives rise to long discussions. Unfortunately, when the focus is on external reporting, cost accounting applications are set up in a much too complicated manner, making it almost impossible for a manager to understand the allocations and accrual postings.

From a management point of view, it is logical that only those costs be included in products/services or in (partially) self-created assets which were also directly caused by these objects. Therefore, in the system presented, only the costs directly caused by a product unit (the proportional product costs) are included in the income statements and in the valuation of inventories of semi-finished and finished goods. In accordance with this principle, only the proportional costs of internal services are charged whereas fixed costs are represented as cost blocks in contribution accounting (see cost cube, Sect. 4.7.1).

This methodology is appropriate in an integrated planning and control system because proportional costs are driven by sales and production quantities, the bills of materials, and the work schedules behind them. Fixed costs, on the other hand, are period costs and should, therefore, be charged to the period in which they are incurred. For example, a director's salary depends on a management decision, not on the quantities produced (See also Sect. 4.7.1).

When preparing financial statements for external users or tax authorities, other considerations come into play. These statements must be prepared in accordance with the appropriate commercial code (or financial reporting requirements) or local tax code. The Swiss Code of Obligations (OR), also used for tax reporting, requires that, "When initially recorded, assets must not be valued at more than acquisition or product costs. In subsequent valuations, assets may not be valued higher than their acquisition or production costs" (translation by the authors). Thus, it is permitted to value inventories of semi-finished and finished goods at proportional product cost. There is no obligation to capitalize portions of fixed costs. This makes it possible to show all purely period-related costs as such in the annual financial statements and for tax purposes.

In other countries, however, and with the better-known accounting standard frameworks, it is required to value semi-finished and finished goods inventories, goods in production and work on capitalized projects and (partially) self-constructed assets **at full product cost.** Examples include:

> *Germany: Section 255 (2) HGB*: "Product cost is the cost of consuming goods and services to produce an asset, expand it or substantially improve it beyond its original condition. This includes material costs, manufacturing costs and special production costs as well as

appropriate portions of material overheads, production overheads and depreciation of fixed assets, insofar as these are caused by production. The cost of production *may be* calculated considering an appropriate share of general administrative costs and an appropriate share of the costs of social facilities, voluntary social benefits and occupational pensions, insofar as these relate to the period of production. Research and distribution costs may not be included" (translation by the authors).

German income tax guidelines: R 6.3 para. 1 EStR (German Tax Law): "The production costs of an asset *must* also include appropriate portions of the necessary material overheads and production overheads as well as the consumption of fixed assets, insofar as this is caused by the manufacture of the asset" (translation by the authors).

Swiss GAAP FER, Valuation principles for the individual balance sheet items, point 9: "Inventories *are* valued at acquisition or manufacturing cost or—if lower—at net market value (lower of cost or market)", p. 30. In the note to this point it is remarked that this refers to full product costs (p. 32, translation by the authors).

IFRS: IAS 2.12: "The cost of inventories comprises the costs directly attributable to the production units, such as production wages. They also *include* systematically allocated fixed and variable production overheads incurred in the processing of raw materials into finished products. Fixed production overheads are those costs not directly attributable to production that are relatively constant regardless of the volume of production, such as depreciation and maintenance of buildings and equipment, and management and administrative costs."

U.S.GAAP, ASC 330-10 is the primary source of guidance on accounting for inventories. As with IFRS, the cost of inventory "... generally includes direct expenditures of getting inventories ready for sale, including overhead and other costs attributable to the purchase or production of inventory" (From: https://www.iasplus.com/en-us/standards/ifrs-usgaap, 2019.).

In accordance with these guidelines, *inventories of semi-finished and finished goods* must be *revalued using pro rata fixed costs* for reporting purposes under commercial and tax law. The fixed cost portions to be allocated are listed in all the specifications quoted. Fortunately, there is no specification in any of the cited standards as to which allocation bases are to be used when calculating full product cost per unit. HGB and IFRS describe the markup calculation (see above), but not in detail. It is therefore in compliance with the law to add the fixed costs of production to the inventories of semi-finished and finished goods with a *single* markup rate (Fig. 6.14).

Allocation of overhead based on a single overhead rate is enough to change from the proportional to the full cost of goods manufactured and sold.

For the example company, a more detailed approach is taken to maintain the fiction of a more "realistic" cost allocation. The starting point is the actual proportional product costs from the sheet "Actualstock," each with its subtotals for semi-finished and finished products. To be added are:

- The fixed costs of the cost centers directly and indirectly involved in the production (sheet "ActualstepwiseCM").
- The inventory changes from the income statement and the value of goods in production.
- The fixed costs of the cost centers 220, 231, and 232 (401,336). They are completely allocated to the semi-finished products; those of the cost centers

Example for simple fixed cost-allocation to present full production cost in the external P&L and balance

as per 12/31/2011

Fixed cost blocks from contribution accounting	Share for manufac-turing	Share semi- and finished goods	Fixed cost from CM-accounting	Allocation share manufac-turing	
CC 220 - 232 semi-finished goods	100%	100%	401,336	401,336	
CC 240 - 260 finished goods	100%	100%	364,572	364,572	Assumption:
Procurement, warehouse	70%	50%	192,251	134,576	30% for merchandise, each 35% for semi- and finished goods
Production management	100%	50%	216,421	216,421	
Buildings & maintenance	70%	50%	148,294	103,806	Assumption: 70% for Production and warehouse
Repair center	57%	50%	15,736	8,970	57% of the repair hours for manufacturing
Energy center	83%	50%	16,616	13,792	83% of KWh fo manufacturing
IT	30%	50%	265,505	79,652	Assumption: 30% IT-cost for manufacturing
Corp. Mgmt. & admin.	25%	50%	674,782	168,696	Assumption: 25% for manufacturing
Total			2,295,515	1,491,819	803,695 remaining fix cost for administration

	Prop. cost units produced	Directly adres-sable	Allocation	Total	Allocation rate
Semi-finished (sheet "Actualstock")	2,353,334	401,336	362,956	764,292	32.5%
Finished goods (sheet "Actualstock")	2,981,581	364,572	362,956	727,528	24.4%
Total	5,334,915		725,912	1,491,819	

Inventory change	internal P&L	Allocation rate	activated fixed cost	full cost inventory
Semi-finished goods		32.5%	-19,533	-79,678
Finished goods	-60,145	24.4%	30,077	153,338
Work in progress WIP	9,885	24.4%	2,412	12,297
Total	73,002		12,956	85,957

Fig. 6.14 Calculation of full product costs with markups for fixed costs

240, 245, 250, and 260 (364,572) are allocated to the finished products (source is again the sheet "ActualstepwiseCM").

- The production-related fixed cost shares of the remaining cost centers are estimated (column "Share for manufacturing") to obtain a distinction between fixed product costs and fixed administrative and selling overheads.
- The fixed costs of the cost centers Repairs and Energy can be distributed based on the services consumed by the production centers (57% and 83%). For the other cost centers the share of the services performed for the production cost centers is a simple estimate.
- For the separation of fixed production costs between semi-finished and finished goods the allocation basis in column "Share semi- and finished goods" (here 50% each) is used. This results in the absolute allocations per cost center group in the last column.
- In the second part of the calculation, the allocations are totaled for semi- and finished goods. The total divided by the proportional costs of the units produced yields the specific markup rate for semi- and finished goods.
- In the third part, these fixed cost allocations are added to the inventory changes, resulting in the inventory at full cost of goods produced.

As a result, the value of the year-end inventories in the HGB and IFRS-compliant balance sheets are to be valued 12,956 higher.

Transformation from the internal to the external profit & loss statement

Profit and loss 2011		Internal	activated fixed cost	Commercial & tax law	Comments
Net revenue		7,050,157		7,050,157	
Inventory change finished goods	+/-	123,262	30,077	153,338	
Inventory change semi-finished		-60,145	-19,533	-79,678	
Work in progress WIP (at year end)		9,885	2,412	12,297	
Change in assets under construction		36,551		36,551	at prop. cost + material
Produced value	=	7,159,709		7,159,709	
Raw material consumption	-	677,966		677,966	
Purchase price variances	-	7,192		7,192	Could also be assigned to product ranges
Merchandise consumption	-	340,273		340,273	
Gross profit	=	6,134,278	12,956	6,147,234	
Personnel costs	-	4,909,599		4,909,599	
Sales commissions	-	77,031		77,031	
Purchasing & shipping costs	-	20,004		20,004	
Advertisement	-	110,000		110,000	
Office supplies	-	12,623		12,623	
Auxiliary and operating materials	-	48,121		48,121	
Telephone, communication	-	34,722		34,722	
El. energy, water, fuel oil	-	60,100		60,100	
Cleaning & conserving supplies	-	3,740		3,740	
Rent	-	30,000		30,000	
External maintenance & repair	-	205,385		205,385	
Other expense, non-activated project costs	-	77,738		77,738	
Software (Lizenzen & Unterhalt)	-	24,000		24,000	
Total cash out costs		5,613,063		5,613,063	
CFBIT Cash Flow Bef.Interest & Taxes	=	521,215		534,171	
Imputed depreciation	-	226,842		226,842	Input depreciation accepted by tax law
EBIT	=	294,374	12,956	307,329	

Other positions to take into account see section 6.7.1

Fig. 6.15 Transformation from internal to commercial profit and loss statement

6.6.3 Income Statement and Balance Sheet According to Commercial Law

In the income statement under commercial law (Fig. 6.15) the three allocation items were added to the inventory values from the operating income statement. As a result EBIT increased by 12,956. This means that this amount of fixed period costs were postponed from 2011 to 2012. As a consequence, Ringbook Ltd. will pay higher income taxes for 2011. Only when the inventory is reduced in the following years will its tax burden be reduced. Also note that if, from an operational point of view, imputed depreciation is set higher than the tax-allowable depreciation in the commercial income statement, the commercial EBIT is increased by the difference.

As mentioned in Sect. 6.6.1, the nonoperational items must also be supplemented, but this is not the case here. Likewise, the imputed RepV depreciation must be replaced by the depreciation of the acquisition value permitted for tax purposes. The change in EBIT (12,956) must also be reflected in the balance sheet.

To determine the operating assets for the external balance the replacement value adjustments made for internal purposes are reversed (column “Other adjustments”). This is necessary because in the external balance sheet the asset residual values are to be calculated from the acquisition values (Fig. 6.16).

Transformation from the internal to the external balance sheet

Balance	Internal balance per 12/31/2011	Activated fixed cost	Other adjustments	Commer-cial & tax law	Comments
Assets					
Liquid assets	210,100			210,100	
Accounts receivable	1,185,385			1,185,385	No delcredere risk deducted (risk for bad debt)
Inventory:				-	
- Raw-/operating material	41,304			41,304	At standard purchase prices, price variance counted in P&L
- WIP Work in progress	9,885	2,412		12,297	
- Merchandise	53,125			53,125	
- Semi-finished goods	116,152	-19,533		96,618	
- Finished goods	271,290	30,077		301,366	
Current assets	1,887,241	12,956		1,900,196	
Fixed assets	2,785,158		-541,000	2,244,158	Accounting value of fixed assets
Assets under constr. /projects, yearly amou	144,051			144,051	
Total fixed assets	2,929,209	-	-541,000	2,388,209	
Balance sum	4,816,450	12,956	-541,000	4,288,405	
Liabilities					
Accounts payable	180,485			180,485	
Bank account	1,293,104			1,293,104	
Provisions for sales commission	77,031			77,031	Interest of 98'577 re-added
Time bonus for employees	107,083			107,083	
Other short term provisions	50,000			50,000	
Current liabilities	1,707,704	-	-	1,707,704	Deferred tax of 37'982 re-added
Long term loan	800,000			800,000	
Long-term liabilities	800,000	-	-	800,000	
Total liabilities	2,507,704			2,507,704	
Replacement value adjustments	541,000		-541,000	-	Dissolution of diff. between repl. value and financial acc.
Reserves/profit carried forward	473,372			473,372	
Share capital	1,000,000			1,000,000	
EBIT	294,374	12,956		307,329	Before interest and def. taxes, amounts deducted from
Equity	2,308,746	12,956	-541,000	1,780,702	bank account and provisions
Balance sum	4,816,450	12,956	-541,000	4,288,405	

Fig. 6.16 Transition from the internal balance sheet to the commercial balance sheet

Overall, the total of all changes made for external reporting leads to profit shifts which distort the result achieved during the year from management's point of view. Additionally, they generate incomplete information regarding the funds needed for operations. Even worse effects arise when impairments must be recognized in accordance with US GAAP or IFRS rules. External reports should therefore only be shown to those managers who are responsible for their content. This also applies to the financial statements of subsidiaries in groups.

The structure of the individual business and of its management is the guideline for devising management accounting systems. Managers of all levels must be enabled to carry out their analyses based on performance and value down to individual items and cost centers.

Planning and control should always come before external reporting!

After Planning Is Before Planning: New Year, New Challenges

7

The owners and management of Ringbook Ltd. met after preparing the annual financial statements to assess the future of the company. It was noted that, although sales and earnings growth were good in 2011, it is questionable as to how the company can remain sustainably successful and develop in line with changes in the market. There are company policy and strategic questions regarding the company's current and future position in the market, as well as the question of what needs to be done to consolidate or expand this position.

7.1 Entrepreneurial Orientation/Corporate Policy

All shares of Ringbook Ltd. are owned by the founding family. As members of the Board of Directors, the shareholders take the overall management of the company very seriously but only partially participate in the operations of the company. The employed managing director is responsible for the implementation of Board policies and strategy.

In the spring of 2012, the owners, together with the managing director, the sales manager, and the production manager, revised the **company policies**, laying the foundations for a new start in strategic planning. The following key stones were agreed upon (compare with Fig. 1.9 in Sect. 1.4.1):

- Ringbook Ltd. is to remain an independent family-owned company.
- The market position is to be strengthened, with market share in Switzerland increased through continuous growth (with the medium-term goal of becoming number 2 in the home market).
- The primary market is to remain in Switzerland. However, exports are important as they increase production volume and consequently reduce average unit costs.
- The stability of the ring binders is rated in the marketplace as being "above average": the mechanism of a fully loaded binder survives undamaged from

L. Rieder, R. Lawson, *Management Control with Integrated Planning*, Management for Professionals, https://doi.org/10.1007/978-3-030-48302-9_7

one-meter falls. Customers particularly appreciate the ability to order binders specifically adapted to their needs (special designs and customer-specific equipment). Therefore, sales efforts will be targeted to higher price market segments.

- Despite electronic and software-related changes in data storage and retrieval, it is still unclear how strongly and by what means electronic storage will be substituted for paper documents and what consequences this will have for the demand for ring binders. The development of an early warning system to monitor this risk is planned.
- To finance future development, shareholders require an average operating result of 10% of the assets invested at replacement values (ROI). No distributions are planned for the time being, as the dependence on loans still appears too high.
- As a liquidity reserve, the equivalent of 2 months of personnel costs is always to be held in the form of assets that can be liquidated at short notice.
- To remain independent of lenders, the equity ratio (equity/total assets) is to rise above 50%.
- All employees, especially managers, are expected to act responsibly in the sense of supporting the whole company. This is based on the conviction that, in an increasingly complex environment, all employees should make an important contribution to the overall result and largely control and steer themselves.
- For this reason, management by objectives (see Sect. 1.2) is the fundamental management methodology to be followed at Ringbook Ltd.
- Active participation of employees in vocational training associations and in associations that promote the development of the private sector is desirable and supported.
- Managers should regularly explain these corporate policy principles to their employees, as well as the outcomes which result from following them.
- In order to learn new findings and procedures for Ringbook Ltd., each coworker is to be invited annually to at least one internal training seminar.

In parallel with the revision of corporate policies, an analysis of the current situation regarding the market position of Ringbook Ltd. was also carried out.

7.2 Market Analysis (with Comparison to Previous Years 2010–2011)

Using figures from the office supplies association and from market surveys, Ringboook Ltd.'s sales manager estimates the volume of its domestic sales of ring binders as follows:

- The number of purchasers of ring binders (private individuals and organizations) rose by approximately 0.5% between 2010 and 2011 due to population growth.
- Despite increasing document scanning, the average number of ring binders purchased per consumer rose by around 2%.

Ringbook market in Switzerland

Exemplary assumptions

Year	2010 actual	2011 actual	
Potential consumers	3,500,000	3,517,500	
Avg. annual demand per customer	3.50	3.57	2% growth assumed
Annual market volume (quantity)	12,250,000	12,557,475	
Ringbook Ltd.	1,627,800	1,720,390	
- of which export	445,700	450,200	
- actually sold in Switzerland	1,182,100	1,270,190	
Market share Ringbook Ltd. (quantity)	9.6%	10.1%	

Fig. 7.1 Estimate of volume–market share development in Switzerland

- This results in a market volume of approximately 12.5 million ring binders in the Swiss market at the end of 2011.
- The export sales of Ringbook Ltd. have to be deducted from total sales to make the domestic revenue figure comparable to that of the prior year.
- If the resulting volume of binders sold in Switzerland is divided by the total market volume, the result is Ringbook Ltd.'s market share.
- The market saturation level is assumed to be 100%. This means that demand is completely "satisfied" by the suppliers.
- An increase in market share from 9.6 to 10.1% seems realistic because two suppliers went out of business in 2011 and Ringbook Ltd.'s sales volume increased by around 7.4% (Fig. 7.1).

The **stationery customer group** is a cause for concern, especially in sales area 201. Many of the customers in this group will give up their business in 2012 and subsequent years because they either retire without successors or do not foresee adequate business volume due to shifts to wholesalers and online purchasing. This was the reason for launching the Ringbook Ltd. online shop project in 2011 (see Sect. 4.6).

Furthermore, "Rack Jobbers" offering low price/low-quality products from abroad to wholesalers are active in the market. They offer to keep point of sales systems up to date and to continuously refill shelves. To keep the large distributors as customers, higher discounts were already granted in 2011 (see sheet on item discounts).

In the medium term, the **sales territories** will also have to be redefined. The sales representative of region 201 (Bauer) will retire in 2016. His sales area is most affected by the shifts in customer structure (reduction of direct sales customers in the stationery sector).

As Fig. 7.2 shows, direct sales to customer companies are developing very well. The expansion of this customer group will be an important task both for the area manager (203/Sahli) and for sales promotion.

Year	Sales region	Gross sales	Net sales	Item discount absolute	Invoice discount absolute	Sales quantity	Change net sales to prev. year
2010	201	2,554,082	2,063,463	358,952	131,667	543,880	
2010	202	2,828,228	2,472,425	166,247	189,557	520,780	
2010	203	606,928	519,862	56,719	30,346	117,440	
2010	204	2,141,340	1,541,765	-	599,575	445,700	
			6,597,514	581,919	951,145	1,627,800	
2011	201	2,582,088	2,063,504	381,831	136,753	563,420	100.0%
2011	202	3,103,968	2,690,213	200,684	213,071	576,230	108.8%
2011	203	742,952	626,371	79,434	37,148	130,540	120.5%
2011	204	2,319,540	1,670,069	-	649,471	450,200	108.3%
		8,748,548	7,050,157	661,949	1,036,443	1,720,390	106.9%

Fig. 7.2 Net sales development in the sales territories (sheet "Salesstatistics")

Product group	PG	Year	Net sales	Gross sales	Sales quantity	Change to prev. year	CM I Standard after commissions	CM I in % net sales
2Ring normal (stock)	1	2010	1,457,952	1,802,810	447000			
2Ring normal (stock)	1	2011	1,500,219	1,870,250	462800	2.9%	974,194	64.9%
4Ring normal (stock)	2	2010	1,368,549	1,733,300	455800			
4Ring normal (stock)	2	2011	1,424,775	1,810,700	476400	4.1%	562,721	39.5%
2Ring special designs	3	2010	1,308,868	1,591,700	289400		-	
2Ring special designs	3	2011	1,362,900	1,669,250	303500	4.1%	833,229	61.1%
4Ring special designs	4	2010	931,549	1,183,840	211400		-	
4Ring special designs	4	2011	983,150	1,251,320	223450	5.5%	501,516	51.0%
2Ring special formats (stock)	5	2010	588,377	716,040	105300		-	
2Ring special formats (stock)	5	2011	644,694	790,840	116300	9.6%	152,113	30.7%
4Ring special formats (stock)	6	2010	575,586	671,160	98700		-	
4Ring special formats (stock)	6	2011	638,928	750,040	110300	11.0%	470,907	73.0%
Merchandise	7	2010	366,633	431,728	20200		-	
Merchandise	7	2011	495,490	606,148	27640	35.1%	279,853	43.8%
	Total	2010	6,597,514	8,130,578	1,627,800	-		
	Total	2011	7,050,157	8,748,548	1,720,390	6.9%	3,774,533	53.5%

Fig. 7.3 Change in product groups (see sheet "Salesstatistics")

Because existing customers are lost for a variety of reasons, the acquisition of new customers will be important in subsequent years. Sales management is aware of the need to expand efforts to attract new customers. In particular, the aim is to generate leads (i.e., invitations for sales representatives to visit a potential customer and convince him to purchase Ringbook Ltd. products).

The **product group analysis** (Fig. 7.3) confirms the trend of previous years. The growth drivers (in percentage terms) are the merchandise and the special formats (the latter are not included in the product ranges of many competitors). If the sales change is compared with the achieved CM I as a percentage of net revenue (see sheet "ActualCMitems"), it becomes evident that the special formats (product groups 5 and 6) have also made a significant contribution to improving earnings. The same applies to the merchandise. Although their CM I as a percentage of net revenue at 43.8% is substantially lower than that of their own products, the merchandise does not have to cover any fixed production costs.

For the sales promotion of own products, the challenge arises to concentrate product-related advertising on two-ring books and four-ring special formats, since a higher CM I percentage of net revenue can be generated with these product groups.

The **ABC analysis** can be derived from the sales statistics and the CM I calculation (Fig. 7.4). First, the item "CM 1 actual after commission" was sorted in descending order and the sales shares of the total sales (net) were calculated. In the "cumulated" column one can find which items represent 80% of the total revenue. These are classified as A items. The items over 80–95% are the B articles and the remaining the C articles.

It is noticeable that the merchandise products (items 120000 ff.) are mainly C items. This is understandable as the range of merchandise has only been available for 3 years. The C and B articles of the company's own products would have to be analyzed in more detail if capacity bottlenecks needed to be addressed. That has not been the case yet.

In the right three columns the same ABC analysis of the achieved CM I was created. The two best-selling items (103000 and 105110) contribute disproportionately to the creation of CM. These items should therefore be brought to the fore in sales talks with customers.

The same procedure can also be used to create a **customer ABC analysis**, which provides essential information for planning sales visits. If product range streamlining should become necessary, a two-dimensional ABC analysis can be developed by customer and item. This enables precise discussions with individual customers in order to convert their C product orders into A product orders.

The analysis of the contribution margins by the customer, again presented in descending order, reveals a smaller cluster risk. The top ten clients generated 3,648,191 net sales, representing 51.7% of total net sales. Sales to the Austrian subsidiary and to the French distributor were not among the top ten as they serve their own markets (Fig. 7.5).

The tracking of incoming orders and order backlogs is not so important at Ringbook Ltd., as customer orders are delivered quickly (at the end of 2011 only one item of sales order 324 was in the order backlog; it was not counted in annual sales).

The **delivery reliability** of Ringbook Ltd. must be improved. The analysis in the sheet "Actualsales" reveals that in 2011 123 of 411 order items were delivered a little late, which corresponds to 30% of all order items. In total, there were 499 days of delay, i.e., an average of 4 days per delayed order.

These examples are intended to show how deep in detail of the individual dimensions of sales and distribution one can go when analyzing revenue and CM creation. Many starting points for improvements are created. The prerequisite, however, is that the relevant data is entered for each order item, as shown in the simulation model. Even when working with Excel and its limitations this can be referred to as Big Data Analysis (around 1350 data records from invoiced items and CM calculation).

ABC-Analysis of the single products , actual 2011

Itemnr	Net sales actual	CM I actual after commission	Share of net sales	Cumu-lated	ABC	CM I share	Cumu-lated	ABC
103000	644,694	470,907	9.1%	9.1%	A	12.5%	12.5%	A
105110	732,952	457,575	10.4%	19.5%	A	12.1%	24.6%	A
104000	638,928	279,853	9.1%	28.6%	A	7.4%	32.0%	A
105010	375,970	246,937	5.3%	33.9%	A	6.5%	38.6%	A
105050	377,011	235,960	5.3%	39.3%	A	6.3%	44.8%	A
101090	486,262	222,995	6.9%	46.2%	A	5.9%	50.7%	A
101100	378,224	216,327	5.4%	51.5%	A	5.7%	56.4%	A
105090	356,235	203,169	5.1%	56.6%	A	5.4%	61.8%	A
105020	240,414	160,695	3.4%	60.0%	A	4.3%	66.1%	A
105120	249,854	157,775	3.5%	63.6%	A	4.2%	70.3%	A
105030	233,282	153,477	3.3%	66.9%	A	4.1%	74.3%	A
101060	322,963	139,021	4.6%	71.4%	A	3.7%	78.0%	A
101070	389,752	120,375	5.5%	77.0%	A	3.2%	81.2%	A
101020	218,940	95,991	3.1%	80.1%	A	2.5%	83.7%	B
101040	161,679	80,714	2.3%	82.4%	B	2.1%	85.9%	B
105080	109,526	69,559	1.6%	83.9%	B	1.8%	87.7%	B
105070	83,334	54,770	1.2%	85.1%	B	1.5%	89.2%	B
101010	114,048	43,488	1.6%	86.7%	B	1.2%	90.3%	B
101120	83,866	43,143	1.2%	87.9%	B	1.1%	91.5%	B
101030	85,104	40,323	1.2%	89.1%	B	1.1%	92.5%	B
101050	124,124	40,213	1.8%	90.9%	B	1.1%	93.6%	B
105060	59,910	39,408	0.8%	91.7%	B	1.0%	94.7%	B
120010	114,675	36,044	1.6%	93.4%	B	1.0%	95.6%	B
120040	68,167	27,714	1.0%	94.3%	B	0.7%	96.3%	C
101110	34,798	19,050	0.5%	94.8%	C	0.5%	96.8%	C
105100	23,859	14,710	0.3%	95.2%	C	0.4%	97.2%	C
105040	20,772	13,388	0.3%	95.4%	C	0.4%	97.6%	C
120110	53,480	12,873	0.8%	96.2%	C	0.3%	97.9%	C
120080	54,387	12,074	0.8%	97.0%	B	0.3%	98.3%	C
120020	35,875	11,259	0.5%	97.5%	C	0.3%	98.5%	C
120030	28,671	11,120	0.4%	97.9%	C	0.3%	98.8%	C
120090	43,029	10,587	0.6%	98.5%	C	0.3%	99.1%	C
120100	35,961	8,964	0.5%	99.0%	C	0.2%	99.4%	C
120060	24,427	8,819	0.3%	99.4%	C	0.2%	99.6%	C
120050	16,985	5,994	0.2%	99.6%	C	0.2%	99.8%	C
120070	14,053	4,909	0.2%	99.8%	C	0.1%	99.9%	C
101080	8,165	2,595	0.1%	99.9%	C	0.1%	100.0%	C
120200	5,780	1,755	0.1%	100.0%	C	0.0%	100.0%	C
Totals	7,050,157	3,774,533	100.0%			100.0%		

Fig. 7.4 ABC analysis of individual products (sheet "Actualsales")

Actual customer CM I

Cust nr	Customer_name	Year	Cust group	Sales region	Sales channel	Gross revenue	Net revenue	CM I standard actual	CM I after commis-sions	CM I in % net revenue	Top ten CM I
400	Ringbuch Ges.m.b.H Dornbirn	2011	6	204	2	1,448,040	1,042,589	455,512	446,402	42.8%	0
160	Papeterie Remund	2011	1	202	1	803,000	690,580	442,232	433,387	62.8%	1
510	Universität St. Gallen	2011	7	202	2	733,900	660,510	349,337	342,350	51.8%	2
395	Classeurs de St. Gall SA Mulhouse	2011	6	204	2	871,500	627,480	310,299	304,093	48.5%	0
380	IBM (Schweiz) AG	2011	4	203	2	505,882	433,144	260,336	255,129	58.9%	3
320	Neue Warenhaus AG	2011	3	201	1	431,132	350,954	213,415	209,147	59.6%	4
190	Matzenauer & Co, AG	2011	2	201	1	456,080	347,224	213,128	208,865	60.2%	5
540	FHS Ostschweiz	2011	7	202	2	353,980	318,582	188,855	185,078	58.1%	6
300	Von Roll AG	2011	4	202	2	298,040	253,334	167,490	164,140	64.8%	7
330	Manor SA	2011	3	201	1	255,000	206,550	130,329	127,722	61.8%	8
290	Rohner AG	2011	4	202	2	174,200	148,070	96,638	94,705	64.0%	9
180	Gimmi & Co. AG	2011	2	201	1	314,164	239,243	96,320	94,394	39.5%	10
390	COOP AG	2011	3	203	2	237,070	193,227	91,929	90,091	46.6%	
310	Siemens AG	2011	4	201	2	200,640	170,544	88,628	86,856	50.9%	
340	EDMZ Eidg. Drucksachen- & Mat.zentrale	2011	5	202	2	191,216	162,534	87,743	85,988	52.9%	
205	Grobet SA	2011	2	202	1	216,000	164,160	79,624	78,031	47.5%	
325	Jelmoli SA	2011	3	201	1	143,128	116,235	76,141	74,618	64.2%	
195	Winterhog Papiere	2011	2	201	1	136,440	103,784	74,783	73,288	70.6%	
375	Kantonsverwaltung Aargau	2011	5	202	2	156,500	133,025	69,358	67,971	51.1%	
520	ETH Zürich	2011	7	202	2	123,660	111,294	53,606	52,534	47.2%	
185	Keller H.J.	2011	2	201	1	127,900	97,204	52,199	51,155	52.6%	
170	Schäfler Pius	2011	2	201	1	134,300	102,698	50,023	49,023	47.7%	
130	Fend Erben	2011	1	201	1	65,998	57,464	36,895	36,157	62.9%	
350	Kant. Verwaltung SG	2011	5	201	2	81,600	69,360	30,916	30,298	43.7%	
140	Jäger Elsa	2011	1	201	1	47,100	40,506	29,760	29,165	72.0%	
530	Schulverwaltung Stadt St. Gallen	2011	7	202	2	53,472	48,125	28,199	27,635	57.4%	
360	Stadtverwaltung SG	2011	5	201	2	81,500	69,275	26,985	26,446	38.2%	
295	Pneu Egger AG	2011	4	201	2	46,980	39,933	23,700	23,226	58.2%	
120	Specker Paul	2011	1	201	1	35,556	30,949	16,138	15,816	51.1%	
150	Wettstein Karl	2011	1	201	1	17,970	15,904	7,339	7,192	45.2%	
110	Hess AG	2011	1	201	1	6,600	5,676	3,704	3,630	64.0%	
	Total	2011				8,748,548	7,050,157	3,851,565	3,774,533	53.5%	

Fig. 7.5 Customer contribution margins (sheet "CustomerCM")

These analyses only provide reliable information if the basic data has been recorded correctly. Managing persons are always responsible for the quality of the data collected. They must check whether their employees enter data correctly, completely, and on time. Neither a controller nor an internal auditor can assume this responsibility, as they are not involved in the data creation process. Nevertheless, the latter can use random samples and test routines to gain an impression of the data quality achieved.

7.3 Customer Benefit Analysis

The question of how existing and potential customers rate Ringbook Ltd.'s products and services in comparison to the competition is of primary importance for the future orientation of Ringbook Ltd. "Who offers the best price/performance ratio for physical (paper) data storage from the customer and user point of view?"

As an introduction to the strategy discussion, a comparison was made between the factors that generate the benefit for the customer and the *costs incurred by the customer*. This resulted in a simple customer benefit analysis (Fig. 7.6). This is not market research in the usual sense. Rather, the staff at Ringbook Ltd. put themselves

Customer Benefit Analysis

	Ratings						Weighted Ratings				
Vendor	Ringbook Ltd.	Biella	Drisag	Leitz	Kolma	Weight	Ringbook Ltd.	Biella	Drisag	Leitz	Kolma
Benefits	Benefits from customers viewpoint										
Strong mechanism	100%	80%	70%	80%	65%	25%	25%	20%	18%	20%	16%
Resilience	100%	90%	80%	90%	75%	10%	10%	9%	8%	9%	8%
Many formats	100%	100%	70%	100%	80%	20%	20%	20%	14%	20%	16%
Many colors	100%	110%	80%	80%	85%	20%	20%	22%	16%	16%	17%
Delivery readiness	100%	90%	50%	110%	100%	5%	5%	5%	3%	6%	5%
Own design possible	100%	70%	110%	50%	80%	20%	20%	14%	22%	10%	16%
Total benefits						100%	100%	90%	80%	81%	78%
Cost	Price level compared to Ringbook Ltd.										
Net sales price to customers	100%	90%	115%	85%	100%	100%	100%	90%	115%	85%	100%
Other cost of use	From customer view all vendors are equal										
Comparison to Ringbook Ltd. (cost and benefits same weight))							0%	0%	-35%	-4%	-22%

Fig. 7.6 Customer benefit analysis (simplified)

in the position of the customers and drew up the following comparison of the suppliers:

- The product features and characteristics customers consider important reveals the list of benefits.
- Ringbook Ltd. sets the standard; therefore, its positions are always 100%. If competitors are rated better, they get a higher percentage, if poorer, a rating of less than 100%.
- In the "Weight" column, the share of 100% of the individual benefit factors is estimated. This is again seen from the customer's point of view.
- In the right half of the table, the estimates were multiplied by the weightings, so that in the "Total benefits" line it can be seen to what extent the total benefits offered by the various providers differ from the position of Ringbook Ltd.
- What is the cost of application in customers view of the different offerings? Here the most important element is the net price paid by the end-consuming customer to his supplier, because the products are largely comparable (all products are similar in terms of functionality). Thus, it was assumed that the end customer would incur the same application costs for all products (space for storage, possible maintenance, or replacement of the ring binders, cleaning).
- In the last line, the balance of benefits is subtracted from the balance of costs. It is therefore assumed that the benefit aspect and the cost aspect are equally important for the customer. It turns out that Ringbook Ltd.'s offer differs only slightly from that of its competitors, i.e., there is largely a "me-too situation." Because Drisag is primarily focused on customer-specific production, its product range drops somewhat; at Kolma, the reason for dropping is mainly to be found in the limited product range and the weakness of their mechanism.

Despite the many (invented) numbers, this comparison is not to be understood as an exact mathematical description of the customer's view. The focus is on identifying the factors that most influence the **customer's purchase decision** (benefits and costs). This should drive future product development and help to increase the competitiveness relative to other providers.

From this customer benefit analysis, it can be deduced that Ringbook Ltd. is well positioned, especially in comparison to the larger providers, and therefore has opportunities to gain market share. However, it remains to be seen how the market for (paper-bound) data storage served today will develop and how this will affect the purpose of the company and subsequently the strategies of Ringbook Ltd.

The presented customer benefit analysis is still incomplete. This is because existing and new customers are increasingly including electronic data filing and storage in their list of purchase decision criteria. They ask themselves what differences will arise between physical and electronic filing in their company. From the buyer's perspective, the following benefit and cost elements could be included in the assessment:

Benefit elements

- Shorter search times thanks to electronic support, less manual data transfer of documents, thus less time required for internal tasks
- Less space required for storage, thus freeing space for other uses
- Savings in the procurement of physical filing media (ring binders, filing boxes)
- Less effort for wastepaper disposal

Cost components

- Hardware and software to be installed at cost, maintenance, and license costs
- System introduction and maintenance, integration of applications into ERP, user licenses, energy consumption
- Employee training
- Risk of complete data loss

The attributes of electronic archiving that appear to be essential to customers need to be added as further columns in the cost/benefit analysis. These benefits and cost elements result in additional lines. The cost/benefit criteria that determine the pure comparison of ring binder providers are thus losing weight in favor of the criteria for electronic offers. The useful elements of physical filing are greatly reduced in comparison to electronic filing, and possible savings in working hours are becoming more significant. In return, the installation and operating costs of the electronic solution are more significant. It is recommended using dynamic investment appraisal to compare the cost components (from the customer's point of view), since comparability can be achieved over a period of several years (see Sect. 4.6.3).

The Generic Decision Modeler from Orengo offers a practical, immediately implementable introduction to an in-depth customer benefit analysis; see M. Orengo, *Customer Orientation in Innovation, Marketing, Sales, Organization and Management*, 2nd (enhanced) edition, 2017, Verlag edition, Hamburg, ISBN 978-3-7345-5098-0 (in German).

If Ringbook Ltd. remains active in the existing markets and tries to gain market share, it must expect that total sales volumes for ring binders will no longer grow in the medium term and that the net sales prices that can be achieved will also fall, as its competitors will try to maintain their positions (also by means of price reductions).

This requires a strong **cost position**. Put simply, Ringbook Ltd. must be able to continuously reduce the average total cost per unit sold, i.e., become more efficient. If Ringbook Ltd. is not successful enough in cost-cutting, a competitor will do better and thus have the potential to generate more and longer positive cash flow in a declining market.

7.4 Product/Market-Strategies Until 2015

The strategic discussion at Ringbook Ltd. is currently largely dominated by unanswered questions. The most important ones include:

- Will there still be an interesting market for ring binders in the foreseeable future?
- Our business today is the filing of documents. To what extent will this still have to be done physically in the future?
- To what extent will new technologies replace the physical filing of documents?
- Will we still generate sales in direct contact between the seller and the customer?
- Does our business purpose need to be redefined?
- Will there be anything left to produce at the existing production site?
- Which employees and which systems are required for our future?
- Who will be our competitors in the future?
- Can the resulting transformation be achieved with the financial resources available?
- What will then be the corporate purpose of Ringbook Ltd.?

Owners and management have already discussed this issue several times but have not yet reached final decisions. The following strategic decisions have been taken so far:

- The existing business must be further developed, considering the corporate policy guidelines that still apply. The aim is to generate results from the operating business that will make it possible to finance the challenges of the future. The results to be achieved should be reflected in the planning (annual and medium-term) according to level (down to the individual cost center).
- Even if in the coming years sales increases become possible, it is to be assumed that the market for ring binders will become smaller, since electronic document

filing is legally accepted to a large extent and increasingly documents are transmitted only electronically.
- An early warning system is to be set up which will provide information for the revision of the strategy every 6 months.
- Since it is to be expected that various competitors will withdraw from the ring binder market in the coming years and price competition will increase among the remaining competitors, improvement of the cost position (by achieving average costs per unit lower than those of the competition) must be pursued with great commitment.
- The land and building capacities are large enough to generate 50% more physical output. However, machine capacities are no longer far from full capacity utilization. This must be considered in operational planning.
- To be able to build up future reserves from the existing business for as long as possible, the annual and medium-term planning is to be expanded in a more target-oriented manner.

7.5 The Crux with the Cost Position

If a company builds up a new product/market combination or expands an existing one, it inevitably finds itself in the situation of having to produce continuously cheaper. "Produce" refers to the total costs of the company, including those that are not directly included in the product (i.e., fixed costs). The "inevitable" refers to two major developments:

- Customers (new and existing) want to purchase the service/product at a lower price so that more money remains available for other needs. Successful products or services already offered are quickly imitated by other organizations.
- Competitors try to achieve higher capacity usage to lower the average total cost per unit. This is done with the help of net sales revenue reductions (yet contribution accounting shows that this procedure generally reduces EBIT or even generates losses). Competitors can also reduce net sales prices so much that other competitors cannot join in, resulting in their losing market share.

Sooner or later, all these developments will lead to lower selling prices and thus to lower contribution margins per unit for the company itself. If profit (EBIT) is to be maintained, more units must be sold (of either existing or new products/services) and/or the product and fixed costs must be reduced.

Improving one's own cost position vis-à-vis the competitors is therefore a must. Despite the erosion of sales prices and the trend toward rising costs for internal tasks, profitability must be maintained or improved to earn cash flows for investments in new businesses.

Cost position improvement is an ongoing task of operational management. Finding and implementing the appropriate measures takes time, usually more than a year, as processes and structures need to be restructured. Cost development goals should therefore be anchored in medium-term (operational) planning. The annual plan must specify which part of the cost reduction target is to be achieved in the coming year. The (partial) results to be achieved should be settled in a measurable form in the annual objectives of every manager (see IMS in Sect. 2.1.1).

7.5.1 What Experience Teaches Us

In 1983, the Motorola Dyna Tac 8000x was the first commercially available mobile phone to come onto the market at a price of $3995. Thirty-five years later, a smartphone with more functions and without being tied to a service provider can be purchased from retailers for around $20, roughly 5% of the earlier price. Similarly, the original IBM Personal Computer was launched in 1981 at a price of $1565. Thirty-five years later PCs are available for well under $100 while being much more powerful than the original and offering more functionality. The HP LaserJet printer was launched in 1984 at a price of $3495. After about 30 years, laser printers were available for $100.

These examples show that products or services that have been successfully launched in the market will soon be copied or further developed by other providers and sold at a much cheaper prices and with greater functionality. If a supplier wants to remain in markets such as these while maintaining profitability, it must try to reduce the average total cost per unit of product in every possible way. Companies that were able to parry sales price reductions through growth and a reduction in average costs have survived and, in some cases, have become global corporations. Other companies have become unprofitable due to a lack of cost reductions and had to give up.

These connections are not new. As a result of his empirical studies, B.D. Henderson presented the **Law of Experience** back in 1974—also known as the *Experience Curve* or Boston Effect (Henderson 1979, pp. 11 & 101). In simplified terms, Henderson proved that for entire industries given the product volumes offered in a market:

> The real (inflation-adjusted), full per unit value-added costs decrease by 20–30% with each doubling of cumulative output.

To transfer this high-level understanding into practical application, the individual elements must be analyzed in a differentiated way:

- The rule applies to any doubling of the *cumulative* output quantity: how quickly a doubling takes place is dependent on market growth and on the company's own growth. In fast-growing markets, the cumulative output (of all suppliers) can be doubled in a few months; in mature markets this can take several years.

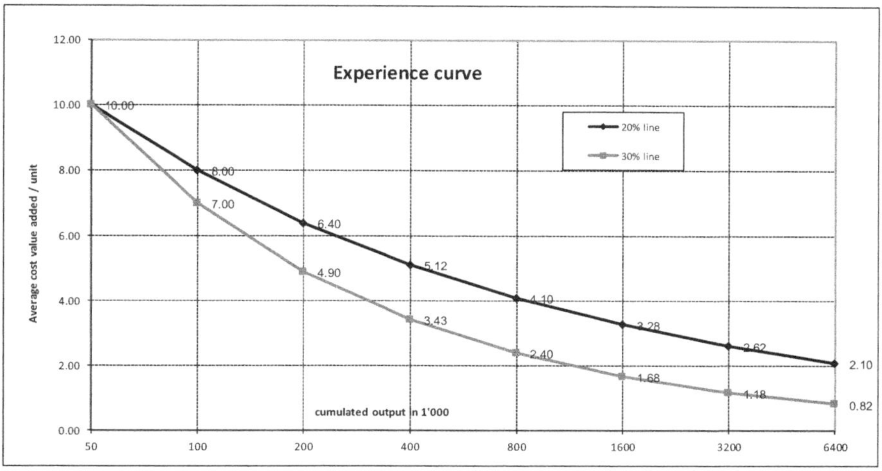

Fig. 7.7 Experience curve as orientation frame

- The relationship between the period for the next doubling and the company's internal cost targets for the next planning year must first be established. In other words, planning within the company must determine how the fixed costs of the functions and the proportional costs of the individual products are to change in the planning years (medium-term and annual planning).
- When it is possible to measure the cost reduction realized in one's own company, it is too late. In the meantime, the competition has already acted. This could lead to shifts in market share, which in turn can give faster growing companies greater opportunities for further cost reductions than in one's own company. *Cost reduction potentials must therefore be actively sought and realized.*
- Cost reduction opportunities are to be found *everywhere* in the company, not only in products. This is because the unit cost decrease is calculated by dividing the value-added costs by the total quantity of goods produced. From an overall cost perspective, a reduction in absolute personnel administration costs reduces unit costs the same as a disproportionately low increase in IT costs in relation to revenue growth over the same period.
- Cost-cutting must start from value-added cost. These are all expenses paid to external suppliers (except direct material costs), the total cost of personnel, as well as imputed depreciation. The formula net sales—EBIT—direct material consumption generates the same figure.

The graph in Fig. 7.7 shows how the value-added costs per unit should develop given an assumed previous cumulative production (and sales volume) of 50,000 units and value-added costs of 10 per unit. The next doubling of the cumulative output quantity will be achieved at 100,000 units. At that time, the average value-added costs per unit should range between 8 (20% line) and 7 (30% line).

Cost reductions are hardly achieved automatically. In most cases, this requires investments in processes, equipment, and time. Employees must learn to handle processes correctly with less deployment time (learning effect). Investments in plants and process improvements as well as product design should lead to processes and functions being operated more cost-effectively (quantity and design effect).

This requires generating ideas and deriving measures and improvement projects from them. The interim targets to be achieved in a plan year are to be quantified and included in the annual objectives of the responsible managers.

The first question to be answered is the **effectiveness** of processes: In what form and to what extent will the handling of a process be necessary in the future? Is work carried out today indispensable? Can lower unit costs be achieved with other input materials or by redesigning the product/service (design change)?

Only then comes the question of **efficiency**: Which cost developments can be achieved in the medium-term planning horizon in the individual cost centers and for the products?

Is it possible to keep the real value-added costs within the empirically determined "development corridor" of minus 20% to minus 30%? This general presentation does not yet show whether the efforts planned by a company in the medium term to reduce its average costs will be effective. For this purpose, it is necessary for a company to *translate the required cost reductions into the annual perspective*.

This is shown below for Ringbook Ltd. where, based on the data for 2011, we calculate the average value-added costs per unit that should be achieved each year if the promises of the experience curve are to be realized. It should be noted that it is not known how competitors' sales volumes will change in future years and how successful they will be in realizing their own cost-cutting potential. It is only possible to determine how the total value-added costs of one's own company, considering revenue growth, needs to change. It is also unknown whether the necessary cost reductions can be achieved through cutting proportional product costs or fixed costs. It is for this reason Henderson referred to value-added cost.

The value-added costs of Ringbook Ltd. for 2011 can be found in the sheet "ActualP&L" (lower part): Gross profit—external service costs (5,839,905). These are divided by the production volume (1,756,330), which gives a rounded amount of 3.33 value-added costs per sales unit (including EBIT).

Initial situation: (Ringbook Ltd. without **merchandise, sheet "ActualP&L" (bottom)**

- Cost of actual value added per finished good unit in 2011 (excluding EBIT): **3.33**
- Planned annual growth rate of sales volume: **3%**
- Cumulated output at the end of 2010: **14 million units**

Application (in Medium-Term/Strategic Planning)

The cumulated output quantity at the end of 2010 (estimate) is the basis for calculating the expected annual doublings factor. Applying the following formula generates in line 5 of Fig. 7.8 the doublings per year factor (from 2012) and in line 6 the cumulative doublings factor.

Transformation to the yearly view

		2010	2011	2012	2013	2014	2015	2016
1	Planned annual growth rate	3%			Value added cost/unit produced, 2011:			3.33
2	Year	2010	2011	2012	2013	2014	2015	2016
3	Units to produce (without merchandise)		1,756,330	1,809,020	1,863,290	1,919,189	1,976,765	2,036,068
4	Cumulative output quantity	14,000,000	15,756,330	17,565,350	19,428,640	21,347,830	23,324,594	25,360,662
5	Doublings per year	-		0.1568	0.1455	0.1359	0.1278	0.1207
6	Cumulative doublings	0	0.00	0.1568	0.3023	0.4382	0.5659	0.6867
7	Value added cost target 10%-line		3.33	3.27	3.22	3.18	3.13	3.09
8	Value added cost target 20%-line		3.33	3.21	3.11	3.02	2.93	2.85
9	Value added cost target 30%-line		3.33	3.14	2.99	2.84	2.72	2.60
10	Required cost reduction (20%-line)			-206,824	-191,056	-178,187	-167,535	-158,616
11	Cumulative required cost reduction (20%-line)			-206,824	-397,880	-576,067	-743,601	-902,218
12	Planned value added cost/unit (objectves of managers) without interest, tax and profit		3.33	3.26	3.19	3.12	3.05	2.98

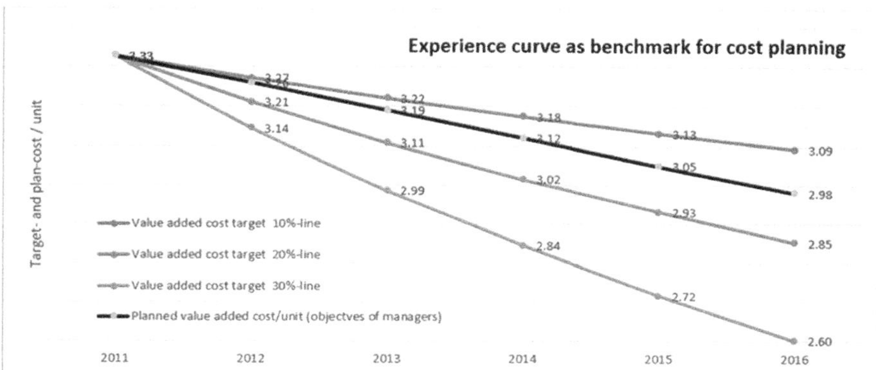

Fig. 7.8 Experience curve target corridor (funnel) and planned value-added costs per unit

$$\text{Annual doubling of cumulative output factor} = \frac{\text{LOG}\left(\frac{\text{cumulative quantity} - \text{plan year}}{\text{cumulative quantity} - \text{previous year}}\right)}{\text{LOG}\ (2)}$$

The cost reductions per unit to be achieved are calculated in lines 7–9. This is—purely mathematically—the application of the formula to Ringbook Ltd. There is one line for each cost reduction range (10, 20, or 30%).

The cost-cutting target of 0.12 for 2012 and for the 20% line is found by multiplying the production volume (2012 = 1,809,020) by the required reduction in value-added costs (3.33 – 3.21 = –0.12) compared to 2011. The 0.12 multiplied by the planned production presents the amount of value-added costs to be reduced (206,824). Line 10 thus quantifies for each year the cost reduction to be achieved in the whole company.

This approach makes it possible to quantify a "funnel" cost corridor for a company: If the company wishes to remain competitive in terms of costs and considering its market position, cost-cutting measures must be implemented. Whether the cost reduction can be achieved by reducing fixed costs or by lower proportional product costs per unit remains to be seen. All managers now have the task of developing ideas, measures, and projects that make these cost reductions a reality.

In line 12, managers enter their estimate of the development of value-added costs for future years (here –0.07/each year). These entries mark the course of the black curve in Fig. 7.8. It should be in the target corridor between the 10% curve (line 7) and the 30% curve (line 9).

The approach outlined here can be used to quantify the costs targets to be achieved for medium-term planning. Annual planning must also be based on this approach.

7.5.2 Starting Points for Cost Reduction

For existing companies, cost reduction is necessary to achieve a competitive cost position as explained. To succeed in this a company needs:

- Many good and feasible ideas
- Decisions that become clear mandates and objectives
- Persistent adherence to the goal of cost reduction
- Measurement of partial results and, where appropriate, corrections
  Cost reductions are to be found everywhere in the company, but the question is where to start first and where the greatest potential can be expected. In Ringbook Ltd., costs are incurred almost equally for the products (proportional manufacturing costs) and for the capacities and structures (fixed costs). Many of the companies known to us have similar cost distributions and are continuously

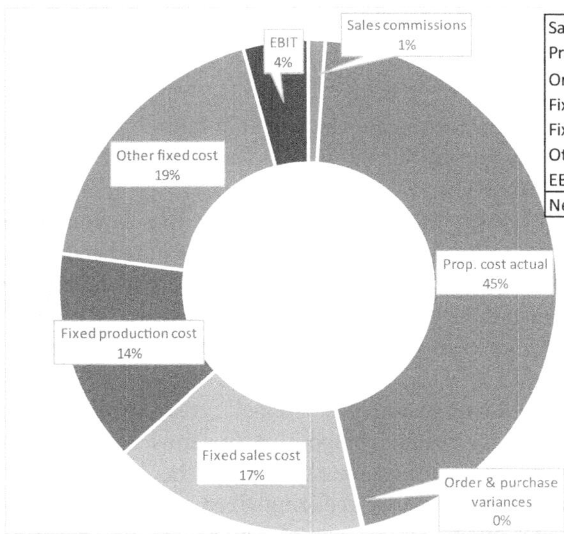

Sales commissions	77,031
Prop. cost actual	3,198,592
Order & purchase variances	5,749
Fixed sales cost	1,178,896
Fixed production cost	982,329
Other fixed cost	1,313,186
EBIT	294,374
Net revenue	7,050,157

Fig. 7.9 Shares of cost and earnings blocks—actual 2011

working to reduce their value-added costs. In most cases, however, these efforts are concentrated on the proportional manufacturing costs, and reducing fixed costs seems to be more difficult (Fig. 7.9).

To focus on the search for cost reduction potentials and to be able to define concrete measuring points, potential starting points are described below along with comments and examples.

7.5.2.1 Cost-Reduction Potentials in Proportional Manufacturing Cost

Proportional production costs are driven by quantities, BOMs and work plans, by processes and lot sizes as well as by the underlying factor prices (material and material costs, personnel costs, energy, possibly quantity-dependent licenses):

- With given sales and production quantities (the plan), it is obvious to first try to negotiate lower *purchase prices for* raw materials. If this is successful, value-added will not be increased, but earnings will improve. To be effective, purchasing negotiations must concentrate above all on raw materials and purchased parts consumed in large quantities and on the more expensive ones. This is, of course, more likely when higher purchase quantities can be negotiated. An essential input for this is reliable annual rough planning (Sect. 4.4.1).
- Material consumption is defined by the BOMs. In our experience, in many companies the parts list data is not up to date. The validity of the *preset quantities* must be checked regularly. It is also important to check whether new materials are available in the market whose use will result in lower cutting losses or scrap given existing procedures.
- A central determining factor for the performance-dependent (proportional) manufacturing costs is the *standard times*. For these too, the data must be updated annually so that the cost center managers receive a suitable comparison between planned and actual performance. Being able to reduce allowed times is a consequence of learning in the process, if no other machines are used.
- If material consumption and working times can be reduced through improved *setup processes*, this leads to lower proportional unit costs just as much as the production of larger lots, resulting in increased added value.
- *Quality control* directly integrated into the cost center and in the processes should result in only good units being passed on to the next processing department. This avoids rework on units of inadequate quality.
- If a company manages to perfect previously incompletely controlled production processes (e.g., wafer production, incomplete chemical reactions, and heat-sensitive processes) in such a way that the proportion of good parts in the first run increases sharply, it not only creates a cost advantage, it can also better meet delivery deadlines.

7.5.2.2 Cost Reduction Potentials in the Fixed Cost-Area

Fixed or step-fixed costs are distinguished from proportional costs by the fact that they are caused by management decisions regarding structures and capacities (Sect. 4.7.1). Because the services provided in the fixed cost areas are often difficult to define, delimit, and measure, it is often only possible to define measurable and verifiable results indirectly.

The tasks of a department are often so varied that they can hardly be quantified in work plans with standard times. As a result, it is seldom possible to plan personnel requirements accurately enough. In addition, many managers often do not know exactly what their employees are really doing, how much time is needed to do it, and which tasks do not have to be done at all. Therefore, in the fixed cost areas additional FTEs are often approved because of numerous complaints that the workload can no longer be handled with existing staff. Yet often it is not clear whether it is necessary to perform the given task to the current degree.

Fixed external costs are also caused by management decisions. Often their amount can only be influenced in periods of more than 1 year, be it because contracts or notice periods have been designed accordingly or that the external services must be provided to maintain operations (e.g., software licenses and maintenance, leasing contracts, calendar-based maintenance work, rents, agency contracts in advertising and sales promotion). This means that cost reduction potentials for these expenses are to be found and realized especially in the planning and budgeting process.

Depreciation is the result of investments in fixed assets and is usually fixed because these assets often are technologically obsolete but still can be used in operation (see Sect. 4.7.7). Depreciation costs are determined at the time of the investment decision and only change when a decision is made to make a replacement investment. Thus, depreciation, from management's point of view, is the type of cost that requires the longest time to change.

Fixed costs are an ongoing issue for the long-term survival of companies because if sales or margin problems arise, fixed cost reductions cannot be realized quickly. These cost reductions need to be worked out and decided in the planning stage. Two instruments are particularly suitable for this purpose:

- *Planning and recording of time consumed for internal tasks*: To better plan and track how much working time is spent on which internal tasks, it was recommended in Sect. 5.1.5.3 to plan and record the corresponding times on a task-related basis. The evaluation of these data generates, especially in multiyear comparison, ideas for the assignment of work to cost centers, for the potential use of data automation (reduction of the working hours required), and for the omission or shortening of evaluations and reports as well as of meetings.
- The *dynamic investment calculation*, as in the application model presented in Sect. 4.6.3, also helps to decide whether contracts leading to expenses can be negotiated more favorably. The cash outflows resulting from an existing service are compared with the cash outflows that would be expected if a new offer were signed. Because an investment calculation depicts the cash flows over the entire planned useful life, it is also possible to depict and compare different contract

durations, one-off and repetitive payments for the various variants. If benefits arise in the form of time savings compared with the actual situation, these are included in the decision template as cash flows. Even if not all figures are available in many decision-making situations, the deciding managers receive an expenditure/benefit analysis for the entire planned useful life before budgeting the expenses item by item and thus releasing the cash outflow.

- In the context of medium-term and annual planning, the question often arises as to whether internal tasks should be outsourced (outsourcing in the fixed cost area). The investment calculation model is also suitable for helping make this decision. This is because the future cash outflows for external costs are compared with the internal benefits of savings in personnel deployment. The appropriate performance agreement can be recorded in a Service Level Agreement (SLA).

7.5.2.3 Combined Levers for Cost Reduction

Cost reduction potentials, whether of a proportional or fixed nature, often arise when changes in the processes are linked to investments. Application examples include product rationalizations, adaptations of the product or the product design, in- or outsourcing of processes, and optimization of lot sizes. Also, the automation of data collection, which means that process and inventory data is captured only at one location but can be integrated into the evaluations of all interested parties, should lead to the realization of cost reduction potentials.

In such decision-making situations, the potential benefits (savings in working hours within the company, more favorable material consumption, lower annual primary costs for external services) are offset by single or multiple cash outflows of investment nature. The instrument to prepare such decisions is again the **investment calculation** or in simple cases a **break-even analysis**.

If initial expenditures (investments) are only necessary in the first year of implementation to realize the cost reduction, a break-even analysis is enough. The investment is divided by the cost reduction per unit, resulting in break-even production volume. If this is already achieved in the first year, profitability is assured. The example uses the figures from the Ringbook Ltd.'s automatic material positioning

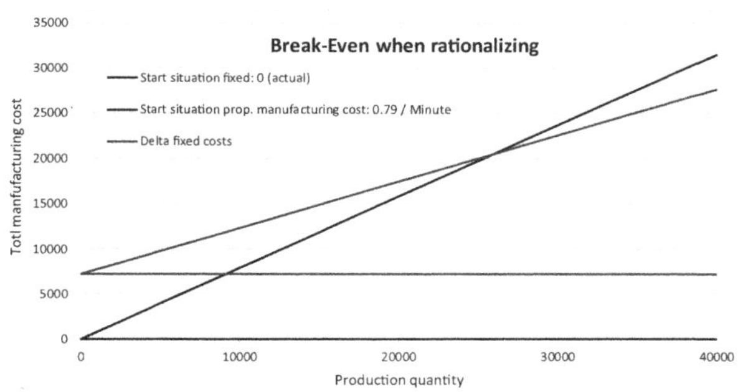

57,493	Project cost (=Investment)
8	Planned useful life (years)
7,187	Depreciation p.a.
0.79	actual prop. manufacturing cost
35%	Reduction of worktime
0.5135	prop. manufacturing cost new / minute
7,187	Delta fixed costs
0.2765	Delta prop. costs / minute
25,991	Break-Even-production quantity

Fig. 7.10 Break-even analysis for the project automatic material positioning

project (see Sect. 4.6.3) but does not yet consider the additional savings in setup times (Fig. 7.10).

If different cost reduction amounts and staggered capital expenditures are expected for the planned years of use, again the investment calculation scheme presented in Sect. 4.6.3 is suitable. Whether and how much cost reduction can be generated from outsourcing or insourcing projects can also be calculated with the investment calculation.

In all these cost-cutting cases, the question has to be answered: "Which costs will be eliminated, which expenses will be added." Expenditures are the cash outflows caused by the project; omitting costs must either be primary costs or proportional costs of internal services provided. If ISPs are discontinued, the underlying costs in the serving costs centers must first also be discontinued before the cash outflow of the project is reduced. An example is the cost reduction project in assembly. Automation leads to lower personnel costs in the assembly cost center. Since the latter receives the personnel services from the personnel pool, expenditure only decreases when the corresponding personnel in the pool is reduced. Any fixed cost allocations are irrelevant for the decision since the cash outflows only become less if the primary costs for the ISP are reduced in the serving cost center.

Finally, *product design* can also make a significant contribution to cost reductions. If it is possible to manufacture a product with cheaper material (e.g., plastic instead of metal) or to integrate more functions directly into a single part or to shorten the test runs of the finished product, the direct material costs and the processing costs can be reduced. In such situations, the investment required to modify the product must be compared with the potential savings (investment calculation). The sales market also plays a role, as customers decide whether they want to continue buying the redesigned product or something else.

The realization of cost reduction potentials and thus the maintenance of a competitive cost position entails a lot of work and requires many decisions considering the overall context. The success of Ringbook Ltd. in making the promises of the experience curve a reality is discussed in Sect. 8.7.

8 Development in Subsequent Years

Changing markets and changes within a company necessitate multiyear planning periods. An integrated planning and control system thus also has the task of depicting planned and actual figures for the medium-term horizon and providing managers at all levels with suitable analysis.

Extension of the Simulation Model to the Years 2012–2015

To provide example performance indicators for multiyear periods, and to derive guidance for the design of medium-term planning, analysis and piloting information, the simulation model was supplemented with data for the years 2012–2015. The model contains plan and actual data for these years in the same granularity as for 2011. The planning and recording instruments described in Chaps. 3–5 are also available for these years, with the figures changed appropriately.

To keep the complexity of the model manageable and to avoid having to repeat all the details again, the following simplifications and changes have been made for the years 2012–2015:

Simplifications:

- No new projects
- No new items
- No change in item and invoice discounts
- No work in progress at the end of the year
- Order entry, delivery, billing, and revenue generation always in the same year (no order backlog at year-end)

Changes:

- Some new customers and some customers who have ceased to exist (in 2012)
- Sales growth with various customers and increased gross prices

L. Rieder, R. Lawson, *Management Control with Integrated Planning*, Management for Professionals, https://doi.org/10.1007/978-3-030-48302-9_8

- Adjustment of planned purchase prices of raw materials
- Other plan and actual amounts for primary cost center costs
- Changes in the headcount of individual cost centers, mainly due to increasing internal tasks
- Salary increases for all employees 2013–2015 (around 2% per year)
- Various new and replacement investments (sheet "Invest&depr")

Due to the database-oriented structure of the simulation model, no new worksheets need to be developed except for additional reports. The previously used worksheets contain the data records for all 5 years. Although this has the disadvantage that the tables for Excel ratios become very extensive, it facilitates orientation in the overall system and allows year-to-year comparisons.

8.1 New Year: Creation of the Management-Relevant Basis for Comparison

In Sect. 3.1 it was postulated that an accounting system suitable for management purposes should always be based on standard values, as this would enable the objectives to be expressed in figures and the managers to be given suitable benchmarks. The target to actual comparison for 2012 must therefore be based on the planned purchase prices, bills of material and work plans, cost center, and sales plans for 2012. The entire budget for 2012 serves as a benchmark for the achievement of objectives in 2012.

This requires the closing balances in the operating balance sheet as of 12/31/2011 be revalued in the opening balance sheet as of 1/1/2012 using the 2012 budgeted figures. Inventories affected by this revaluation include:

- Raw materials (revalued to planned purchase prices for the coming year)
- Work in process (material already on the shop floor and production times already completed valued at planned values for the coming year)
- Merchandise (revalued to planned purchase prices for the coming year)
- Semi-finished products (planned purchase prices, planned cost rates of cost centers, standard quantities, and standard times valued at planned prices for the coming year)
- Finished products (planned purchase prices, planned cost rates for cost centers, standard quantities and standard times, and consumption for setup and scrap valued at planned consumption for the coming year)

The largest revaluation amount of –33,679 from 2011 to 2012 is for finished goods (sheet "Actualbalance"). This is attributable to the project Automatic Material Positioning in the assembly department, as this project should reduce the assembly costs per unit by around one-third from 2012 on. The opening inventories of finished goods as of 01/01/2012 must therefore be revalued to the standards of 2012 so that a correct target to actual comparison can be made in 2012.

The revaluation of the closing stocks to the rates applicable for the planned year is carried out only in the management view. As already shown in Sect. 6.6, this evaluation has no influence on external reporting. If the quantities of the closing stocks of the actual year are known and the standard cost objectives for the planned year are available, the revaluation is carried out automatically from 12/31 to 1/01 of the following year. In the simulation model the necessary calculations are carried out in the Closing balance sheet (Revaluation to standard 2012 column). The valuation of opening balances at the same rates as in the standard cost estimates ensures that managers can compare the same with the same.

8.2 Analysis of Profit Development 2011–2015

The ex post analysis is approached top-down for the entire period. Based on the operating income statements and balance sheets, it is determined which factors have had a positive or negative impact on the change in earnings.

To see the overall impact on the financial statements, the income statements and balance sheets for the period 2011–2015 are presented in Figs. 8.1 and 8.2. The large size of the tables in the workbook requires a substantial reduction in their size when presented in these two figures. The originals can be seen in the Excel workbook sheets "ActualP&L" and "Actualbalance."

A first glance at the operating profit and loss accounts reveals that a major reason for the improvement in EBIT is sales growth. This success was reduced in 2013 by an economic dip (a slump in sales from 2012 to 2013 and corresponding decline in EBIT). The items WIP and Change in Value of Assets under Construction remained empty in 2013–2015 because, as mentioned above, no new projects were completed and all production orders were completed at year-end. Because of the growth in sales, inventories of semi-finished and finished goods also had to be increased to ensure constant readiness to deliver.

The projects and investments (see sheet "Invest&depr") as well as the moderate index adjustments for determining replacement values have led to an increase in the imputed depreciation required for operations of around 50% over the 5 years (from 226,842 to 340,463).

For the plan to actual comparison, the planned values specified in the 2011 plan (for 2011–2015) were used (sheets "P&Lplan" and "Balanceplan" as well as Figs. 4.70 and 4.72). This means that plan adjustments made in 2012 and later are not included in the comparison. The actual data for the 5 years, on the other hand, correspond to the actual performance (in the simulation model). This allows the tracking of the changes in the income statement and balance sheet ratios over 5 years.

The development of the key figures shows that Ringbook Ltd. was quite successful in the values relevant for operating success. Despite the decline in 2013, profitability developed positively (see ROS, ROI, and ROCE). The stability of the company also improved. This is demonstrated by the change in the equity ratio (partly because no dividends were paid out). It should be noted that at the beginning of 2012 only 74% of the fixed assets were covered by equity, but despite the

			Actual internal Profit and loss statement			Total cost method			management-oriented								
			Plan	Actual	Difference	Plan	Actual	Difference	Plan	Actual	Difference	Plan	Actual	Difference	Plan	Actual	Difference
		PR#	2011	2011	12/31	2012	2012	12/31	2013	2013	12/31	2014	2014	12/31	2015	2015	12/31
60 Net revenue			6,794,141	7,050,157	256,016	7,293,023	7,434,170	141,146	7,659,411	7,401,950	-257,461	7,879,393	7,927,976	48,584	8,404,095	8,367,353	-36,741
61 Inventory change finished goods	+/-	2	50,249	123,262	73,013	34,888	143,308	108,420	-90,780	50,744	141,524	156,269	77,746	-78,524	82,112	211,889	129,776
62 Inventory change semi-finished		1	-1,955	-60,145	-58,190	43,009	-10,492	-53,502	71,452	126,727	55,275	106,865	58,825	-48,040	72,376	42,892	-29,484
63 Work in progress WIP (at year end)				9,885	9,885		(9,989.85)	-9,990		-	-		-	-		-	-
64 Change in assets under construction			33,866	36,551	2,685	-	-	-	-	-	-	-	-	-	-	-	-
Produced value	=		6,876,300	7,159,709	283,409	7,370,920	7,556,995	186,075	7,640,084	7,579,421	-60,662	8,142,527	8,064,547	-77,980	8,558,583	8,622,134	63,551
Raw material consumption	-	3	665,307	677,966	12,658	740,749	752,675	11,926	767,070	762,164	-4,906	866,902	878,205	11,303	948,534	961,148	12,613
Purchase price variances	-			7,192	7,192		-11,713	-11,713		-23,398	-23,398		-61,837	-61,837		-40,070	-40,070
Merchandise consumption	-	6	243,530	340,273	96,743	379,532	461,226	81,694	415,921	701,147	285,226	733,924	483,532	-250,392	498,704	570,473	71,768
Gross profit	=		5,967,462	6,134,278	166,816	6,250,639	6,354,806	104,167	6,457,093	6,139,507	-317,585	6,541,701	6,764,647	222,946	7,111,344	7,130,583	19,240
1 Personnel costs	-		4,802,516	4,909,599	-107,083	4,975,936	4,794,813	181,123	4,944,108	4,932,948	11,160	5,128,340	5,123,015	5,325	5,298,179	5,278,405	19,775
2 Sales commissions	-		74,872	77,031	-2,159	84,552	85,789	-1,237	88,666	82,536	6,130	87,369	89,651	-2,282	95,227	93,852	1,375
3 Purchasing & shipping costs	-		20,000	20,004	-4	22,600	22,620	-20	23,700	23,400	300	25,500	24,120	1,380	26,700	25,200	1,500
4 Advertisement	-		110,000	110,000	-	114,000	126,360	-12,360	119,000	126,840	-7,840	116,000	127,920	-11,920	119,100	130,500	-11,400
5 Office supplies	-		13,730	12,623	1,108	13,860	13,192	668	14,630	12,823	1,808	14,690	13,632	1,058	14,830	13,897	933
6 Auxiliary and operating materials	-		52,270	48,121	4,149	53,570	51,184	2,386	54,380	50,374	4,006	54,380	53,294	1,086	56,520	54,267	2,253
7 Telephone, communication	-		34,860	34,722	138	35,270	36,299	-1,029	36,100	36,537	-437	36,400	37,817	-1,417	37,700	38,466	-766
9 El. energy, water, fuel oil	-		67,800	60,100	7,700	71,300	70,140	1,160	72,400	70,320	2,080	73,600	72,900	700	70,800	74,400	-3,600
8 Cleaning & conserving supplies	-		4,080	3,740	340	4,200	3,828	372	4,300	3,630	670	4,400	3,982	418	4,550	4,070	480
10 Rent	-		30,000	30,000	-	30,000	30,000	-	30,600	30,000	600	30,600	31,200	-600	31,600	31,800	-200
12 External maintenance & repair	-		222,575	205,385	17,190	223,595	214,896	8,699	228,770	206,026	22,744	229,520	223,623	5,897	262,550	235,483	27,067
13 Other expense, non-activated project costs	-		82,860	77,738	5,122	83,000	81,684	1,316	84,000	76,688	7,312	85,300	85,005	295	86,920	86,759	161
14 Software (Licenses & maintenance)	-		24,000	24,000	-	25,000	24,480	520	25,600	25,200	400	25,100	25,440	-340	25,600	25,956	-356
Creation of other new provisions			-	-	-	-	-	-	-	-	-	-	-	-	-	-	-
Total cash out costs			5,539,563	5,613,063	-73,500	5,736,883	5,555,285	181,598	5,726,254	5,677,322	48,932	5,911,199	5,911,599	-400	6,130,276	6,093,055	37,221
CFBIT Cash Flow Bef.Interest & Taxes	=		427,900	521,215	93,316	513,757	799,521	285,765	730,839	462,186	-268,653	630,502	853,048	222,545	981,067	1,037,528	56,461
31 Imputed depreciation	-		226,842	226,842	-	266,382	273,521	-7,139	283,299	295,908	-12,610	298,724	317,251	-18,528	315,590	340,463	-24,873
EBIT	=		201,058	294,374	93,316	247,375	526,000	278,626	447,540	166,278	-281,263	331,779	535,796	204,018	665,477	697,065	31,588
EBIT in CM-accounting				294,374			526,000			166,278			535,796			697,065	
Difference				0.00			0.00			(0.00)			(0.00)			-	
				5,762,873			5,743,017			5,890,694			6,139,200			6,339,667	

Value added incl. EBIT (gross profit - third party costs)	6,760,711	7,029,490	6,801,345	7,463,580	7,851,382
Sales quantity (incl. merchandise)	1,720,390	1,786,972	1,686,465	1,848,980	1,890,565
Value added / unit	3.93	3.93	4.03	4.04	4.15
of which EBIT / unit	0.17	0.29	0.10	0.29	0.37
Value added cost (incl. merchandise)	5,839,905	5,828,806	5,973,230	6,228,851	6,433,518
Quantity produced (production level 3)	1,756,330	1,856,000	1,679,910	1,863,700	1,986,680
Value added cost / unit	3.33	3.14	3.56	3.34	3.24
Value added cost target (20%-line/unit exp. curve)	3.33	3.21	3.12	3.02	2.94
Difference	-	(0.07)	0.44	0.32	0.30

Fig. 8.1 Operating income statement over 5 years (sheet "ActualP&L")

Balance sheet change (actual)

Assets	PR#	Opening balance 01/01/2011	Operation	Money flow	2011 Internal balance 12/31/2011	
Liquid assets		210,100	-	-	210,100	
Accounts receivable		1,001,514	7,050,157	-6,866,286	1,185,385	
Inventory:						
- Raw-/operating material	3	68,400	-685,158	658,063	41,304	
- WIP Work in progress			9,885		9,885	
- Merchandise	6	20,516	-340,273	372,882	53,125	
- Semi-finished goods	1	176,297	-60,145		116,152	
- Finished goods	2	148,028	123,262		271,290	
Current assets		1,624,854	6,097,728	-5,835,341	1,887,241	
Fixed assets		2,791,000	-226,842	221,000	2,785,158	1
Changes replacement value			-		-	
Assets under constr. / projects			36,551	107,500	144,051	1
Total fixed assets		2,791,000	-190,291	328,500	2,929,209	
Balance sum		4,415,854	5,907,437	-5,506,841	4,816,450	
Liabilities						
Accounts payable		179,940	626,432	-625,888	180,485	
Bank account		1,171,542	4,802,516	-4,582,377	1,391,681	2
Provisions for sales commission		-	77,031		77,031	3
Time bonus for employees			107,083	-	107,083	4
Other short term provisions		250,000	-	*-160,841*	89,159	5
Current liabilities		1,601,482	5,613,063	-5,369,105	1,845,440	
Long term loan		800,000		-	800,000	
Long-term liabilities		800,000	-	-	800,000	
EBIT			294,374	-294,374	-	
Interest				*98,577*		6
EBT				*195,796*		
Deferred tax liabilities				*39,159*		6
Annual profit				*156,637*	156,637	7
Replacement value adjustments		541,000	-		541,000	
Reserves/profit carried forward		473,372			473,372	8
Share capital		1,000,000			1,000,000	
Equity		2,014,372	-		2,171,010	9
Balance sum		4,415,854	5,907,437	-5,506,841	4,816,450	
Net revenue		6,794,141			7,050,157	
Checksums		-	-	-	-	

management-oriented · Home · 2012

Assets	Revaluation to standard 2012	Rebooking at the beginning of the	Opening balance 01/01/2012	Operation	Money flow	Internal balance 12/31/2012
Liquid assets			210,100	-	-	210,100
Accounts receivable			1,185,385	7,434,170	-7,350,565	1,268,990
Inventory:			-			
- Raw-/operating material	1,670		42,974	-740,963	758,463	60,474
- WIP Work in progress	105		9,990	-9,990		-
- Merchandise	1,007		54,132	-461,226	486,898	79,803
- Semi-finished goods	1,101		117,253	-10,492		106,761
- Finished goods	-33,679		237,611	143,308		380,918
Current assets	-29,796		1,857,444	6,354,806	-6,105,205	2,107,046
Fixed assets		144,051	2,929,209	-273,521	237,000	2,892,688
Changes replacement value			-	71,555		71,555
Assets under constr. / projects		-144,051	-	-	-	-
Total fixed assets			2,929,209	-201,966	237,000	2,964,242
Balance sum			4,786,653	6,152,840	-5,868,205	5,071,289
Liabilities						
Accounts payable			180,485	674,683	-660,374	194,794
Bank account			1,391,681	4,876,486	-4,995,805	1,272,362
Provisions for sales commission			77,031	85,789	-77,031	85,789
Time bonus for employees			107,083	-81,673	-25,410	-
Other short term provisions			89,159	-	*83,283*	172,443
Current liabilities			1,845,440	5,555,285	-5,675,337	1,725,388
Long term loan			800,000		-	800,000
Long-term liabilities			800,000	-	-	800,000
EBIT				526,000	-526,000	-
Interest					*109,584*	
EBT					*416,416*	
Deferred tax liabilities					*83,283*	
Annual profit		-156,637	-		*333,133*	333,133
Replacement value adjustments			541,000	71,555		612,555
Reserves/profit carried forward	-29,796	156,637	600,213			600,213
Share capital			1,000,000			1,000,000
Equity			2,141,213	71,555		2,545,901
Balance sum			4,786,653	6,152,840	-5,868,205	5,071,289
Net revenue			7,293,023			7,434,170
Checksums		-	-	-	-	-

2013

Assets	Revaluation to standard 2013	Rebooking at the beginning of the	Opening balance 01/01/2013	Operation	Money flow	Internal balance 12/31/2013
Liquid assets			210,100	-	-	210,100
Accounts receivable			1,268,990	7,401,950	-7,394,385	1,276,555
Inventory:			-			
- Raw-/operating material	1,260		61,734	-738,767	756,353	79,320
- WIP Work in progress	-		-	-		-
- Merchandise	1,463		81,266	-701,147	730,770	110,889
- Semi-finished goods	2,529		109,289	126,727		236,017
- Finished goods	9,593		390,512	50,744		441,256
Current assets	14,845		2,121,891	6,139,507	-5,907,262	2,354,136
Fixed assets		-	2,892,688	-295,908	187,500	2,784,279
Changes replacement value			71,555	55,958		127,513
Assets under constr. / projects		-	-	-	-	-
Total fixed assets			2,964,242	-239,950	187,500	2,911,792
Balance sum			5,086,134	5,899,557	-5,719,762	5,265,928
Liabilities						
Accounts payable			194,794	661,838	-645,694	210,938
Bank account			1,272,362	4,932,948	-4,884,661	1,320,649
Provisions for sales commission			85,789	82,536	-85,789	82,536
Time bonus for employees			-	-	-	-
Other short term provisions			172,443	-	*12,532*	184,974
Current liabilities			1,725,388	5,677,322	-5,603,612	1,799,097
Long term loan			800,000		-	800,000
Long-term liabilities			800,000	-	-	800,000
EBIT				166,278	-166,278	-
Interest					*103,618*	
EBT					*62,659*	
Deferred tax liabilities					*12,532*	
Annual profit		-333,133	-		*50,128*	50,128
Replacement value adjustments			612,555	55,958		668,513
Reserves/profit carried forward	14,845	333,133	948,191			948,191
Share capital			1,000,000			1,000,000
Equity			2,560,746	55,958		2,666,831
Balance sum			5,086,134	5,899,557	-5,719,762	5,265,928
Net revenue	7,659,411					7,401,950
Checksums		-	-	-	-	-

2014

Assets	Revaluation to standard 2014	Rebooking at the beginning of the	Opening balance 01/01/2014	Operation	Money flow	Internal balance 12/31/2014
Liquid assets			210,100	-	-	210,100
Accounts receivable			1,276,555	7,927,976	-7,849,420	1,355,112
Inventory:			-			
- Raw-/operating material	6,414		85,733	-816,368	786,913	56,278
- WIP Work in progress	-		-	-		-
- Merchandise	2,059		112,948	-483,532	558,965	188,381
- Semi-finished goods	10,710		246,726	58,825		305,551
- Finished goods	15,107		456,363	77,746		534,108
Current assets	34,289		2,388,425	6,764,647	-6,503,542	2,649,530
Fixed assets		-	2,784,279	-317,251	186,500	2,653,528
Changes replacement value			127,513	59,929		187,441
Assets under constr. / projects		-	-	-	-	-
Total fixed assets			2,911,792	-257,323	186,500	2,840,969
Balance sum			5,300,217	6,507,324	-6,317,042	5,490,499
Liabilities						
Accounts payable			210,938	698,933	-706,350	203,521
Bank account			1,320,649	5,123,015	-5,422,123	1,021,541
Provisions for sales commission			82,536	89,651	-82,536	89,651
Time bonus for employees			-	-	-	-
Other short term provisions			184,974	-	*85,953*	270,927
Current liabilities			1,799,097	5,911,599	-6,125,057	1,585,640
Long term loan			800,000		-	800,000
Long-term liabilities			800,000	-	-	800,000
EBIT				535,796	-535,796	-
Interest					*106,032*	
EBT					*429,764*	
Deferred tax liabilities					*85,953*	
Annual profit		-50,128	-		*343,811*	343,811
Replacement value adjustments			668,513	59,929		728,441
Reserves/profit carried forward	34,289	50,128	1,032,608			1,032,608
Share capital			1,000,000			1,000,000
Equity			2,701,120	59,929		3,104,860
Balance sum			5,300,217	6,507,324	-6,317,042	5,490,499
Net revenue			7,879,393			7,927,976
Checksums		-	-	-	-	-

2015

Assets	Revaluation to standard 2015	Rebooking at the beginning of the year	Opening balance 01/01/2015	Operation	Money flow	Internal balance 12/31/2015
Liquid assets			210,100	-	-	210,100
Accounts receivable			1,355,112	8,367,353	-8,291,102	1,431,363
Inventory:			-			
- Raw-/operating material	1,996		58,274	-921,078	934,500	71,696
- WIP Work in progress	-		-	-		-
- Merchandise	3,555		191,936	-570,473	558,965	180,428
- Semi-finished goods	6,211		311,762	42,892		354,654
- Finished goods	11,300		545,408	211,889		757,297
Current assets	23,062		2,672,592	7,130,583	-6,797,637	3,005,539
Fixed assets		-	2,653,528	-340,463	172,000	2,485,065
Changes replacement value			187,441	63,949		251,390
Assets under constr. / projects		-	-	-	-	-
Total fixed assets			2,840,969	-276,514	172,000	2,736,455
Balance sum			5,513,561	6,854,069	-6,625,637	5,741,993
Liabilities						
Accounts payable			203,521	720,799	-708,504	215,815
Bank account			1,021,541	5,278,405	-5,736,405	563,541
Provisions for sales commission			89,651	93,852	-89,651	93,852
Time bonus for employees			-	-	-	-
Other short term provisions			270,927	-	*121,198*	392,125
Current liabilities			1,585,640	6,093,055	-6,413,362	1,265,332
Long term loan			800,000		-	800,000
Long-term liabilities			800,000	-	-	800,000
EBIT				697,065	-697,065	-
Interest					*91,077*	
EBT					*605,988*	
Deferred tax liabilities					*121,198*	
Annual profit		-343,811	-		*484,790*	484,790
Replacement value adjustments			728,441	63,949		792,390
Reserves/profit carried forward	23,062	343,811	1,399,481			1,399,481
Share capital			1,000,000			1,000,000
Equity			3,127,922	63,949		3,676,661
Balance sum			5,513,561	6,854,069	-6,625,637	5,741,993
Net revenue			8,558,583			8,622,134
Checksums		-	-	-	-	-

Financing / definancing

		2011			2012		2013		2014		2015
Creation of other new provisions			-	without income tax		-		-		-		-
Dissolution of other provisions			200,000	200'000 provisions paid via bank, deferred tax liab. added to provisions.		-		-		-		-
Debtor days	53		53	Assumption: Actual debtor days are calculated in receivables acctg.		53		53		53		53
Inflow accounts payable			2,165,817			2,337,528		2,531,254		2,442,249		2,589,784
Creditor days			30			30		30		30		30
Accounts payable payed			1,985,332			2,142,734		2,320,316		2,238,728		2,373,969
Change of long term loan			0			0		0		0		0
Interest on loan and opening balance bank credit		5%	1,971,542		5%	2,191,681	5%	2,072,362	5%	2,120,649	5%	1,821,541
Tax rate (income tax)		20%			20%		20%		20%		20%	

1 Rebooking finished projects & assets under construction
2 Payment of personnel & social welfare
3 Change of liability for sales commissions
4 Change of liability for time bonus
5 Dissolution of provisions
6 see financing/definancing
7 Rebooking of annual profit in reserves
8 Correction of profit carried forward with revaluation of inventory
9 Incl. annual profit
For simplification the annual profit is added to reserves (no dividend payment).

Fig. 8.2 Development of the internal balance sheets 2011–2015 (sheet "Actualbalance")

investments and the higher replacement values, the asset coverage ratio I increased to 134%. Finally, the liquidity situation also improved significantly, with net current assets rising to 1.74 million. This was due to sales growth and to the good increase in profitability (Fig. 8.3).

For a more in-depth analysis of the reasons for these improvements, see the more detailed reports in the management accounting system.

8.3 Development of Contribution Margins and Cost Structure

The actual management accounting complete overview (sheet "CMoverview") summarizes the step-by-step contribution accounting for each year in one column. According to the P&L for 2011–2015, net sales rose from 7,050,157 to 8,367,353. This corresponds to an increase of around 18.7%.

The overview of the Sales Success Statement further shows:

- At 24.3%, CM I (after commissions) grew faster than net sales. This is primarily attributable to the cost reduction in assembly from 2012 (due to the automated material positioning project).
- The product group CM and the total sales CM (28.8%) grew even more than CM I as a consequence of the disproportionately low increase in fixed sales costs. These are economies of scale.
- The purchase price and order-related variances had only an insignificant impact on the positive development of CMs in 2011 and 2012. The strongly positive purchase price variances 2013–2015 are attributable to the fact that the planned price increases did not occur or only occurred subsequently.
- In 2012, months 1–3, cost center 250 assembly shows a total of –15,513 working time variances. This is because the introduction of automatic material positioning took 3 months to function smoothly. For this reason, the specified times in various orders were not adhered to (to be seen in the sheet "ActualstepwiseCM" and as well by order in the sheet "Productionorders").
- Further economies of scale were achieved in the area of fixed production costs. In 2012, fixed production costs rose disproportionately because the pool workforce was not immediately reduced despite the shortened processing times in assembly and because some employees continued to be employed until their final retirement age. From 2013 onward, production structure costs (including the increase in imputed depreciation) developed at a disproportionately low rate compared to CM I growth (109.5% compared with 124.3% for CM I).
- The other fixed costs increased 122.7%, slightly slower than the CM I (124.3%). This improvement occurred despite a sharp increase in imputed depreciation for administration and IT because the number of IT employees was kept constant. However, Corporate management and administration had to increase its staff from 6 to 7.5 FTEs (+25%).
- Because of all these factors, EBIT in 2015 was around 2.3 times higher than in 2011 (Fig. 8.4).

Key ratios in the internal P&L and balance	2011	2012	2013	2014	2015	Formula:
Return on Sales	4.2%	7.1%	2.2%	6.8%	8.3%	EBIT / Net sales
Capital turnover	1.46	1.47	1.41	1.44	1.46	Net sales / balance sum
Return on Investment ROI	6.1%	10.4%	3.2%	9.8%	12.1%	EBIT / balance sum
Capital Employed	4,362,691	4,618,263	4,787,480	4,926,401	5,039,962	Balance sum - "free capital" (accounts payable, provisions)
Return on Capital Employed ROCE	6.7%	11.4%	3.5%	10.9%	13.8%	EBIT / Capital Employed
Equity ratio	45.1%	50.2%	50.6%	56.5%	64.0%	Equity / balance sum
Asset coverage ratio 1	74.1%	85.9%	91.6%	109.3%	134.3%	Equity / fixed assets
Asset coverage ratio 2	101.4%	85.9%	119.1%	137.4%	163.6%	(Equity + longrange liabilities) / fixed assets
Quick ratio	75.6%	85.7%	82.6%	98.7%	129.7%	(Liquid means + accounts receivable) / shortrange liablilities
Net current assets	41,801	381,658	555,039	1,063,891	1,739,966	Current assets - shortrange liabilities

Fig. 8.3 Profitability, stability, and liquidity indicators 2011–2015

		Management accounts complete overview					2015 % of
	Actual year	2011	2012	2013	2014	2015	2011
CM I after sales commissions	KOSnr	3,774,533	4,270,946	4,121,048	4,476,823	4,692,792	124.3%
Fixed costs product ranges	101	159,381	161,618	165,018	169,605	170,639	
	102	151,143	160,290	160,652	165,030	169,249	
CM product ranges		3,464,009	3,949,038	3,795,378	4,142,188	4,352,904	
Fixed costs sales organization		868,373	912,563	983,021	1,007,612	1,010,896	116.4%
Sales mgmt. & office	100	550,530	593,638	663,552	687,318	690,046	
Eastern Switzerland	151	120,076	120,351	120,522	120,708	120,897	
Western Switzerland	152	91,923	92,491	92,673	92,858	93,047	
Business clients (direct)	153	105,843	106,083	106,274	106,729	106,906	
CM sales		2,595,637	3,036,475	2,812,358	3,134,576	3,342,007	128.8%
Purchase price variances		-7,192	11,713	23,398	61,837	40,070	
Material quantity variances		-1,093	-	-	-	-	
Working time variances		-790	-15,513	-	-	-112	
Lot-size variances		3,236	1,556	-2,189	1,409	1,874	
Yield variances		91	-	-	-	-	
Sum purchase and production variances		-5,749	-2,244	21,209	63,246	41,832	
Fixed costs production		982,329	1,118,672	1,198,495	1,104,909	1,075,934	109.5%
Plant mgmt. & work scheduling	200	216,421	204,439	254,914	260,900	265,585	
Stamping	220	93,726	60,922	88,340	87,864	112,942	
Wire rolling	231	26,734	27,471	27,978	30,822	31,253	
Wire bending & forming	232	280,876	290,445	309,970	302,654	322,671	
Cardboarding	240	60,555	63,492	63,740	68,994	66,493	
Personnel pool 240-260	245	241,686	381,185	353,223	253,209	172,786	
Assembly	250	42,861	66,428	67,740	71,639	74,716	
Film welding	260	19,470	24,290	32,592	28,828	29,488	
Other fixed costs		1,313,186	1,389,559	1,468,794	1,557,116	1,610,841	122.7%
Procurement & warehouse	210	192,251	203,629	219,669	224,227	230,059	
Buildings & maintenance	320	148,294	148,902	151,754	157,507	161,618	
Repair center	330	15,736	16,188	16,886	18,145	18,744	
Energy center	340	16,616	30,326	31,876	32,488	40,220	
IT	300	265,505	305,041	311,369	318,404	327,059	
Corp. management & admin.	900	674,782	685,474	737,240	806,344	833,140	
non-activated project costs		0	-	-	-	-	
Creation of other new provisions		-					
EBIT contribution accounting		294,374	526,000	166,278	535,796	697,065	236.8%

Fig. 8.4 Compressed stepwise CM accounting

It can also be concluded from the analysis that economies of scale can mainly be generated by better use of existing capacities and by consistently constraining increases in structural costs.

The presentation of the changes in the cost blocks and the EBIT in graphic form confirms the impact of these changes even more impressively. The total of all stacked bars of a year corresponds to net revenue. The assignment of the cost centers to the individual cost blocks (see Fig. 8.5) corresponds to the functional area assignment in the sheet "CCassignment."

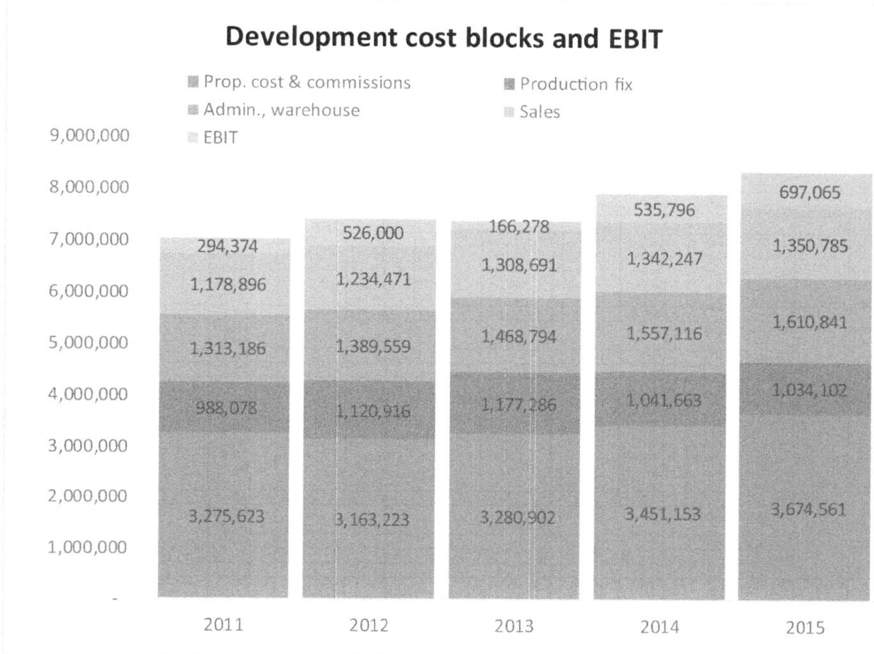

Fig. 8.5 Development of cost blocks and EBIT over the reported years (sheet "Salesefficiency")

8.4 Development in the Sales Dimensions

Since the analysis of real sales and its growth is always prepared based on the single billing items (see sheet "Actualsales"), it can also be aggregated by sales area for the multiyear view. This was done in the sheet "RegionalCM":

- Figure 8.6 shows for each reporting year how much CM I Actual was achieved before and after sales commissions, how much fixed costs were clearly attributable to the respective sales region, and the net contribution achieved by each sales region. No fixed costs were allocated to exports and the onlineshop, as these areas are managed by the head of sales and his office staff.
- Furthermore, in Fig. 8.6 the sales area CM was compared with the working hours of the sales representatives (from the sheet "Actualinternaltasks"). This shows that CM I actual per working hour has increased in all areas, indicating an increase in efficiency.
- If the Sales-CMs (after deduction of all influenceable fixed costs of the entire sales organization) are analyzed in relation to the working hours spent on them, the key figure Sales-CM actual/hour is obtained (column far right in Fig. 8.6). In 2011, an average of 171.90 CM per hour of work was achieved after the

Actual sales success **By sales region** by sales channels at the end of the table

Data origins: "Actualsales", "CCtotals", "Actualinternaltasks"

Year	Sales rep	CCnr	Sales region	Gross revenue actual	Net revenue actual	CM I standard actual	Sales com-missions	CM I after commission	Actual cost own CC	CM sales region	Hours worked int. tasks	Net revenue / hour	CM I actual / hour
2011	201	151	Eastern Switzerland	2,582,088	2,063,504	1,170,406	23,408	1,146,998	120,076	1,026,922	1700	1,213.83	688.47
2011	202	152	Western Switzerland	3,103,968	2,690,213	1,563,081	31,262	1,531,820	91,923	1,439,896	1700	1,582.48	919.46
2011	203	153	Business clients (direct)	742,952	626,371	352,265	7,045	345,220	105,843	239,377	1700	368.45	207.21
2011	204	100	Sales mgmt. & office	2,319,540	1,670,069	765,812	15,316	750,496		750,496			
			Total	8,748,548	7,050,157	3,851,565	77,031	3,774,533	317,843	3,456,691	5,100	1,054.92	605.05
2011			Fixed cost of product range	101	Finished goods					159,381	1700		
2011				102	Merchandise					151,143	1500		Sales-CM
2011			Sales mgmt. & office	100						550,530	6800		actual /hour
			Sales- CM							2,595,637	15,100		171.90

Year	Sales rep	CCnr	Sales region	Gross revenue actual	Net revenue actual	CM I standard actual	Sales commission	CM I after commission	Actual cost own CC	CM sales region	Hours worked int. tasks	Net revenue / hour	CM I actual / hour
2012	201	151	Eastern Switzerland	2,625,402	2,089,541	1,220,317	24,406	1,195,911	120,351	1,075,560	1710	1,221.95	713.64
2012	202	152	Western Switzerland	3,251,209	2,809,179	1,767,599	35,352	1,732,247	92,491	1,639,756	1700	1,652.46	1,039.76
2012	203	153	Business clients (direct)	884,831	744,765	458,321	9,166	449,154	106,083	343,071	1710	435.53	268.02
2012	204	100	Sales mgmt. & office	2,420,324	1,694,227	843,215	16,864	826,351		826,351			
2012	299		Online shop	96,458	96,458	67,283	-	67,283		67,283			
			Total	9,278,224	7,434,170	4,356,735	85,789	4,270,946	318,925	3,952,021	5,120	1,102.24	673.09
2012			Fixed cost of product range	101	Finished goods					161,618	1690		
2012				102	Merchandise					160,290	1560		Sales-CM
2012			Sales mgmt. & office	100						593,638	7600		actual /hour
			Sales- CM							3,036,475	15,970		190.14

Year	Sales rep	CCnr	Sales region	Gross revenue actual	Net revenue actual	CM I standard actual	Sales commission	CM I after commission	Actual cost own CC	CM sales region	Hours worked int. tasks	Net revenue / hour	CM I actual / hour
2013	201	151	Eastern Switzerland	2,708,498	2,148,802	1,192,822	23,856	1,168,965	120,522	1,048,443	1710	1,256.61	697.56
2013	202	152	Western Switzerland	3,155,056	2,721,501	1,692,295	33,846	1,658,449	92,673	1,565,777	1710	1,591.52	989.65
2013	203	153	Business clients (direct)	877,399	740,605	413,388	8,268	405,121	106,274	298,847	1710	433.10	241.75
2013	204	100	Sales mgmt. & office	2,400,920	1,680,644	828,281	16,566	811,715		811,715			
2013	299		Online shop	110,398	110,398	76,798	-	76,798		76,798			
			Total	9,252,271	7,401,950	4,203,584	82,536	4,121,048	319,468	3,801,580	5,130	1,093.74	642.98
2013			Fixed cost of product range	101	Finished goods					165,018	1700		
2013				102	Merchandise					160,652	1530		Sales-CM
2013			Sales mgmt. & office	100						663,552	8640		actual /hour
			Sales- CM							2,812,358	17,000		165.43

Year	Sales rep	CCnr	Sales region	Gross revenue actual	Net revenue actual	CM I standard actual	Sales commission	CM I after commission	Actual cost own CC	CM sales region	Hours worked int. tasks	Net revenue / hour	CM I actual / hour
2014	201	151	Eastern Switzerland	2,658,377	2,098,009	1,225,990	24,520	1,201,470	120,708	1,080,762	1710	1,226.91	716.95
2014	202	152	Western Switzerland	3,369,358	2,909,225	1,800,274	36,005	1,764,269	92,858	1,671,410	1710	1,701.30	1,052.79
2014	203	153	Business clients (direct)	1,109,816	937,852	562,923	11,258	551,665	106,729	444,936	1660	564.97	339.11
2014	204	100	Sales mgmt. & office	2,659,340	1,861,538	893,358	17,867	875,491		875,491			
2014	299		Online shop	121,351	121,351	83,928	-	83,928		83,928			
			Total	9,918,242	7,927,976	4,566,474	89,651	4,476,823	320,295	4,156,528	5,080	1,170.29	706.53
2014			Fixed cost of product range	101	Finished goods					169,605	1700		
2014				102	Merchandise					165,030	1530		Sales-CM
2014			Sales mgmt. & office	100						687,318	8640		actual /hour
			Sales- CM							3,134,576	16,950		184.93

Year	Sales rep	CCnr	Sales region	Gross revenue actual	Net revenue actual	CM I standard actual	Sales com-missions	CM I after commission	Actual cost own CC	CM sales region	Hours worked int. tasks	Net revenue / hour	CM I actual / hour
2015	201	151	Eastern Switzerland	2,760,367	2,194,526	1,279,570	25,591	1,253,979	120,897	1,133,082	1710	1,283.35	748.29
2015	202	152	Western Switzerland	3,536,675	3,051,284	1,869,456	37,389	1,832,067	93,047	1,739,020	1710	1,784.38	1,093.25
2015	203	153	Business clients (direct)	1,120,841	947,564	572,430	11,449	560,981	106,906	454,075	1710	554.13	334.75
2015	204	100	Sales mgmt. & office	2,911,290	2,037,903	971,127	19,423	951,705		951,705			
2015	299		Online shop	136,077	136,077	94,060	-	94,060		94,060			
			Total	10,465,250	8,367,353	4,786,644	93,852	4,692,792	320,850	4,371,942	5,130	1,207.29	725.43
2015			Fixed cost of product range	101	Finished goods					170,639	1700		
2015				102	Merchandise					169,249	1530		Sales-CM
2015			Sales mgmt. & office	100						690,046	8600		actual /hour
			Sales- CM							3,342,007	16,960		197.05

Fig. 8.6 Contribution margins of the sales areas (sheet "RegionalCM")

deduction of all fixed sales costs. In the crisis year 2013, this figure fell to 165.43, but then rose to 197.05 by 2015. Here also considerable progress was made in productivity.

- Figure 8.7 documents how the sales region CM and the entire sales CM have changed over the 5-year period. The increase in Sales CM is the main reason for the EBIT increase over the years.
- The sheet "CustomerCM" (only in the simulation model) shows how the revenues and CM of the individual customers changed during the reporting period. Sorting was chosen in descending order, as this also resulted in an ABC-overview. In addition, it can be shown how the order of the ten largest customers shifted over the years (the subsidiaries were each marked with rank 0).

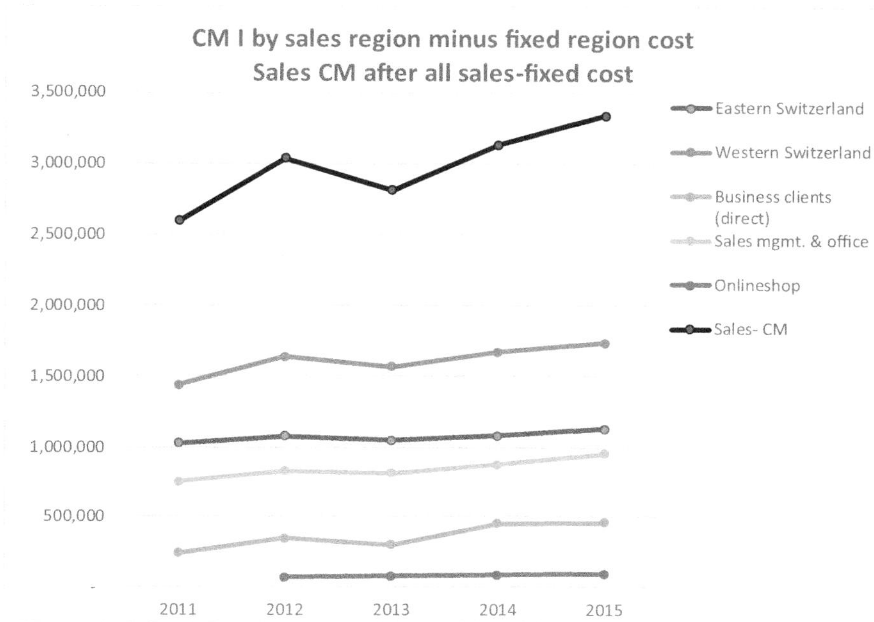

Fig. 8.7 Contribution margin development of the sales regions and total (not cumulated)

- In the sheet "CustomerCM," it was further evaluated which and how many new customers could be acquired and how their sales developed. This overview is just as necessary for the management of the sales area as the overview of lost customers and the causes of these departures (these examples can all be found in 2012).

The positive CM development is also reflected in the reclassification according to sales channels (Fig. 8.8). A look at the development of the CM I in the three sales channels produces a forewarning for the future. Most of the 18 new customers were acquired in the direct sales channel, while the 4 lost customers were all dealers (see sheet "CustomerCM"). As a result, the share of direct sales is becoming increasingly important for overall success (64.9% of CM I in 2015). Six of the top revenue and CM bringer companies were direct sales customers in 2015 (see sheet "CustomerCM"). These shifts must be kept in mind so that cluster risks do not grow unnoticed.

The strong sales and CM growth from 2011 to 2015 has left its mark on the internal tasks, especially in the cost center Sales Management (100). The number of employees had to be increased in partial steps from four to five persons. It should be noted that this also includes the work for the onlineshop (800–1400 hours p.a., see sheet "Actualinternaltasks"). 68.34 was the average presence hour rate in cost center 100 in 2015. This results in estimated personnel costs for the support of the onlineshop of $1400 \times 68.34 = 95{,}676$ (see sheet "Personnelcosts"). In 2015, the

Year	Sales channel nr	Sales channel	Gross revenue actual	Net revenue actual	CM I standard actual	Sales commissions	CM I after commission	Share of revenue	Share of CM I	Compared to previous year
			Actual sales success				**By sales channel**			
2011	1	Dealers	3,190,368	2,569,132	1,522,031	30,441	1,491,591	36.4%	39.5%	
2012	1	Dealers	3,100,791	2,466,816	1,512,452	30,249	1,482,203	33.2%	34.7%	99.4%
2013	1	Dealers	3,034,018	2,393,184	1,400,147	28,003	1,372,144	32.3%	33.3%	92.6%
2014	1	Dealers	3,142,539	2,480,874	1,518,521	30,370	1,488,151	31.3%	33.2%	108.5%
2015	1	Dealers	3,283,270	2,606,704	1,584,001	31,680	1,552,321	31.2%	33.1%	104.3%
2011	2	Direct customers	5,558,180	4,481,025	2,329,533	46,591	2,282,943	63.6%	60.5%	
2012	2	Direct customers	6,080,975	4,870,895	2,777,000	55,540	2,721,460	65.5%	63.7%	119.2%
2013	2	Direct customers	6,107,855	4,898,368	2,726,639	54,533	2,672,106	66.2%	64.8%	98.2%
2014	2	Direct customers	6,654,351	5,325,751	2,964,024	59,280	2,904,743	67.2%	64.9%	108.7%
2015	2	Direct customers	7,045,903	5,624,573	3,108,583	62,172	3,046,411	67.2%	64.9%	104.9%
2012	3	Online shop	96,458	96,458	67,283	-	67,283	1.3%	1.6%	
2013	3	Online shop	110,398	110,398	76,798	-	76,798	1.5%	1.9%	114.1%
2014	3	Online shop	121,351	121,351	83,928	-	83,928	1.5%	1.9%	109.3%
2015	3	Online shop	136,077	136,077	94,060	-	94,060	1.6%	2.0%	112.1%

Fig. 8.8 Development of CM I in the various sales channels (bottom of sheet "RegionalCM")

onlineshop generated a CM I of 94,060 (see sheet "RegionalCM"), which means that after 4 years of operation it is still a source of losses, as its contribution margins cover neither the estimated personnel costs nor the imputed depreciation.

8.5 Development in Production

Automatic material positioning in the Assembly cost center made the greatest contribution to increasing production efficiency since 2012. This is first and foremost due to the reduction in absolute proportional manufacturing costs in assembly from 1,069,393 in 2012 to 837,662 in 2015 (sheet "CCefficiency", column proportional manufacturing cost). These amounts already include the costs incurred by the higher production quantities. At the other production sites, the allowed times per unit and the setup times remained the same in all years.

Figure 8.9 shows that although the directly attributable fixed costs in most production cost centers rose in absolute terms (column fixed costs), fixed costs as a percentage of the proportional manufacturing costs mostly decreased. The absolute

Development of cost center efficiency

Medium-term development of actual (fixed) costs of the internal functions and KPI's

Data origin: "CClist, CCtotals Invest&depr, ActualCMitems, Presencetime"

Year	PR#	CCnr	Description	Function	Fixed cost	Of which imputed depreciation	Controllable fixed cost	CM I after commissions	Prop. manufacturing cost	Actual hours worked	Avg. personnel (FTE)	**Fixed cost percentage of prop. manuf. cost**
2011	2	200	Plant mgmt. & work scheduling	Production	216,421	5,250	211,171	3,622,421		3,520	2.1	9.4%
2012	2	200	Plant mgmt. & work scheduling	Production	204,439	5,408	199,032	4,045,768		3,296	1.9	10.0%
2013	2	200	Plant mgmt. & work scheduling	Production	254,914	5,766	249,148	3,779,052		4,270	2.5	13.0%
2014	2	200	Plant mgmt. & work scheduling	Production	260,900	6,081	254,819	4,253,855		4,270	2.5	11.9%
2015	2	200	Plant mgmt. & work scheduling	Production	265,585	6,203	259,383	4,416,825		4,250	2.5	11.3%
2011	2	220	Stamping	Production	93,726	13,063	80,664		302,853	6,876	4.0	30.9%
2012	2	220	Stamping	Production	60,922	14,704	46,217		330,514	6,756	4.0	18.4%
2013	2	220	Stamping	Production	88,340	20,623	67,717		319,034	6,832	4.0	27.7%
2014	2	220	Stamping	Production	87,864	21,348	66,516		361,167	7,544	4.4	24.3%
2015	2	220	Stamping	Production	112,942	25,025	87,917		376,296	8,160	4.8	30.0%
2011	2	231	Wire rolling	Production	26,734	14,000	12,734		195,941	-	-	13.6%
2012	2	231	Wire rolling	Production	27,471	16,170	11,301		211,826	-	-	13.0%
2013	2	231	Wire rolling	Production	27,978	16,493	11,484		209,525	-	-	13.4%
2014	2	231	Wire rolling	Production	30,822	19,023	11,799		226,665	-	-	13.6%
2015	2	231	Wire rolling	Production	31,253	21,204	10,049		246,641	-	-	12.7%
2011	2	232	Wire bending & forming	Production	280,876	12,000	268,876		165,369	10,976	6.5	169.8%
2012	2	232	Wire bending & forming	Production	290,445	14,610	275,835		177,895	11,860	7.0	163.3%
2013	2	232	Wire bending & forming	Production	309,970	16,802	293,167		174,004	11,785	6.9	178.1%
2014	2	232	Wire bending & forming	Production	302,654	17,138	285,516		190,238	11,956	7.0	159.1%
2015	2	232	Wire bending & forming	Production	322,671	17,731	304,940		206,372	12,750	7.5	156.4%
2011	2	240	Cardboarding	Production	60,555	15,000	45,555		275,311	-	-	22.0%
2012	2	240	Cardboarding	Production	63,492	17,200	46,292		289,684	-	-	21.9%
2013	2	240	Cardboarding	Production	63,740	18,794	44,946		313,799	-	-	20.3%
2014	2	240	Cardboarding	Production	68,994	21,370	47,624		329,218	-	-	21.0%
2015	2	240	Cardboarding	Production	66,493	21,797	44,696		352,730	-	-	18.9%
2011	2	245	Personnel pool 240-260	Production	241,686	-	241,686			37,752	22.2	0
2012	2	245	Personnel pool 240-260	Production	381,185	-	381,185			34,280	20.2	0
2013	2	245	Personnel pool 240-260	Production	353,223	-	353,223			31,598	18.6	0
2014	2	245	Personnel pool 240-260	Production	253,209	-	253,209			31,598	18.6	0
2015	2	245	Personnel pool 240-260	Production	172,786	-	172,786			31,450	18.5	0
2011	2	250	Assembly	Production	42,861	16,000	26,861		1,069,393	-	-	4.0%
2012	2	250	Assembly	Production	66,428	23,725	42,703		731,600	-	-	9.1%
2013	2	250	Assembly	Production	67,740	25,399	42,340		679,197	-	-	10.0%
2014	2	250	Assembly	Production	71,639	26,157	45,481		758,918	-	-	9.4%
2015	2	250	Assembly	Production	74,716	26,931	47,785		837,757	-	-	8.9%
2011	2	260	Film welding	Production	19,470	13,750	5,720		243,478	-	-	8.0%
2012	2	260	Film welding	Production	24,290	16,913	7,378		258,797	-	-	9.4%
2013	2	260	Film welding	Production	32,592	18,251	14,341		219,155	-	-	14.9%
2014	2	260	Film welding	Production	28,828	18,866	9,962		268,723	-	-	10.7%
2015	2	260	Film welding	Production	29,488	20,743	8,745		282,311	-	-	10.4%

Fig. 8.9 Efficiency increases in the production cost centers (sheet "CCefficiency")

Year	Function	Purchase price & order variances	Fixed cost incl. variances	Fixed cost % of CMI (after com-missions)	
2011	Production	-5,749	988,078	27.3%	from CM I finished goods
2012	Production	-2,244	1,120,916	27.7%	
2013	Production	21,209	1,177,286	31.2%	
2014	Production	63,246	1,041,663	24.5%	
2015	Production	41,832	1,034,102	23.4%	

Fig. 8.10 Percentage of fixed production costs of CM I Actual

increases are mainly due to the growth of imputed depreciation. The latter also explains why the proportion of fixed costs has risen in assembly and film welding.

In Personnel pool 245, absolute personnel costs (column fixed costs) first rose from 241,686 to 381,185, but then fell to 172,928 by 2015. This is the result of the change in full-time equivalents in the personnel pool. In 2011 the number of employees in cost center 245 was 22.2 FTE. In 2012 it was reduced to 20.2 FTE. In 2013 three retirements (a bit late) made it possible to lower the average FTEs to 18.6. In 2015 on average 18.5 FTE were on duty. As a result, the cost of unused personnel capacity (fixed cost) was lowered substantially.

Due to higher production volume and the resulting higher demand for planning and scheduling work, plant management (200) had to increase its workforce somewhat. This increased the share of this cost center of the total costs of production (last two columns).

Overall, the aggregation of all production cost centers, including all variances in production shows that the share of fixed production costs of CM I actual of finished goods fell from 27.3 to 23.4% (Fig. 8.10).

8.6 Development in the Support Functions

The directly attributable costs in the cost center Purchasing and Warehousing increased in absolute terms, but at a slower rate than CM I's development. This is due to the fact that the quantity of procurement processes grew slower than the turnover (sheet "Actualpurchases") while the number of employees only increased by 0.3 FTE.

The cost centers Buildings and Maintenance, Repairs and Energy Center were mainly affected by the greater imputed depreciation due to the investments. As there was no need to increase staff levels, the necessary CM I share for these cost centers only increased insignificantly.

The cost center IT (300) also saw an increase in imputed depreciation by almost 50% over the years. Fortunately, it was possible to manage the development and operation of the entire IT system with the same number of employees, which resulted in a roughly constant share of IT costs of CM I (Fig. 8.11).

Year	PR#	CCnr	Description	Function	Fixed cost	Of which imputed depreciation	Controllable fixed cost	CM I after commissions	Actual hours worked	Avg. person-nel (FTE)	**Fixed cost percentage of prop. manuf. cost**	**Fixed cost percentage of actual CM I**
2011		210	Procurement & warehouse	Admin., warehouse	192,251	15,000	177,251		3,664	2.2	10.9%	Compared
2012		210	Procurement & warehouse	Admin., warehouse	203,629	17,200	186,429		4,006	2.4	10.6%	to
2013		210	Procurement & warehouse	Admin., warehouse	219,669	18,444	201,225		4,270	2.5	10.2%	purchased
2014		210	Procurement & warehouse	Admin., warehouse	224,227	19,063	205,165		4,270	2.5	11.0%	value
2015		210	Procurement & warehouse	Admin., warehouse	230,059	20,344	209,715		4,250	2.5	10.3%	
2011		300	IT	Admin., warehouse	265,505	24,625	240,880	3,774,533	4,170	2.5		7.0%
2012		300	IT	Admin., warehouse	305,041	27,239	277,802	4,270,946	4,350	2.6		7.1%
2013		300	IT	Admin., warehouse	311,369	30,284	281,086	4,121,048	4,270	2.5		7.6%
2014		300	IT	Admin., warehouse	318,404	31,514	286,890	4,476,823	4,270	2.5		7.1%
2015		300	IT	Admin., warehouse	327,059	34,644	292,415	4,692,792	4,250	2.5		7.0%
2011		320	Buildings & maintenance	Admin., warehouse	148,294	24,400	123,894	3,774,533	1,752	1.0		3.9%
2012		320	Buildings & maintenance	Admin., warehouse	148,902	25,632	123,270	4,270,946	1,656	1.0		3.5%
2013		320	Buildings & maintenance	Admin., warehouse	151,754	26,395	125,359	4,121,048	1,708	1.0		3.7%
2014		320	Buildings & maintenance	Admin., warehouse	157,507	27,756	129,751	4,476,823	1,708	1.0		3.5%
2015		320	Buildings & maintenance	Admin., warehouse	161,618	29,311	132,307	4,692,792	1,700	1.0		3.4%
2011		330	Repair center	Admin., warehouse	15,736	7,625	8,111	3,774,533	1,704	1.0		0.4%
2012		330	Repair center	Admin., warehouse	16,188	8,479	7,709	4,270,946	1,704	1.0		0.4%
2013		330	Repair center	Admin., warehouse	16,886	8,961	7,926	4,121,048	1,708	1.0		0.4%
2014		330	Repair center	Admin., warehouse	18,145	9,890	8,255	4,476,823	1,708	1.0		0.4%
2015		330	Repair center	Admin., warehouse	18,744	10,588	8,156	4,692,792	1,700	1.0		0.4%
2011		340	Energy center	Admin., warehouse	16,616	2,567	14,050	3,774,533	-	-		0.4%
2012		340	Energy center	Admin., warehouse	30,326	2,810	27,515	4,270,946	-	-		0.7%
2013		340	Energy center	Admin., warehouse	31,876	3,033	28,843	4,121,048	-	-		0.8%
2014		340	Energy center	Admin., warehouse	32,488	3,261	29,228	4,476,823	-	-		0.7%
2015		340	Energy center	Admin., warehouse	40,220	3,492	36,728	4,692,792	-	-		0.9%
2011		900	Corp. management & administration	Admin., warehouse	674,782	11,000	663,782	3,774,533	10,675	6.3		17.9%
2012		900	Corp. management & administration	Admin., warehouse	685,474	17,530	667,944	4,270,946	10,205	6.0		16.0%
2013		900	Corp. management & administration	Admin., warehouse	737,240	18,881	718,359	4,121,048	11,310	6.7		17.9%
2014		900	Corp. management & administration	Admin., warehouse	806,344	19,458	786,886	4,476,823	12,164	7.2		18.0%
2015		900	Corp. management & administration	Admin., warehouse	833,140	20,847	812,292	4,692,792	12,974	7.6		17.8%

Fig. 8.11 Cost development in the administrative and support areas (sheet "CCefficiency")

Fig. 8.12 Hourly requirements and derived personnel costs in administration and management

Year	CCnr	Actual presence time	Hours internal taks adjusted	Personnel costs actual year	Actual presence time rate / hour	Personnel costs internal tasks
2011	900	10,675	10,675	641,862	60.13	641,862
2012	900	10,205	10,205	639,209	62.64	639,209
2013	900	11,310	11,310	707,368	62.54	707,368
2014	900	12,164	12,164	762,514	62.69	762,514
2015	900	12,974	12,974	796,108	61.36	796,108
Change 2011 - 2015			121.5%	124.0%		124.0%

In absolute terms, the fixed costs of the Management and Administration cost center (900) rose by around 158,000 over the 5 years (Fig. 8.11). This is mainly due to the increase (21.5%, Fig. 8.12) in the number of working hours required for internal tasks (including traceability of transactions, increase in statistics to be supplied outside the Group, applications and reports, coordination work in management processes). Because of this change, the number of FTE rose from 6.3 to 7.6 (Fig. 8.11).

In the general overview, the change in cost compared to net sales is as in Fig. 8.13 (see sheet "Salesefficiency").

The trend lines derived from the original values indicate that:

- CM I developed very positively due to process improvements in production.
- Production-related fixed costs rose less than CM I in percentage terms due to better utilization of available personnel capacities (jumpers).
- The whole sales organization became more productive as its cost increased at a lower rate than net sales.
- The costs of the Administration and Purchasing/Warehouse functions rose disproportionately to net sales. This will have a strong negative impact on contribution margins and thus on EBIT, if net revenues fall due to more favorable offers by competitors. Breaking this rising trend of structural cost blocks for Administration and Management is difficult and can only be achieved over a period of several years.

8.7 Improvement of the Cost Position

The ex post analysis of the annual results 2011–2015 showed that Ringbook Ltd. has made a big leap forward in terms of net sales and EBIT. EBIT in 2015 was around 2.4 times higher than in 2011. However, the question as to whether the company has also succeeded in realizing the promises of the experience curve and thereby achieving a stronger cost position vis-à-vis its competitors remains to be answered.

It can be seen from sheet "Articlemaster" that Ringbook Ltd. has adjusted the list prices of the individual items each year based on the estimated inflation rate. The production volumes of own products grew by an average of around 3.1% year-on-

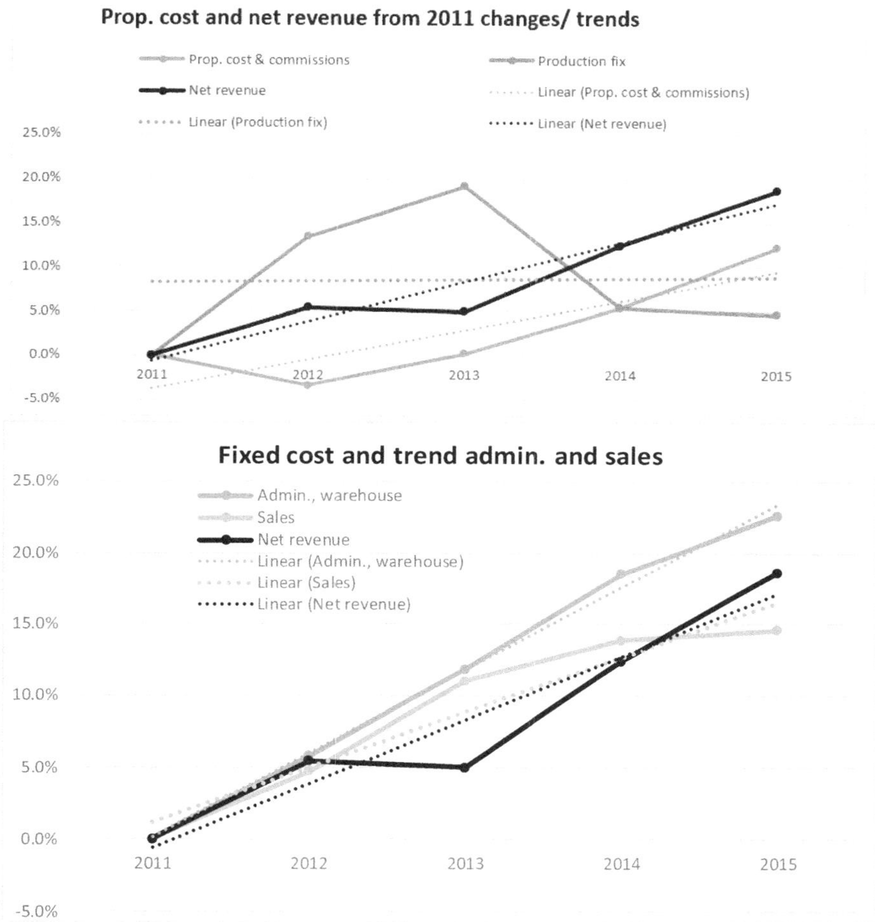

Fig. 8.13 Change in actual structural costs of individual functions compared to net sales

year, which also led to correspondingly higher production volumes (Fig. 8.14) and inventories as well as to higher EBIT. In Ringbook Ltd. it is assumed that the overall market has grown by approximately 3% annually as described in Sect. 7.5.2. It follows from this that Ringbook Ltd. has gained a bit of market share in 2011–2015 (Sect. 7.2).

Since the exact sales and turnover figures of the competitors are not available, it is unknown whether and which competitors have been able to achieve higher sales and thus have created a better basis for the realization of their experience curve. If this were the case, there would be a great risk that these competitors could use price reductions to try to force other suppliers, possibly including Ringbook Ltd., out of the market.

1	Avg. annual growth rate (actual)	3.13%	Value added cost/unit produced, 2011:				3.33
2	Year	2010	2011	2012	2013	2014	2015
3	Units to produce (finished goods)		1,756,330	1,856,000	1,679,910	1,863,700	1,986,680
4	Cumulative output quantity (actual)	14,000,000	15,756,330	17,612,330	19,292,240	21,155,940	23,142,620
5	Doublings per year	-		0.1607	0.1314	0.1330	0.1295
6	Cumulative doublings	0	0.00	0.1607	0.2921	0.4251	0.5546
7	Value added cost target 10%-line		3.33	3.27	3.22	3.18	3.14
8	Value added cost target 20%-line		3.33	3.21	3.12	3.02	2.94
9	Value added cost target 30%-line		3.33	3.14	3.00	2.86	2.73
10	Actual value added cost/unit acc. to P&L without interest, tax and profit		3.33	3.14	3.56	3.34	3.24
11	Difference (20%-objective - actual)		-	0.07	(0.44)	(0.32)	-0.30
12	not exploited cost-cutting potential		-	125,191	-739,886	-592,783	-596,659
13	Cumulative unexploited cost-cutting potential			125,191	-614,695	-1,207,479	-1,804,137

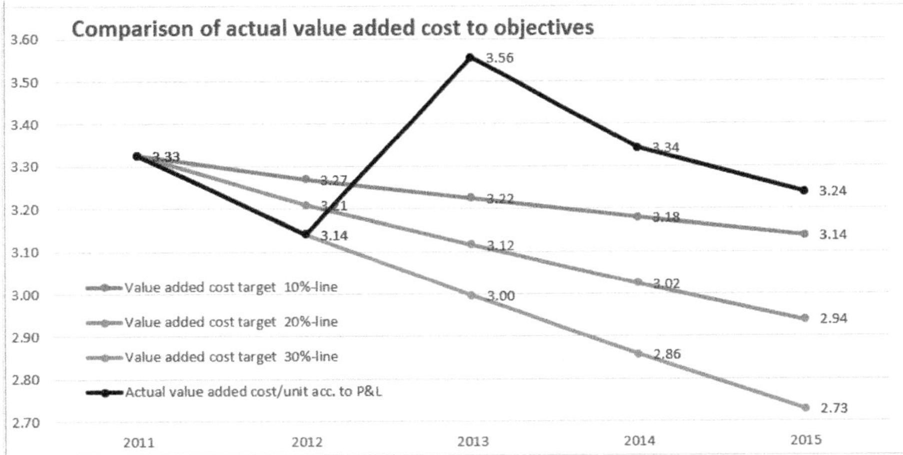

Fig. 8.14 Development of cost value added in comparison to the experience curve (ex post)

In the absence of reliable market data, Ringbook Ltd. only has the option of checking whether it was able to realize the cost-cutting potential according to its own experience curve according to the quantities it produced. This consideration is quantified in Fig. 8.14 using the experience curve funnel of Sect. 7.5.2:

- In line 1, the average value-added cost of 3.33 per unit produced was used as the starting point (source: "ActualP&L"). In addition, the real growth rate of the company's finished goods production volumes 2011–2015 was calculated (around 3.1% annually).
- The cumulated output at the beginning of the ex post analysis (row 4) is based on an estimate in most companies. The point is to assess the cumulative experience with the products/services offered today as a starting value. If the cumulated output quantity in the sheet "Experiencecurve" is changed by 20% upwards or downwards, the targeted cost value added (20%) only changes in the "hundredth range." The "funnel" of cost reduction is only slightly shifted as a result.
- The initial quantity and the actual sales quantities result in recalculated doublings per year in line 5 (see Sect. 7.5.2) and the corresponding cumulations in line 6.
- Lines 7–9 show the values for the target cost value-added "funnel" for 2012 on, based on the doublings achieved by the company.
- The actual value-added costs per unit produced in line 10 are also taken from sheet "ActualP&L."

Thanks to the automation project in the Assembly cost center, it was possible to achieve the 30% cost reduction line in 2012. In later years, however, the experience cost targets were far from being met. The reasons for this are that as of 2012:

- No new cost-reducing projects were implemented (to keep the numerical model simpler).
- Calculated depreciation rose continuously despite the slump in sales.
- From 2013 onward, annual wage increases of around 2% were granted (see sheet on personnel costs).

Lines 11–13 quantify which cost reduction potentials 2012–2015 were not exploited, underlying the actual sales (production) volumes achieved by the company itself. Line 11 calculates the difference between the actual and target value-added costs (20%-line). In row 12, this value is multiplied by the production quantities for the year and cumulated in row 13.

This mathematical derivation shows how important it is for a company to continuously realize the (statistically promised) effects of experience curves.

If the approximately 1.8 million reduction in value-added costs missed in the years 2012–2015 are divided by net sales 2012–2015 of own products of approximately 27.8 million (sheet "ActualCMitems"), this amounts to roughly 6.5%. It can thus be seen that an average price reduction of 6.5% by a competitor could have been parried if the value-added costs had been reduced accordingly, with EBIT remaining the same in 2012–2015.

Continuous improvement of the cost position is essential for organizational survival because, especially in mature markets, competitors regularly try to drive other suppliers out of the market by lowering prices. Realizing cost reduction potentials is exhausting and takes time. Many approaches can only be implemented over a period of several years. This means that medium-term planning will be given greater weight in the integrated planning and control system and that it will be just as important in terms of quantity and performance as annual planning. The tools must enable all managers to monitor whether and to what extent they have succeeded in improving effectiveness and efficiency in their area over the years.

Many of the performance indicators presented in this analysis chapter reflect the change in various aspects of performance over the years. In the following paragraphs some of these will be examined in greater detail, as they can be used for piloting to sustainable success at the appropriate level.

Sales Area

If the ratio of fixed costs of the sales territory divided by (net) sales becomes smaller, this means an increase in efficiency, as the total fixed costs of the territory increase slower than net sales (turnover). It is even more informative to divide these fixed costs by the achieved CM I standard, because this figure also includes the rebates and other benefits granted by the salespersons to the customers and because only the planned proportional product cost (standard) is deducted (purchase price and production variances remain in the purchasing and production area, see sheet "Salesefficiency").

Since the available working hours often represent the main bottleneck in customer acquisition and support, the CM I ratio per sales employee should be given a high weighting (efficiency). The presentation of the achieved revenues and CM I by customer in descending order enables ABC-type analyses and an indication of the effectiveness of the sales staff (see sheet "CustomerCM").

It is important that the defined cost centers correspond to the CM-steps in contribution accounting. The fixed costs directly assignable to a specific sales area are related to the CM I standard actual for the area because they are controlled there. The fixed costs of sales promotion for finished goods can only be related to the CM I standard actual for all finished goods as they are incurred in supporting these sales. Finally, the fixed costs of the sales management and the office staff are assigned to the entire CM I standard and actual since the sales manager in the example company is responsible for all sales staff as well as for exports, the onlineshop, and his complete staff.

To know the CM I standard of new customers for the year or to evaluate the losses from terminated customer relationships (sheet "CustomerCM") requires that each billing item be stored individually in the database. With regard to new customers, the time required to acquire them and to support existing customers should be compared with the realized revenues and CM to see if the improvement in sales efficiency should be assessed (These are not analyzed separately here).

Production Area

Productivity gains are achieved in the production area if the total costs clearly traceable to the area (without allocations) increase at a lower rate than output. To be able to measure and assess this progress in an appropriate way, the cost split (proportional and fixed) must first be introduced (see Sect. 4.7.1). The proportional product costs are driven by processes, materials used, and manufacturing quantities, the fixed costs of the production area are the result of management decisions (see Sects. 4.7.1 and 7.5.2).

In the sheet "Actualpropcostitems" the change in the proportional manufacturing costs per good unit can be analyzed over time. There it also can be seen how the proportional cost center rates have changed over the years. Both indicators serve to track the achievement of medium-term efficiency improvements.

In the sheet "CCefficiency" the ratio of fixed costs as a percentage of the proportional manufacturing costs is calculated for each production cost center. This percentage should decrease over time as imputed depreciation and personnel costs for internal tasks grow at a lower rate than the growth rate of proportional manufacturing costs. As with increasing automation in a cost center, where proportional manufacturing costs per unit fall while fixed costs concurrently rise, increases in efficiency only occur if the average directly controllable total costs per good unit fall. This key figure can be found in sheet "CCefficiency," column "Complete manufacturing/good unit." However, this figure has the shortcoming that it does not consider changes of the share of an item manufactured in this cost center compared to all items manufactured items here. In all cases, the total fixed costs of all production cost centers should increase at a lower rate than that for all proportional manufacturing costs.

Management and Support Areas

The fixed costs in the management and support cost centers for the overall view are mostly related to the earned CM I volume after commissions. This shows, after all, whether the share of the realized CM I consumed by the support areas will decrease over time. This key figure does not consider, however, that sales are mainly responsible for the CM I standard actual. Without the performance of the support areas all other areas are unable to generate their contributions. Individual, performance-related productivity benchmarks therefore need to be utilized for the individual support cost centers whenever possible.

From a management perspective, it is essential that company-specific and cost center-specific conditions be considered when establishing efficiency indicators. On the cost side, only those cost elements should be included for which a cost center manager is directly responsible. These include proportional manufacturing costs and the fixed costs of the manager's cost center (without any allocations). The reference/comparative quantity to be searched for is a value or a quantity that the cost center manager can also influence as directly as possible.

The small size of the example company Ringbook Ltd. means that most of the support tasks are performed in the IT and Administration and Management cost centers. The people working there take on various tasks in parallel and can therefore only inaccurately allocate their time required for internal tasks to individual activity types. Therefore, it can only be observed whether the hours spent on internal tasks and the resulting costs increase or decrease in relation to the total costs. Alternatively, it can also be observed how administration costs change in comparison to the CM I volume.

While searching for piloting parameters, it is necessary to consider whether "handier" key figures can be found if (in a larger company) a finer cost center structure becomes possible.

8.8 Compatibility with Other Managerial Costing Frameworks

8.8.1 The Costing Levels Continuum Maturity Model

Gary Cokins developed the Costing Levels Continuum Maturity Model "...to measure two key capabilities of costing systems: (a) the modeling capabilities of an approach ... and (b) the robustness of the marginal/incremental information an approach provides" (Cokins 2009, p. 6). In this model he starts with data won from pure financial accounting transactional systems (Level 1) and structured the development steps of management accounting in 12 levels. "Organizations that plan at Level 12 have arguably attained the highest level of cost planning. Simulation can come in many flavors and degrees of sophistication" (ibid, p. 17). Level 11 integrates Resource Consumption Accounting (RCA), forward capacity planning, and giving cost control feedback to managers for corrective actions. Level 12 adds simulation.

Larry White (2009) presented the details of the *RCA Methodology*. He notes the importance of the following elements of RCA:

- Managers are the primary users of management accounting information, but not of the external financial statement (p. 63).
- Resources are the cause of all costs and revenues. Resources have three fundamental characteristics: (1) Capability, (2) Capacity, and (3) Cost structure or cost behavior (p. 65). The starting point in RCA is thus resource consumption, not the general ledger (p.72). Splitting costs in their proportional (variable) and fixed portion is necessary for decision-taking in planning and control (p. 67–70).
- Quantities and associated monetary amounts are never separated (p. 72). This is important as the quantity information is gathered in several ERP modules whereas financial amounts are entered in the ledger systems.
- The principles for modeling resource consumption and costs are: (1) Causality, (2) Responsiveness, and (3) Work (p. 67).

- If a causal relationship between consumption and cost cannot be established, the respective (fixed) costs are not allocated to a product unit or from one cost center to another (p. 67 and pp. 74–76). Fixed costs should never be reflected in product cost.
- Overall, the approach RCA takes to acquiring the operational and cost data needed for management support makes it radically different from other management accounting techniques.

Chapters 1–3 of this book discussed the need of managers for a holistic management control system. In Chaps. 4–6 a methodology to generate the part ascribed to the management accounting system was presented in detail. A comparison of the presented management accounting system and RCA results in more or less a complete match. *Our presentation is thus compatible with RCA.* This match is not surprising as the methodology on which both systems are based is the same, Grenzplankostenrechnung (GPK). This concept was invented by H.G. Plaut and presented for the first time in 1953 (see bibliography)! Many of these still relevant ideas find their representation in today's ERP-offerings and can be used to realize RCA or our detailed propositions.

In Chaps. 4–6 of this book all the elements of Resource Consumption Accounting are represented: The elements are combined with capacity planning. The development of the presented system for integrated planning and control always starts from the needs of the customers. The simulation model allows the estimation of the financial and capacity-related consequences of managerial decisions. It can thus be stated that the management accounting system presented here is *fully at Level 11.*

Level 12 is reached as well, as indicated by the included simulation model. Concerning simulation, it was shown several times that fully automatic calculations help a great deal in planning, but that managers at all levels must make decisions about how many units to sell and to produce and about the personnel and machine capacities they are willing to engage in the planned periods. These decisions form the boundaries within which suitable simulation outcomes are possible.

The presented management accounting system covers many aspects of operational management and control during the year. Still missing to achieve comprehensive management control is planning for mid-term operational management consistent with the organization's strategies. This is the topic of Chaps. 9–11.

8.8.2 The IMA Conceptual Framework for Managerial Costing

The IMA's (Institute of Management Accountants) *Conceptual Framework for Managerial Costing* (CFMC) provides a framework for managerial costing that seeks to outline the principles, concepts, and constraints necessary for effective cost modeling, which provides a monetary representation of the organization's resources, processes, and products/services. The principles of the CFMC are in many ways similar to those described in this book. These include:

- Addressing the need for Management Control Systems to provide managers clear insight into the quantities of resources applied to their managerial objectives, the capacities of their resources and supporting resources, and the fixed and proportional costs of those resources.
- Viewing cost allocations as creating distorted information. Allocating costs with weak or noncausal relationships to a managerial objective distorts the quality of decision-support information.
- An emphasis on the principle of causality, i.e., the importance of cause-and-effect relationships.
- An understanding that operational quantities need to be modeled before they are represented in monetary terms (i.e., cost information).
- Understanding the need to have defined managerial objectives for all levels of managers and supervisors, with managerial objectives expressed in both nonfinancial and financial terms (i.e., Management by Objectives MBO).
- Employing causal depreciation schedules based on useful economic life and replacement value rather than a noncausal schedule dictated by financial accounting rules.
- Not allocating the cost of idle/excess capacity expenses to individual products or services. These costs must be "covered" from the revenue of all products and services for the company to earn a profit. One cannot "calculate" idle capacity costs into a product unit.

A major difference between the management control framework in this book and the CFMC is that the latter focuses solely on costing and does not discuss revenues, an important part of a holistic management accounting system.

"Success stories" in business literature often describe *bright strategic decisions* that have laid the foundation for exponential corporate development. However, to make these successes happen in every case required "**operational excellence**." In our opinion, the basic elements of successful corporate management are fine-tuning details, mastering processes, distinguishing between "necessary" and "nice to have," and continuously improving implementation in sales and distribution, persistently pursuing improvement of the cost position. An important component in achieving financial success is also the identification and tracking of operational piloting information.

9 Pilot Control and Early Warning

Increasing complexity of corporate management often leads to longer decision-making and preparation periods. In addition to planning for the coming year, there is also an increasing need to think ahead about medium-term changes and the corresponding necessary planning. Managers should be aware of decisions and actions that have to be taken for the annual plan-year, the consequences of which will only unfold in later years (Fig. 9.1).

On the one hand, this requires parameters that are mainly derived from **internal data** and largely indicate predictable medium-term (>1 year to approximately 5 years) developments. These are referred to here as **piloting control variables.** On the other hand, **early warning indicators** (Sect. 9.4) can be obtained from sources **outside the company** which indicate possible or already emerging changes in the corporate environment. Both early warning and piloting information are inputs for strategic and medium-term planning.

In the section on Basic Terms, a default setting is referred to as a control that is fixed without regulating feedback (open-loop control). Before the actual control and regulation, awareness must be generated that controlling intervention is necessary. Piloting information is intended to point out to the individual manager that problems could arise in his area of management if developments are ignored or only rudimentarily noted and corrective action is not taken.

Improvement in the performance and cost parameters over the 5-year period led, as shown in Chap. 8, to gain in the key performance indicators for efficiency improvement. Although derived from historical data, these indicators point to developments that will require future action. Pure cost/performance analysis cannot, however, suffice for management support. Additionally, it is necessary to look for indicators that point out emerging developments in the managed area to the responsible persons. These indicators should enable the assessment and monitoring of implementation. This shifts the emphasis in feedforward control to qualitative elements and assessments.

L. Rieder, R. Lawson, *Management Control with Integrated Planning*, Management for Professionals, https://doi.org/10.1007/978-3-030-48302-9_9

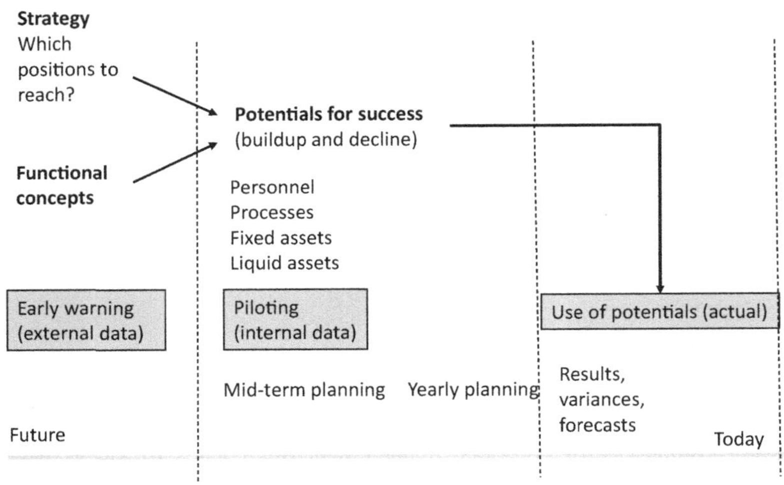

Fig. 9.1 Early warning, pilot control and buildup of potentials

Piloting information and parameters are intended to help:

- Remind managers of any decisions that are important to their area and prevent postponing of those decisions
- Avoid bottlenecks of all kinds
- Continuously improve processes
- Strengthen competitiveness through increased efficiency

If findings from piloting information are incorporated into objectives and annual planning, it makes it easier for managers to fulfill their responsibility for QQDR (quantities, qualities, deadlines, and results). In every company all work is performed in cost centers, on projects, or on orders (i.e., in working groups). For this reason, generally valid cost center and project-related piloting parameters must first be found. After that comes the search for function-specific piloting parameters. Finally, it must be considered whether input control parameters can be found that are particularly suitable for subareas such as profit centers, strategic business areas, or for the overall management of the organization.

Not all the proposals for piloting parameters mentioned in the following sections are relevant to every organization. Managers will need to derive suitable parameters for their own area. In this way it is possible to analyze which of the necessary data can be obtained and evaluated from the existing information systems (management accounting, ERP, and CRM) and for what purpose one's own databases need to be built up.

9.1 General Piloting Information for Cost Center and Project Managers

Managers manage one or more **cost centers** and/or **projects**. In this function, they ensure that AMPLE (Sect. 1.1.1) is used properly in their own area. This means that they ensure that the annual objectives are achieved and that the workplace is attractive for their employees as well as the positive development of their areas.

Various variables are appropriate for monitoring this. The items listed in Fig. 9.2 provide suggestions for cost center and project managers; these should be considered as examples and not as an exhaustive list. The collection of the data for these parameters requires little additional effort since most of the information is collected in a company anyway:

- Parameters 1–3 result from direct discussions with employees, from company-wide surveys and from the data to be collected in the HR department.
- Parameters 4–6 can be obtained from the payroll accounting data.
- A cost center manager records the data for parameters 7–9 himself in employee appraisals and forwards it to the personnel department.

Nr.	Contribution to:	Piloting topic	How often?	Comment	Who?
1	Attractivity	Employee satisfaction	every 2 years	Indications of change in acceptance and esteem of managerial behavior	CC-mgr.
2	Attractivity	Reasons for leave	when quitting	Obtained by personnel administration at the exit interview, provides input for improvement in managerial behavior	Pers. dept.
3	Attractivity	Unwanted leaves	yearly	Provides indications of why good managers and skilled people leave. Requires that aptitude of furtherance is captured in the documents of personnel administration.	Pers. dept.
4	Attractivity	Annual fluctuation in FTE per cost center	yearly	Number of hires needed annually per cost center, an indicator of recruiting and education costs.	Pers. dept.
5	Attractivity	Amount of compen-sation balance (hours and value)	quarterly	Legal specifications observed? Obtain employee feedback during performance appraisals. Quantify costs, see section 6.5 and sheet "Personnelcosts".	CC-mgr.
6	Attractivity	Open vacation days	quarterly	Can the employees really take their vacations? Integrate vacation plans in yearly planning process.	CC-mgr.
7	Attractivity	Further education and training	biannual	Check during the appraisal interview whether the planned activities for further education and training were completed. Gives clues regarding the accuracy of current managerial knowledge	CC-mgr.
8	Attractivity	Employee-potential	yearly	Are employees with managerial development potential or professional expertise identified and documented in the personnel file?	Pers. dept.
9	Attractivity	Substitution	yearly	Are deputies for management positions named, actualized and documented?	CC-mgr.
10	Due-dates	Ordered compared to effective delivery-date	yearly	Extent to which due dates of production and internal orders and SLAs are met. (Data in the sheets "Completemessages, Actualprojects" and Service Level Agreements)	CC-mgr.
11	Evolution	Hours spent for internal tasks	yearly	Analysis of hours spent for groups of internal tasks (data ins sheet "Actualinternaltasks")	CC-mgr.
12	Evolution	Process improvements	quarterly	Search and assess documentation of publications concerning new or improved processes (procurement, production, sales, administration)	CC-mgr.
13	Evolution	New control applications	quarterly	Evaluation of new tools for improving planning and control	CC-mgr.

Fig. 9.2 General piloting factors for cost center and project managers

- A comparison of desired and actual dates can be obtained from the order data (sales and production as well as projects) and from the target to actual comparison of personal annual objectives. All needed data should be available.
- The development of the time consumption for internal tasks is obtained by evaluating operating data.
- To be up to date on further evolutionary topics, a cost center or project manager must familiarize himself with the specialized press and record early warnings.
- The table does not include the "upcoming retirements" and "planned transfers" of existing employees to other cost centers.

The column "How often?" indicates the suggested frequency of observation and thus also survey periods for input variables. The Comment column roughly describes what is to be collected or interpreted. In most cases, these are qualitative assessments in text form. Finally, it must be specified who is to collect and store the data (the "Who?" column).

The listed general piloting factors are also largely relevant for **project managers** because they pilot the success of the project in terms of deadlines and costs. As most project members can only spend part of their working time on projects given their primary work responsibilities for their master cost center, project progress assessment needs to record the working time of individual project members effectively available for project processing. If project members are assigned other tasks, the risk of running into delays for the project increases. Expected delays on the supplier side can also endanger the success of the project on schedule. Such changes should be recorded because they may also affect project costs and investment volume.

The list of general piloting factors presented here forms the starting point for each manager. However, it is not exhaustive; further specific factors can be added on a cost center-specific basis.

9.2 Function-Related Piloting Information

We now discuss which area-specific or task-specific piloting parameters are to be collected for the holistic management of the functional areas in addition to those already mentioned for cost centers and projects.

9.2.1 Directly Market-Related Functions

The following persons or divisions (groups) work directly in the marketplace:

- Sales Representatives
- Sales Manager, Regional Manager, Country Managers
- Key Account Managers
- Product Managers
- Customer Project Manager responsible for results

Nr.	Piloting topics	Data source, computation, presentation
	Concerning customers and products	
1	Quality of leads	Number of lead addresses provided / invitations for presentation
2	Offers sent	Quantity and average value
3	Offering success rate	Offers accepted / offers issued (quantity and value)
4	Order entry	Monthly total
5	Orders on hand	Order backlog / Average monthly sales
6	Average order size (executed)	Turnover / number of orders
7	New customers (number and revenue)	Sales to new customers this year
8	Lost customers (number and revenue)	Previous year customers not ordering this year
9	Reorder rate	Number of orders per customer compared to previous year
10	Customer complaints	Number, value, reasons
11	Revenue growth	Actual compared to previous year
12	Top-ten-changes	Top-down list of customers or items (net revenue & contribution)
13	Contribution margin per hour	Analysis of contribution margin generated per hour worked (per sales person or group)
14	Development of sales deductions	Net revenue & net proceeds development (by sales region, channel, customer group, product group)
	Concerning products	
15	Sales by itemnr. (quantity, net revenue, CM I	Appraisal of sales statistics
16	Out of stock items	Number and value of item numbers not available at appointed date
17	Best and worst selling items	CM I of the 10 best and the 10 worst selling items

Fig. 9.3 Piloting information to be obtained from the sales statistics

- Sales Channel Managers
- Internal sales organization
- Customer Consultants
- Marketing

The sales managers also belong to this group. They are all dependent on being able to track the factors that determine sales and net revenues over time so that they can react to changes in pricing and conditions, arrange sales promotions and further marketing efforts, and so that the important topics in customer discussions are set correctly.

The most important databases for obtaining this piloting data are sales statistics based on the individual billing items and the CRM (Customer Relationship Management) application. The necessary granularity of these evaluations is determined by the processing of market information. The most granular data are item and customer. Summarization takes place according to the market dimensions (product group, sales promotion by customer group, salesperson, sales channel, region, country) of the organization under consideration.

The indicators listed in Fig. 9.3 are intended to help continuously improve effectiveness (serving the right customers with the right products) and efficiency (increasing the sales CM, Sect. 8.3). If this is successful, the entire sales and distribution organization will become more productive as it generates more contribution margin per hour used.

In larger organizations, efficiency gains must be sought and realized in even smaller organizational units (e.g., cost centers). For this purpose, the working hours spent on the following internal tasks should be tracked:

- Average time spent entering, processing, and billing a sales order
- Time spent on recording and processing customer data, including determination of creditworthiness
- Time spent on planning and implementing the media plan, including advertising
- Time spent on preparing and supporting other marketing efforts, including follow-up actions.

9.2.2 Production and Research and Development

In addition to the generally valid piloting factors in Sect. 9.1, cost center-specific relations can become important.

Production Cost Centers

To realize cost reduction potentials, production management requires information as to which cost centers will reach their capacity limits in the medium term, which can trigger investments. This requires tracking the ratio of output to available capacity (actual activity level/normal capacity) and establishing a sequence of **bottleneck cost centers** (Fig. 9.4).

Unplanned overtime, that is overtime that is not included in the personnel planning of the cost center, leads to variances and often indicates in which cost

Nr.	**Piloting information**	Task / question	Formula
1	Bottleneck cost centers	In which cost centers is the activity level near the available capacity?	Actual activity level / Normal capacity (RFU) per cost center
2	Overtime	Unplanned overtime should decline	Actual overtime hours / planned overtime hours in the personnel cost plan
3	Standstill times	Do they change due to processes, machines or employees?	Standstill times per cost center and reason
4	First Pass yield	Is the share of good units increasing compared to the gross production quantity?	Output quantity / Input quantity (if necessary as a value relation)
5	Scrap rate development	Share of scrap costs compared to proportional manufacturing costs should decline	Scrap costs / proportional standard product costs good of units produced
6	Warehouse scrap	Share of scrap costs compared to proportional manufacturing costs should decline	Write-downs on semi- and finished goods in stock, because not saleable anymore / proportional standard cost of good units
7	Lot size development	Change in setup costs compared to proportional product costs	Setup costs / proportional product costs
8	Product quality complaints	Hints of manufacturing process- or material-deficiencies	List sorted per cost center and items
9	Customer complaints	Hints of organizational, material- or manufacturing-deficiencies	List sorted per cost center and items

Fig. 9.4 Pilot control for manufacturing CCs from PPSS and management accounting

centers process flow problems are to be addressed. Downtimes are caused by machine or tool breakage or maintenance work. They should be reduced so that the full capacity of a machine or cost center can be utilized. This requires measurement of the standstill time per machine by means of the FDC.

Improvement of the ratio of good units produced to input quantity (e.g., first pass yield) is a result of better process control. This results in a decrease in the amount of scrap. In a multiyear comparison the yield rates should improve in order to lower product costs per unit. Another way to lower product costs is increasing lot sizes, as this spreads setup costs over a larger number of units.

Scrap costs also arise when inventory is removed from the stock of semi-finished and finished goods because goods have been produced incorrectly or when too much was produced, and their sale is no longer expected.

The cause of scrapping stock is often to be found in the placing of orders:

- Producing a greater quantity than the amount ordered in the hope that a customer will accept the parts later, or
- Processing all material delivered to the cost center (e.g., rolls, coils) so that no raw material remnants have to be moved back to stock

Complaints often relate to the quality delivered (to the warehouse or to customers) and to missed deadlines. Eliminating the causes of this is another starting point for improving the cost position.

Plant Management/PPSS/Work Preparation

The analysis of plant management and scheduling costs in Sect. 8.5 indicated that they grew faster than total proportional manufacturing costs (Fig. 8.9). This is due to the increase in working hours used for internal tasks from 3400 in 2011 to 4250 in 2015 (sheet "Actualinternaltasks"). The use of ERP systems greatly helps to contain the time required to perform these functions. Nevertheless, to strengthen an organization's cost position in these areas as well it is necessary to look for possibilities to constrain the time required for planning, scheduling, and support to a lower percentage of the value of the production output provided. For this purpose, the recording of working times in the FDC system can be used for internal tasks (Sect. 5.1.5.3). The aim is to identify the "time wasters" and, if possible, to contain this work. Plant management can create this database itself by introducing extra service types for its specific tasks and structuring its own service recording accordingly (as in Fig. 9.5).

If the more detailed measurement of the time consumed in this cost center is not implemented the reasons for the incremental expansion of the workforce cannot be substantiated. In that case a plant manager's request to hire another employee can only be judged and decided based on the manager's assertions.

Research and Development (R&D)

R&D departments often struggle with delays in meeting milestones and order completion deadlines. An R&D manager wants to know whether these are due to

Nr.	Piloting topics	Task / question	Computation
1	New entries, mutations of items, bills of material, work plans into the ERP	Time required per entry over the years	Time spent / number of entries
2	Executed production orders	Change in time required per production order over the years	Time spent / number of entries
3	Yearly production plan	Time needed for coordination with sales, quantity and lot size-planning	Time spent compared to previous years
4	Product development and improvement	Time requirde for planning, clearances, approvals ant tests (without projects)	Time spent compared to previous years
5	Technical support	Time spent with supporting cost center managers	Time spent compared to previous years
6	Answering customer requests	Requests to be answered during the offering process and the exploitation (number and time)	Time spent compared to previous years
7	Responses to requests fom associations or public administration	Forms, reports, proofs, security attests to be filled in	Time spent compared to previous years
8	Collaboration on projects (rebuildings, extensions, process routings	Change in time required	Time spent compared to previous years

Fig. 9.5 Special piloting factors for production management and scheduling

insufficient staffing, late deliveries from suppliers, or unsuccessful trials and tests. To be able to analyze and report the consequences, he should be able to recognize in an overview of all orders:

- Which milestones and other dates were reached late.
- How long the delay was (in days or weeks).
- Which costs were incurred for follow-up (research working time).

The data necessary for creating the overview are created in the project plans and post-calculations (see Sect. 4.6.2 and sheets "Projectplan and Actualprojects"). The change of the performance indicator "number of R&D orders placed/Headcount" indicates to the R&D manager whether, in the medium-term range, he will be able to process all orders. The same parameters can also be used in a design department.

9.2.3 Procurement, Warehousing, Logistics

Piloting information for the Procurement area is intended to draw attention to emerging changes in supplier selection and the likely consequences thereof. This requires continuous monitoring and evaluation of supplier quality over several years (adherence to delivery dates, complaints, price, and condition comparisons).

Excessive dependence on individual suppliers can affect, among other things, the company's ability to supply its own customers and the proportional manufacturing costs of its products. To avoid cluster risks in procurement, it is advisable to monitor the change in supplier concentration, to purchase raw materials from various suppliers, and to keep possible alternative sources of supply up to date.

Nr.	Piloting topics	Task / question	Computation
1	Adherence to schedules	Share of on-time deliveries by supplier	Punctual deliveries / all deliveries (by supplier)
2	Supplier concentration	Dependency from single suppliers	Purchases from the 5 biggest / total purchases
3	Supplier quality	Number of complaints	List of complaints by supplier and year
4	Replacement suppliers	Possible sources of supply	List of possible suppliers, time spent for
5	Receiving inspections	Number of quality checks needed	Number and time spent in total
6	Procurement costs	Change in the procurement cost rate	Procurement costs billed by the suppliers / total
7	Average cost per purchase	Change in the controllable and fixed procurement costs	Controllable costs of the cost center Procurement / number of issued order-positions
8	Picks per hour	Change in picking performance	Worke time in the warehous /number of in/out-movements (production and sales)
9	Internal warehousing and transportation costs	Disproportionate increase in logistic costs compared to output	Controllable fixed costs Logistics / number of in/out-movements

Fig. 9.6 Piloting information for purchasing, warehousing, and internal logistics

The purchasing department should contribute to improving the cost position by reducing the average (fixed) costs per order (improvement of the input/output ratio). The controllable costs of a purchasing department cannot be assigned to the purchased items according to cause. The purchasing staff procures raw materials, auxiliary materials, and services using the available ERP functionalities. Because several purchase order items can be contained in the same delivery, the delivery costs cannot be uniquely assigned to the individual purchased products. However, in a comparison over several years, an analysis can be made as to whether the average fixed costs per order item are reduced. This is also an indication of an improved input/output ratio (numbers 6 and 7 in Fig. 9.6).

The medium-term change in warehouse productivity can also be measured by using measures such as:

- Order picking for internal and external deliveries
- Time needed for internal transports

Utilizing continuous improvement processes (Kaizen), productivity can be improved, increasing the number of process units without increasing warehouse staff.

9.2.4 Human Resources (HR)

Some personnel-related piloting clues were already listed for the cost centers (items 1–9 in Fig. 9.2).

These involve monitoring changes in the whole company as well as in its larger subunits. The database is created in the personnel function and can be analyzed by evaluating payroll accounting and attendance records. These include records regarding unwanted dismissals, reasons for leaving, fluctuation rate, absences as well as overtime, vacation, and compensation credit overviews.

Nr.	Piloting topics	Task / question	Computation
1	Employee satisfaction	Changes of personal attitudes of the employees towards their work, their supervisors and the company	Biannual employee attitude surveys
2	Unwanted departures	How many potential carriers (specialists and managers) resigned?	List of employees leaving with the note "Potential" in their personnel file?
3	Fluctuation rate	Annual employee turnover	Number of leaves / total headcount (structured by reasons such as retirement, termination by employer, resignation)
4	Reasons for resignation	Why do employees leave?	List structured by reasons (wage level, work content, superior, colleagues). Must be obtained during the exit interview.
5	Absenteeism	Change in the share of the non-performed contractual net working time	Analysis by reasons for absence (per cost center, over the years, hours and personnel costs).
6	Potential managers	Relation between potential and actual managers	Qualified potential managers / total number of managers
7	Potential for skilled professionals	Share of skilled employees with potential for a professional career	Number of skilled persons with potential to become professionalists / total no- managing staff, plus named list
8	Balance of compensation hours	Are surplus hours worked (compared to contract) compensated in due time?	Analysis of the payroll and of the flextime balance (by cost center). Hint for future personnel dotation.
9	Change in overtime balance	Where do high overtime hours arise frequently? Probably not sufficient number of staff.	Unplanned overtime YTD / Unplanned overtime YTD previous year. Planned overtime has to be included in the staff-planning of a cost center.
10	Development of the vacation day balance	Are unexpected vacation replacements required? (by cost center)	Vacation credit days per cost center. Evaluation is especially important for managers as the number of days could be a clue to overload or to problems with personal time-management.
11	Age structure in management	How many executive an management positions are to be replaced in the next year?	Named list by year and cost center. Percentage of replacements compared to total managerial positions.
12	Management capacity needed	How many additional management positions are needed according to the strategic and operational plans?	List of management positions to be added by functions and regions according to mid-term planning.
13	Number of apprentices	How many apprentices are to be engaged per year?	Analysis by profession, year of apprenticeship and department
14	Development of wage level	Are we paying competitive wages and salaries?	Comparison of the own wage/salary structures and levels to other local employers and to the industry.
15	New legal prescriptions	What will be the consequences of new laws and regulations for the personnel costs?	Judgement of the expected additional charges and calculation of the cost consequences of changing legal requirements.

Fig. 9.7 Piloting information for the personnel area

The basis for evaluations of the existing structure and the positions to be filled (apprentices, managers, upcoming retirements, and transfers to other cost centers) is mainly found in the HR master data (Fig. 9.7). Demand figures for new positions can be derived from an analysis of the medium-term change in the divisions and functional areas. The primary addressees of these reports are the members of the Executive Board, enabling them to have an overall view of personnel changes.

New legal regulations often result in higher social security contributions. The expected changes need to be estimated as input for the medium-term planning (and entered in the annual working times sheet).

If an organization is to grow, its management and specialist potential must also be expanded (IMS, right upper quadrant, Fig. 2.1). In this case, it is necessary to consider and record which positions and how many additional training courses are required, as these will anticipate management change and development of further training courses.

Human resources work becomes more efficient when the time spent on the care, support, promotion, and payment per employee is reduced. Independent cost centers should be set up for training and additional education as well as for management development if staff can be clearly allocated to these areas and specific course-related costs are incurred. Whether the planning and processing efficiency improves can be tracked through the change in the time required for these internal tasks. The effectiveness of training courses can be assessed by skill-related questions in the course evaluations. Whether the right skills and abilities have been imparted, however, only becomes clear in the field.

9.2.5 Buildings and Internal Services

Strategic and medium-term planning determines the requirements for plots of land, all types of premises, and the work required to maintain their operational readiness. Thus, piloting factors are primarily plans of other areas:

- Plans for production enhancements or changes to the production layout (showing where existing rooms can be converted).
- Necessary capacity expansions of internal service areas (such as warehouses, laboratories, maintenance, vehicle fleet, IT, access roads).
- New locations for sales and administration offices (both domestic and abroad).
- Personnel requirement planning helps predict future space requirements (including, for example, sanitary facilities, break rooms, and staff restaurants).

Further data is required for potential changes in existing facilities:

- List of rental agreements, with details of the rent and the next possible termination dates. In the event of organizational changes, rental costs may be reduced by relocating to owned buildings.
- Legal regulations on the design and equipping of sanitary areas, staff restaurants with their kitchens, as well as regulations regarding fire protection and environmental protection. Such specifications, as well as building code requirements regarding access and departure, often lead to additional investment requirements for buildings and land.

Monitoring the piloting factors for "Facilities" should lead to a reduction in costs for constructing and maintaining buildings per available square foot (or square meter). A possible key ratio could be:

Controllable cost of buildings and maintenance including imputed depreciation/ available area in square feet (or square meters)

The requirements for workshops, maintenance services, laboratories, internal transportation, and garages are also geared to the medium-term plans of sales, production, and administration. To maintain the required level of service, separate documentation is required, which can be used for performance planning:

- Installed assets and expected replacement dates as indications for pending replacement investments
- Maintenance and upkeep plans for all machines and systems
- Spare parts that must be available immediately (including the effect on inventory levels)
- Required expertise which must always be available in the company (e.g., programming capacities for process control of plants and for avoiding downtimes)
- Preventive maintenance of systems; repair of systems in the event of damage
- Areas in which preventive maintenance should be carried out automatically by the (external) machine supplier
- Agreed reaction times with external craftsmen and service technicians and monitoring of these
- Service work which should completely be performed internally for reasons of availability or secrecy

The proportional costs of these internal service centers are passed on to the receiving cost centers by the internal services provided ISP. Efficiency improvements will be achieved in these areas if the remaining fixed costs can be reduced. The assessment is based on the change of the controllable fixed costs plus the imputed depreciation of the corresponding cost centers.

If a decision must be taken as to whether services should be provided with the company's own personnel or purchased externally, it is advisable to prepare a comparative investment calculation (see Sect. 4.6.3) as planning preparation. The expenses for external procurement (one-off and performance-related) for the planned useful life should be compared to the value of the company's own resources that would potentially be consumed (including facilities that would otherwise be vacant).

9.2.6 Information Technology (IT)

Data and its evaluation are becoming increasingly important and indispensable for corporate management. Forward-looking planning is therefore a must for IT. The needs of internal and external customers are the most important input information. These include:

- Expansion plans for further data integration (processes to be integrated, interfaces, databases, reports)
- Required specialist knowledge and skills needed by IT employees in the future
- Additional IT personnel needed due to requests by internal IT customers
- Requirements of customers and suppliers, including the form and speed with which they want to receive their data
- Future storage capabilities/requirements (e.g., scanning of all documents, data warehouse)

- New applications (e.g., integration of smartphones and other portable devices into recording and reporting applications, new payment methods, big data analysis, cybersecurity)
- Wage level compared to local employers
- Changes in legal regulations (e.g., data protection, working hours)

With mutually integrated applications and automated interfaces an IT cost center can make a significant contribution to gaining a better cost position. Very often this contribution emerges in the form of efficiency increases in all receiving cost centers since those can handle more of their own processes with the same personnel deployment. This makes it nearly impossible to quantify the financial success of improved IT-processes. IT performance must be assessed based on compliance with the requirements of the Service Level Agreement (SLA).

9.2.7 Controller Service and Finance

Controller services are used, among other things, to prepare data for planning and control decisions and to support managers in making business decisions as rationally as possible. As management partners, controllers ensure that a large proportion of the piloting factors listed in the other management functions are collected and evaluated. Together with the managers, they interpret the data and use their managerial understanding to provide suggestions for improvement. As a result, the controllers additionally need only those piloting measures that affect their own work. Examples include:

- Change in the time needed for the discussion of plans and results with managers of all levels compared to the time invested into devising and producing reports
- Time required for cooperation in planning (systems, meetings, planning coordination)
- Time required for completion and presentation of the overall plans (planned year and medium-term)
- Time required for strategic planning and measurement of target achievement

The controller service becomes more efficient if the time required to support managers in planning and making decisions, including the associated reports, grows at a slower rate than the CFBIT (Cash Flow Before Interest and Taxes) generated by the complete business. The latter amount cannot be controlled by controllers, but they do support managers' achieving the CFBIT and its growth.

CFOs are usually responsible for maintaining the capability to pay on time, for optimizing the tax burden, and for the cost-efficient handling of operational payment processes (incoming and outgoing payments) as well as for external reporting. Corresponding piloting data can include:

- Financing needs in the medium-term horizon
- Specifications for determining transfer prices for deliveries of goods and services within the group
- Amount of workload generated to validate the correctness of transfer prices
- Compliance with new tax law requirements in the countries in which the company does business
- Monitoring of changes in insurance terms and conditions and assessment of risk coverage options
- Exchange rate changes and interest rate conditions
- Changes in (international) accounting standards

The financial sector will become more efficient if its controllable fixed costs grow slower than CFBIT. The comparison with the CFBIT is also appropriate here as the finance department works for the entire enterprise.

9.3 Piloting Information for Managers with Overall Responsibility

Managers with overall responsibility include persons who manage a legal entity (stock corporation, limited liability company, cooperative, state institution). Such functions are assumed by the supervisory board, the board of directors, the CEO, the managing director. Additionally, overall managers can be heads of independent operating profit centers or division heads who do not simultaneously manage their own legal entity. All these persons need a general overview of upcoming developments, be it early warning information or piloting factors.

If managerial engagement of board members is high, they will also need the (x) information.

The piloting factors for these management positions, summarized in Fig. 9.8, are largely the same, but with different degrees of aggregation. To differentiate from early warning information only information requests that can be obtained from internal data are listed. In the specific application case it must be agreed with the respective receiver which of this data is to be reported, how often, and in what degree of detail.

The databases for obtaining this piloting information are the operating systems, mainly financial accounting and customer-related data. Since it should be analyzed whether the need for action has increased, usually the change of the individual indicators is shown in a multiyear comparison.

Adressees-->	Board of Directors	CEO (corporation)	Heads of divisions-, SBU's, profit centers	Heads of legal entities
Forecast for the year end	x	x	x	x
State of project completions (successes, problems, meeting milestones)	(x)	x	x	x
State of strategy implementation (successes, problems, meeting the milestones)	(x)	x	x	x
Incoming orders and orders on hand (if relevant)	(x)	x	x	x
Share of new product sales compared to total revenue	(x)	x	x	x
Potential revenue risks (top ten customers)		x	x	x
Change in repurchase rates, customer frequency and average order size		x	x	x
Customer complaints and their reasons	(x)	x	x	x
Insights from market research and customer surveys	(x)	x	x	x
Potential raw material supplier risks (top ten suppliers and their replacement)	(x)	x	x	x
Status of investments (versus budgeted plans)		x	x	x
Change in interest rates, actual situation with banks, open credit limits	(x)	x	x	x
Change in proportional product costs and total fixed costs as a percentage of net revenue over time (cost position)	(x)	x	x	x
Violations of compliance rules	x	x	x	x
Assessment of covered (by insurance) and uncovered risks (product liability, accidents, fire and water, theft, vandalism, business interruption)	x	x	x	x
Unwanted leaves (management and professionalists)		x	x	x
Job vacancies (structure and quantity)		x	x	x
Unmanned management positions (all hierarchical levels), positions to be filled within 3 years	(x)	x	x	x
Overview of support staff (who for whom?)		x	x	x
Number of applications per advertised position (attractivity)		x	x	x
Share of part-time employees in management functions		x	x	x
Change in employee satisfaction	(x)	x	x	x
Impending changes in purchasing behavior	(x)	x	x	x
Upcoming legislative changes		x	x	x

Fig. 9.8 Piloting information for managers with overall responsibility

9.4 Early Warning

> Every development in business happens only once. The next Bill Gates is not programming an operating system. The next Larry Page or Sergey Brin won't make a search engine. And the next Mark Zuckerberg won't create a social network. If you are copying these guys, you aren't learning from them (Thiel 2014, p. 7).

As important as this insight is, it often leaves managers, who are thinking about the future challenges their company or department will face and whether the organization must be partially or completely restructured, puzzled. Although managers know that the future is unpredictable, they need "early information." What changes/transformations in the corporate environment might require adapting one's own organization for it to survive successfully and sustainably? Early warning and early detection systems serve this purpose.

An early warning system is an "... information system for the detection of risks that may arise in the foreseeable future; it is used in various areas, such as the military, in medicine and in companies. If opportunities can also be identified with the help of such an information system, it is an early detection or early clarification system. External (e.g., economic, technological, social and political data) as well as internal early indicators (e.g., sales, financial, personnel and production indicators) can be considered as signals for the early detection of relevant changes in the environment of a company and in the company itself." (translation from www.Wirtschaftslexikon24.com, Term Early Warning System, accessed 10.9.2018).

9.4.1 Pilot Control or Early Warning?

Regarding the structuring of the content of the management control system, a distinction is made here between piloting and early warning. The piloting data described in Sects. 9.1–9.3 mainly consist of internal operational information and parameters obtained by evaluating internal company data. The evaluations are intended to "explain" foreseeable internal changes. Examples include sales changes, order intake changes, quality problems in procurement or production, new management positions to be filled, looming liquidity issues. Such information can trigger actions but does not say anything about whether other external factors, e.g., new technologies, will determine the potential success of a company in the future.

An early warning system, on the other hand, collects external data regarding (presumed or foreseeable) changes in the corporate environments and prepares it for decision-making. This data forms the input for managers who are considering whether and how to update the company's purpose, strategies, or functional concepts so that the entire organization can adapt to changing environmental conditions in good time.

Because the need for early warning is so important, many publications on the development of early warning systems have appeared in recent years. The internet contains numerous catalogs of parameters and software for the development of early warning systems. In our opinion, however, these are usually only structured catalogs of operational internal key figures to be recorded, combined with suggestions as to which external parameters should be tracked.

9.4.2 Early Warning Indicators and Networks

A clearly structured example of the development of an early warning system is given by Achim Bossler (2010, p. 637 ff.). He notes that an early warning system must be set up on a company-specific basis, since it must be clarified individually which interest groups have what expectations of the company in question and which variables characterize the competitive situation in which the company operates.

For this purpose, Bossler (2010, p. 643 ff.) creates company-specific **networks**. To do this, he first develops the basic cycle, the "engine" of the company under

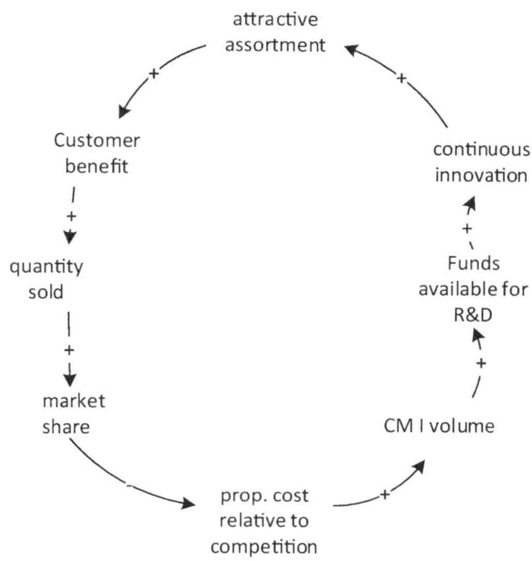

Fig. 9.9 Basic circuit of the Swatch network

consideration (Fig. 9.9). The example of Swatch watches illustrates how the attractiveness of the assortment influences the quantity sold and how this then leads to even greater assortment attractiveness via several intermediate factors (cycle). In Fig. 9.9 the arrows are drawn according to their direction of action (according to the understanding of those who draw the network). A + sign in the arrow means a strengthening effect, a minus sign a dampening effect.

The group working on the network supplemented this basic engine in several steps. Since many internal and external factors influence the success of a company it is necessary to limit the size of the network. In the Swatch example the number of factors was limited to 50.

Because the development was based on the internal "engine," the direct environmental influencing factors are located at the outer edges of the network (Fig. 9.10). The circled factors are the resulting external **early warning indicators**. Those not encircled are either influenced by the company itself or are the result of changes in early warning parameters. From this it can be concluded that the early warning indicators are to be found in the **corporate external environment.**

Four main conclusions can be drawn from the consideration of Fig. 9.10:

- At the top left are the assessments of **customers** and "not yet customers." Their change can only be ascertained through (opinion) surveys. Qualitative early warning indicators are developed.
- The middle left can be summarized under the title **Competition Observation**. However, it is to be kept in mind that new (technological) developments may not yet be identified because their products or producers are not yet recognized as competitors (e.g., replacement of mobile phones by smartphones).

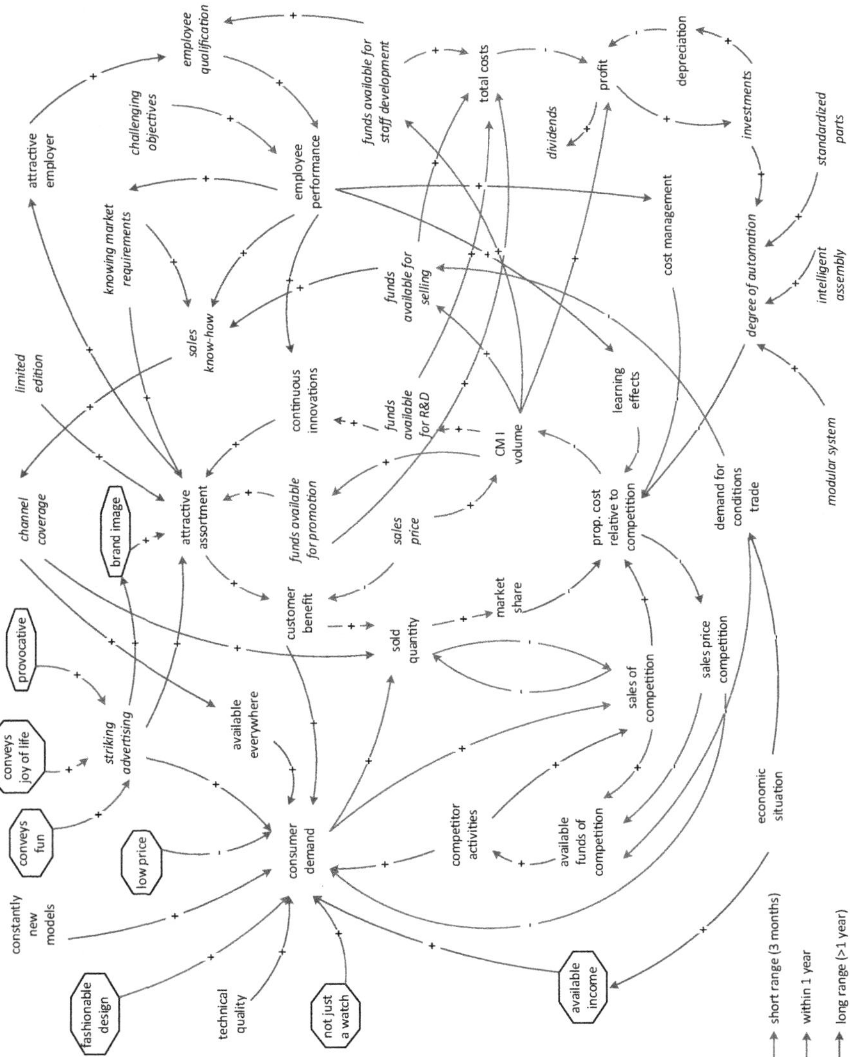

Fig. 9.10 Derivation of early warning indicators from the entire Swatch network

Environmental Changes to be Observed	Examples of Changes
Market	
Changes of attitude of buyers	Degree of attention to brands
Strong revenue gains by competitors	Competitors cost reduction potentials and economies of scale
Mergers of competitors	Stronger market presence, advertising, range of products
Change in net revenues	New discount types and deductions
New distribution channels or changes in the existing ones	Online sales, shop-in-shop, rent instead of purchase, leasing
New dealer structures	Integration into large online portals, direct sales
Resources	
Raw material shortages, supplier capacities, business leaves	Insufficient availability; delivery times increasing
New raw materials, semi-finished products	Quality improvements, reduced cost of production
School graduates	Shifts in the choice of vocational training and degree programs, new occupational profiles
Technologies	
Production processes	Changes in processing, such as bonding instead of welding, thin-film process, 3D manufacturing, energy storage
Integrated systems	Robots, production lines, lot size 1
New and expiring patents	Opportunities and risks for new processes and products, possible licensing, potential new research topics
Reports from professional meetings and training courses	New market development, ERP and planning and control systems, financing and payment procedures
Data processing	New ERP functions, CRM, payment transactions, customer data, findings from social media
Regulatory environment	
New laws and regulations	New technical regulations, hazardous ingredients, batch tracking, Cybersecurity, international transfer prices, tax law, attendance time recording, labor law, social insurance, vacation regulations
Possibilities for legal objections	Delays due to objection processes, rapid or slow processing of inquiries by the authorities
Barriers to trade	Import restrictions, customs duties, technical specifications
Political shifts	
Government debt, exchange rate trends	Realizable sales prices in various markets
Political changes	Foreseeable legislative changes, restrictions on entrepreneurial freedom
Personal settings / behaviors	
Work-life balance	Leisure requirements, entry into working life, childcare
Single-person households	Space requirements, risk of poverty, accessibility of persons
Propensity to consume	Consume or save, income available for food, health, housing, travel, and vacation
Means of shopping	Online shopping versus shopping in a physical store.
"Healthy" life	Changes in consumer demand resulting from a desire for a heathier lifestyle
Natural environment	
Avoidance of environmental damage	Avoid /reduce ecological damage
Green house gas emissions	Reducing or avoiding activities that contribute to greenhouse gas emissions
Free areas	Restriction of building sizes, traffic routes, and maintenance of natural areas
Recycling	Integration of reuse of disposed products into the lifecycle process

Fig. 9.11 Examples of topics for early warning information

- At the bottom left are the more **macroeconomic/social** indicators. Whether these will change can be deduced from reports on the economy, exchange rates, purchasing indicators, and similar indicators.
- New applications, technologies, raw materials form the fourth group of developments to be observed (not shown here).

Early warning from the environments, filtered to the essentials, are essential for corporate guidance. Managers gain time to adapt to new developments and needs, generate new products and new sales opportunities, and focus on avoiding bad investments. The Swatch example shows that any early warning system must be “tailor-made” since the importance of the various factors is dependent upon a company’s specific situation.

The list of environmental areas to be observed in Fig. 9.11 is not exhaustive. It is intended to serve as a template for a company’s own early warning system, enabling it to monitor potential opportunities and risks.

10 Consequences for Medium-Term Planning

In Sect. 1.4.3 medium-term planning was defined as the link between strategy, functional concepts, and annual planning. It provides a comprehensive preview of the desired overall development of a company. In this way, it becomes input for the next annual plan.

Input data for medium-term planning includes:

- Strategic plans, including adjustments resulting from early warning indicators
- Functional development concepts (see Sect. 1.4.2)
- Piloting factors
- Annual results from past years

With regard to the scheduling of activities, after completion of the annual planning and fiscal year change, the strategic planning and the concepts for the functional areas must first be updated before the update of the medium-term planning can begin.

Medium-term planning is limited in most companies to updating the profit and loss accounts and the balance sheets based on prior annual results and the current annual plan. This is insufficient in an integrated planning and control system as medium-term planning is intended to provide essential quantity- and performance-related input for the next annual plan. Without the link between strategies, functional concepts, and medium-term planning projects and operational changes that are to be implemented in subsequent years are not or only incompletely considered. In addition, the proportion of the efficiency improvements (in the cost centers) to be achieved is missing.

A procedure for obtaining a performance- and value-related medium-term plan is outlined below, including an explanation on how implementation is possible with the simulation model.

L. Rieder, R. Lawson, *Management Control with Integrated Planning*, Management for Professionals, https://doi.org/10.1007/978-3-030-48302-9_10

10.1 Required Depth of Planning

From a bird's eye perspective, the purpose of medium-term planning is to see whether the link between strategy implementation and the operational jobs to be done will "work out" and lead to appropriate financial results. To achieve strategic objectives and implement functional concepts, projects and internal orders are planned. Their implementation requires personnel, machine capacities, and money. This means that the operational planning dependencies described in Sect. 4.2 are also relevant for the medium-term planning process. However, it needs to be clarified whether and which "abbreviations" are justifiable for the faster and less time-consuming preparation of medium-term plans. The starting point for this consideration is the presentation of the planning process (Fig. 4.10). A simplified structure is presented in Fig. 10.1 based on the following assumptions:

- Production quantities and sales quantities are the same, i.e., no change in inventory is planned.

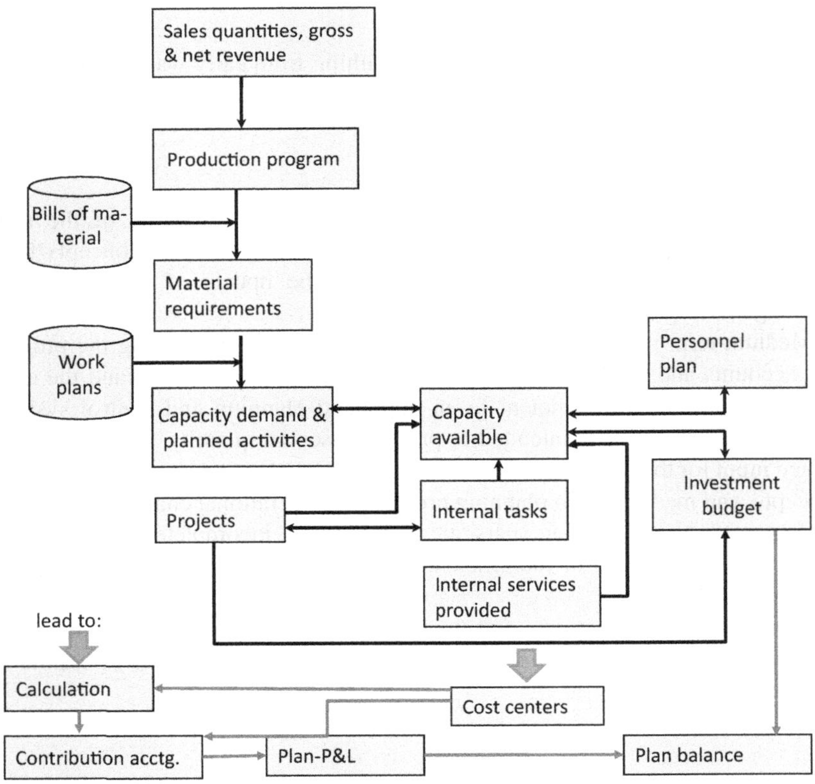

Fig. 10.1 Planning dependencies as a starting point for medium-term planning

- Projects are important because they are derived from strategic planning and improvements in operational functions and often take several years to complete.
- For the valuation processes from product costing to cost center accounting, from profitability analysis to balance sheet, the schemata set up in Chap. 4 are adopted.

The black arrows represent data flows in the ERP system. These data are prerequisites for the plan-calculations in management accounting (blue arrows).

In annual planning, each salesperson was required to specify the planned sales quantities per product group in their sales area. That was less than ten entries per year in the model. This number can also be required for multiyear planning, as the salesperson must consider which customers he will lose and how many new customers he must win each year when determining the planned quantities. Each salesperson can enter the planned sales quantities per product group and year directly in the sheet “Regionalsales.”

In the example, the sales manager determined the gross sales prices of individual items and the item and invoice discounts to be granted. It is also the responsibility of the sales manager to outline a means for increasing net revenues for the next planning years. While it would require less effort if salespeople and sales managers only indicated the change of total sales they expect, this would prevent quantifying the effects on production and contribution margins in a sufficiently granular way.

If the planned sales quantities are available, the production quantity of the finished products can be calculated. This allows the manager in charge of production to roughly determine the adjustment of the production quantities (in the sheet “Productionplan”). The simulation model automatically calculates the subsequent requirements for the preceding production stages, since the target setup and scrap quantities are already stored. If new items are added during the planning period, they must be created by inserting new rows in the sheet “Articlemaster.” This is the prerequisite for the subsequent creation of the corresponding BOMs and work plans.

The adaptation of BOMs and work plans is somewhat more complex. On the one hand, efficiency targets must be incorporated into the specifications. On the other hand, projects or process improvements can lead to far-reaching changes in the specified quantities and times (e.g., the effects of the Automatic Material Positioning project in Sect. 4.6.2):

- When using materials, an efficiency improvement results either in lower specified quantities (bills of material), lower process-related scrap, or lower setup material requirements (both to be maintained in the sheet “Articlemaster”). If the use of a different raw material would reduce consumption, the changes would also have to be made in the worksheets mentioned above.
- If a machine runs faster due to a process improvement, this reduces the allowed time of all items produced with the machine to the same extent. This makes it possible to reduce the specifications for all affected routing items (work plan sheet). If the setup process can be shortened, adjustment is possible in the same worksheet.

- A process improvement can also result in fewer operators working on a machine at the same time (e.g., by using a handling robot). This adjustment can be stored in sheet “Costcenterplan” in column “Personnel multiplier.”

For the planning and calculation of internal services provided (ISP), expected changes are recorded in sheet “ISPplan” as these shifts can affect the cost rates of the cost centers working directly on the product. If maintenance and servicing work previously performed by an ISP cost center is outsourced the service relationships in the “ISPplan” sheet need to be deleted. Alternatively, the expected external costs can be included in the sheet “Primarycostplan.”

The planned time required for internal tasks is recorded in sheet “Internal-taskplan” for all plan years. From there the sums for each cost center are transferred to the sheet “Costcenterplan.” In the latter, the total demand for personnel services (including downtimes and planned activity) is calculated and compared with the planned headcount (normal capacity of all employees). The difference is displayed in the column “Capacity bottleneck personnel,” where a field is colored red if a bottleneck occurs. Regardless a cost center manager must enter the annual planned workforce in full-time equivalents himself because the manager determines the personnel requirement.

Based on staffing requirements, the personnel department enters the gross wage totals to be planned in the plan years in the sheet “Personnelcosts.” Upcoming new hires must be entered in the personnel list with “No Name” items so that the planned wage total meets the requirements. If changes in sales commissions are to be planned, the data can be adjusted accordingly in sheet “Salesstructure.”

Missing as planning input are, finally, the costs for direct and auxiliary material, including:

- The planned purchase prices for raw materials, recorded by the purchasing manager, as the expected purchase prices for the merchandise items in the sheet “Articlemaster” for each year to plan.
- Budgeted amounts for each auxiliary material cost-type recorded by center managers (in sheet “Primarycostplan”)
- The primary cost budgets for sales promotion measures, marketing and advertisement as well as for trade fair appearances
- The planned external purchases for projects (entered as collective items in sheet “Projectplan”). If new projects are to be considered in the planning horizon, the projects, their planned purchasing budgets, and the estimated internal consumption can be prepared for entry by inserting new lines.

Figure 10.2 gives a summary overview of where the input elements of medium-term planning are to be updated.

Data maintenance for mid-term planning

Planning subjects	Granularity	Worksheet	Pro	Comment
Sales quantities	Per sales region and product group	Regionalsales		Including new and lost customers
Gross sales price	By item number	Articlemaster		Complement new items (sales manager)
Sales commissions	Rate per sales and year	Salesstructure		Commission rate for all sales reps and year
Invoice discounts	Rate per customer group and year	Salesstructure		Update customer groups (sales manager)
Item discounts	Rate per range, customer group and year	itemdiscounts		Update customer groups (sales manager)
Personnel costs	Per employee and year	Personnelcosts		Yearly gross wage/salary
Non wage labor costs	rate per year	Workingtime		Yearly markup rate
Purchase prices raw material	Price per year and item number	Articlemaster		Yearly planned
Primary cost center costs	Amount per Year, cost type, cost center	Primarycostplan		Individual entry per position
Planned investments	Amount per year and cost center	Invest&depr	*	Also investments in projects
Setup and scrap quantities	Objective per item and year	Articlemaster		Changes for every year
Bills of material	Preset quantity per item and year	Billsofmat		Efficiency objective per year
Work plans	Allowed time per item and year	Workplans		Yearly efficiency objective per item (also setup)
Internal tasks	Planned time per activity type, cost center, year	internaltaskplan		FTE's required for internal tasks
ISP activities	Planned activity per receiving/performing CC, year	ISPplan	*	Planning of exchanged services
Sales promotion	By cost center and year	Primarycostplan	*	Sales promotion budget
Advertisement	By cost center and year	Primarycostplan	*	Budget for Marketing, exhibitions, advertising
Column "Pro": In the lines marked with * primary costs and ISP activities can be planned project-wise (sheet "Projectplan")				

Fig. 10.2 Data elements to be entered per worksheet and stored results

10.2 Results from Medium-Term Planning

The large number of input elements listed in Sect. 10.1 makes the effort involved in drawing up an integrated medium-term plan much more extensive than simply updating the profit and loss account and the operating balance sheet. Still, it is to be noted that this effort is necessary if reasonably reliable plans are to be generated. Examples include:

- Merely defining sales or net revenue targets to be achieved cannot show how personnel and machine capacities are to be expanded in the planned years. This is due to missing the linkage from sales to planned activities.
- In most cases, it is to be expected that the sales prices achieved for a product will not change in the same way for all products, across all product groups and sales channels. Similarly, shifts in the net revenue share of the sales territories in the overall business are normal as customer structures change. Such shifts affect production planning, cost center planning, and investment planning.
- If simple value-based budgets are set for projects or restructurings, it cannot be inferred from these which personnel changes can be expected in the ISP cost centers and those in the fixed cost centers.
- Some cost centers still have capacity reserves, others are already fully utilized with existing orders.
- Without including planned material consumption and material consumption from the warehouse the effects of projects on working hours and machine times can only be roughly estimated.

To scrutinize purely value-based planned income statements and balance sheets for decision-making, managers need to consider information regarding quantities and cost center activities contained in additional auxiliary plans not integrated into the overall system. Otherwise the organization only has the rough forward projection of revenue and expense items from the past to use.

The efforts required for preparing the auxiliary plans can be performed directly in the simulation model. The planning results obtained from the simulation model show that this approach is worthwhile:

- Net revenue planning provides information on how sales territories, sales channels, customer groups, and product groups are to grow.
- The standard cost calculations of the individual items are automatically updated for each planned year by using the structures from annual planning across all production levels.
- Stepwise contribution accounting can be created multidimensionally just as in the annual planning process because the splitting into proportional and fixed costs is reemployed and because the primary costs are planned by the cost center manager or the personnel department on a yearly basis.
- Project costs and investments are integrated into the overall view. This also applies to the costs of marketing and sales promotion.
- As standard costs become available, the expected change of warehouse inventories can be displayed in quantity and value.
- The transfer to the company P&L and balance sheet functions automatically (as shown in annual planning).
- The extent to which the strategic product/market objectives can be achieved can be assessed on a planning basis, as they are broken down into "annual targets" via sales and revenue planning.
- The CM calculation and the investment budgets show in which years the strategies and the projects for functional change will have a major impact on liquidity and profitability.

With the simulation model, the operationalization of strategic plans in implementation-oriented medium-term planning is successful since market position targets are converted into annual planned sales. The projects resulting from the functional concepts are presented according to their realization horizon with deadlines, time requirements, costs, and investments and include expected overall change.

Medium-term planning should be updated annually to include:

- An additional year's experience
- Adjustment of planning entries that have already been entered due to strategy or project changes
- A "budget kneading phase" to reconcile the needs of the planners and managers

If the medium-term planning is developed in the simulation model, the template for the next planning year can be used directly in the annual planning process. This accelerates the operational annual planning and saves time because only the changes must be recorded.

All Systems Coordinated?

11

The purpose of this book is to provide a system for the integrated, holistic planning and management of an organization. In such a system the focus must be on the manager, regardless of whether he is a team leader or the top executive. This requires a **focus on managerial relevance** in the system implemented. While requirements for external reporting were considered, they are of secondary importance when designing such systems.

11.1 And the KPIs?

Key Performance Indicators (KPIs) are "general indicators in business administration that refer to the success, performance or capacity utilization of a business, its individual organizational units or a machine. . .Based on their performance reference, [KPIs] serve management to control and evaluate business processes, individual projects or departments. Depending on the perspective taken (e.g., management accounting, customers or management), different parameters are used as KPIs." (Gabler's business encyclopedia, available at https://wirtschaftslexikon.gabler.de/definition/key-performance-indicator-kpi-52670/version-275788, translated by the authors).

KPIs can be used to both assess the change in specific individual processes, e.g., the number of agreed framework agreements with suppliers per unit of time, and overall performance in terms of value (Return on Investment, ROI). R. Kaplan and P. Norton note in their book *The Strategy-Focused Organization* (2000, p. 3) that it is necessary to make the strategy measurable by means of balanced scorecards which define KPIs in such a way that employees know what they have to do well in order to contribute to strategy realization (Kaplan and Norton 2000, p. 103f.). To our knowledge, however, an overall KPI system that would need to be developed for the sustainable successful management of a company is not yet available.

L. Rieder, R. Lawson, *Management Control with Integrated Planning*, Management for Professionals, https://doi.org/10.1007/978-3-030-48302-9_11

Utilizing the AMPLE performance controls and referencing the Integrated Management Model (IMS) as well as to the Viable System Model (VSM), it was described how management control systems need to be set up so that they can sustainably support successful corporate management. The indicators derived in Chaps. 3–9 can almost all serve as KPIs in the sense of Kaplan and Norton if they are used in a future-oriented manner and adapted to the corresponding management level. However, it would be foolish to describe the presented key variables as complete. Environmental and internal company changes will repeatedly lead to process results being measured differently.

11.2 Lessons Learned for Complete Integration

A company can become and remain successful if it meets the needs of existing and potential new customers better than its competitors. To succeed, environmental changes must be continuously coordinated with those within the company. The AMPLE framework (Sect. 1.1.1) provides orientation for doing this. Chapters 1, 2, and 9 set out in more detail the requirements for a comprehensive management control system. This resulted in some **design maxims**:

- Think from market into company (no customers → no sales → no willing employees → no profit).
- Objectives are results to be achieved.
- Objectives are always personal, as people manage organizational parts.
- Each manager is responsible for QQDR (quantities, qualities, deadlines, and results) in his area. But he only controls what he can influence directly himself. He cannot be responsible for more than that.
- Planning is indispensable in management, as it is the prerequisite for coordination. This begins with the definition of the company's purpose and continues through to operational and tactical control.
- Every strategy must be implemented operationally. This means that each strategic objective is to be specified with enough preciseness so that it can be reflected in operational objectives and thus in the annual plans.
- Plans and target values should be determined according to the **countercurrent principle** (see Sect. 1.5 and glossary), so that acceptance is created, and unrealistic specifications are avoided.
- **Operational Excellence** is indispensable to generating real and sustainable success from strategies. Executives are mainly concerned with realizing this operational excellence. To achieve this they need the appropriate instruments.

Integrated planning and control requires a **management control system**. In Sect. 0.4 this system was divided into three main parts:

- **Management accounting system**: This builds on the results of all the quantitative and performance-related plans and links them to value measures in order to

present the overall picture in a manner appropriate to management. To do this, it must be able to map the value types Plan, Target, Actual, and Forecast. Furthermore it shall be able to aggregate plans and actual results from the lowest level to the overall result and to structure them according to areas of responsibility (billing items, customers, cost centers, cost elements). This kind of accounting for management was discussed in Chaps. 3–6.
- **Piloting and early warning system**: In an integrated planning and control system, addressing medium to long-term changes is as important as achieving short-term success. These changes should be considered in operational planning with piloting input (based on internal data) and with early warning information (from the corporate environment). In many cases, internal company changes resulting from the interpretation of piloting and early warning data require implementation periods of several years. As a result, medium-term planning must become more and more performance-related, similar to the management accounting system. It must ensure that the resource potentials necessary for the future (e.g., employee qualification, junior managers, plants, market access, efficiency improvements) are available in a timely manner. The contents of this system were described in Chaps. 7–11.

With the **simulation model** for the example company Ringbook Ltd., the management accounting system can be experienced. Excel was chosen to avoid barriers to entry. Most people interested in the topic of integrated planning and control can work with Excel and have the application available on their devices. The large size of the model as well as the possibility to change plan or actual input data and to track the consequences over a period of 5 years lead to slightly increased response times (depending on the available memory and processor).

From an integration point of view, it is important to indicate in an integrated planning an control system where management decisions need to be made by those persons who will subsequently assume responsibility. The many yellow fields in the model (apart from the basic data) show that pure simulation cannot be effective without input from managers.

The Controller Zentrum St. Gallen CZSG has already been able to accomplish the implementation of the management accounting system described above in many companies. This was always done by connecting the installed ERP system with SQL Server databases and Business Intelligence tools.

While topics such as liquidity, financing, transfer pricing, and the design of external reporting were only lightly touched upon, that is not to say they are unimportant. The focus of this book is on designing systems to enable integrated planning and control of an operational company both in the short term and for strategic time horizons.

Quotation costing, which involves generating a price quotation for a customer, was not dealt with. Although the cost data is provided by management accounting, it is always the market that drives prices, not a company's costs. Those costs may form a basis to assist the salesperson in determining the offer price, but the main factors influencing the customer's purchase decision are the competitive situation and the benefits from the customer's point of view, not the supplier's costs.

Increasing **digitization** (Industry 4.0) increases the need for integration between processing systems while also enabling faster integration of management systems. Some changes to be observed:

- Customer-specific quotations can be created more quickly because technical systems (design, layout) grow together with the ERP functions.
- Preparation- and setup-times are reduced through automation of tool change and material feed. This allows smaller lot sizes and faster customer-specific production. (This also applies to the service area.)
- Storage/retrieval and picking are accelerated by the immediate availability of data. (This also applies in retail.)
- Through the integration of production planning and purchasing, it is increasingly possible to order according to demand, which reduces inventories.
- Feeding robots can work unattended, allowing for "ghost shifts."
- Numerical programming (NC programs for machines) can either be planned and recorded as an ISP for production systems or directly as a work plan position for a production order. With this possibility their cost becomes part of the proportional costs.
- The share of fixed costs in total costs will tend to rise because investments in hardware, software, and machinery are necessary.
- The measurement of the real quantity and time consumption is increasingly carried out automatically. This simplifies production data collection, which enables faster order-related evaluations in management accounting. This enables management to detect and implement suitable corrective measures quicker in the event of variances.
- Business intelligence and big data analysis tools enable faster and more comprehensive evaluations, which will also influence the decision-making behavior of managers.
- Ensuring data quality, especially in master data and transaction data, is becoming increasingly important, as the databases are the only way to exploit the advantages of digitization. Every manager must be directly responsible for the accurate and timely collection and maintenance of data. There must therefore be regular reviews of the quality and timeliness of data collection by management.

The "higher speed" to be expected in fulfilling management tasks (due to digitization) requires annual and multiyear plans as well as strategic definitions which serve as orientation in the hectic pace of daily events. The outlined Accounting for Management makes it possible to translate objectives into figures and to prepare the orientation in a level-appropriate and up-to-date way by means of target to actual comparisons and forecasts.

Our experience in medium-sized, owner-managed companies shows that the medium- to long-term effects of piloting information are still not sufficiently considered and collected. In our opinion, this leads to too little concern with the future of the company and setting the company's course, and also to "hurried actions" when reliable employees retire. For this reason, the chapters on piloting and early warning indicators are just as much a part of integrated planning and control as operational excellence.

In the next crisis—be it internal or external—you will neither have the time nor the money for the enhancement of your Management Control System.

Start implementing integrated planning and control now!

Executives operate Management Control, controllers provide the necessary Management Control System.

Documentation of the Simulation Model 12

12.1 Purpose of the Model

The purpose of the simulation model is to provide an application example of an uncompromising management accounting system with planned, target, and actual data. It focuses on continuous performance and quantity orientation. It:

- Presents the interaction of basic (master) data with the necessary calculations and the necessary evaluations.
- Describes the integration of multidimensional sales/turnover planning, production, purchasing, capacity, and cost center planning as well as projects with activity-related plan-cost-accounting.
- Presents opening and execution of production and sales orders and illustrates target and actual reports.
- Provides bottom-up presentation of target to actual comparisons for orders, projects, cost centers, inventories in all management relevant dimensions up to the overall result.
- Describes transfer from the performance and cost-related view to the operating profit and loss statement and the operating balance sheet. Presentation of the adjustment postings for the preparation of the balance sheet and P&L for external reporting are provided.
- Describes necessary inventory revaluations at the end of the year to maintain management orientation.
- Presents the necessary data structures in a multiyear presentation.
- Analyzes changes in sales, manufacturing, and cost center efficiency.
- Derives key figures for efficiency control and improvement of the strategic cost position.
- Provides guidance on the design or further development of your own integrated planning and control system. For this purpose, all formulas used are disclosed and replicable.

L. Rieder, R. Lawson, *Management Control with Integrated Planning*, Management for Professionals, https://doi.org/10.1007/978-3-030-48302-9_12

- Provides a template for the analysis of necessary functions of a new ERP system to be introduced or extended.
- Describes the use of data and structures for the construction of training examples.

12.2 Why an Excel Model?

The entire system is a comprehensive model that can be extended at any time. The simulation model was developed completely in Excel so that, as far as possible, *no barriers to entry* restrict access. Excel is a widely used application, installed in many companies and on a huge number of computers.

No in-depth knowledge of Excel is required to operate the model. Persons with some familiarity using formulas and simple data structures can reconstruct all the calculations and the details in the formulas. No additional applications (e.g., PowerPivot) were used so that the application can be used with a standard Excel installation (even for users without specific ERP-experience). The entire model is summarized in a single, very extensive file, which greatly facilitates orientation and comprehension of the calculations.

The overall model is structured similarly to a professional ERP-database application. However, some standard functions available in programmed database management systems are not included due to Excel-technical reasons and in order not to increase the dimensions of the model too greatly. All basic data contained in the delivery state (protected) can be changed (designations, prices, quantities, times, etc.). In all worksheets, the quantitative, performance, and value-related consequences of the change can be immediately traced. These features allow the model to be extended, particularly to generate additional evaluations or to depict more complex relationships.

12.3 Scope of the Model

To be able to present integrated planning and control in as much detail as possible in a comprehensible way requires a detailed application:

- The entire course of business is planned in detail over 5 years, provided with actual data and documented with the corresponding target to actual comparisons.
- To consider all calculations and evaluations for 54 items, 54 customers and 60 employees, about 30,000 lines for the planning calculations and for the recording of actual data are included. For the resulting evaluations, a further 20,000 or so lines are created.
- In total, the simulation model consists of well over 500,000 individual cells.

12.4 System Operation

- The openness for adaptations and extensions, combined with the requirement to combine everything in a single Excel model, means that the entire system is recalculated every time an input is made. Depending on the performance of the processors and the available RAM, this results in somewhat long response times.
- If it is not necessary to be able to understand the effects of changes step by step, the automatic recalculation can be switched to manual. The model will be recalculated on command (by selecting Menu formulas/Calculation options/Manual, then F9 for the recalculation).
- The individual (working) sheets are password-protected so that formulas are not erroneously overwritten or changed. The password for the individual worksheets can be obtained from the authors if required.
- The starting point is always the "Menu"-sheet. All (over 80) worksheets are listed there and can be accessed directly by double-clicking on the worksheet name. Each worksheet has a "Home" button in the upper left corner. A click on it leads back to the menu. Alternatively, you can navigate to the individual worksheets by clicking on the worksheet tab.
- "Auto filter" is installed in many sheets. This allows you to select the columns by which to sort the rows. Another click on the filter symbol restores the original state.
- As far as it makes sense in the application, users can also format rows, columns, and cells themselves (display, colors, size) in the protected version.
- For simulations it is recommended to work with several windows (view/new window) and, if possible, on two screens. The effect of a change is thus immediately traceable.
- The model can be extended by adding customers, input materials, products, cost centers, parts lists, work plans, etc. However, because Excel does not support full data inheritance from parent databases, new items or customers must be added manually by inserting rows in each worksheet affected by this addition. The model largely works with dynamic data ranges, named "dber." As a result, when a new row is inserted, the formulas of the individual columns are automatically adopted.

The formulas used are not secret. They can be viewed at the top of each editing field. This allows the users to follow at all times how a given cell result was calculated and to use these calculations also for their own applications.

12.5 Navigation, Recorded Data, and Evaluations in the Simulation Model

The following tables (Figs. 12.1 and 12.2) give an overview of what data is recorded in the various worksheets (yellow, green, red). From there the simulation model automatically imports the data into the sheets for further calculations. To make

Documentation of the purposes of all worksheets.

Worksheet:	Capture of:	Storage of computed results:
Basic data:		
Orgchart	Structural organization of the sample company	
Salesstructure	Customer groups, sales channels, regions & commissions, sales representatives and respective cost centers	
Customers	Number, address, sales channel, sales representative, customer group	
Itemdiscounts	Discount rates according to customer group and product range	
Ranges Pgroups	Product ranges, product groups, sales promotion cost centers	
Articlemaster	Itemnr. & description, quantity unit, link to product range and group, year of introduction, opening inventory, reach target, setup & scrap demand, planned lots per year, planned purchase price, list price	Standard proportional product costs, opening quantities and values per item and year
Billsofmat	Item to produce, input items, preset quantities	
Workplans	Itemnr, cost center, allowed time/unit, setup time per lot	
CClist	Cost center nr., description, reference factor unit RFU, opening replacement value, planned useful life, ISP cost centers, company holiday	
CCassignment	Assignment of cost centers to regions, ranges and functions	
Costtypes	Description, primary and secondary cost tyes	
Activitytypes	Description, link to internal service provider	
Workingtime	Target presence time, average absence times, planned rate for non wage labor costs	Planned rate for non wage labor costs
Invest&depr	Investments, imputed depreciation, replacement values (planned)	Replacement values: actual, new, residual, replacement value reserves
Openingbalance	Internal balance sheet positions, opening inventory in units per item	Opening values of inventories at planned prices of the plan-year
Planning input:		
Regionalsales	Planned sales quantities per product group and sales region	Planned sales quantity per item (statistically derived)
Plansales	Adaptations of planned quantities per item by sales persons	Statistical and corrected sales quantities
Productionplan	Planned production units per item and year	Material requirements
Purchaseplan	Planned purchase quantities per item and year	Planned purchase values
Costcenterplan	Manager, full time equivalents FTE, reference factor unit RFU, number of planned shifts, personnel pool, cost center specific absences, planned standstill	Planned activity,need for internal services, planned proportional cost rate, proportional and fixed planned costs (amount)
Primarycostplan	Cost type, amount	Planned activity level, proportional and fixed cost per cost type
ISPplan	Serving and receiving cost centers, activity type, performance and non-performance related internal services	Planned cost for internal services provided
Intclearingplan	Cost type, charged and discharged cost center, primary costs	Primary costs to be charged and discharged per cost center and cost type
Internaltaskplan	Internal tasks per activity type and cost center	
Projectplan	Project identification, milestones, planned consumption of material, services and investments	Project budget
Investmentappraisal	Target ROI, sales quantities and prices, prop. cost per unit, additional fixed cost of the project, investment and divestment	Net present value and internal rate of return of an investment, money flows
Actual data input:		
Actualsales	Ordernr., customer, order date and due delivery, actual delivery date, item,	Revenue and CM I per billed item-position
Productionorders	Production ordernr., month, lot size change	
Actualmaterial	Per order position: material consumed	Consumption and variance of material per production order
Completemessages	Good units deliverd to stock, partly or total completion messages	Value inventory entry, yield and lot size variance per production order
Actualprodtime	Actual cost center services performed for orders and projects	
Actualpurchases	Month, quantity, actual purchase prices	Purchase price and variance per item
Actualinternaltasks	Actual time for internal tasks per cost center and activity type	Time spent for nternal tasks per cost center and year
Actualprimarycosts	Primary costs per cost center and cost type	Total primary costs per CC, cost-type, month
ActualISP	Serving / receiving cost center, cost type, quantity provided	Monthly charges for internal services provided from cost center to cost center
Actualprojects	Material consumption, milestones actual, activation of investments	Actual project costs
Personnelcosts	Gross salary and time bonus per employee	Planned presence-time rates, actual personnel costs, provisions for time bonus, valuation differences for the following year
Presencetime	Actual presence time per employee and month	Actual personnel costs
Actualclearance	Actual charge and discharge of primary costs between cost centers	
Experiencecurve	Yearly growth rate, start cumulated ouput, value added cost plan and actual	Experience curve targets to be reached per year

Fig. 12.1 Data elements to be entered per worksheet and cached results

calculations of subsequent stages faster, many calculations are stored back in basic or plan tables. Which data elements these are is noted in the third column. In the protected (delivered) version, all yellow fields can be changed.

The pure evaluation sheets (light blue, Fig. 12.2) require no further input. They are automatically generated from the preceding sheets. The same applies to the proofs (white sheets, not listed here).

Reports:	Storage of computed results:
Avgdiscounts	Average planned discounts for the plan year
Plansales	Planned sales quantities and revenue per itemnr. and sales region
Revenueplan	Gross, net revenue, average discounts per itemnr planned
Acualmanufcost	Planned and actual manufacturing cost per workplan-position
Yearlyitems	Direct material, proportional cost of semi- and finished goods per itemnr. and year (plan)
Yearlybillsofmat	Material requirements per item and year, including setup and scrap
Stockplan	Planned development of inventory (quantities and values)
Directmatcalc	Planned proportional cost per good unit including setup & scrap
Capacityplan	Planned proportional manufacturing cost per workplan-position and itemnr.
Secondarycostplan	Planned proportional and fixed cost for ISP in receiving cost centers
Propcostitems	Standard costs per itemnr.
CMplanitems	Contribution margin CM I standard before and after sales commission
StepwiseCM	Stepwise contribution margins after deduction of directly controllable fixed costs (per product group and per sales region)
CCcostplan	Planned cost totals per cost center (primary, secondary and internal clearance)
Ctypeplan	Planned cost type totals
P&Lplan	Planned profit & loss statement of the year
Balanceplan	Planned balance sheet of the year

Fig. 12.2 Contents of the standardized evaluations plan and actual

Glossary

Activity-Based Costing Activity-Based Costing (ABC) is an approach to costing that focuses on activities as the fundamental cost objects, then uses the cost of these activities as the basis for assigning costs to other cost objects such as products, services, or customers. In the Management Accounting System proposed here this cost charging happens only based on the planned proportional costs of the serving cost centers. The managers of the receiving objects are neither responsible for the fixed costs not for the variances in the serving cost centers.

Actual cost proof Enables the cost center manager to access all documents that led to cost debits in a period.

Bill of materials A specification of the quantities of raw materials, purchased parts, and semi-finished products required to produce one unit or a released production order.

Charging internal services provided (ISP) This occurs when the following prerequisites are fulfilled:

- The issuing cost center must plan costs that are directly caused by its activity level,
- The receiving cost center can decide for itself if it wants to consume the service or there is an automatic mechanism that with more units in the receiving cost center, more activity has to be performed by the performing cost center (for example, maintenance work required after every 1000 operating hours).

In the best-case scenario, the receiving cost center can decide for itself whether it procures the service from internal or external contractors.

Check A check is a necessary but not sufficient element of feedback-loops. The actual results of any activities are assessed and compared with the corresponding target values. This is followed by a variance analysis and the decision as to with which corrective actions the targeted situation can be restored (Ulrich and Fluri 1995, p. 146 f.).

CM II or CM 2 Misleading term in multilevel and multidimensional contribution accounting. CM II is reported by various ERP vendors as the difference between net revenue and full product cost. Due to the allocations necessary to calculate the full product cost, this CM II is no longer a real contribution margin. In the relevant literature, e.g., Kilger (1988, p. 73) or Kilger et al. (2002, p. 531), CM

L. Rieder, R. Lawson, *Management Control with Integrated Planning*, Management for Professionals, https://doi.org/10.1007/978-3-030-48302-9

II does not occur with included fixed costs. As described in Sect. 6.3, we recommend using descriptive names for the levels after CM I, since other fixed costs are to be deducted from CM I in the product dimension than in the customer dimension.

Controller Controllers provide management support to managers at all levels. They develop and implement all necessary instruments and systems that managers need for performance and value-based integrated planning and control (see the Controller's Dictionary, CWB).

Controlling Controlling means having your business "under control." Controlling is therefore a management task. With their instruments and advice, controllers enable managers at all levels to carry out controlling.

Cost of sales method Under this method the net revenues for the period are compared with the product costs of the products sold during the period. The product costs of changes in inventories of semi-finished and finished goods are reported in inventories.

Cost position A company has a better cost position than that of its competitors if its value-added costs per unit are lower. While it may not be possible to precisely calculate this figure, cost-cutting opportunities must be sought constantly and everywhere in the company in order to survive price competition and to maintain profitability.

Customer benefit Ratio of the benefits that a customer expects from his purchase decision to the disadvantages he incurs with the purchase (his own application costs). Also known as the cost/benefit ratio.

Delivery reliability Measure of the degree of compliance with agreed delivery dates. Delays are usually measured in days or hours. This key figure can be used for vendors, production items, warehouse receipts, and deliveries to customers.

Disburdening costs Costs charged from one cost center to another or to orders (like with credit and debit accounts in financial accounting). This transfer of costs leads many cost center managers to believe that it is good if they can pass on their own costs (including those allocated) in full or even with a surplus to others.

From a business point of view, disburdening makes no sense. Costs are budgeted and incurred in the serving cost center and should be controlled there. The proportional costs of the services rendered are charged to the receiving cost centers or orders. The planned fixed costs and the spending variances remain in the origin cost center. From there, they are transferred by means of stepwise contribution accounting.

Flexible budget/Should-be costs The flexible budget is the planned cost adapted to the actual activity level of a cost center. Calculation formula: Planned fixed costs + (Actual activity/planned activity × proportional plan costs).

The flexible budget thus indicates what costs (in total) a cost center manager should have incurred at an actual activity level. In other words this figure represents the costs that "should have been." This is the suitable yardstick for comparison with the actually incurred costs, as it aligns the plan to the actual performance.

Free samples Samples of a company's product distributed free, often as an introduction to potential customers. They are part of the costs of a sales order or of a customer agreement. Since inventory withdrawals are necessary for these, the proportional standard costs per unit are to be used for the evaluation.

Functional concepts Medium-term plans to develop support functions needed to successfully support the achievement of strategic product/market objectives. Functional concepts (functional strategies) are always derived from product/market strategies.

Functional diagram Two-dimensional representation of tasks and the persons or organizational units involved in their fulfillment. The tasks are listed in the rows, the participants in the columns. The contribution of the position is entered in the resulting fields by means of an abbreviation. Example:

Position:→ Task:↓	Cost center manager	Chief	Controller	Management
Cost planning	Building the plan P	Decision D	Execution E: Preparation of plan/target/actual comparison, information	Check C

Good unit or piece Product unit that meets all qualitative specifications and can be placed in stock.

Holistic Integral, integrated, to look at something in its entirety.

An integrated performance management system must take a holistic view of a company's activities, including all its dimensions, including changes in the current and future (partial) environments of the company.

Internal tasks All work performed in the cost centers that is neither directly caused by the manufactured and sold products, nor requested by other cost centers according to their free will.

Key figure system Mathematically or logically linked combinations of several key figures (absolute or relative numbers with a special meaningful value). Key figures can be derived from planned values or from actual data and serve as a yardstick to represent the cause and effect of processes in a causal relationship (CWB, p. 140 f.).

Key Performance Indicators (KPI) Quantifiable measurements that reflect the critical success factors of an organization. (*IMA Management Accounting Glossary*)

Machine-hour rate A machine-hour rate is formed to charge the directly performance-related machine costs (energy, preventive maintenance, lubricants) as well as the performance-related personnel costs of the machine cost center to the products and orders.

Management control An organized, integrated process and structure through which management attempts to achieve enterprise goals effectively and efficiently. It provides well-defined units of measurement and evaluation, measures actual performance, and emphasizes continuous comparisons of actual with planned or budgeted performance, and taking corrective action and forecasting. (*IMA Management Accounting Glossary*)

Management Control System (MCS) Consists of the instruments needed to practice management control. The instruments can be divided into three main groups: (1) Management accounting for operational planning and control; (2) Piloting information for planning and control of mid- to long-term internal developments; and (3) Early warning information from outside the company to support decision-taking for the future development within the changing environment (strategy).

Material quantity variance The difference between the precalculated and actual quantity of a raw material or semifinished good used to produce a given output, valued at standard proportional cost per unit.

Net proceeds Gross selling price less all possible sales deduction items. See Sect. 4. 3.2.

Plan To intend, be determined, be willing, aim, have in mind, seek. "Planning" is understood here as a creative act that leads to the determination of the results to be achieved together with the allocation of necessary resources as well as the denomination of procedures needed. A plan also serves as a basis for comparing what has been achieved with what has been intended (feedback-loop).

Planned activity level The product-related activity that a cost center is to perform in the planned year. It is derived from production planning. Planned activity level is specified with the reference factor unit (RFU) of the cost center that describes the cause of the costs (usually employee hour).

Production planning (Rough planning, Order planning) Planning the quantities of each product to be produced for a year. For this purpose, the products must be broken down into their individual parts according to the bill of materials so that it can be seen how many units are to be produced per item. The capacity requirements per cost center are then calculated using the standard times in the work plans. Rough planning is intended to show whether the available production capacities will be sufficient to process the demanded program. The capacity requirements are then the planned activities of the individual cost centers.

Real production orders are created based on the current requirements. They contain the order-specific BOM and the work plan. This information is used to reserve capacities in the cost centers (dispatching). The production order data is the technical basis of the preliminary costing of an order.

Purchase price variance Occurs when the actual purchase price for a raw material or service differs from the planned (standard) price at the time of purchase. The variance should be reported so that internal consumers (production, cost centers, sales) can distinguish between the share of the variance due to market effects and the share due to their own variances (material and working time).

Rolling plans (Also called Continuous Planning) If new orders are received with due dates, they have to be included in production planning for the next period. Cost center plans and item-related standard costs should not be changed in management during the year, as they contain the objectives to be achieved. The incorporation of new or unplanned influences happens in the precalculation of orders and in the forecast (for the target- and result-oriented area). A forecast is made based on the expectations of the forward-looking manager, not on the basis of projections (Sect. 1.2.1).

In medium-term planning with a multiyear horizon, rolling plans are the norm, since the existing plans for subsequent years are drawn up based on the current results achieved and considering the changes that have occurred since the last plan adjustment.

Routing variance This is the cost-consequence of a production run that was performed in other cost centers or on machines other than planned in the precalculation. See Sect. 6.1.

Sales deductions Reductions of the price received from the customer which the company has to bear (e.g., bonuses, reimbursements, cash discounts) as well as cost elements to be borne by the company because of the contractual arrangement with the customer (e.g., non-invoiceable freight, transport insurance, transport damage).

Service level agreement (SLA) An agreement or a point of intersection between a customer and the service provider for recurring services. The aim is to make the control possibilities transparent for the client by describing in detail the guaranteed performance characteristics, such as the scope of services, reaction time, and speed of processing. An important component here is the quality of service (service level).

Service providers can be external contractors, or one or more cost centers. The ordering party is the community of cost centers receiving the services. SLAs regulate quantities, qualities, deadlines, and availabilities. Cost allocation to the receiving parties should not be part of an SLA, since the costs are to be controlled by the service provider.

Spending variance The difference between "should-be costs" (i.e., flexible budget costs) and actual incurred costs. If the actual costs in a cost element are higher than the target costs, this results in a negative variance because the difference has a negative effect on the company. A positive variance shows the size of realized productivity improvement in a cost center.

Strategy The way that an organization positions and distinguishes itself from its competitors. It is the basic business approach an organization follows to meet its goals. A strategy defines the product/market combinations to be reached and the future potentials for success to be built up in a measurable and verifiable form. A strategy is formulated for a Strategic Business Unit based on customer needs. This means that a corporation can follow several strategies at the same time. Strategy implementation always requires operational planning and its execution. To do so, changes in the functional areas are often a prerequisite. These are planned in the Functional concepts (see Sect. 1.4.2).

Sustainable The ability of a company/system to continue to exist successfully despite changes in its surrounding environment.

Total cost method A method for the presenting of an income statement that compares the net revenues of a period with the total costs/expenses incurred in the period, broken down by cost type. Since revenues refer to the quantity sold, but costs are incurred based on the quantity of goods produced, the change in the value of inventories must be shown to make the basis for reporting revenues and costs consistent.

Value-added The difference between net sales and all purchased and consumed inputs (material, energy, all external services purchased against invoice or cash).

Variable costs These correspond to proportional product costs. However, the term "variable" should not be used, since all too often the proportionality of the costs to the quantity produced is confused with the controllability of costs (CWB, p. 200).

Wage provision Wage provisions must be booked if work has been performed but not yet settled and paid out to the employee (holiday pay, overtime, flextime). Such positions reduce the monthly result and must therefore be recorded.

Work plan A description of the processes to be carried out during the manufacture of a product, indicating the cost center and the time allowed to carry out the individual tasks (similar to the preparation descriptions in a cooking recipe).

Working time variance Occurs when the allowed (target) times according to the work plan are different from the actual services on the order.

Cited Literature[1]

Ashby, W. R. (1956). *An introduction to cybernetics*. New York.
Beer, S. (2008). *Diagnosing the system for organizations* (Malik ed.) (imprint). Malik Management Zentrum St. Gallen.
Bossler, A. (2010). Aufbau und Einführung eines Frühaufklärungskonzepts. In L. Rieder (Herausgeber), *Controller-Leitfaden (Praxishandbuch)*. Zürich, 637 ff.
Cokins, G. (2009). *Evaluating the costing journey: A costing levels continuum maturity* model. Information paper, published July 2009 by the Professional Accountants in Business Committee of the International Federation of Accountants. New York.
CWB International Group of Controlling IGC. (2010). *Controller's dictionary* (CWB), g/e, e/g (4th ed.). Stuttgart.
Deyhle, A., & Hauser, M. (2011). *Controller practice volume 1+2* (15th ed.). Freiburg.
Doerr, J., & Duggan, K. (2017). *OKR objectives & key results. Measure what matters*. Penguin.
Dörner, S. (2016, March 4). *Das Google-Prinzip für die Mitarbeiterführung*. die Welt.
Fässler, K., Rehkugler, H., & Wegenast, C. (1980). *Lexikon Kostenrechnung und Controlling* (4 völlig erweiterte und überarbeitete Auflage). München.
Forrester, J. (1961). *Industrial dynamics* (Student ed.). Cambridge, MA: Massachusetts Institute of Technology.
Gablers Wirtschaftslexikon. https://wirtschaftslexikon.gabler.de
Grochla, E. (1973). *Unternehmensorganisation*. Reinbek/Hamburg.
Henderson, B. (1979). *On corporate strategy*. New York: Abt Books.
Horngren, C., Bhimani, A., Foster, G., & Datar, S. (1999). *Management and cost accounting*. London: Prentice Hall.
IMA. (2014). *The conceptual framework for managerial costing*. Available at www.imanet.org/-/media/df27d1327c4b4f9dbc0b5a43537bcc7f.ashx
Kaplan, R., & Norton, D. (2000). *The strategy-focused organization*. Boston, MA: Harvard Business School Press.
Kilger, W. (1988). *Flexible Plankostenrechnung und Deckungs beitrags rech nung* (9. Verbesserte Auflage). Wiesbaden.
Kilger, W., Pampel, J., & Vikas, K. (2002). *Flexible Plankostenrechnung und Deckungs beitrags rech nung* (11. vollständig überarbeitete Auflage). Wiesbaden.
Malik, F. (1981). *Management-Systeme*; die Orientierung Nr. 78, Bern (Original, in German).
Malik, F. (2008). *The right corporate governance*. (3rd ed., Frankfurt, translated from German by Jutta Scherer). Munich.

[1]As far as possible, original works are quoted. While many of these provide good proposals to support integrated and holistic leadership and have been around for many years, they are still insufficiently applied in science and practice.

L. Rieder, R. Lawson, *Management Control with Integrated Planning*, Management for Professionals, https://doi.org/10.1007/978-3-030-48302-9

Odiorne, G. (1965). *Management by objectives: A system of managerial leadership*. New York.
Odiorne, G. (1987). *The human side of management*. Lexington, MA.
Orengo, M. (2011). *Re-Organisation von Unternehmen mit Hilfe des Viable System Models (VSM)*. SEM Radar, 2011/01.
Orengo, M. (2017). *Kundenorientierung in Innovation, Marketing, Vertrieb, Organisation und Führung* (2. erweiterte Auflage). Verlag tredition Hamburg.
Plaut, H. G. (1953). *Die Grenz-Plankostenrechnung, Teil I und II*. Zeitschrift für Betriebswirtschaft, Hefte 6 und 7.
Rieder, L. (2004). *Kosten-/Leistungsrechnung für die Verwaltung*. Bern.
Rieder, L. (Herausgeber). (2010). *Controller-Leitfaden* (Praxishandbuch), Zürich.
Rieder, L. (2012). *Benefit commission, St. Gallen*. Available free at https://en.management-control.eu
Rieder, L., & Berger-Vogel, M. (2015). *360°-Management für alle Funktionen und Führungsstufen: Ziele, ihre Kennzahlen und Frühwarngrössen*. Zürich.
Schmalenbach, E. (1963). *Kostenrechnung und Preispolitik* (8. Auflage). Köln und Opladen.
Seiler, A. (1999). *Accounting, BWL in der Praxis I* (2. Auflage). Zürich.
Simons, R. (1995). *Levers of control*. Cambridge, MA: Harvard Business School Press.
Stöger, R. (2011). *Wirksames Projektmanagement* (3. Auflage). Stuttgart.
Swiss GAAP FER. (2007). *Fachempfehlungen zur Rechnungslegung*, Stiftung für Empfehlungen zur Rechnungslegung, Zürich 1/1/2007.
Thiel, P. (2014). *Zero to one*, with B. Masters. London.
Ulrich, H. (1987). *Unternehmenspolitik* (2. Auflage). Bern.
Ulrich, P., & Fluri, P. (1995). *Management*. Bern: Paul Haupt.
Ulrich, H., & Krieg, W. (1974). *SGMM, St. Gallen management model* (3. verb. Auflage). Bern.
Welch, J. (1995, May 29). Interviewed in *Fortune* 131(10), S.73–75.
White, L. (2009). Resources consumption accounting: Manager-focused management accounting. *Journal of Corporate Accounting and Finance, 20*(4), 63–77.

Index

L. Rieder, R. Lawson, *Management Control with Integrated Planning*, Management for Professionals, https://doi.org/10.1007/978-3-030-48302-9

The manufacturer's authorised representative in the EU is Springer Nature Customer Service Centre GmbH, Europaplatz 3, 69115 Heidelberg, Germany. If you have any concerns regarding our products, please contact ProductSafety@springernature.com

Printed and bound by CPI Group (UK) Ltd, Croydon, CR0 4YY

30/09/2026

02225505-0012